*Truth in History*

# Truth in History

## OSCAR HANDLIN

THE BELKNAP PRESS
OF HARVARD UNIVERSITY PRESS
Cambridge, Massachusetts,
and London, England

Library of Congress Cataloging in Publication Data

Handlin, Oscar, 1915–
  Truth in history.

  Includes index.
  1. Historiography. I. Title.
D13.H288      907′.2      78–24157
ISBN 0–674–91025–7

Designed by Mike Fender

*To*
*Lilian*
*for life, for love, for learning*

# PREFACE

## *The Abuses of History*

HISTORIANS, like other scholars in the United States, long occupied themselves in self-justification. The lachrymose call for appreciation expressed the insecurity and self-pity of people without confidence in their own values, who needed reassurance by the approval of others. And in a society which calibrated all measures by a single standard, the proof of worth was usefulness.

The 1970s added an economic dimension to the plaintive apologetics. Since most historians earned their livelihood by teaching, they suffered during that unhappy decade when education abruptly became a buyers' market. Persuaded of the need to choose relevance, students shopped avidly for the best bargains in learning; and in many institutions the study of history suffered. To protect their jobs, historians, like other faculty members, set about demonstrating the utility of the subject matter they purveyed. A long tradition of dreary argument gave them material for the sales pitch: history turned out future statesmen, loyal citizens, intelligent voters, good neighbors, and stable, well-rounded, liberally educated individuals.[1] The sell was hard. Having in the lush 1960s heedlessly generated a massive brood of new Ph.D.'s, the older scholars faced the uncomfortable obligation of finding a larger number of new places for their progeny, at precisely the time when opportunities contracted.

In the frenzied effort to cope, prospective teachers struggled to sharpen performing and teaching skills—to innovate. A few aging

[1] Rehearsals of the traditional case of history may be found in William H. Cartwright and Richard L. Watson, Jr., *The Reinterpretation of American History and Culture* (Washington, 1973), 4 ff.; Robert V. Daniels, *Studying History: How and Why,* 2d ed. (Englewood Cliffs, N.J., 1972), 6 ff.

radicals still threatened to tear the world down, but the most common response was assertively to promise that the subject would equip citizens with the nostrums to dissolve current and future problems. "Perhaps," a professor wistfully wrote, "the criteria for organizing introductory courses in history may emerge from present-day ecological interest." Ecology, which treated "the shape of things, both in the beginning and in an approaching end," offered "a new and attractive alternative to the remnants of the traditional histories."[2]

The effort to float with that particular fashion was doomed to futility, as were earlier frantic scratchings for substance, in femininity, ethnicity, and population. The obvious practical rewards students valued were not within the power of departments of history to bestow. The study of the past was not pre-anything; it did not promise ready entry into a lucrative profession; it did not offer direct access to positions of prestige or authority. Nor would slick audiovisuals stir the interest of an audience reared since childhood on TV offerings. Stuck with a product not easy to sell, the historians and their professional organizations tumbled into a scramble for customers which for earnestness would have gladdened the heart of any PR man, and for awkwardness would have saddened his sense of technical competence.[3]

A pity. The misdirected search for clients obscured the genuine values of the discipline. History could not compete for attention on any terms but its own. Other, more flexible departments of knowledge could always outbid it in a marketplace geared to relevance. In the rivalry for audiences likely to be attracted by quick cures for the ills of personality or society or pulled by entertaining images on a screen, the historian was at a hopeless disadvantage. What remained, therefore, was the plea from unemployment, a plea more likely to evoke sympathy than support, because all too often it implied that the use of history was to feed historians.

Standing on that uncertain ground, blinded by the urgencies of the academic marketplace, the historians of the 1970s neglected the true value of their subject. The crisis they perceived was but

2 Henry Bausum, "Social Function of History," *AHA Newsletter*, XV (September 1977) , 7.

3 Robert S. Feldman, "Historical Role Playing: An Alternative Teaching Strategy," *AHA Newsletter*, XV (November 1977) , 4.

the surface manifestation of a deeper, less readily visible ill that sapped the vitality of the profession.

While scores of Ph.D.'s without academic jobs drifted off into other occupations, desirable posts went unfilled for the lack of scholars adequately trained to fill them.

Therein lay the true crisis. Erosion of the basic skills, atrophy of familiarity with the essential procedures, dissipation of the core fund of knowledge left stranded many worthy individuals, who simply did not know what they were doing or why. Only a reversal of the trend could redeem the discipline and lead to an understanding of the true uses of history.

The pages which follow address the issue. They emanate from a half-century's experience of reading, writing, teaching, research, and publishing my own works and those of others, in a variety of fields and in several disciplines (or so it might seem in the perspective of 1978). Personal reflections present the grounds both for pessimism and for optimism and open the way to consideration of some long-term trends affecting the thinking about history in the United States. A succession of brief analyses of the problems of handling historical material, illustrated by examples from my own work, show what history is and can do. It will be possible thereafter to ask, and answer, the question: Of what use is history?

# Contents

Preface. The Abuses of History     vii

*Personal Reflections on a Calling*     1
1.   A Discipline in Crisis     3
2.   Living in a Valley     25

*The Central Themes of American History*     41
3.   A History of American History     43
4.   Theories of Historical Interpretation     85
5.   Historical Criticism     111
6.   An Instance of Criticism     145

*Dealing with the Evidence*     163
7.   How to Read a Word     165
8.   How to Count a Number     194
9.   Seeing and Hearing     227
10.   History in a World of Knowledge     252

*Persistent Themes and Hard Facts*     291
11.   Political Theory and Popular Thought     293
12.   Man and Magic     316
13.   Good Guys and Bad     332
14.   The Two-Party System     353

*The Uses of History*     369
15.   The Diet of a Ravenous Public     371
16.   Ethnicity and the New History     383
17.   The Uses of History     403
     Acknowledgments     417
     Index     421

# Personal Reflections
# on a Calling

SUBTLE LINKS join subjective to objective elements in the practice of the historian's craft. While the world of the elapsed past has its own reality, independent of who attempts to view and describe it, and is thus objective, the scholar's vision is subjective, at least to the extent that his own point of observation and the complex lenses of prejudice, interest, and preconception shape what he discerns and therefore what he can portray. The historian consequently must know not only how to explore the sources and how to fit together the data garnered from them, but also the internal and external constraints which affect the performance of those tasks. As a result, he depends both on a command of techniques and on self-understanding. A manual of rules and procedures may ease the difficulties of research, analysis, and writing; application of the rules still requires self-understanding. And the compiler of this book, making no pretense to dispassion, recognizes that only an awareness of his own situation can offset the distortions of a limited perspective.

Hence this work begins with two distinctly personal essays—the one the product of a first perception of the crisis in the historical profession in 1970, the other an effort at stocktaking in 1977. Both are distinctly personal documents; yet each is relevant to the writing and reading of history.

# 1

## A Discipline in Crisis

THERE WAS A TIME when no one was more faithful than I in attendance at the annual meetings of the American Historical Association. But toward the end of the 1950s I stopped going because these gatherings, pleasant as they were in other respects, had moved so far from the proper business of the historian as to empty the ritual of justification. I came back once more in December 1970, partly out of nostalgia and partly in response to an invitation suggesting the retrospection appropriate to advancing age. The occasion did not convince me I need soon return.[1]

The first A.H.A. convention I attended assembled a third of a century ago at Providence, Rhode Island. I was young and, no doubt, naive, a third-year graduate student. I had one foot in at Harvard, but most of me was still in Brooklyn which perhaps accounted for the excitement of the sessions, the exhilaration of talks with men whose names graced the title pages of books I had read. Ideas seemed everywhere in circulation through the corridors of the Biltmore; and I recall to this day the cordiality of older men—Howard K. Beale, Paul Lewinson, Eugene Anderson, Hans Rosenberg—who made me feel at once involved in a group of shared values and interests. It was to edge into this fellowship that I had joined the Association while still an undergraduate; and this token of fulfillment of the desire to be a historian was ample reward for the costs I could then ill afford.

Had I known then what I know now, I might well have chosen a different line of endeavor.

[1] Oscar Handlin, "History: A Discipline in Crisis?" *American Scholar*, XL (Summer 1971) , 447 ff.

My dissatisfaction has not been personal. I am not aggrieved at the status I have achieved or the position I hold; I have completed some of the work I wished to do; and the number and the quality of the students with whom I have had the good fortune to associate has been gratifying. My discontent focuses on the state of the discipline. Not that there are fewer good scholars now than then, or fewer good books; and comparisons of the relative merits of the ancients and moderns are, in any case, beside the point. Nor is it simply the Oliver Twist reflex—that, having gotten something, we want more. The annoyance arises rather from expectations unfulfilled—expectations that were perhaps unrealistic, although not unworthy.

I embarked upon historical research as an explorer conscious that every great discovery was one that revealed a continent of ignorance, the importance of which would unfold from subsequent discoveries. I had not yet written anything, but I hoped, in time, to produce a book, the value of which would be measurable by its location in a living stream of thought composed of the works that followed as well as those that preceded it. I would not have expected then that, almost three decades after its appearance, that first book would still stand not outdated—literally inconsequential. And now in retrospect I perceive that this was the fate of the best historical writing of my generation.

A comparison that is, on the face of it, immodest and exaggerated is nonetheless illuminating. It is evidence of strength, not of weakness, that the work of the physicists of the 1930s has long been outdistanced. That history developed differently is an indication, at the very least, that the discipline does not conform to the pattern of other sciences; and that calls for an examination of the assumption that it does or should.

The expectations I inherited in the 1930s had been nurtured for perhaps a half-century. They were professional, transmitted through a small group of men and women, internally cohesive and held together by adherence to common standards and convictions. The convention of 1936 was large by the criteria of the times, but its nine hundred and fifty-six registrants were together guests at a lunch given by Brown University, a gesture that was symbolic of a sense of unifying purpose that overrode differences in background, interpretation and points of view.

It is hard to convey the sense of that unifying purpose other than in personal terms. Four of my teachers—Charles H. McIlwain, Frederick Merk, S. E. Morison, and Arthur M. Schlesinger—had treated the American Revolution, each in a distinctive fashion. Yet the student, confronting that array of divergent viewpoints, found no cause to doubt that a common standard of scholarship animated all four historians. Indeed, McIlwain's presidential address at the Providence meeting emphasized the continuity and integrity of the historical enterprise. When later I encountered Charles Peirce's description of the "community of investigators" laboriously inching the world toward truth, it seemed the perfect term for our company.[2]

I retained the faith in that community through most of my career. I believed that I associated with co-workers laboring toward an end that was the same for all of us; it simply never occurred to me to take account of ethnic, religious, or ideological factors in dealing with a student or colleague or with any scholar and prospective scholar whom I could help. If John Higham came to talk with me about his dissertation or Staughton Lynd sent me something he had written, I thought I responded solely out of a desire to further their own work, not out of calculation of what might come of it or with the intention of exerting influence upon the product. In the past thirty years I have read some thousand manuscripts, not counting the papers and dissertations of my students, at an enormous cost in time for no conceivable reward other than the furtherance of a common purpose. I went fifteen years without a leave of absence, while expending the funds that gave leaves to more than a hundred other historians, and did not count the opportunity wasted since a common effort involved us all.

A change has occurred, and I may have been slow to perceive it. I can recall the blank incomprehension with which I learned that we were expected to think not of historians, but of schools or types or parties among historians, cut apart from one another in

---

2 Charles H. McIlwain, "Historian's Part in a Changing World," *American Historical Review*, XLII (January 1937), 207 ff.; Charles Sanders Peirce, "How to Make Our Ideas Clear" (1878), *Collected Papers* (Cambridge, 1960), V, 249.

criteria of judgment and objectives by ideology or other sectarian factors. I was surprised in 1968 at the request that I recommend teachers not according to ability but according to race and political orientation. The dissolution of the sense of community proceeded so rapidly that I was not surprised in 1970 to find the American Historical Association Council suggest that nominations take into account "age, sex, ethnic background and employing institution." Hence the crisis, which comes not by assault from without but by decay from within. The need to reexamine objectives may be cathartic and salutary; or it may reveal a deep-seated malady. But the consequences of pretending it does not exist will certainly be fatal.

Part of the change is the product of sociological forces that have expanded the numbers, altered the status, and modified the position of the historical profession in the academic world, in the publishing business, and in society. I do not underestimate the importance of these factors, but I prefer to concentrate here upon another aspect of the transformation: the intellectual pressures emanating from within that have fragmented the discipline, loosened its cohesive elements, and worn away the consciousness of common purpose. These pressures, which have blurred accepted guidelines and values, are at the root of this crisis.

The strategic location of history in the world of learning was secure in the 1930s. That world was worldwide, small enough so that everyone, more or less, knew his colleagues everywhere. Although travel was less frequent and more strenuous than it was to become later, contact among historians and across national boundaries was firmer than in the 1970s. Furthermore, the process of defining the profession that began in the late nineteenth century had been fortunate in outcome. History was a social science, linked in the structure of universities and in academic practice with economics, political science, and sociology. But it was also one of the humanities, linked as well with literature, fine arts, and philosophy. The dual aspect was visible organizationally in the place the American Historical Association held on both the Social Science Research Council and the American Council of Learned Societies. More important, the dual orientation was evident in the substance of what historians actually did.

History in the United States was a social science, one of the group of disciplines that gave professional form to the study of the life of man in society. But its practitioners, regarding themselves as custodians of the record of the human past, believed that their role was distinctive. Economics, sociology, and political science treated institutionally distinct subject matters in a fashion that was basically analytical; history was a foundation for them all. It was the laboratory that churned out data and supplied information from which subsequent generalizations would arise, and that, at the same time, tested the hypotheses formulated by the analytical scholars. The importance of this role was evident in *The Encyclopedia of the Social Sciences,* edited by E. R. A. Seligman (1930–1935), which, in sharp contrast to its successor, drew historical materials intimately into the whole fabric of presentation. *A Charter for the Social Sciences,* a report produced under the auspices of the A.H.A. at about the same time, articulated the same point of view. This document, which was to have been a point of departure for subsequent generations of work, proved ironically a memorial to the wishes of a generation that was passing on. But it showed the strong anchorage that held history to the social sciences.[3]

The association had special importance within the line of scholarly research with which I identified. In the United States since the turn of the century, the search for a new history that would break away from the institutional rigidities of the old had drawn Arthur M. Schlesinger, among others, to a definition of the subject encompassing every aspect of human behavior and aimed at a unifying formulation that would establish the connections among politics, economics, religion, the family, and ideas. A parallel tendency in France led Lucien Febvre and Marc Bloch in a quest for *synthèse historique,* for the products of which their journal, *Annales,* provided an outlet. In this context, history was at once a body of knowledge important in itself, a means of establishing the linkages among the social sciences, and, by way of the generalizations it supported, an instrument useful in the definition of current policy.[4]

3 Charles A. Beard, *Charter for the Social Sciences* (New York, 1932).

4 Charles A. Beard, *Nature of the Social Sciences in Relation to Objectives of Instruction* (New York, 1934), 50 ff., 214 ff.

Individual efforts were therefore parts of a larger process of cumulation. A scholar was conscious of his ties both to those who had taught him and to those whom he would teach. If he could see farther than his predecessors, it was because he stood on the shoulders of giants. And it would be a measure of his own growth that those who stood on his shoulders would see farther than he. History was subject to the same beneficent laws of improvement as were the other sciences, and the individual's merit lay in involvement in it. This conviction was so thoroughly part of the assumptions of my generation that I could hardly believe it when one of my students of the next generation asked me whether a critical comment would offend my teacher Arthur M. Schlesinger. It seemed to me supererogatory to explain that it was a normal expectation of scholarship to renew itself by later work.

Yet, although historians viewed themselves as participants in a scientific process that new information and insights kept in constant flux, they enjoyed an offsetting prop to the ego in the consciousness that they were also practitioners of a literary art. They stood in a tradition that antedated the science of history, that went back through Francis Parkman to George Bancroft and Thomas Macaulay and, indeed to Thucydides. So that the hope of still being read tempered for many the consciousness that passage of time would inevitably supplant their works as science. They had, that is, the best of both worlds—or thought they had.

To appraise the outcome of these faded expectations, it is necessary to abandon the conventional stratagem of science that interprets every change as improvement and that uses past errors not as cautions of future fallibility but as evidence of present superiority.

The judgment of history as a literary art is the easier to deliver. The average effort requires little comment; it bears the impersonal marks of a competently edited clinical or laboratory report. The best contemporary writing within the genre deserves more attention. It is clear, and it is sometimes amusing, but it is usually frozen in patterns inherited from the past, sometimes actually in antique idiom. The reviewers' conventional term of approval is "readable." By whom? Actually, the word usually means "undemanding," so that it is praise to say of a book that it is easily read or skimmed. The language structure comes intact from the nineteenth century except insofar as the influence of journalism has simplified it.

Now there were great writers among the nineteenth-century historians. But there was a congruence between the styles of Macaulay or Parkman and the modes of expression of their contemporaries in fiction or poetry. The style of each was distinctive, but Macaulay shared the language of Carlyle and Thackeray just as Parkman shared the language of Lowell and Melville. No such congruence exists today; the historians have locked themselves apart from the changes that have transformed the English language since the time of Joyce, Eliot, and Pound.

Dead style is not just a matter of external form. It is related to what the historians have to say. We do not demand of Faulkner or Pound that they make easy reading, because we know that intricacies of exposition, obscure allusions, and unusual diction are the means of communicating complex ideas. Do historians never feel the same need? Are there no complexities in the development of institutions, in the action of culture upon personality, in the operations of contingency, past as well as present? We enjoin ourselves repeatedly to extend the human experience by a display of imagination, empathy, and the ability to understand situations and characters other than our own, that is, by precisely the same qualities needed by any writer. Yet, without boldness of artful literary expression, we fall back upon the bland language of the weekly newsmagazine and remain insensitive.

Imagination and empathy are personal qualities. They call for the involvement of the writer—including the historian—with his subject. They call for icy passion, not always in accord with the methods of science that pull the investigator toward detachment, toward an impersonal, uninvolved stance. The historian is thus subject to the tension of a choice, as it were, between learning the language of English prose or of Fortran. By pretending that there was no need for choice, by grossly underestimating the difficulty of either task, three generations of historians resolutely shut their eyes to problems we still face and for which we are less prepared than they were. No advice was ever easier to give than to occupy both stools; its plausibility explains in part our present sprawling posture.

The discipline has also fallen far short of fulfilling the scientific aspirations of the 1930s. It is no simple task to equip a historian in the 1970s. The checklist of requirements for his preparation is long and growing—and more honored in form than in performance. The task of training the historian is not made easier by casual curtailment of the course of preparation to raise productivity as measured by the number of degrees granted.

In part, the difficulty of equipping the historian springs from the methodological and conceptual dependence of history upon related bodies of knowledge, a dependence frequently explained by the excuse that the discipline had only recently acquired the attributes of a science. As great a historian as Marc Bloch sounded the familiar lament: "This newcomer in the field of rational knowledge is also a science in its infancy." I do not know by what standard of chronology history is more youthful than political science or sociology, but I suspect that the infant-science argument, like infant-industry or young-nation pleas, conceals inner insecurities and self-doubt. If only we were mature enough to handle the big tools, then the difficulty of managing the pen might be less oppressive![5]

The hankering after new methods, to be supplied, it was hoped, by the other social sciences, is not recent. Twenty-five years ago historians were already turning to Weber, Michels, Sorokin, Mannheim, Durkheim, Freud, Schumpeter, Pareto, and Keynes for guidance. The search for the saving social science reaches back from the present beyond Beard and Carl L. Becker at least to Turner's clutch at Achille Loria.[6]

I share the longing of my colleagues, past and present, and more, I have not merely talked about those methods but have actually turned my hand at their use. The gains are almost self-evident, the losses almost imperceptible, but real.

Who will deny the beneficence of the computer? Certainly not one who spent months laboriously transcribing 43,567 entries

[5] Marc Bloch, *Historian's Craft* (New York, 1953) , 13. See also Chapter 10.

[6] Frederick Jackson Turner, "Significance of the Frontier in American History" (1893) , *Frontier in American History* (New York, 1920) , 11; Lee Benson, *Turner and Beard: American Historical Writing Reconsidered* (Glencoe, Ill., 1960) , 2–40.

from manuscript schedules, hand-sorting and finger-counting them. I bless the new hardware and software, the programs and printouts, the data banks and shared-time devices that ease the tasks of computation. Gladly have I signed the vouchers! But I cannot strike the balance of the results, for losses as well as gains have followed from the effort to harness quantitative methods to historical investigation.[7]

Take account of some of the elements. At worst, we find elaborate ways of telling time by algebra. More generally we encounter studies that make modest contributions to the understanding of problems posed by examining conventional sources. Quantification at this level involves classifying and counting; and technology makes the task more expeditious but demands no shifts in conceptualization. The years that separate Crane Brinton's *The Jacobins* (1930) from Charles H. Tilly's *The Vendée* (1964) have increased methodological sophistication but have brought no substantial alteration in point of view. Here I refer to techniques, not substance, for each of the books made useful contributions to the understanding of the French Revolution.

More elaborate techniques than these are also valuable. Certainly they add precision to many statements formerly left shadowy. But I cannot wholly agree that historical problems that hinge on the question "how many?" are always better solved by numerical answers. The more precise statement is not always the more accurate one. In 1813 John Adams tried to estimate how many colonists were for independence and hazarded various guesses—nearly equally divided; a third; five to two.[8] It would no doubt be more precise to be able to say 39 percent were for, 31 percent against, and 30 percent neutral, or to plant a good solid decimal point with a long series of digits behind it. But it would be less accurate to do so, for the data does not support that degree of refinement; and the Adams statement itself I believe to be less accurate, given the present state of our knowledge,

[7] Oscar Handlin, *Boston's Immigrants*, rev. ed. (Cambridge, 1959) , 234 ff.; Chapter 8 at note 16.

[8] To William Plumer, March 28; to Thomas McKean, August 31; to Thomas Jefferson, November 12; Thomas McKean to John Adams, September 28, November 15, January 14, 1814, John Adams, *Works*, 10 vols. (Boston, 1850–56) , X, 35, 63, 74, 79, 81, 87.

than a still vaguer partitive formulation: most, some, others. Every effort at quantification, in the end, operates within the parameter set by the limitations of the observed data, and the more venturesome the attempt, the greater the risk of slipping over the edge. Which is no reason for not taking the risk, but is a warning about the precautions necessary in doing so.

The historian who moves unequipped into these strange territories is at the mercy of interpreters and surrenders his freedom to judge what is and is not feasible. We have long known the danger of depending on translators; we must now learn the danger of depending upon programmers. I have seen the products of research swirl out of control, and a work that started to deal with one subject turn into something altogether different—better or worse—as the remorseless printout carried the scholar where he had no intention of going.

There is another peril. The mounting piles of printout raise a barrier between the author and his subject. We know that numbers are not people; aggregations suppress particularities, and, in gaining what we can about the sums, we lose something about the constituent integers. In the dreary process of copying and sorting, I got to know my forty-three thousand Bostonians—where they lived and how they worked—with an intimacy Sam Warner could not match in his excellent study of Philadelphia, for he dealt with the residents of wards and I with the residents of homes, and, while he was able to do some things I could not, he was not able to do others that I could.[9]

And often in the end, after the calculations are in, we still revert to a literary issue: the choice of adjectives. I watched closely and with admiration the manner in which Stephen A. Thernstrom handled the highly complex technical problems involved in estimating the rate of social mobility in nineteenth-century Newburyport. His conclusion seemed to me sound, although I was amazed to learn that so many sons of unskilled laborers moved upward in occupation. Some years later, however, I was even more amazed to find a historian draw from the same figures an unwarranted conclusion about how few moved upward: "Thanks to

[9] Sam Bass Warner, Jr., *Private City: Philadelphia in Three Periods of Its Growth* (Philadelphia, 1968), 226 ff.

Thernstrom we now know that in at least one nineteenth-century city, Newburyport, there is no solid basis in fact for the widely held view that social mobility was a significant reality."[10]

Now the precise number had receded from my consciousness; but I wondered what difference it made. Suppose it were 22 percent; one could write *only* 22 percent or *fully* 22 percent with equal plausibility. Or if it were 78 percent, one could still say *only* or *fully*.

Of course, if this number were one in a series, we could make a different kind of judgment—*more* or *less*. And Thernstrom did gather up nine other estimates, produced by varying methods and covering various areas at various times. But the evaluation still depended on the mastery of material external to the quantitative data.

Theory at this juncture is a useful crutch. A fully articulated and well-agreed-upon theory of social mobility might supply models against which to match particular findings. Theory might also suggest means of compensating for the deficiencies of data, as it did for Alfred H. Conrad and John R. Meyer in their study of "The Economics of Slavery in the Antebellum South." But even if the appropriate theory is at hand, the historian must know it well enough to judge the fit to his own evidence and to his own sense of the particular situation.

To add to his obligations, we are told by Robert W. Fogel and others that the historian must also take account of counterfactual propositions. To judge the consequences of railroad development, we must estimate the results that would have followed from building canals instead; and his own probings in that direction I find stimulating. Indeed, it would be possible to extend the number of counterfactual propositions indefinitely. Suppose a strong federal authority had insisted that there be one Boston–New York route, not four? Suppose the first railroad corporations had been authorized, as the turnpikes were, to maintain the roads for the use of competing common carriers? A great mass of computation would follow, of which the historian would have to take account, but which would not solve his problem. Unfortunately,

---

10 Merle Curti, *Human Nature in American Thought* (Columbia, Mo., [1968]), 104; Stephan A. Thernstrom, *Poverty and Progress* (Cambridge, 1964). See also Chapter 8 at note 29.

his task would still be to explain how and why the railroads developed as they did.[11]

The quantitative techniques make the greatest display and account for the most lavish grants. But they are not alone among the weapons in the historian's armory. Other varied instruments have long stood in the corners, for their popularity seasonally waxed and waned through the decades. It is good to see the rediscovery, if not the fully successful use, of the techniques of historical demography, too much neglected since they served A. M. Carr-Saunders, R. R. Kuczynski, and D. V. Glass in the 1930s. It would be better if one could be sure that old mistakes were not being repeated in new forms.

Geography, on the other hand, has largely receded from the historical consciousness in the United States, despite the recent valiant efforts of Harry R. Merrens and Raleigh A. Skelton and other practitioners of that discipline. Even the renewal of interest in urban studies has not recalled attention to the leads of Pierre Laveden, left unexplored since his day.

A minor revision of terminology, and we find ourselves among the behavioral sciences, confronted by psychology. There is no need to repeat here what was so forcefully stated in 1958 in William L. Langer's thoughtful presidential address about the importance for historians of the techniques and concepts of psychology. Similar pleas reached us earlier from Lucien Febvre and others, although in less sophisticated forms. It is far easier, however, to make than to implement such suggestions, for more is required than a simple plastering over of gaps in the evidence with patches of theory. Dependence upon the concepts of Erik Erikson or R. D. Laing provides no more support in the 1970s than Freud did in the 1920s. The need exists; it long has. The tools of analysis deserve careful study; they long have. But efforts to treat the data of the past with them have not commanded confidence. Note, for instance, the bitter controversy that followed upon a recent diagnosis of the illness of George III. Or William C.

---

[11] Alfred H. Conrad and John R. Meyer, *Economics of Slavery and Other Studies in Economic History* (Chicago, 1964) , 3–84; Robert William Fogel, *Railroads and American Economic Growth: Essays in Econometric History* (Baltimore, 1964) ; Fritz Redlich, " 'New' and Traditional Approaches to Economic History and Their Interdependence," *Journal of Economic History,* XXV (December 1965) , 480 ff.

Bullitt's Wilson. Or the first volume of David Donald's Sumner
or Stanley Elkins' Sambo. Or the challenges that should have
greeted the facile generalizations in Michel Foucault's history of
insanity. Or what is said and left unsaid about the emotional and
other nonrational aspects of human behavior in the past.[12]

I am far from having exhausted the list of techniques we have
either neglected or misused. Erwin Panofsky and Francis Yates
in their own fields have demonstrated the illuminating potentialities of iconography; but we have hardly begun effectively to exploit the mass of artifacts of the past three centuries. As a result,
the crude conclusions that offset the useful insights of Philippe
Ariès, who blundered upon some of these materials, met uncritical
acquiescence. An occasional essay like Carl Schorske's on Vienna
makes analogies with music; but I had to go back to Wilhelm
Dilthey's work of more than eighty years ago for a serious effort
to use the content of music as evidence of the experience of those
who created or listened to it.[13]

We have been deficient also in the way in which we use the
rudimentary units with which we work: words. For almost a
century anthropologists, linguists, philosophers, and literary critics have devoted sustained attention to language and its surface,
symbolic and hidden meanings. Yet the currents of thought generated by Bertrand Russell, I. A. Richards, or Claude Lévi-Strauss
have not perceptibly altered the way in which historians look at
documents or analyze texts. In a different, although somewhat
related, field we may have retrogressed in the past three decades;
we have gone no farther now in the history of ideas than did A. O.

12 William L. Langer, "Next Assignment," *American Historical Review*, LXIII
(January 1958), 283 ff.; Charles Chenevix-Trench, *Royal Malady* (New York, 1964);
Ida Macalpine and Richard Hunter, *George III and the Mad-Business* (London,
1969); Sigmund Freud and William C. Bullitt, *Thomas Woodrow Wilson* (Boston,
1967); David H. Donald, *Charles Sumner and the Coming of the Civil War* (New
York, 1960); Stanley M. Elkins, *Slavery* (Chicago, 1959); Michel Foucault, *Madness
and Civilization*, trans. Richard Howard (New York, 1965).

13 Philippe Ariès, *Centuries of Childhood*, trans. Robert Baldick (New York,
1962); Irene Q. Brown, "Philippe Ariès on Education and Society," *History of Education Quarterly*, VII (Fall 1967), 357 ff.; Carl E. Schorske, "Politics and the
Psyche in *fin-de-siècle* Vienna," *American Historical Review*, LXVI (July 1961),
930 ff.; Wilhelm Dilthey, *Von Deutscher Dichtung and Musik* (Leipzig, 1933),
189 ff.

Lovejoy and Perry Miller in this country or Friedrich Meinecke and Ernst Cassirer in Europe.

The mere multiplication in the number of tools at his disposal has not therefore helped the historian. While he hastily learns to use one, others rust neglected; new models constantly appear, and the old have scarcely paid for themselves when they are obsolete. Imagine the frustration of a scholar trying to use in the 1970s the statistics or psychology he learned in the 1930s, if he did not really keep up with change in those fields; and if he did, how the process of doing so would have eaten into the time for his other work.

Of necessity, consequently, insofar as history claimed to be a science, its sole instrument for advancing knowledge was the monograph. However productive of insights the analytic essay or the discursive narrative might be, only the monograph on a defined and necessarily circumscribed subject afforded the scholar the medium for assembling, evaluating, and weighing the total evidence yielded by his research. This was the only available counterpart of the experiment or the controlled observation on which other disciplines depended.

In traditional fields with a canon defined through the decades or centuries, monographs fall within a mosaic that provides a standard for assessing their contributions. The *kriegschuldfrage,* the French, American, and English revolutions, monasticism— such issues tolerate alterations of detail and broad efforts at continuing reinterpretation. Even the intrusion of nonspecialists sometimes has beneficial results, for the mobilization of resources to beat back novelty requires at least an effort at stocktaking. In Europe the small number of scholars and strict professorial control over students' subjects limit the consequences of fragmentation. But in subjects without defined boundaries or questions, and particularly in the United States, where numbers are large and where tutelary controls scarcely exist, monographs spin in space without reference to any particular orbit. The most impressive do not touch off chains of investigation to verify, extend, or amend the interpretations advanced. Six years later in the one case, and eight in the other, we still had no comparable studies against which to test Thernstrom's conclusions about social mobility in Newburyport or Warner's about the suburbs of Boston.

Could we hope to do better with analyses of the demography of Andover or violence in the Kansas cattle towns?[14]

The discontinuity of research—the fact that the questions raised and answers given fail to stir the attention of historians other than their authors—enlarges the dangers of specialization. The distension of knowledge and the academic organization of American and, increasingly, all universities make some degree of specialization unavoidable, as does the growing complexity of techniques. We now have specialists by country and by period, with lines becoming ever finer, and also by method employed and subject treated. Even to be a generalist now is a kind of specialty, as if there could be a breed apart working not intensively on a narrow subject but spread thin over a broad area. We approach an ideal in which each scholar rules a little domain without concern for what happens over the fence.

Unhappily the subject is not so readily divided. The important developments insist on crossing boundaries, not only of time and space and language, but also of techniques and systematic analysis. We cannot be intellectual historians without occasionally needing to know about demography or agriculture; or economic historians without knowing something about law. The tendency toward specialization more seriously than ever inhibits the search for connections, for the synthesizing aspects, highly valued in the 1930s.

We have long attempted to offset the damage done by discontinuity and specialization through conferences, sponsored research, serial publications, and other devices to encourage teamwork or collaboration, or at least through comparative studies to focus attention on common questions. These devices have not worked. I do not say that they cannot work or should not work, but they have not, and I speak not only from experience, but from reflection on the evidence of others. I looked recently at the list of Needs and Opportunities for Research prepared by a committee of the American Historical Association in 1932. It was a good list. It still is. The needs and opportunities still exist, most of them still virgin territory. In fact, joint efforts now are more difficult

---

14 Thernstrom, *Poverty and Progress;* Sam Bass Warner, Jr., *Streetcar Suburbs* (Cambridge, 1962) ; Philip J. Greven, Jr., *Four Generations* (Ithaca, 1970) ; Robert R. Dykstra, *Cattle Towns* (New York, 1968) .

than they were seventy years ago; compare the tasks of A. B. Hart in readying the American Nation Series and Lord Acton, the old Cambridge History, with those of their more recent successors. Moreover, the assumption that nationalism would cease to exert a divisive influence upon the discipline turned out to be utterly naive.[15]

To compound our difficulties we stagger beneath a burden, bequeathed by our intellectual progenitors, of making ourselves useful in the solution of society's ever-changing problems. Allied to the analytical social sciences with their commitment to questions relevant to current policy, historians felt both internal and external pressures to refocus their attention with every change in the headlines. One unintended result was a massive maldistribution of manpower. The historians of the 1930s emphasized the primacy of scholarship and denied the obligation of the scholar to take account of "the possible applications of his findings to practical affairs." They intended to "cover the wide world and all time with their searchings." Nevertheless, their emphasis on the discipline as a social science diverted disproportionate energy into the study of the recent past and of the United States. A second result was a faddishness in the subjects that attracted graduate students, with alterations in taste as radical and as frequent as those in clothing, and the discontinuities more abrupt than ever.[16]

Hence the disarray of the discipline. Learning, like power, is susceptible to infeudation and, in the one case as in the other, to abuse. The most serious is the decline of craftsmanship. With every historian free to putter in his garden to his heart's content without interference or criticism, with many of them engaged in areas in which the evidence is partial and the rules for its use imperfect, it often seems not to matter how sloppy the job is. I speak here not of the complex problems of interpretation but of the simpler ones that involve the verification of statements of fact.

15 American Historical Association, Committee on the Planning of Research, *Historical Scholarship in America: Needs and Opportunities* (New York, 1932). Publication of the American Nation Series (28 vols.) took fourteen years (1904–18), of the Cambridge Modern History (13 vols.), ten (1902–12). In a considerably longer period their successors remained incomplete.

16 Charles A. Beard, *Charter for the Social Sciences* (New York, 1932), 5, 6.

I do not have a reliable index for measuring the precise frequency of error over time; I offer only an impression, and not proof, but illustrations. Furthermore, I do not wish to imply that I consider myself to have been free of sin. Having written more than most, I have probably committed more errors than most. No one knows better than I the mischief the occurs in the transfer of a name or number from the source to the note, thence to the holograph copy and on, by way of successive typists and compositors, to the printed page. I address myself not to such human failings, but to an attitude that treats the fact either as irrelevant or as susceptible to manipulation toward an end dictated by some more general logic.

The first illustration is personal. Shortly after my return to the United States in the fall of 1970, I noted the review in which Robin W. Winks hailed David Hackett Fischer's *Historians' Fallacies* as an important book, perhaps the most important to have appeared in recent years, in terms of helping an entire generation of scholars who profess to have lost confidence in being historians. Not these laudatory phrases, however, but a reference to my own work caught my attention. In due course, therefore, I turned to the book's index and then to the pages referred to, where I found a discussion of *argumentum ad nauseam*. Nauseating was the proper word. The utter stupidity of the comments was not surprising. Nor was the fact that they showed no evidence that their author had read any of the books alluded to. But I was shocked that he could not copy the titles correctly. I do not suggest that he should have looked at the title pages on the chance that some riffling of the pages might have offered him a clue to the contents, although he might thus have refrained from citing as my work a UNESCO symposium of which I was *rapporteur*. It would have been a matter of simple prudence in laying about at antagonists, some of whom have a modicum of polemic skill, to keep a guard up. If he chose instead to stride unzipped into battle, it was because the mere matter of accuracy was less important than getting graduate students "chortling over one passage or another in the stacks" (Mr. Winks's terms of praise) .[17]

Taxed with these errors at the December 1970 meeting of the

17 Robin W. Winks, "Hardly a Major Historian Escapes Unscathed," *New York Times Book Review*, May 10, 1970, p. 2. See also Louis O. Mink, review of *Historians' Fallacies* in *History and Theory*, X (1971) , 107 ff.

A.H.A., Fischer offered to correct the titles. He did not offer to read the books to which he had referred or to examine the accuracy of the statements he made about them. Christopher Lasch, who shared the platform, was more prudent; he did not argue that misquotation did not matter, as he did in 1965 when a perceptive reviewer exposed the careless blunders in *The New Radicalism in America, 1889–1963*. I hope that his silence was a token of acquiescence, in principle at least, with the basic proposition that there can be no scholarly discussion of any broader matter until there is agreement—total, unqualified, and unconditional— on the ineluctable and binding quality of the data.[18]

Softness on this issue conforms to other manifestations of the decay of professional standards—the decline, on the one hand, of the quality of documentation and, on the other, of critical capacity, the assignments undertaken and never completed, the grants accepted and never complied with, the shifty letters of reference and the equivocal evaluations.

The profession, Peirce's community of investigators, has failed to do anything to halt the erosion of standards. I am not suggesting that a few good, juicy public scandals would be desirable; I am suggesting the need for the internal discipline that arises out of accepted standards of practice and malpractice and out of the tokens of recognition that provide guidelines to the aspiring. We lack those standards or guidelines as long as a notice in the New York *Times* or the *New Yorker* is more important in establishing a career in history than a review in the *American Historical Review* or the *Journal of American History;* as long as promotions and appointments rest on strategic or ideological considerations rather than on merit; and as long as prizes are awarded according to the caprice and prejudice of judges rather than as recognition of excellence.

An ingenious essay informed us of the death of the past. "The strength of the past in all aspects of life is far, far weaker than it was a generation ago," says J. H. Plumb. "Indeed, few societies

---

18 John P. Roche, "Profiles in 'Tsoores,'" *New Leader*, XLVIII (Aug. 16, 1965), 14, and the rejoinders, *ibid.* (Sept. 13, 1965), 33 and (Sept. 27, 1965), 34, 35; Chapter 6 at note 12.

have ever had a past in such galloping dissolution as this." The obituary is premature. Although it may no longer serve the particular purposes he ascribed to it, the sense of the past is as live as ever.[19]

I thumb once more through John Fowles's *The French Lieutenant's Woman*. What conceivable merit earned it a place on the best-seller lists of two countries I do not know; but certainly a considerable element in its popular attractiveness was its antique décor—the sense of distance from characters and setting, which also repeatedly crops up on stage and screen, and in all the aspects of contemporary culture devoted to "camp." Nor, I believe, would an examination of the rhetoric of the decades after 1955 reveal that the past ceased to be a source of myths—although those current in the 1970s differed from those Plumb described, and they swayed broader sectors of the society. Actually, his moving peroration could itself be read as a plea for another/different/better/ newer myth. On quite another level, it is significant that the analytical social sciences, which a generation earlier were content with static models, increasingly sought a time dimension.[20]

I agree with Plumb in perceiving an inverse relationship between the past in his sense and history. Only, while he finds the one dead and the other strong, I find the one still vigorous and the other weak.

The crisis in history is the result not of the death of the past but of its misappropriation. Its negligent guardians have lost command. Confused by new gadgets, internally divided and distracted by the racket outside, they have allowed their subject to slip into the hands of propagandists, politicians, dramatists, novelists, journalists, and social engineers. I wish that I could share the easy, unreflective optimism of the introduction to the Winter 1971 issue of *Dædalus*, "Historical Studies Today," the editor of which delivers the casual judgment that "professional historical investigation is flourishing, and is as robust as it has ever been." That more people that year earned a living by calling themselves historians consoles me not at all. That as much good honest work as ever, or more, may be getting done consoles me only slightly

19 J. H. Plumb, *Death of the Past* (Boston, 1970) , 15.

20 See Chapters 15, 17.

more, for the obstacles to identifying and learning from the first-rate product in any field are more formidable than before.[21]

Mostly I draw comfort from the reflection that, whatever may happen to the community of investigators, the historian, when all else is stripped away, remains a creative individual.

Of that I remind myself daily when I pass the ancient dicta-phone, vintage about 1936, that stands at the entrance to my office. The first such instrument I acquired was a castoff discarded by one of the deans in 1950. I well recall my first essay in creation by way of this medium. Having carefully read the instructions, I extracted from its protective case a clean wax cylinder which I mounted on the roller. I connected the feedline, threw the switch, adjusted the needle, and pressed the release pedal. Nothing happened. I checked all the connections; still nothing. Something was missing. It then became clear to me that, however ingenious the equipment, it would not work unless I had something to say.

The historian will not find it by borrowing tools or slogans from scientists or propagandists, from the wielders of power or those who seek to gain it. He will find something to say as a historian only through the creative tension that arises from exercising the full power of his imagination and understanding against the unyielding evidence that survives the past. He can continue to do so as an individual even if the crisis in the discipline should leave him without a community of investigators of which to be part.

In my youth I feared the fate of the dusty little men in dusty little rooms, who hoarded up the dusty little learning no one valued. Hence, I wished to believe that a net of connections with what had gone before and what would follow would support my book in the open air.

My fears now fasten on a more grotesque image: a super, super, super market, in which shiny, shiny men stock the endless shelves, indiscriminate, inarticulate, each to his own pitch—with no questions asked about the contents of the boxes. Hence, I try now to read and write each book as if it stood totally alone, following

---

[21] The editors' preface to the book version, Felix Gilbert and Stephen Graubard, *Historical Studies Today* (New York, 1972), vii–x, remains resolutely sanguine, although in another form.

nothing, with nothing to follow, its worth set solely by its own contents.

The crisis may pass, and chaos may prove to be the present appearance of new forms sturdier than any of their predecessors. The historian may nurse that much hope. But he must not confuse wish with reality, and he cannot pretend to be one of a community that no longer exists.

*Postscript.* The audience that heard the words above first spoken considered them unduly pessimistic. The intervening years, alas, have validated the bleakness of the appraisal.

The trends apparent in 1970 deepened thereafter and transformed the professional life of historians in the United States. The growth in numbers which enrolled almost twenty thousand members in the American Historical Association turned that organization from a body devoted to preserving and advancing knowledge into a group which labored to further the interests of its members.

Altered forms of governance measured the breadth of the change. As long as it was a society of scholars who shared common standards, it designated officers by recognition as rewards for achievements in writing or teaching. The mere suggestion, as in 1945, of political or other extraneous considerations in the choice shocked the membership, which decisively rejected it. The shift to contested elections, with tickets balanced to reflect internal diversities, revealed the disappearance of the old, shared common standards and the inability to recognize achievement without reference to ideology or the special interests of various constituencies. The annual meetings, although still making place for learned papers, devoted increasing attention to the welfare not of history but of historians. Thus, the 1971 program chairman called for close contacts with the mass media, "not as a public relations gimmick" but to educate the public "about the importance of history as a discipline and the worth and function of historians."[22]

The drift toward trendy relevant subjects and the deterioration of standards continued. Doctoral dissertations, which measured

22 *AHA Newsletter,* X (September 1972) , 14.

the direction of future scholarship, revealed the growing popularity of twentieth-century American topics and the contraction of
interest in ancient, medieval, and renaissance history. The decade
of the 1960s produced 5,884 doctorates, as compared with 7,695
for the whole period 1873–1960; and of those trained recently,
fewer than 29 percent were products of the seven universities
which before 1960 had produced more than 44 percent of the
degree holders. Miraculously, good work continued to be done—
although the deterioration of all standards of performance complicated the task of discovering it.[23]

23 Warren F. Kuehl, *Dissertations in History* . . . *1873–1960* (Lexington, Ky.,
1965), and *Dissertations in History* . . . *1961–June 1970* (Lexington, Ky., 1972), x.

# 2

# *Living in a Valley*

PEOPLE WHO LIVE in the mountains view landscapes different from those exposed to the people of the plains.[1]

The statement is simple. Perhaps it seems unexceptionable to the point of being commonplace. Yet its implications deserve exploration; they have much to say to the historian.

The contrast made a deep impression upon me because I came to the mountains after having spent my childhood and youth entirely in the plains.

When I now think of the plains, my thoughts run first to the rural prairies—the long stretches of open fields of the American Middle West, the Russian steppes, or the Low Countries. And yet none partook more of the quality of the plains than the section of urban Brooklyn in which I grew up.

The area was level. The real-estate developers who had filled in the swamps just before the First World War had packed the land down, aiming for, and attaining, the absolute in flatness. Furthermore, they had imposed upon their tracts an immense rectilinear grid that crushed all sense of variety in the landscape. Long, straight lines extended rigidly into the indefinite distance. Position on that grid defined the place. We belonged to 62nd Street and 20th Avenue; that intersection was the center of our neighborhood. From it the rows of houses, much alike, crisscrossed away at right angles for ever and ever. Beyond 62nd lay 63rd, then 64th, and so on, for all we knew to infinity.

1 Oscar Handlin, "Living in a Valley," *American Scholar*, XLVI (Summer 1977), 301–312.

When I grew somewhat older, I explored. I walked west, beyond 65th and 66th, number after number, then got to 86th
Street and discovered the bay at its farther edge. And across the
bay, I knew, was Staten Island, where no doubt the numbers
continued on in their own way indefinitely.

Only in that direction did my explorations reach a satisfactory
conclusion. I once tried going north, from 20th to about 8th
Avenue—into a region of Italian kids so tough that even I beat a
cautious retreat. To the east the forbidding barriers of Washington Cemetery and to the south a baffling maze of parkways frus-
trated boyish efforts at discovery. But then, it was characteristic
that very few of my neighbors, young or old, knew much about
the alien spaces bordering the neighborhood. Their travel did not
take the lateral form that would have revealed the configuration
of the territory. Daily they left home for work or school, great dis-
tances away; but they moved by the subway, which obscured both
topography and people. A voyage through dark tunnels that began with a descent down one hole and terminated with an ascent
up another, miles away, left no sense whatever of what intervened.

With such initial impressions of space I blundered innocently
into another world. My first encounters with the mountains were
shocking and disturbing, for they exposed me not only to a novel
set of sights, but also to modes of thinking totally different from
my own.

In the mountains, aphorisms coined on the plains become
either irrelevant or false. The wisdom of the one place does not
apply to the other. The sun rises in the east and sets in the west.
A truism. But in the mountains the first light glistens off the
western peaks; only later does the ball of fire appear in the east.
At dusk the eastern summits still gleam, while shadows cover
those in the west. A straight line is the shortest distance between
two points—in the plains, not in the mountains. Whoever has
viewed the way in which paths switch back and forth up the
slopes, or snake around natural obstacles, will understand why
linear measurements have little meaning here. Indeed, away from
the plains I lose altogether the habit of calculating distance in
blocks, meters, or miles; the gauge of hours and minutes is far
more significant.

So, too, nomenclature in the mountains follows distinctive

rules, different from those of the plains. Not that the terms up there are necessarily more specific. On the contrary, some words are maddeningly vague and inclusive. The word *Alp,* for instance, refers to the entire chain of mountains that extends from France across to Austria. It can also refer to a high-altitude meadow or field. Still again, it can refer to a building in that field. The word would thus seem to lack precise definition. But, as understood by mountain people, it does have a clear meaning, derived from its relation to a whole function that is an important part of their way of life. While undifferentiated in the sense required by plainsmen, for whom a place is a place is a place, the word has clear connotations for those familiar with the animal husbandry of the mountains.

By contrast, other words have a particularity far beyond that to which the people of the plains are accustomed. Down below, the word "meadow" has a broad, inclusive meaning. And in some cases no doubt the people of the mountains also use it in a general way. They will, for instance, write *Wiesen* on signs posted to warn the tourist away from the growing grasses they will harvest into hay. But among themselves, the mountain people use a much greater number of words; not only *alp,* but *Au, Rüti, Schwendi, Sass, Trift, Boden, Heuberge, Maienfeld, Maiensass.* When you add to these the propensity for diminutives and for descriptive prefixes and suffixes, the result is an imposing array of words that apply to the fields they know. This of course is apart from the fact that each specific field has its own patricular name. People are not very good at explaining the meaning of the differences they recognize; as nearly as I can make out, the term applied to a meadow depends on its situation—whether it lies above or below the tree line, whether it gets the morning or the afternoon sun, whether it was an opening in the forest always, or at least as far as memory ran, or whether it was the product of fire in historic times. Such distinctions hardly matter in the plains; they have tremendous importance in the mountains, where habits of abstraction, in these matters at least, are lacking.

As a plainsman who derives linear, lateral impressions of space from an inspection of maps, I am again and again struck by the sensory quality of apprehension up there. Years ago I felt as lost as Hans Castorp did on his magic mountain when snow obscured the markers. The mountain people need no man-made guideposts. I can chart by compass point the *joch* or *fenêtre* or *fürkli;* they see, without consciously seeking, the yoke, the window, the saddle. In September I was cutting downward through an unmarked wood when I found myself veering off on the flat in search of a path. I wondered why, for I was not conscious of having made a decision to do so. Then I became aware that I could hear a stream below, so I must have known, without knowing it, that on unfamiliar terrain it was more prudent not to come too far down off a beaten trail lest I find myself at the edge of an unpassable gorge.

⤸

This preliminary suggestion that the ways of thinking in the mountains differ from those in the plains has perhaps been needlessly lengthy; but the point deserved the making because we usually derive our impressions from writers who are people of the plains.

Three little stories illustrate some of those distinctive ways of thinking. These stories happen to be true, and they are the products of my own observations. If need be, I could supply you with witnesses and evidence, even documents. The fact that the stories are susceptible of proof does not matter. For even had I the fictive imagination to make them up, they would still be true in what they say about mountain folk mentality. What they signify, if anything, is another matter.

The first story deals with the residents of a village just beyond the forest, part of the same commune but distinctly set off from the place in which we lived. The people there carried about a half-hidden fear of avalanches. Not that they had had one in recent years, or even within the actual memory of anyone then alive. But more so than other folk—and why I do not know—they dreaded the possibility. When asked, they repeated what everyone knew, that there had quite recently been an avalanche in Davos. Davos was a big city, and it stood to reason that a disaster which damaged so large and powerful a town would overwhelm a little hamlet. Something had to be done.

I have never been quite sure about the precise allocation of governmental responsibility over there in matters such as these. A federal research institute devoted itself to the study of avalanches; and apparently, under some circumstances, those authorities were willing to assist. But appeals from this village were unavailing; as far as science could foretell, the avalanche danger was slight. Nor did the cantonal officials help, although they seemed forever involved in numerous petty details connected with control of the forests and of the roads. The commune of which the village was a part did extend a little aid, but I suspect less out of conviction than out of a desire to pacify a significant bloc of voters in the assembly.

All in all, however, outside support counted for little; the men of the village did the work themselves. In periods of relatively low activity, during the summer and late in the fall, they were up high above, antlike, beaverlike, day after day erecting a barrier to halt any future fall. To supplement the heavy timbers ordinarily used, they somehow secured a supply of old steel beams or rails, which they laboriously dragged up into place.

Thus the toil went on from year to year. Although few actually shirked their share of the task, the young men grumbled; and the complaints grew louder with the passage of time. Nothing had happened, and this work came to seem unnecessary to the youths. They had, after all, received assurances from the highest level of authority that the effort was not needed; and they, unlike their elders, could think of more diverting ways of using time than in repetition of a labor that was never finished. For it was in the nature of the barrier—or rather, by the time we saw it, of the set of barriers—that improvements could always be imagined: supporting lines above and on the flanks, more strength at the base, and the like. Meanwhile, nothing tested the worth of what had now become one of the chief preoccupations of the village.

One night in the early spring the test did come. There were warnings. Two days before, the cantonal police arrived and ordered the people of one of the lateral valleys to evacuate their homes and take up lodgings in town. But the village, they insisted, would remain safe. Then, before dawn, the avalanche defied science, swerved unexpectedly, and came down across the eastern corner of the hamlet. The flow of ice and snow carrying masses of rock with it, swept away an ancient forest, cut deep gashes into the lower meadow, and demolished a cluster of houses, burying the sleeping occupants. As for the barrier, it was in the right place but totally ineffective, wiped out in a matter of seconds.

Later, when the danger of further slides had subsided, people came soberly to look, and there was much shaking of heads. But the general tone was acquiescence. So the mountain behaved; we did what we could, but defeat was not surprising.

Still later began the immense job of clearing away the debris. Then, late in the summer and on into the fall, the men once more climbed upward and resumed the task of constructing the barrier. That was not surprising.

What was surprising was that the sons now ceased to grumble. We knew well one of the modern young men, son of a peasant of average means. The youth had somehow acquired a locksmith's skill. He did not actually practice that trade, but worked in a metal factory about fifteen miles away where he designed hinges, handles, locks, and other products of iron and brass. His income was good; he had contacts with the world away from the village; and he maintained those contacts with a snappy Fiat equipped with speakers, back as well as front, that announced his presence in the neighborhood. In the long summer evenings and on weekends he hastened from the factory to put in a few hours on the barrier.

Since he had earlier been one of the leading malcontents, I asked why he now put in the time and effort. He had evidently given no thought at all to the question and stared in astonishment that it should be asked.

"But," he said, "there is much to do before the winter sets in, and the fathers will not be able to do it all alone. Help is necessary."

Neither he nor anyone else, then or later, considered the evidence: if an avalanche did come, the barrier built with the toil of years would be ineffective. That judgment simply did not enter into their calculation. An avalanche would come again some day, and one did what one could, without weighing the chances of success.

I draw no conclusions from this story, which, however, reminds me of another.

When we paid the rent for our house we went around to the tavern over which our landlady presided. Formality required then

that we spend some time there—a drink, a snack—which was not
in itself unusual, except that this particular tavern was much fre-
quented by locals and somewhat off the beaten track for outsiders.
Generally, a card game was in progress around the big table by
the stove. And invariably one middle-aged man, rather battered,
was an onlooker, never a player. He hoisted his beers cheerfully,
but after a point, we noticed, the waitresses ceased to take his
orders.

We once asked our landlady why he never played. She shrugged
off the question: he is the man who takes care of the pigs and
therefore he has to leave early. Why? Because to take care of the
pigs he must get up well before dawn each morning, collect the
slops from a wide area, and bring them up to the rather out-of-the-
way corner where he tended the needs of his own pigs and those
others in his charge. All this he had to do before the active life of
the village began.

In the months that followed, nothing changed in the relationship of the man who took care of the pigs to his neighbors. He
remained a solitary, morose figure, and we began to feel that he
was somewhat put upon. We saw him as the community's helpless,
victimized underman.

Not at all, expostulated the landlady, when we expressed these
sentimental observations. The man who took care of the pigs
owned land on the northern slope worth millions.

Originally, it seems, this land had been swampy, difficult to
drain, and not suitable for tillage. Now, however, that whole area
was much improved; better management of the river flow had
dried out the bordering plots. The tracts held by the man who
took care of the pigs were as good as any in the valley.

In any case, that was not the issue—not any longer, that is, not
since those people from Zurich turned up who wished precisely
that plot on which to build a mammoth condominium. Apparently from their point of view the low-lying situation was ideal.

Why did he not sell?

As to that, there were divisions of opinion. The people from
the city had told him how much better off he would be. He could
sleep late; he could drink what he liked; and he could gamble to
his heart's content—even play in the casino at Lucerne. Some of
the wealthier residents had confirmed this to him. They, after all,

knew that the Commune would gain taxes from the new construction; and those in turn would lower their own.

But to all these arguments he gave a single response: And who will take care of the pigs?"

And most of the men in the tavern agreed with him, which is why they did not wish him too sorely tempted by drink or cards.

The third story occurred in another village, in the west rather than in the east, in a poorer place situated on a gorge the slopes of which were so steep that they accommodated, properly speaking, no roads. There was not a beast of burden on the mountain; everything that moved men carried on their backs or dragged on carts.

There were not very many carts, and most of them were much alike: two axles, four wheels, a single shaft. One was different; it was mounted with two shafts so that, drawn by its owner, it left the clear impression it had been meant for the harness of a horse or donkey.

We had learned by then how to ask questions, and how to be patient while answers slowly emerged, sometimes weeks later.

"Why such a curious cart for up here?"

"Oh, that belongs to the man who talks to his horse."

So it seemed there had once been a horse. How the horse got up there, or why the man sustained him, we never heard explained. One story had it that the owner had ridden in the Swiss cavalry, which had allowed him to take his horse home like a gun or saber. This was plausible—there was a Swiss cavalry— but we could not be sure that was truly the practice.

In any case, there had been a horse; and the name of the horse had been Max; and the man had spent a great deal of time talking to Max. The man was a person of some intelligence; for instance, he read, really read, the *Journal de Genève,* and no doubt discussed its contents with Max.

Now, it seems that originally there had not been a cart, just Max. But the peasants had disapproved. The horse ate like a horse—that is, he consumed more than a human being did—and it was not proper that Max should live in idleness while everyone else worked. In time, all this censorious gossip reached the ears of the man who talked to his horse, and he decided to do something about it. His response had profound consequences for the village. He purchased the cart and offered to deliver fresh bread from the baker every morning to such households as wished it. One result was to legitimize Max. Another was a change in dietary habits. The peasants, who had formerly consumed hard dark bread, which remained edible for weeks on end, now acquired a taste for gray or half-white or even white bread baked fresh daily.

But where was Max?

Well, it seemed that Max had died some years before. Now the man who talked to his horse talked to himself, and himself pulled the cart.

But why should he do so, since it was no longer necessary to legitimize the presence of the horse?

Well, was the answer, who would deliver the bread?

*～～*

I will not presume to sum up the meaning of these stories, other than to reflect that they show something about the distinctive way of thinking of the people who live in the mountains.

Yet I have a sense that the cast of mind here revealed is laden with significance for historians, most of whom are people of the plains and therefore fail to read the lessons the mountains teach.

There is the matter of perspective, for instance, as important to the historian as to the painter. The image of the mountain viewed from below is that of the panoramic postcard; the tourist sends home a picture of Mt. Blanc, or of the Matterhorn, or of the Jungfrau, each a conical peak rising in grandeur toward the sky.

Yet the men of the mountain know that Mt. Blanc viewed from across the lake to the north presents one appearance; seen from Val d'Aosta to the south an entirely different one. Both are equally true; that is, both are equally false. The picture imprinted on a postcard depends upon the perspective—that is, upon the interpretation and the position of the photographers, which, after all, is a phenomenon often troubling to historians who worry about their objectivity and about the biases of their points of view.

And yet, there really is a mountain. Only the observer does not get to know it by looking at postcards any more than the historian can master an event or an era by pondering the outlines of great overarching interpretations. To those familiar with its ridged and wrinkled flanks, with its spread of jagged stone, and with the immense variety of its restless streams, the mountain is far from displaying a clear, conical shape. It offers, rather, the sum of many particular visual impressions—slopes of wood and stone and grass, lines of rock and water, huddled buildings, gaps of sky—which merge in the mind of the viewer endowed with patience and imagination. As do the numerous scraps of evidence hoarded by the historian. All those problems about objectivity and point of view that trouble historians dissolve in the mountain atmosphere.

Which brings me at last to the great Edward Gibbon the bicentennial of whose monumental work coincided with those of the Declaration of Independence and the *Wealth of Nations*. I have nothing to add to the eloquent words of appreciation already lavished upon this man of many talents, whose mastery of the pen matched perfectly his understanding of the past. I speak of Gibbon only as an observer of the mountains. And in that capacity he was sadly deficient—content to sit in Lausanne and look across the lake. He never ventured to foot the trail; the cultivated people of his generation had not yet acquired the taste for strenuous peasant activity, and he was personally less inclined to physical exertion than most of his contemporaries. Yet, had he ventured a score of miles from his languid habitation, he might not have slipped into the disastrous use of the metaphor that shaped the character of his masterpiece.[2]

We have had careful studies of the evolution of the concept of decline and fall of civilizations; but no one has yet pointed out that the underlying metaphor is fundamentally erroneous. It assumes an analogy between the development of a civilization, or a society, or a state, and the shape of the mountain. The very

[2] G. W. Bowersock, John Clive, and Stephen P. Graubard, eds., *Edward Gibbon and the Decline and Fall of the Roman Empire* (Cambridge, 1977), 87 ff., contains Peter Burke's essay on the idea of decline; Walther Kirchner, "Mind, Mountain, and History," *Journal of the History of Ideas*, XI (June 1950), 412 ff., surveys the idea of mountains from antiquity. Jules Michelet, *Montagne*, 3d ed. (Paris, 1968), is one in a series of natural histories which also includes volumes on birds, the sea, and insects; it also contains the incidental observations of a sensitive historian.

concept of decline implies a slope pointing downward and leading to an ultimate fall—over the edge of a cliff perhaps. Its antithesis is rise, an ever-upward gradient leading to a culminating peak. These are the figures of speech appropriate to a resident of Lausanne who looks across the lake.

Those who know the mountain, however, see an entirely different set of images. They cannot imagine a steady upward climb as a metaphor for civilization, because they know that ascent to the top exposes only a blank. From the peak I have usually seen nothing, unless, on a rare clear day, I could look down at the clouds below. Then, too, those captivated by the figure of speech never think of what comes after the summit. Of all the lowland romantics who rhapsodized about progress, only William Godwin worried about what would happen after attaining the peak. And he quickly brushed off the problem in the certainty that once disease and death had disappeared man would never have to go over the top. Yet, in actuality, he who reaches the peak can do nothing but descend and is constantly in danger, exposed to every form of discomfort. The meanings attached to their peaks by those who have attained them vary with their personalities; but I cannot imagine it ever a symbol of civilization.

It is the same, I suppose, with all suggestions of height. My first airplane flight was in a trimotor Ford, at between a thousand and two thousand feet. Skimming the rooftops as it were I could see everything, the color of cars, the movement of pedestrians. Taking the fast flight from Boston to Chicago, with stops at Albany, Rochester, Buffalo, and Cleveland, the pilot thrilled the dozen passengers by all but brushing against the falls at Niagara. Flight at thirty-five thousand feet offers no comparable sensation; a window seat, even on a clear day, opens on no view of detail in the world far below. Being up is being away.

People who live in the mountains know that it is getting down to the valley that brings them to civilization. It is of the essence of the mountain that it enfolds valleys. Therein it differs from the plain, which neither thrusts upward nor plunges downward. And in the valley, where streams merge into rivers, the towns glisten in the fascination of the unfamiliar.

The process of reaching the goal is by no means simple. A writer familiar with the mountains has expressed some of the

complexity of getting there: "You are on the summit of a hill
and dawn has not yet come, and your path goes on before you.
You can think that all is flat in front of you because the darkness
is ahead where anything can be imagined. But gradually day
dawns and, behold, now you see before you at first a little valley
that grows deeper, and behind this land other valleys, than mountains, peak after peak, far into the distance. I do not lack courage.
Men do not lack courage. I think that I will go down into the
valley, mount the slope on the opposite side, and gradually, with
my courage and my strength and my hope, I'll climb up the path
over the highest mountains. But now the light grows brighter, and
deeper and deeper sinks the valley before me. The first valley, the
one that is quite close to me, that just now was full of night and
in which the road seemed to lie as straight as a rod. There it drops
deeper and deeper. What I thought a while ago to be the bottom
was only a sheet of mist; the bottom is far below. And now in the
brighter light I see bushes and undergrowth on the sides of that
slope, and forests and thorns, and the tracks of wild beasts, and
ravines and walls of rock. And the light grows brighter, and something tells me that it will continue to grow brighter from moment
to moment to all eternity, revealing more and more thorns and
walls, and obstacles, and lurking dangers, and crossings, and impediments."[3]

I recalled this passage not long ago when, coming up from the
valley of the Landwasser, I climbed over the Strella Pass and made
my way down to a place called Tritt. From that point I could see,
actually see, Arosa, which was my destination. But then the path
dipped so that the goal was out of sight, and when finally my way
rose again and approached a cluster of houses, it was not Arosa
at all but Medergen, still a long distance off. So, when Arosa next
came into sight, I was already conscious that there was far from being a direct line to it but rather fold after fold, with slopes leading both up and down.

A transient, I reached the town and passed through intact. But
mountain people fear the hazards and tend to play it safe. Tradi-

---

[3] Jean Giono, *Joy of Man's Desiring* (New York, 1940) , 395–396.

tion, tenacious devotion to inherited tasks, and an intuitive sense of place, traits admirable in the highlands, become encumbrances below. Down there the sun does rise in the east and set in the west; a straight line, driven through space, becomes the shortest distance between two points; men calculate in abstractions—all of which are qualities of civilization. Therefore, only the most venturesome risk the descent; others cling to the villages on the upper slopes until some external force dislodges them.

In our day modernization is such a force, its effects evident in patterns of life, habits, even language. When I first came to the Valais, people spoke their own version of French: they said *septant* and *nonant,* pronounced the "x" in Crettex and Chamonix, and softened the "i" in Finhaut. Now television has taught them to talk like Parisians: they say *soixant-dix* and *quatre-vingt dix* and pronounce Crettex and Chamonix and Finhaut as the city people do. I came down into Champex and asked about the bus to Orsières. It would leave in an hour. Years before, I had walked down to Orsières; but the place had changed so much I could not remember where the path started. To my inquiry they responded, "But it is not dear, the autobus," as if lack of means were the only reason for walking. But then I do not insist that they cling to old values in order to gratify the onlooker's sense of the picturesque.

In the past intrusions from outside took other forms. Ancestors of the families I knew had resisted and, when dislodged, had retreated to high places elsewhere to escape the misfortune of change. I speak of course of but a tiny corner of the earth, but not an inconsequential one. Here from the glaciers the two rivers rise: the one, the Rhone, to flow generally westward and then, looping through the lake, southward to the Mediterranean; the other, the Rhine, to flow eastward, then north to the Low Countries and out to the sea. Here much of the history of Europe took form.

The Walzer made themselves known first in the west, in villages like those of the man who talked to his horse. To escape the oppressive bishops who were their overlords, they drifted eastward to ever higher ground, then discovered and moved through the passes to lands as yet unoccupied. They got as far as places now called Schlappin and Monbiel, where their descendants took care of the pigs and feared the avalanches. Here they stopped, for down below a powerful monastery blocked further advance. And when the Reformation enabled them to drive away the monks and level the cloister, they found that another folk stemming from the Arlberg had preempted the lower valley. Here the Walzer remained, therefore, and remain to this day.[4]

The wisdom of the mountain people recognizes the lay of the land; it is among the greatest of their misfortunes to distinguish what is feasible from what is yearned for. "So one gives up the hope of scaling those peaks where, however, the light is sparkling like the leaping of a wild goat. And so one gives up thinking that one's strength and courage and hope will permit one to descend even into the first little valley that deepens from one moment to the next. But now, in despair, one cries within one's self: 'let me take only one step forward. That is all that my strength will permit!' and the light keeps growing brighter!"

In their own way the valley people are also timid, ringed in as they are by fearsome forests and by mountains to which they cannot retreat, having lost the ancestral skills of survival. Not for nothing does the word *alp* for them have an additional meaning: nightmare. Exposed to the comings and goings of strangers, they must learn to deal flexibly with the ever unexpected and to make the most of contingencies, however much they may strengthen their fortifications and subject themselves to internal discipline. Or, alternatively, for some of them at least, the situation demands fresh venturing and new efforts at ascent and descent.

Where are we? Had I the skill of analysis of those historians who play with long sweeps of the past, I could perhaps draw meaningful analogies between the mountain landscape and the modern experience. That is not my style.

I conclude, therefore, with a comment which is simply personal.

My own lifetime spans more than six decades of wearying endeavor, with many a steep climb upward and not a few precipitous clamberings down. So that now we find ourselves in a valley, aching for ease to enjoy our achievements. Whether we shall be indulged in that hope is largely beyond our control.

But the light has grown immeasurably brighter in the interval since my birth. We know now that no simple journey will bring

4 Paul Zinsli, *Walser Volkstum* (Frauenfeld, 1969) .

us to the summit. Indeed we cannot be sure where the summit lies, or in fact whether it exists at all, for our valley is high enough to reveal the complexity of the surrounding ranges. Therein we are both more, and less, fortunate than our predecessors only a generation ago.

We can take only one step forward. That is all our strength will permit.

But the challenging light keeps growing brighter. And when I falter, hesitate to take that next small step, I remind myself that it is not from failing strength, or lack of skill, or want of courage, but because the light is brighter and reveals the perils on the way.

# The Central Themes of American History

HISTORY, as a body of knowledge, as a mode of interpreting the past, and as a pattern of critical practices, is independent of national affiliations and group loyalties. But historians, like other scholars, only escape the limitations of their culture by recognizing and understanding the social and intellectual constraints under which they operate.

The particular way in which the United States developed deeply influenced the American understanding of the past. Popular images and formal histories alike revolved about a few central themes which reflected the impact of the land and the experience of its population. The history of efforts to cope with those themes shaped the context within which scholars confronted more general problems of interpretation and criticism.

The essays which follow outline the history of the subject in the United States, sketch the prevailing theories of historical interpretation, discuss some of the important principles of historical criticism, and conclude with a note illustrating the difficulties in the appropriate use of evidence.

# 3
# A History of American History

THE DISTINCTIVE CULTURAL DEVELOPMENT of the New World made history one of the early forms of American literature and shaped the guiding assumptions in terms of which people wrote and read about their past. Traces of the concern with uniqueness persisted even after the historians absorbed the influences emanating from Enlightenment Europe, even after acceptance of later standards of scientific scholarship.[1]

From the start Americans believed in a special purpose to their experience as a people. Whether their singularity was actual or not, faith in it affected the way in which chroniclers viewed the past. The felt lack of common antecedents and of common roots and the continuing need to justify departures, desertions, and rebellions against Europe generated prolonged elaborations of the theme of exceptionalism.

The very conditions of settlement in that part of the New World which later became the United States raised troubling questions about the reasons for migration. The seventeenth-century histories answered by expressing confidence in the destiny of the new, feeble plantations. The issue of purpose cropped up over and over again in successive generations. Why had the wanderers left the homes of their ancestors to settle in a strange and empty place?

Americans always had to explain who they were in a sense rarely compelling to other men who took for granted a connection that

---

[1] Oscar Handlin et al., *Harvard Guide to American History* (Cambridge, 1954), 3 ff.; Oscar Handlin, "Les Américains devant leur Passé," *Diogène*, VI (April 1954), 27; Oscar Handlin, "The Central Themes of American History," *Relazioni del X Congresso Internazionale di Scienze Storiche*, Vol. I: *Metodologia* (Florence, 1956), 141 ff.

ran to a time out of mind, between a specific place and themselves
and their families. Even after many generations, the descendants
of those who had occupied the New World felt the recurrent obligation to account for their presence in a land that had not always
been theirs.

Later, too, only a minority of Americans ever knew the attach-
ment to a territory that came from awareness that it was home to
them, and had been home to their parents and grandparents.
Transatlantic migration was a continuous process that carried
wave after wave of newcomers to unfamiliar scenes, where they had
to wonder why they were where they were. In addition, an all but
empty continent, unstable frontier institutions, and ceaseless internal movement again and again compelled restless wanderers to
consider why they were in Ohio rather than in Connecticut, or in
Iowa, or in California. Lacking identification with place, they
searched the past to account for their presence where they were.

Furthermore, migration and settlement were always harsh.
Never was arrival a triumphal conquest—not for the first Englishmen who came to Roanoke or Jamestown, nor for the Pilgrims at
Plymouth, nor for any of their successors in the next three centuries. Not for the families who wandered into the Great Valley
of Virginia or for those who ventured into the Nebraska prairies.
Whether at the first landing on the still unknown continent or
emerging from the steerage of steamships in New York or Boston,
whether passing through gaps in the Appalachians or Rockies,
new arrivals understood that a life of unremitting hardship lay
before them.

The fears were fully realized. The physical and material difficulties were most visible. But the emotional hardships were not the
less painful for being less close to the surface. The suffering caused
by the desertion of familiar scenes and faces cried for explanation
and led to a search for the personal as well as the social significance
of the journey and of life in the New World. Each individual
examined his antecedents and the course he had come in order to
understand why he was where he was; and the whole group or its
literate spokesmen searched the past for meaning about itself.
These quests persistently affected the writing of history in the
United States.

The special circumstances of the area of first settlement deepened the need for justification. This raw wilderness offered new-

comers no such immediate rewards as had Mexico and Peru, but only a field for hard labor. Whoever described this adventure took as a subject not a glorious conquest but the desperate scrabbling for survival.

That very circumstance subjected the earliest historians to the additional pressure of a need to attract followers. Chafing under the isolation, eager to establish connections, aware that success would justify their own migration, they tried to persuade others to join them, to add to the population further streams of people from the Old World or from the East. This motive injected a promotional quality into American historical writing; a desire to display the virtues of the land and stress the edifying experience of the people generated the boosterism that became a recurrent element in writings about the United States. The good fortune of those who came—descriptions of which often stood in luminous contrast with actual experience—was a theme to which every group repeatedly reverted.

In seventeenth-century Virginia such practical considerations moved the more literate settlers to take up their pens and compose contemporary history. Promoters eager to attract newcomers and to convince potential investors wrote glowing accounts of the plantations. John Smith and others mingled descriptions of the country with narratives of travels and with history in the narrower sense. They also on occasion mingled hopes with realities and fiction with fact. Similar considerations influenced New England writers.[2]

These pressures generated habits of thought that long affected Americans. The historians were conscious of their transatlantic heritages, whether or not they had themselves made the crossing. But migration which foreshortened the available past affected the way they thought and wrote. Moreover, the land contained no ancient monuments and its few existing inhabitants had no recorded history, so that what had been seemed less important than what would be.

For a long time the only subject accessible to historians was the

[2] Alden T. Vaughan, *American Genesis: Captain John Smith and the Founding of Virginia* (Boston, 1975), 173 ff.; Philip L. Barbour, *Three Worlds of Captain John Smith* (Boston, 1964), 283 ff.; Laura P. Striker and Bradford Smith, "Rehabilitation of Captain John Smith," *Journal of Southern History*, XXVIII (November 1962), 474 ff.

fate of the ordinary settlers. The exceptional number of learned men among them made the seventeenth-century Puritans the first serious historians in this sector of the New World; and they took their own experience as their subject. Since their migration involved deep religious motives, they wished to explain why they had moved by an answer general enough to reveal the wishes of the God they knew governed the universe. They described a vast providential design in which the migration of a Pilgrim people to America was the pivotal element. The ascription of a moral quality to their history habituated them to regarding the New World as the battlefield of saints and sinners, a mode of thought which persisted long after the original Calvinist impulse faded.

William Bradford and Edward Johnson examined social reality and endowed it with cosmic significance. Bradford's *Of Plymouth Plantation,* a carefully detailed circumstantial history of the settlement its author helped to establish, discerned universal significance in what happened to the people who accompanied him. Yet the account was realistic. Bradford described the ever-present toil and danger, as well as the rewards and achievements of life in the colony, then inquired why "sundry notorious sins," especially drunkenness and incontinency and even "sodomy and buggery (things fearful to name) ," intruded in "a land where the same was so much witnessed against and so narrowly looked unto, and severely punished when it was known."

He gave three reasons for the frequency of these transgressions. Perhaps the devil bore "a greater spite" against these churches, "that he might cast a blemish and stain upon them in the eyes of the world." Again, it might have been with wickedness as with waters when their streams were dammed up: "When they get passage they flow with more violence . . . than when they are suffered to run quietly in their own channels." Or it might have been that there were actually not "more evils in this kind" than elsewhere, but they were "here more discovered and seen and made public."

Pondering these issues, Bradford moved from the conventional religious aspect to more practical considerations. He recalled that men in a wilderness, who required much help in building and planting, "when they could not have such as they would, were glad to take such as they could." They thus brought over "many untoward servants," both men and women who, when their times expired, became families themselves. Finally, the transport of passengers and their goods became a trade, and the enterprisers, "to make up their freight and advance their profit, cared not who the persons were, so they had money to pay them. And by this means the country became pestered with many unworthy persons." Other profligates came, sent by friends who hoped for reform or at least to be eased of their burden and kept from shame at their dissolute course at home. By one means or other, after twenty years it was a question "whether the greater part be not grown the worser." The intrusion of an economic motive thus undermined the original religious solidarity of the colonists. The need for labor softened scruples about the kind of people admitted and injected strange, uncontrollable elements into the community.[3]

The same detailed realism infused Edward Johnson's *Wonder-Working Providence* when it dealt with the lives of the people which he, more explicitly than Bradford, connected with a grand providential design. Johnson lingered over the hardships of the settlers who, "in the misse of beere supplied themselves with water" and resorted to the mussels and clam banks for their food. The winter's frost being extracted from the earth, they fell to tearing up the roots and bushes with their hoes; "even such men as scarce ever set hand to labour before." Cutting down the woods, they enclosed corn fields and began to draw their sustenance from their soil. Then this poor pilgrim people erected a college in order "to make the whole world understand, that spiritual learning was the thing they chiefly desired." To make the meaning clear, Johnson compared this poor despised people with their ancient forerunners who were led by the hand from Egypt to Canaan through that great and terrible wilderness. The one migration, like the other, showed the operation of a wonder-working providence. The numbers were small in the modern as in the ancient case, but the history of the New Englanders would affect the Dutch, the French, the Germans, the Italians, the Spaniards, the Portuguese, indeed all the nations of the world. If Christ had done such great things "for these low Shrubs," what would "his

[3] William Bradford, *Of Plymouth Plantation, 1620–1647*, ed. Samuel Eliot Morison (New York, 1952), 316 ff., 321 ff.

most Admirable, Excellent and wonderfull worke" be for the
towering kingdoms of the earth? These poor New England people
were the forerunners of Christ's army and the marvelous provi-
dences were the very finger of God. The Lord had sent "this
People to Preach in this Wildernesse, and to proclaime to all
Nations, the neere approach of the most wonderfull workes that
ever the sonnes of men saw."[4]

                                      ✎

The historians of Christian Europe, and notably Bossuet, also
saw the operations of Divine Providence in the unfolding events
of past, present, and future. But Bradford and Johnson cast the
people as the chief actors in the drama, the profound meaning of
which the Book of Daniel and the Revelation of Saint John suggested and Calvinist theology explained. Human history, preor-
dained by God's will, began with Satan's fall and would conclude
with the transformation of the kingdom of this world into the
kingdom of God. The Puritans knew that, after an era of un-
exampled tribulations, "the son of man" would appear to lead
the armies of the holy in the climactic battle of Armageddon.
Then would begin the last stage in earthly history as the defeat
of Satan opened up a thousand-year millennium of peace and
redemption.[5]

The Reformation had been the modern turning point. But all
had not gone well. The Puritan experience in England showed
that a reaction had set in. Although continuing to believe in that
country's particular destiny—as Jonathan Edwards did even in the
eighteenth century—colonial ministers understood that the battle-
fields had shifted to the empty spaces of the New World, providentially reserved for the purpose. God had always singled out a
chosen people. The burden now rested on the migrants to America. They were pilgrims not only in the sense that they had
wandered from an Old World to a New, but also in the divine
mission on which they had been dispatched. They would lead the

---

[4] Edward Johnson, *Wonder-Working Providence,* ed. J. F. Jameson (New York,
1910) , 60–61, 77, 85, 187, 198–202.

[5] Sacvan Bercovitch, *Puritan Origins of the American Self* (New Haven, 1975) ,
35 ff. For a simpler, less subtle, account, see Peter Gay, *Loss of Mastery: Puritan
Historians in Colonial America* (Berkeley, 1966) , 3 ff.

way to redemption for all mankind; hence their history had universal significance. Their errand explained their migration, their sufferings, their trials, and also their achievements. To write that history was to convey to the whole world the glad tidings of future redemption.

The seventeenth-century writers could not translate these aspirations into concrete terms. Literary skill and human understanding enabled them to render faithfully the events and the people they described. But their grand imaginative design was schematic because they lacked the techniques to connect the over-all vision with the details of their story. The narratives were discontinuous and disjointed, with the unusual, the abnormal and the picturesque taken as providential and therefore significant. Yet, the attention they called to the history of the people and the theme of mission long influenced their successors.

The concept of a saintly people endured well into the eighteenth century. In William Hubbard's *General History* (1680) it was the central element in the New England experience; in the hands of Cotton Mather it became the spine for a succession of biographies; Beverley treated a somewhat different setting in Virginia. In the 1750s President Thomas Clap of Yale still proposed, in a work he never completed, to show the hand of providence guiding the history of Connecticut.[6]

By then, however, historical writing had changed drastically. The Enlightenment made familiar a conception of natural law operating in a universe of systematic occurrences. The events of the past were not each the product of a particular providence, but links in a continuous chain of causes and effects. Even those Americans who, like Jonathan Edwards, still thought a general providence shaped the ends of human history, nevertheless believed also in the regularity and order of immediate events. In the En-

---

[6] William Hubbard, *General History of New England*, 2d ed. (Boston, 1848), xi; Robert Beverley, *History and Present State of Virginia* (London, 1705), ed. Louis B. Wright (Chapel Hill, N.C., 1947); Cotton Mather, *Magnalia Christi Americana*, ed. Kenneth B. Murdock and Elizabeth W. Miller (Cambridge, 1977); Louis L. Tucker, *Puritan Protagonist: President Thomas Clap of Yale College* (Chapel Hill, N.C., 1962), 261.

lightenment universe, reason could make out general patterns by searching not for assertions of divine will but for operations of natural causes.[7]

Eighteenth-century histories, especially of the newer colonies, were still promotional. But the most important writers sought, though imperfectly, to illustrate general laws and to describe the influence on society of the natural environment. They took pains to assemble the relevant documentary material, emphasized secular rather than religious concerns, and attempted to be judicious and impartial. The nature of sources usually made the story of a particular colony the convenient vehicle: thus Robert Beverley's Virginia, John Callender's Rhode Island, Thomas Hutchinson's Massachusetts Bay, William Smith's Pennsylvania, and Alexander Hewatt's South Carolina and Georgia. But Cadwallader Colden's *The History of the Five Indian Nations* explored the experience of the Americans who antedated the English; and the Quaker Samuel Smith did somewhat the same in his history of New Jersey.[8]

The concepts of providence and mission persisted, although in a secular form. John Adams' *Dissertation on the Canon and Feudal Law* (1765), for instance, showed a clear relationship to seventeenth-century beliefs and rhetoric in its interpretation of European history. Religious corruption permitted a confederacy of priests and nobles to hold the people in bondage until "God in

---

[7] There is a nice statement of the general position in John Winthrop, *Lecture on Earthquakes Read in the Chapel of Harvard-College, November 26th 1755* (Boston, 1755). See also Douglas J. Elwood, *Philosophical Theology of Jonathan Edwards* (New York, 1960), 38 ff., 45 ff.; Morton White, *Science and Sentiment in America* (New York, 1972), 41 ff.; Stow Persons, *American Minds* (New York, 1958), 110 ff.; Chapter 4 at note 2.

[8] John Callender, *Historical Discourse Colony of . . . Rhode-Island* (Boston, 1739), ed. Romeo Elton (Providence, 1838); Thomas Hutchinson, *History of the Colony of and Province of Massachusetts Bay* (London, 1765), ed. L. S. Mayo, 3 vols. (Cambridge, 1936); Bernard Bailyn, *Ordeal of Thomas Hutchinson* (Cambridge, 1974), 28, 346; William Smith, *Brief State of the Province of Pennsylvania* (London, 1755); Alexander Hewatt, *Historical Account of the Rise and Progress of the Colonies of South Carolina and Georgia* (London, 1779); Cadwallader Colden, *History of the Five Indian Nations* (London, 1747); Wilbur R. Jacobs, "Cadwallader Colden's Noble Iroquois Savages," in Lawrence H. Leder, ed., *Colonial Legacy*, Vol. III: *Historians of Nature and Man's Nature* (New York, 1973), II, 34 ff.; Samuel Smith, *History of the Colony of Nova-Caesaria, or New-Jersey* (Burlington, N.J., 1765), 69 ff., 135 ff., 440 ff.; L. F. S. Upton, *Loyal Whig: William Smith of New York & Quebec* (Toronto, 1969); Roger J. Champagne, "William Smith's History of the Province of New York," in Leder, *Colonial Legacy*, III, 156, 157.

his benign providence raised up the champions who began and conducted the Reformation." Thereafter knowledge gradually spread, especially in England; and, as it did, ecclesiastical and civil tyranny lost their strength. A note in his diary (February 1765) explained why Adams viewed the next step "with Reverence and Wonder." The settlement of America opened "a grand scene and Design in Providence, for the Illumination of the Ignorant and the Emancipation of the slavish Part of Mankind all over the Earth."[9] The same certainty breathed through the histories, though smothered by clumsily bunched heaps of detail and stilted modes of expression. When a polemic wedge intruded, the faith in uniqueness bubbled forth as in the contrary views of William Douglass and Samuel Smith over whether the imperial connection had been beneficial to the colonies.[10]

The American Revolution provided the decisive evidence. In Europe as in America, liberty became the secular equivalent of Providence. In a widely read work of 1785, an Englishman, Richard Price, treated independence as a step ordained by providence. All the families of the earth would be blessed by the Americans as they had been by the Jews. "Perhaps, there never existed a people on whose wisdom and virtue more depended." Mercy Otis Warren calmly stated the general theme of histories written in the next half-century: the Revolution was the first step in the worldwide spread of republicanism. Loyalists deplored the tendency; patriots extolled it. All recognized it.[11]

[9] John Adams, "Dissertation on the Canon and the Feudal Law" (1765) , *Works,* ed. Charles Francis Adams, 10 vols. (Boston, 1850–56) , III, 451, and *Papers of John Adams,* ed. Robert J. Taylor et al., 2 vols. (Cambridge, 1977) , I, 103 ff., and *Diary and Autobiography,* ed. L. H. Butterfield et al., 4 vols. (Cambridge, 1961) , I, 257.

[10] William Douglass, *Summary, Historical and Political, of the British Settlements in North America,* 2 vols. (Boston, 1755) , II, 126; Smith, *History of the Colony of Nova-Caesaria.*

[11] Richard Price, *Observations on the Importance of the American Revolution and the Means of Making It of Benefit to the World* (London, 1785) , 7, 8; Mercy Otis Warren, *History of the Rise, Progress and Determination of the American Revolution,* 3 vols. (Boston, 1805) , III, 298, 326–327, 401; Thomas Jones, *History of New York During the Revolutionary War* (New York, 1879) ; William Smith, Jr., *History of the Province of New-York* (London and New York, 1757–1826) , ed. Michael Kammen, 2 vols. (Cambridge, 1972) , I, xxv; Champagne, "William Smith's

David Ramsay (1749–1815), a Pennsylvanian educated at Princeton, who had practiced medicine in Charleston, South Carolina, before his service in the Continental Congress, discerned both the causes and effects of the Revolution in an examination of the life of the people. "When the war began, the Americans were a mass of husbandmen, merchants, mechanics and fishermen," utterly dependent upon the mother country. Religion and social structure, however, nurtured a love of liberty. From the Puritans, Americans inherited a deep hostility to tyranny; and since they "were all of one rank," a sense of equality united them in a common cause from the success of which they all expected to gain. The war threw them upon their own resources, exposed talents which would otherwise have been lost, and stimulated political, scientific, artistic, and religious life. Those judgments showed awareness of the necessity for understanding the total context of independence, although Ramsay's performance fell considerably short of the aspiration.[12]

The Revolution marked no break with the eighteenth century in historical method. Although preachers and philosophers before long predicted that literature springing up in the virgin soil of America "would bear new fruits, and, in some respects, more precious fruits" than elsewhere, historians, still listening "to the courtly Muses of Europe," did not venture to walk on their own feet, speak their own minds. They were more likely than not to follow the injunction of the much-read Scot, William Robertson and treat "dignified events and characters." The subject, moreover, was only slowly acquiring definition; the word history still

---

History," in Leder, *Colonial Legacy*, III, 161 ff.; Lawrence H. Leder, ed., *Colonial Legacy*, Vol. I: *Loyalist Historians* (New York, 1971); Arthur H. Shaffer, *Politics of History: Writing the History of the American Revolution, 1783–1815* (Chicago, 1975), 49 ff., 67 ff.; Gordon S. Wood, *Creation of the American Republic, 1776–1787* (Chapel Hill, 1969), 55 ff.; Alan Heimert, *Religion and the American Mind from the Great Awakening to the Revolution* (Cambridge, 1966), 395 ff.; *Impact of the American Revolution Abroad* (Library of Congress Symposia on the American Revolution, Washington, 1976). Lawrence J. Friedman, *Inventors of the Promised Land* (New York, 1975), 3 ff., links spread-eagle patriotism to a need to create myths of perfection and rootedness to offset American insecurity, but he is unaware of prerevolutionary antecedents and of the extent to which secure Europeans shared the same judgments.

12 David Ramsay, *History of the American Revolution*, 2 vols. (Philadelphia, 1789), I, 31, II, 315; also Samuel Williams, *Natural and Civil History of Vermont* (Walpole, N.H., 1794), vii; Ralph N. Miller, "Samuel Williams' History of Vermont,'" *New England Quarterly*, XXII (March 1949), 73 ff.

applied occasionally to fiction or to travel accounts or to descriptions of nature.[13]

The trends of the colonial period continued on into the first half of the nineteenth century. Like the practitioners of other literary genres, the historians of the new nation accepted the mission of expressing the ideals of the Republic. The affirmation of the virtues and the glorious destiny of the United States which Barlow's *Columbiad* put into verse, Parson Weems, John Marshall, and other occasional dabblers in history and biography expressed in prose. The favorite subjects were the men and events of the Revolution.[14]

The authors of the early Republic outreached themselves. They did not know how to name, much less handle, the subject they aspired to treat—a nation, a people, a civilization. Like their eighteenth-century predecessors and like the more skillful writers and more learned scholars of Europe, the high-flown intentions of the title page and preface generally led into the usual political chronicle. The great Voltaire had done no better. In the United States grandiose themes and emphasis upon the heroic individual quite crowded out attention to the usual life of the people which Bradford and Johnson had not been able to overlook. Furthermore, frail memories and imperfectly organized sources limited the available material; pathetically, Thomas McKean and John Adams, not historians but participants in the Revolution, in 1813 searched around for information about the Albany Congress which had met in their youth.[15]

༄

The idea of mission thrived in the second quarter of the nineteenth century, nurtured by the spread of the frontier and by the

13 William Ellery Channing, "On National Literature" (1830), *Works* (Boston, 1843), I, 267; Ralph Waldo Emerson, "American Scholar" (1837), *Works* (Boston, 1883), I, 114; John Burnett Black, *The Art of History* (London, 1926), 131; Williams, *Natural and Civil History of Vermont*, chs. 1–6.

14 Joel Barlow, *Columbiad: A Poem* (Philadelphia, 1807); Mason L. Weems, *Life of Washington* (1806), ed. Marcus Cunliffe (Cambridge, 1962); John Marshall, *Life of George Washington*, 5 vols. (London, 1804–07); Samuel Williams, *History of the American Revolution* (New Haven, 1824).

15 John Adams to Thomas McKean, August 31, 1813, Adams, *Works*, X, 60, 62; also Daniel R. Gilbert, "John Marshall and the Development of a National History," Lawrence H. Leder, ed., *Colonial Legacy*, Vol. IV: *Early Nationalist Historians* (New York, 1973), IV, 184, 185.

ideological justification for expansion. Manifest Destiny, the later formulation, bore overtones of both Puritan and Enlightenment antecedents and had a direct effect upon the writing of history.

John L. O'Sullivan in 1839, bluntly stating the theme, linked the future to an interpretation of the past. With independence, "a new history" began, marked by the "untried political system" of the United States. Chosen for a "blessed mission to the nations of the world," which had until then been shut out from the light of truth, that country would establish on earth the moral dignity of man and the beneficence of God. Its example would "smite unto death, the tyranny of kings, hierarchs, and oligarchs and carry the glad tidings of peace and good will where myriads" endured an "existence scarcely more enviable than that of beasts of the field."[16]

His contemporary Herman Melville, in *White Jacket* (1849) was also explicit: The Americans were teachers to posterity. This "peculiar, chosen people," the modern Israel, guarded "the liberties of the world." God had predestined, mankind expected, great things from this advance guard "sent on through the wilderness of untried things." Almost for the first time in history, national selfishness was unbounded philanthropy; "for we cannot do a good to America, but we give alms to the world." In *Years of the Unperform'd* Walt Whitman perceived America, "Liberty's nation," and other nations as well, "advancing with irresistible power upon the world stage." Never was the average man "more like a God," everywhere urging the masses on, colonizing the Pacific, interlinking all geography, all lands, "with the steam-ship, the electric telegraph, the wholesale engines of war" and "the world-spreading factories."[17]

Later politicians, statesmen, and publicists down to Josiah Strong and Albert J. Beveridge continued to think of the history of America in terms of conquest of the continent and ultimately of the diffusion of its ideology throughout the world. Toward the

---

16 *United States Magazine and Democratic Review*, VI (November 1839), 2–6; Frederick Merk, *Manifest Destiny and Mission in American History* (New York, 1963).

17 Herman Melville, *White Jacket* (New York, 1865), ch. 36; Walt Whitman, *Drum-Taps* (New York, 1865), 53; and, in general, Ernest L. Tuveson, *Redeemer Nation: The Idea of America's Millennial Role* (Chicago, 1968).

end of the century the concept of mission became ensnarled in racism and linked to imperialism. But those entanglements had not previously been essential to faith in the uniqueness of the promised land, a faith that many black, immigrant, and Catholic writers accepted and never surrendered.[18]

The same assumption infused the writings of historians, whatever their subjects. Its imprint was as perceptible, though not as bold, in John L. Motley's *Rise of the Dutch Republic* (1856) as in his speech to the New-York Historical Society (1868), which explained that destiny had put the United States "more immediately than any other nation in subordination to the law [of progress] governing all bodies political as inexorably as Kepler's law controlled the motion of the planets." A generation later Woodrow Wilson expressed equal certainty.[19]

The concept of mission was the theme of the most widely read of the nineteenth-century histories, that by George Bancroft, a Jacksonian intellectual and politician who, between 1834 and 1882, composed a monumental account of the origins of the American people down to the making of the Constitution. Bancroft embodied the best qualities of the historiography of his age; more than his predecessors, he reached out widely for his sources and he recognized the natural continuity of immediate events. But he still believed that God was visible in history, and that a divine providence guided the affairs of men. Although specific incidents followed each other in orderly sequence, progress was part of a larger plan which determined their ultimate direction.

Bancroft's theme was the providential reservation of the New World for its destined purpose as the stage for the role of the American people. His first edition pointed out that it was "but little more than two centuries since the oldest" of the states had received its first permanent colony. "Before that time the whole territory was unproductive waste. Throughout its wide extent,

18 Leonard I. Sweet, *Black Images of America, 1784–1870* (New York, 1976), 69 ff.; Francis L. Broderick, *W. E. B. DuBois* (Stanford, 1959), 44; Samuel Spencer, *Booker T. Washington and the Negro's Place in American Life* (Boston, 1955), 93–94; Mary Antin, *Promised Land*, 2d ed. (Boston, 1969), xii, xiii; Maurice F. Egan, *Columbia Jubilee* (Chicago, 1892).

19 John Lothrop Motley, *Historic Progress and American Democracy* (New York, 1869), 6; Woodrow Wilson, *History of the American People*, 5 vols. (New York, 1902), V, 299 ff.

the arts had not erected a monument. Its only inhabitants were a
few scattered tribes of feeble barbarians, destitute of commerce
and of political connection. The ax and the plowshare were unknown. The soil, which had been gathering fertility from the re-
pose of centuries, was lavishing its strength in magnificent, but
useless vegetation. In the view of civilization the immense domain
was a solitude." To explain the change, Bancroft proposed "to follow the steps by which a favoring providence, calling" American
institutions into being, had conducted the country to "happiness
and glory."[20]

A striking gap in Bancroft's exposition remained characteristic
of the writings of later historians. The people were the protago-
nists, yet they did not appear in the chapters that followed the
preface. The actual narrative treated political and diplomatic
events and focused on the activities of statesmen, while other folk
receded into a vast abstraction not described but taken for granted
and justifying the acts of the principals by their mere presence.
In the gap between rhetoric and detail, Bancroft and his contemporaries stood in sharp contrast to seventeenth-century
historians.[21]

Sydney George Fisher a generation later took issue with Bancroft, yet fell victim to the same disjunction of rhetoric from detail. Fisher insisted that the men who had made the American
Revolution were British and that their heritage accounted for the
traits that made them rebels and independent. In actual writing,
however, Fisher in his general books was no more capable than
Bancroft of dealing with or understanding the life of the people.[22]

To a considerable extent the difficulty was technical. The influences that played upon Bancroft and his contemporaries emanated less often from the formal philosophies of history that then
occupied their contemporaries across the Atlantic than from ideas
transmitted in literary forms. Scott and Byron more often supplied

---

[20] George Bancroft, *History of the United States,* 10 vols. (Boston, 1834–74) , I,
1–3; also David W. Noble, *Historians against History: The Frontier Thesis and the
National Covenant in American Historical Writing since 1830* (Minneapolis, 1965) ,
18 ff.

[21] David Levin, *History as Romantic Art* (Stanford, 1959) , 3 ff.

[22] Sydney George Fisher, *True History of the American Revolution* (Philadelphia,
1902) ; below, note 32.

the concepts for the generation of American historians after 1820 than did Hegel, Michelet, or Macaulay. The popular novels and poems gave currency to a pattern of attitudes historians accepted and incorporated into their own writings: the hero as a protagonist striving against large, hostile forces; the clash of conflicting ideas through the past; the ponderous influence of nature; and the power of an undefined fate inherent in the character of men and nations.

These romantic influences emphasized trends already apparent in such works as Marshall's life of Washington. History required composition on an epic scale, for it had to deal with the efforts of great characters, noble or evil, to assert themselves in nature, and it needed room to set forth the clash of conflicting or discordant ideals. History achieved its goals, as did other forms of literature, by emphasis upon the narrative; the story chronologically told supplied its own organization and permitted the component parts of the whole to fall into their appropriate places.[23] Like Bancroft, John G. Palfrey, the historian of New England, William H. Prescott, who dealt with Latin America, and John L. Motley, whose subject was the Dutch Republic, gave high value to literary presentation and wrote to reach a large audience. To tell an exciting story that would win and hold attention they adhered to a strictly chronological exposition, setting forth the events of the past in the order in which they occurred. Since the historians, like the novelists of their day, wished to trace a simple plot knotting together recognizable characters, they fixed their attention upon politics and statesmen, however insistently theory summoned them to deal with the people. As a result, simple conceptions of motivation and of causation were the usual features of the narrative form, even in the volumes of Richard Hildreth, who understood that there was a relation between economic and political forces. Francis Parkman alone achieved a more illuminating analysis of the events he described. His strong sense of drama and his power of expression broke through the limitations of purely narrative exposition.[24]

23 Marshall, *Life of George Washington*, I, v, xi ff.; Bancroft, *History of the United States*, II, 452 ff.; Gilbert, "John Marshall," 177 ff.; Levin, *History as Romantic Art*, 49 ff.

24 Donald E. Emerson, *Richard Hildreth* (Baltimore, 1946) , 85 ff., 141; Mason Wade, *Francis Parkman: Heroic Historian* (New York, 1942) , 368 ff., 379 ff.

With Parkman, the narrative style reached its high point; but it still served James Ford Rhodes, Theodore Roosevelt, and James Schouler; and it continued to supply a medium for Samuel Eliot Morison, Bruce Catton, Allan Nevins, and others down through the third quarter of the twentieth century. It shaped most biographical writing and, in the 1880s and 1890s, had to its credit such substantial achievements as the American Statesmen series.[25]

While the writers of narrative histories evaded many problems of organization and interpretation, they nevertheless emphasized the necessity of precise method. Their great nineteenth-century achievement, the *Narrative and Critical History of America,* edited by Justin Winsor, was a monument to meticulous scholarship, although its critical apparatus swamped the narrative text. Jared Sparks, George Ticknor, J. R. Brodhead, Peter Force, and others were persistent builders of libraries, accumulators of documents, and publishers of source materials. Working with old and new historical societies, they influenced many town and state histories and eased all future research.[26]

Futhermore, American historians remained sensitive to the responsibility inherited from the nineteenth-century narrative writers, to address not a small group of peers only, but the whole public. Consistently American scholars fought the spread of jargon or esoteric terminology or abstruse style. Though other factors made it difficult after 1900 to attract a wide general audience, the obligations toward popular education and edification remained a heritage from the narrative tradition.

In the last decades of the nineteenth century fresh impulses transformed the writing of American history. Until then history had been the avocation of gentlemanly scholars, journalists, and litterateurs, working as individuals; only a few, beginning with

---

[25] James Schouler, *History of the United States under the Constitution,* rev. ed., 7 vols. (New York, 1894–1913) ; J. F. Rhodes, *History of the United States from 1850,* 7 vols. (New York, 1893–1906) ; Edward Channing, *History of the United States,* 6 vols. (New York, 1905–25) ; E. P. Oberholtzer, *History of the United States since the Civil War,* 5 vols. (New York, 1917–37) ; Allan Nevins, *Ordeal of the Union,* 8 vols. (New York, 1947–71) .

[26] Justin Winsor, *Narrative and Critical History of America,* 8 vols. (Boston, 1884–89) .

Jared Sparks, had taught the subject in universities. Now it became a profession and found a recognized place, of growing consequence, as one of the rigorous disciplines in college curricula.

There was no clear turning point. Herbert Baxter Adams established his seminar at Johns Hopkins in 1876, almost at the same time that Henry Adams began to teach at Harvard and Charles Kendall Adams at Michigan, and shortly before Hermann E. von Holst came from Germany to lecture at Johns Hopkins, Cornell, and Chicago. From these sources, and through young men who studied across the Atlantic, American historians acquired a new sense of the scientific potentialities of their craft.

With considerable success they sought to establish the professionalism of the subject, not only to assure the refinement and transmission of skills from one generation to another but also to attain public recognition of the unique qualifications of the trained scholar. The latter task was particularly important in a field which remained open to amateurs, journalists, and politicians, many of them writers of intelligence and ability.

As in other professions, the university was the instrument for establishing standards and credentials. Instruction in the seminars and workshops of the developing graduate schools aimed to prepare teachers and investigators by conveying a fund of knowledge and of research techniques in a specialty. The Ph.D. degree certified the readiness of the recipient. Organization within departments prevented powerful individual professors from dominating an area as their counterparts did in Europe and also assured some degree of uniformity in requirements and criteria of judgment.

The American Historical Association, formed in 1884, was the most important of the groups within which the members established a sense of common identity and tried to define standards of performance on a national scale. The Ph.D. was by no means a license; hiring authority remained in the hands of the schools and colleges, and the purchasers of books paid little attention to degrees. But the learned societies sponsored meetings and published journals and monographs which recognized merit according to a canon in which all scholars had a stake. The associations were voluntary and possessed no legal power; but an internal and informal network of authority evaluated credentials and maintained standards. In theory any university chartered by a state could award the doctorate; and all Ph.D.'s were equal. But in practice the diplomas were worthless without the recommendations to gain posts for their possessors. In practice, too, a handful of institutions awarded almost all the degrees; and a few score professors who knew one another personally decided which among their students deserved prizes, fellowships, and positions in the highly varied array of American institutions of higher learning.

Faith in the universality of history as a discipline sustained its scholarly quality. Since truth was one and equally accessible to investigators of all origins and beliefs, the scientific historians regarded themselves as members of a worldwide community and aimed to surmount all national and creedal divisions. They hoped to get away from exclusive preoccupation with their own country's past, and they wished to apply within the United States such criteria as would command respect anywhere in the world.

The concern with the pasts of societies other than their own both stimulated and reflected the influence of scientific history. The consciousness of continuities—between modern American constitutional practice and thirteenth-century England or between contemporary religious problems and events in the Near East centuries before—compelled scholars to know about events in remote times and places. To do so they needed a command not only of the languages but also of the methods of the advanced schools in Britain, Germany, and France. And Americans who dealt with those subjects exposed their writing and teaching to the scrutiny of critics whose perspective was different from their own and whose equipment and training were often superior. The reputations of George Burton Adams, Edward P. Cheyney, Charles Gross, and Charles H. Haskins rested, in part at least, upon international recognition.

The primary contribution of the scientific historians was not the notion of objectivity. That was already an ideal in the eighteenth century; as an actuality it was never fully attained. The more significant achievements of these scholars sprang rather from their attitude toward, and from their concern with, the technique of handling facts. Earlier writers, their attention fixed on the large sweep of history, had often been casual in matters of detail. In the interests of what they knew was the larger truth, they were willing to sacrifice literal verity, as when Bancroft urged the engraver to remove the warts from Franklin's nose or when Jared Sparks took the liberty of improving the grammar of Washington's letters. To the scientific historian the fact was absolutely intractable; whatever flights of fancy his interpretation might take, he accepted the obligation of scrupulous factual accuracy.

A new preoccupation with the methods of critical analysis and verification of data replaced the rough-and-ready commonsense approach of the past. The form of writing shifted from the loose discursive narrative to the heavily footnoted monograph focused on a clearly defined problem. Henry Adams and Edward Channing, and later Herbert L. Osgood, Charles M. Andrews and Ellis P. Oberholtzer, still responded to the impulse to compose longer works; but even those partook of monographic qualities. More generally the historians of these generations, in their more extended efforts, preferred the collaborative series, like the American Nation (edited by Albert Bushnell Hart), in which specialists pooled their talents.

The scientist specialized. To know, that is, to master all the relevant facts, required the investigator first to circumscribe the subject of inquiry. Increasingly historical research, like that in the physical sciences, dealt with manageable problems, that is, with subjects limited by the nature of the sources and the needs of interpretation. Carl L. Becker, Charles H. McIlwain, and Charles H. Haskins did not hesitate to choose subjects on either side of the Atlantic; but usually it made evident good sense for one historian to concentrate on France and another on Germany, because national lines conformed to the requirements of language and the organization of archives and of publishing activities. It also made sense to specialize upon one type of subject, because even modern France or early modern Germany was too large for an analysis that would permit historians to answer the questions they now wished to ask.

J. B. Bury's declaration that history had ceased to be "a branch of literature" and had joined the sciences which dealt "objectively with the facts of the universe" created a furor in England, but not in the United States, where the transformation proceeded placidly. Increasingly, as Darwinian influence spread in American thought, historians tried to explain development—a task that required them to treat continuities as well as changes over time. To do so they had to define the entity with which they dealt in some meaningful way. The natural scientists spoke of the evolution of species and genera; the historians' equivalent was the evolution of institutions. John Fiske, long a Darwinian, thus turned to history in mid-career to trace the evolution of American institutions to their European sources. Inspired by John Richard Green's history of the English people, he rejected old-fashioned history, which, "retaining the marks of its barbaric origin," dealt "with little save kings and battles and court intrigues." Fiske aimed to describe the development of a democratic polity.[27]

The definition of an institution was sometimes pragmatic: Congress was an institution in the sense that the body which met in 1890, while no longer composed of the same individuals who had met in 1790 and in many respects different, had demonstrably descended from its predecessor. The definition also could acquire clarity from the nature of such entities: Congress was an institution in the sense that it shared the characteristics of legislative bodies which evolved under nineteenth-century conditions.

Institutional specialization was a fruitful tactic in the half-century after 1880. It permitted historians to isolate and intensively mine discrete bodies of material, using for the purpose tools of analysis sharpened by the related social sciences. Instead of dealing with the state generally they dealt with constitutional, legal, political, diplomatic, or military history. Economic history developed as a separate field, with subdivisions that were either regional or topical—Western, Southern, agricultural, financial. The same approach affected religious, cultural, intellectual, and family history.

The institutional historians established an accepted chronology and periodization and posed questions that long framed the organizing concepts of their subjects. They applied the conclusions of their monographs to general problems given system and significance by reference to the social sciences. History was thus the handmaiden of political or economic science, but its role was

[27] John B. Bury, "Science of History," *Selected Essays,* ed. Harold Temperley (Cambridge, 1930), 9, 11; Milton Berman, *John Fiske* (Cambridge, 1961), 145. On institutions, see also Chapter 10 at note 35.

nonetheless vital. Those analytical disciplines were moving away from their earlier orientation which had been predominantly theoretical and abstract. Under the influence of Spencer, of the other Darwinists, and to some degree of Comte, the moral philosophers in process of becoming social scientists no longer searched for deductions from absolute principles and now considered it their proper task to describe the nature of development. The new interest increased the importance of the time perspective and gave historical data a fresh scientific significance.

By the opening of the twentieth century most American scholars regarded it as their function to trace the evolution of social institutions back to their origins. The figures of speech employed —germ, evolution, development—revealed an understanding of the institution as largely self-contained and self-generating, affected but slightly by the surrounding environment, and governed by its own inherent rules of growth.

The interests of the institutional historians were mainly political; H. B. Adams often reminded the students in his Johns Hopkins seminar of Freeman's dictum, "History is past politics." In part that emphasis was international; Freeman was after all English. But concentration on constitutional and governmental development conformed also to the existing popular interest in politics and to the belief that most significant achievements of the United States had been connected with democracy. The contributions to colonial history by H. L. Osgood, G. L. Beer, C. M. Andrews, and the "Imperial School" rested upon that premise.[28]

The institutional approach applied with equal consistency and with as much success in other fields as well. The treatments of law and of constitutional change followed lines quite different from those of political development. W. J. Ashley and E. F. Gay, both products of European training, established a vigorous school of economic history that made notable contributions to that subject in the first quarter of the new century; and Albion Small and other sociologists encouraged historical research in that field.

28 Persons, *American Minds,* 316 ff.; H. L. Osgood, *American Colonies in the Seventeenth Century,* 3 vols. (New York, 1904–07) , and *American Colonies in the Eighteenth Century,* 4 vols. (New York, 1924–25) ; G. L. Beer, *Origins of British Colonial System* (New York, 1908) , and *Old Colonial System* (New York, 1912) , and *British Colonial Policy* (New York, 1907) ; C. M. Andrews, *Colonial Period of American History,* 4 vols. (New Haven, 1934–38) .

The formalism of the institutional historians was a source of intractable problems. The world they described had not, in actuality, fallen into the divisions they accepted; yet they could not readily deal with the areas of intersection and overlap. Technology, movements of capital and labor, the nature of the market and of transportation were important in the development of manufactures. But so, too, were government policies on tariff and immigration; attitudes toward work, enterprise, and savings shaped by religion and culture; the relations among states that affected the flow of goods and people; and the assumptions about family life that influenced who would earn, where, and why. Such aspects of their subject escaped the institutional historians. Despite his obeisance to Green, Fiske wrote essentially political history.

Moses Coit Tyler exemplified the dilemma. His subject was the history of literature. But the writings he examined for the colonial period (1878) were minor, viewed in the context of the masterpieces of seventeenth-century English prose and poetry. They acquired importance only as they illuminated the intellectual history of the nation. Fifteen years later, when he turned to the decades after 1763, the discrepancy between intellectual and literary criteria was even more striking. Tyler's *Literary History of the American Revolution,* therefore, aimed "for the first time" to set forth the inward history of the struggle for independence, to describe "its ideas, its spiritual moods, its motives, its passions, even . . . its sportive caprices and its whims, as these uttered themselves at the time, whether consciously or not, in the various writings of the two parties of Americans who promoted or resisted that great movement." Notwithstanding these ambitions, Tyler did little more than stitch together a succession of biographical sketches bundled up in chapters with unifying general titles.[29]

An awareness of the need for some broader synthesizing principle remained, especially among writers who sought to describe and explain their own society, still growing, still changing. The continuing consciousness, despite all professions of scientific aloofness, of some unique significance to the product of the great migration to America directed attention at the subjects of Bradford

[29] Moses Coit Tyler, *Literary History of the American Revolution, 1763–1783,* 2 vols. (New York, 1897), I, vii.

and Johnson, that is, at the people rather than at statesmen and rulers.

Interest in these problems had never died. From Isaac Backus onward, writers who traced religious developments treated the communicants rather than the princes of the churches. From Franz von Löher and Thomas D'Arcy McGee onward, authors who celebrated the achievements of exceptional immigrants also perforce dealt with ordinary people.[30] From Benjamin Trumbull and Jeremy Belknap onward, chroniclers of the states tucked sections on education, literature, religion, manners, and customs into their books.[31] Sydney George Fisher's *Pennsylvania* handled science, the mechanic arts, and ethnic groups more successfully than did his better known works on a national scale.[32] Indeed, local histories through the nineteenth century found room to describe popular ways of life, if for no other reason than out of boosterism; and the growing interest in American genealogy and antiques also increased interest in the historical context of these objects.[33]

Some of the narrative historians had dealt with similar materials. James Schouler, for instance, tried to describe life in the colonies in 1776. Fired by enthusiasm after having read Macaulay's chapter on England in 1685, J. B. McMaster resolved to write a history of the people of the United States, "to describe the dress, the occupations, the amusements, the literary canons of the times; to note the changes of manners and morals; to trace the growth of

[30] Isaac Backus, *History of New England, with Particular Reference to Baptists,* 3 vols. (Boston, 1777) ; Franz von Löher, *Geschichte und Zustände der Deutschen in America* (Cincinnati, 1847) ; Thomas D'Arcy McGee, *History of Irish Settlers in North America,* 2d ed. (Boston, 1850) ; Charles W. Baird, *History of the Huguenot Emigration to America,* 2 vols. (New York, 1885) .

[31] Williams, *Natural and Civil History of Vermont,* 311 ff.; Benjamin Trumbull, *Complete History of Connecticut,* 2 vols. (New Haven, 1818) ; Jeremy Belknap, *History of New Hampshire,* 3 vols. (Boston, 1791–92) ; Jere Daniell, "Jeremy Belknap and the History of New Hampshire," in Leder, *Colonial Legacy,* IV, 241 ff.; H. H. Bancroft, *California,* 7 vols. (San Francisco, 1884–90) .

[32] Sydney George Fisher, *Making of Pennsylvania* (Philadelphia, 1896) .

[33] Justin Winsor, ed., *Memorial History of Boston,* 4 vols. (Boston, 1880) ; J. E. A. Smith, *History of Pittsfield, 1734–1876* (Boston and Springfield, 1869–76) ; Charles E. Banks, *History of Martha's Vineyard,* 3 vols. (Boston, 1911–25) ; Oswald Tilghman, *History of Talbot County, Maryland* (Baltimore, 1915) . See also George H. Callcott, *History in the United States* (Baltimore, 1970) , 25 ff., 175 ff.; David D. Van Tassel, *Recording America's Past* (Chicago, 1960) , 59 ff., 95 ff., 121 ff.; Robert R. Dykstra, *Cattle Towns* (New York, 1968) , 364.

that humane spirit which abolished imprisonment for debt, which reformed the discipline of prisons and of jails, and which has, in our time, destroyed slavery and lessened the miseries of dumb brutes." He also proposed to describe the long series of mechanical inventions and discoveries and tell how, under the "benign influence of liberty and peace, there sprang up, in the course of a single century, a prosperity unparalleled in the annals of human affairs."[34] An occasional institutional historian also crossed over into this area, as William B. Weeden did.[35]

But too often those who sought to treat the life of the people stressed the antiquarian, the quaint, and the curious. Like Michelet, they believed that "to know the life of the people," they had but to interrogate their memories.[36] Unable to formulate the appropriate problems, they found themselves in the position of Tolstoy's deaf man answering questions no one had asked. Useful as their work was, it lacked consistency of theme or of interpretation in the absence of a definition of the subject that supplied a guide to what was worth studying and why. In J. B. McMaster, for example, the effort to cram a great variety of diverse data into a single work led to a total sacrifice of narrative qualities. The mounting accumulation of facts threatened to overwhelm the historian, unless approached in a selective fashion through clearly formulated questions, the answers to which provided him a coherent basis of organization.

The deficiency was particularly striking in the most accomplished of the late-nineteenth-century historians of the United States, Henry Adams. Adams intended his study of the administrations of Jefferson and Madison to be a test of the experiment in democratic government. He therefore began his first volume with

34 John B. McMaster, *History of the People of the United States*, 8 vols. (New York, 1881–1913), I, 2, 3; Eric Goldman, *John Bach McMaster* (Philadelphia, 1943), 105 ff.; James Schouler, *Americans of 1776* (New York, 1906).

35 William B. Weeden, *Economic and Social History of New England, 1620–1789*, 2 vols. (Boston, 1890).

36 Jules Michelet, *People*, trans. George H. Smith (New York, 1846), 9. For later gropings toward synthèse, see William R. Keylor, *Academy and Community: The Foundation of the French Historical Profession* (Cambridge, 1975), 157 ff.

six chapters on the United States in 1800, within which he described, in cross section, the society he expected to examine thereafter. But the rest of the book reverted to the familiar materials of political and diplomatic history. Its closing pages left Adams aware that he had not been able to arrive at the conclusion he sought. Like his contemporaries and his ancestors, he recognized a theme, but possessed neither the technical nor substantive means for providing it with flesh and blood. No more than McMaster, or for that matter Macaulay, could he handle the dynamics of social history. A skillful writer could describe society in 1800 or in 1685. It was another problem entirely to move that cross section through time.[37]

The American who came closest to portraying the people of the past was not a professional historian but a novelist. Edward Eggleston had learned as a writer of fiction that abstract characters were neither comprehensible nor effective in furthering the plot of a story; he had used the details of local color to flesh out his narratives and had realistically depicted manners, motives, and way of life to make the men and women on his pages credible. The same standards of judgment served him when he composed a history of the origins of his country's civilization. He never precisely defined the concept of civilization, which he identified with what the Germans called cultural history. Apart from the general belief that "the real history of men and women" revealed the evolving character of each age, Eggleston adhered to no abstract theory. But the search for authentic detail pressed him toward intensive research in the sources in a fashion which met the rigorous criteria of the professionals and earned their tolerance for what he labeled "The New History" in his 1900 presidential address to the American Historical Association.[38]

Eggleston, in fact, did not write what the Germans called cul-

---

[37] Henry Adams, *History of the United States, 1801–1817*, 9 vols. (New York, 1889–91) ; William H. Jordy, *Henry Adams, Scientific Historian* (New Haven, 1952) , 75 ff.

[38] Edward Eggleston, *Beginners of a Nation* (New York, 1897) , and *Transit of Civilization from England to America in the Seventeenth Century* (New York, 1900) ; and "New History," American Historical Association, *Annual Report, 1900* (Washington, 1901) , I, 37 ff.; William P. Randel, *Edward Eggleston* (New York, 1946) ; Charles Hirschfeld, "Edward Eggleston: Pioneer in Social History," in Eric F. Goldman, ed., *Historiography and Urbanization* (Baltimore, 1941) , 190 ff.

tural history. That strain in Europe reached back to the eigh-teenth-century efforts of J. J. Winckelmann to situate the great achievements of classical art in time. More than a century of work along these lines had produced occasional works well known in the United States, among them Jakob Burckhardt's *Die Kultur der Renaissance in Italien* (1860). Two decades after Eggleston spoke, Johan Huizinga employed that still vital mode of analysis in his *Waning of the Middle Ages* (1919). The scholars in that tradition examined the products of the plastic and literary arts as symbols or expressions of the underlying practices, attitudes, and beliefs of a society.

Americans did not follow that line of inquiry; their own past was not rich enough in works of high art to encourage it, and the dominant mode of academic criticism tended to abstract cultural objects from their context rather than to integrate them. Nor be-tween 1900 and 1920 was there significant attention to the "real history of men and women." Eggleston was an isolated figure; lacking a university base, he had no students and few successors.

Instead, after his address, interest in social history revolved about two familiar themes: the assumption that the American experi-ment had a special purpose in human progress; and the Manichean view of history as a struggle no longer of saints and Satan but nonetheless of heroes and villains, of angelic and demonic forces. The Puritans and Quakers had ascribed ignorance, poverty, war, and injustice to the intrusion of unregenerate outsiders and to involvement by weak-willed, greedy men and women in a con-spiracy of evil. Reformers of the Progressive era located the ob-stacles to progress in the selfishness of individuals and special groups that heedlessly pursued wealth. Offended by the excesses of the robber barons of the gilded age, stirred by the revelations of muckrakers, yet animated by unyielding faith in the future, the progressive historians used the past to demonstrate the inevitabil-ity of improvement when not impeded by personal or class selfishness.[39]

---

[39] Perry Miller, *New England Mind from Colony to Province* (Cambridge, 1953), Book One, and *Errand into the Wilderness* (Cambridge, 1956), 217 ff.; and *Nature's Nation* (Cambridge, 1967), 14 ff.; Joseph E. Illick, III, "Robert Proud and the History of Pennsylvania," in Leder, *Colonial Legacy,* I, 175, 176; Arthur M. Schlesin-ger, Jr., misunderstood the two aspects of this view of history and treated them as

The creed of progress animated James Harvey Robinson and Charles A. Beard, who became spokesmen of "the new history," a title to which they gave their own meaning. Discontented with their own training—heavily weighted toward politics—they sought a type of history that would serve reform objectives. The subtitle of the widely used high school textbook on which they collaborated revealed their intention: *The Development of Modern Europe: An Introduction to the Study of Current History.* They borrowed Eggleston's term to describe a narrative that would go beyond military and diplomatic events to treat man's advance in civilization, by which they meant a condition embracing the social changes they advocated. But since they had no experience in treating material on the life of the people, their textbook fell into the usual political framework, with occasional paragraphs interspersed on economic, cultural, and, to a lesser extent, social developments. The work, nevertheless, struck a responsive chord in an audience intellectually prepared to revolt against institutional formalism and politically ready to vote for progress in 1912.[40]

Robinson did not pursue the idea further except in broad discursive essays. The new preface to his study of Petrarch showed awareness of the problem, but no steps toward its solution. Beard, the more prolific writer, further simplified the concept of a new history, which he made into the story of conflict between competing economic groups running back from his own day to the country's origins. His books on the ratification of the constitution (1913) and on Jeffersonian democracy (1915) and *The Rise of American Civilization* (1927), written with Mary R. Beard, articulated commonly shared prejudices and had considerable popular success, as did Vernon L. Parrington's *Main Currents in American Thought* (1927–1930), which explicitly applied to literature populist ideas derived from the political scientist J. Allen Smith. The

---

alternative and successive rather than as reciprocal and simultaneous—"America: Experiment or Destiny?" *American Historical Review,* LXXXII (June 1977), 505 ff. See the more perceptive essay by David Levin, "Forms of Uncertainty: Representation of Doubt in American Histories," *New Literary History* (Autumn 1976), 59 ff.; also Chapter 13.

40 James H. Robinson and Charles A. Beard, *Development of Modern Europe* (Boston, 1907–08); James H. Robinson, "Sacred and Profane History," American Historical Association, *Annual Report, 1899,* I, 529 ff.; and *New History* (New York, 1912).

drama of a continuing battle between mercantile and agrarian interests influenced some citizens but had almost no scholarly consequences. Robinson continued to hold his post at Columbia but did not teach in this area, and neither Parrington nor Beard, who resigned from the University to devote his full time to writing, had students.[41]

Down to 1920 the great bulk of scholarly writing about America and about Europe remained locked into the institutional framework. Politics and diplomacy, the sources of most abundant archival material, attracted the greatest attention; and even works on the productive system and culture fell within the conventional pattern. As earlier, biography was a popular medium.

Marxism, to which historians in Europe were at least sensitive, did not significantly affect scholars in the United States before 1920.[42] Discontent with institutional history more often took a form indigenous to the United States and derived from the concepts of the frontier and of sectionalism associated with Frederick Jackson Turner.

Turner was scarcely conscious of the long-term effect of his words when he read his famous paper on the significance of the frontier in American history in 1893. Then and later he sometimes spoke of the frontier as if it were itself an institution, and some of his followers accepted the "frontier interpretation" dogmatically and thus misunderstood the larger meaning of his ideas.

The frontier and the West as concepts in 1893 were already familiar though the efforts of Lyman Draper, H. H. Bancroft, R. G. Thwaites, and Theodore Roosevelt. Turner did more than extend those ideas. He was less interested in furthering any particular interpretation than he was in achieving a view of events in whole context. He pleaded, in essence, that to treat the institutions of politics, of economics, or of religion as if their development were entirely self-contained and self-generating was misleading; these could only be understood in terms of the interconnections

[41] James H. Robinson, *Petrarch: The First Modern Scholar and Man of Letters* (1898; New York, 1914) ; Richard Hofstadter, *Progressive Historians* (New York, 1968) ; also Chapter 4 at notes 11, 29.

[42] Early faulty Marxist works included Algie M. Simons, *Social Forces in American History* (New York, 1911) ; Herman Schlüter, *Lincoln, Labor and Slavery* (New York, 1913) ; and, in a sense, A. W. Calhoun, *Social History of the American Family,* 3 vols. (Cleveland, 1917–19) . See also Kent and Gretchen Kreuter, "Vernacular History of A. M. Simons," *Journal of American Studies,* II (October 1968) , 65 ff.

among them in any given time and place. The most suggestive work of Turner and his students examined precisely such connections between geography and politics, between the productive system and religion, and the like. These interpretations enabled the authors of monographs to investigate the intersection, on a limited plane, of forces institutional works could not readily treat; examinations of the relation of politics to the regional and economic context were particularly important. Turner's situation as a trainer of graduate students further maximized his impact on the interests of the next generation.[43]

The First World War created no marked break in American historiography. Instead, its immediate result was to direct increasing attention to diplomatic, military, and political history; these became the most relevant of fields alike to scholars committed to the new history and to those loyal to the institutional approach.[44] But the historians who moved to positions of prominence in the 1920s were eager for a new kind of history—new, more often in the sense used by Eggleston than in that used by Robinson and Beard. *New Viewpoints in American History* by Arthur M. Schlesinger (1922) articulated the desire to shift the emphasis in subject matter to such issues as immigration, women, economic history, and the city; and the developing social sciences promised to provide a means by which to do so. Historians accepted the obligation to treat their data, not simply as interesting curiosities, but as revelations of patterns of behavior that extended through the whole life of a society. The *History of American Life* series thus dealt with the literature, the art, the religion, and the economy of the United States as parts of an integral whole.[45]

[43] Frederick Jackson Turner, *Frontier in American History* (New York, 1920), and *Significance of Sections in American History* (New York, 1950) ; Ray Allen Billington, *Frederick Jackson Turner* (New York, 1973) ; Wilbur R. Jacobs, ed., *Frederick Jackson Turner's Legacy* (San Marino, Calif., 1965), 151 ff.; Carl L. Becker, "Frederick Jackson Turner," *Everyman His Own Historian* (New York, 1935) , 191 ff.

[44] Carol S. Gruber, *Mars and Minerva: World War I and the Uses of the Higher Learning in America* (Baton Rouge, La., 1975) .

[45] Arthur M. Schlesinger, *New Viewpoints in American History* (New York, 1922) ; Arthur M. Schlesinger and Dixon R. Fox, eds., *History of American Life,* 13 vols. (New York, 1927–48) .

In retrospect, it was easy to take the virtues of that series for granted. It was a mistake to do so. It drew together and gave a kind of organization to a wide variety of materials, drawn from disparate sources. Moreover, its volumes were not catalogues, in the sense that those of McMaster often were. The specifics fell into a framework and signified something, although the framework was limited and appeared at its best in chapters, or rather parts of chapters, rather than in the volumes or in the series as a whole.

Offsetting those solid merits was a schematic, simple plan that assigned each volume a fixed time span, within which quite uniform chapters treated set topics. The lack of any integrating quality was not surprising, given the disparity of the authors. All the volumes reflected their origins in the progressive, reform tradition and referred frequently to "rise" and "progress," to the neglect of countertendencies. And its editors were no more successful than earlier social historians had been in solving the problem of how to move their cross sections through time. The result at best was a succession of stills—but not motion.

The *American Life* series was representative of the best scholarship of the quarter-century after 1920. Impressive monographs added steadily to information about fields theretofore neglected, but the investigators who turned to social history learned that more was demanded of them than to discover subjects not previously written about. And neither the legacy of Turner nor borrowings from the analytical social sciences in themselves provided coherent interpretive schemes.

Sectionalism proved a useful focus of study in the case of the South, where common social and cultural characteristics and a continuing sense of regional identity offered a basis for fruitful research. There also the Civil War—more critical as a social experience than elsewhere—furnished scholars with a stimulating point of departure. With William E. Dodd the study of Southern history moved beyond apologetics, although overtones of the ancient war issues lingered. Serious students set their hands to the task of understanding the society of the South; the contributions of Woodward, Abernethy, Buck, and Cash went a long way toward doing so.[46]

46 William E. Dodd, *Cotton Kingdom* (New Haven, 1921); T. P. Abernethy, *From Frontier to Plantation in Tennessee* (Chapel Hill, N.C., 1932), and *Three Virginia Frontiers* (Baton Rouge, La., 1940); C. Vann Woodward, *Tom Watson*

The West, however defined, did not present the opportunity for as many original contributions. W. P. Webb's *Great Plains* was suggestive and enlightening, despite its weakness of detail. However, the great mass of monographs dealing with this area filled gaps in information, but did little more. Promising indications that a closer study of the ecology of the region might supply new insights into its history were still no more than promises. Some of the most useful works on the West came from writers whose studies focused not on the region as such, but on the more general developments in which it was a factor.[47]

The other sections of the nation proved less fertile still. Apart from occasional studies in its commercial and manufacturing history, the story of New England after the seventeenth century suffered from neglect; and the middle states never fitted Turner's category in any sense meaningful to historians. With only few exceptions, therefore, the conception of the section was not a useful point of departure, although scholars who learned to take account of sectional considerations sometimes found them convenient tools in treating economic or constitutional or diplomatic problems.[48]

Social science did not fill the gap left by the lack of an organizing principle in social history. Historians respectfully paid homage to the related disciplines in programatic essays, but rarely were familiar enough with the issues to apply them to their own work. And indeed the social sciences, between the wars, increasingly narrowed their interest to static models without room for a time dimension, so that they offered little guidance to outsiders.[49]

The inability to assimilate Marxist patterns of thought cut Americans off from concepts which might have helped clarify the problems of class and social structure. The few crude adherents of historical materialism in the United States commanded little attention and less respect. Under Stalinist auspices, the Orthodox

---

(New York, 1938); Paul H. Buck, *Road to Reunion* (Boston, 1937); W. J. Cash, *Mind of the South* (New York, 1941).

[47] Walter P. Webb, *Great Plains* (Boston, 1931).

[48] For example, Frederick J. Turner, *United States, 1830–1850* (New York, 1935).

[49] Harry Elmer Barnes, *New History and Social Studies* (New York, 1925); Chapter 1 at note 6; Chapter 10 at note 1.

doctrine hardened into a mold which alienated some careful scholars like Pokrovskii and persuaded others like Tarlé to conform, and which was certainly inapplicable to the New World. The more flexible speculations of Horkheimer and the Institut für Sozialforschung came from outside organized academic life and therefore were hardly known across the ocean. An occasional diplomatic history—perforce international—drew upon the insights of Marx and Max Weber and earned the respect of Americans. But, in general, there was little communication between scholars in Europe like those connected with *Annales* and those who moved in the same direction in the United States.[50]

Instead, American historians commonly thought in terms of the division of interests described earlier in the century by the Populists and by Beard and the progressives, a division that aligned the agrarian against the mercantile elements in the nation's social order. But James Truslow Adams and other heirs of that interpretation viewed social groups in the mirror of politics, devoting their attention to the organizations, the grievances, and the conflicts of farmers and laborers, not to the composition and the conditions of life and work of the tillers of the soil or the artisans or the factory employees or the merchants.[51]

Groupings based on ethnic ties received more rewarding consideration. T. C. Blegen, George M. Stephenson, and, above all, Marcus L. Hansen dealt broadly with aspects of immigration; and W. E. B. DuBois in *Black Reconstruction* not only treated the Negro with awareness and understanding but also used the Marx-

---

[50] Philip S. Foner, *Business and Slavery* (Chapel Hill, N.C., 1941); Herbert Aptheker, *American Negro Slave Revolts* (New York, 1943); also the standard Marxist text, Georgii V. Plekhanov, *Materialist Conception of History* (1897; New York, 1940); Jesse D. Clarkson, introduction, Mikhail N. Pokrovskii, *History of Russia* (Bloomington, Ind., 1966), xxii–xxvii; Edgar Hösch, *Evgenij Viktorovič Tarlé* (Wiesbaden, 1964), 18, 100 ff.; Bertram D. Wolfe, "Operation Rewrite: The Agony of Soviet Historians," *Foreign Affairs*, XXXI (October 1952), 39 ff.; C. E. Black, ed., *Rewriting Russian History* (New York, 1956), 9 ff.; Martin Jay, *Dialectical Imagination: A History of the Frankfurt School* (Boston, 1973), 253 ff.; William L. Langer, *Diplomacy of Imperialism* (New York, 1935); Eckart Kehr, *Schlachtflottenbau und Parteipolitik, 1894–1901* (Berlin, 1930).

[51] James T. Adams, *Revolutionary New England* (Boston, 1923), and *New England in the Republic* (Boston, 1926). The most important monograph of the period, Arthur M. Schlesinger, *Colonial Merchants and the American Revolution* (New York, 1918), dealt with political attitudes not with social or economic characteristics.

ist approach more successfully than any other American scholar.[52]

Above all, the aspiration toward social history did not counteract the professional drift toward specialization. The monographs as written treated a single theme within some limited area of research and rarely resisted the tendencies toward fragmentation. Those who worked on a reform movement or a group or a city often lost sight of the relation to other such subfields, the number of which proliferated. The topics differed from those of the earlier generation, but still fell within institutional lines. When it came to explaining change, their authors traced the unfolding of self-contained intellectual, reform, or religious forces as their predecessors had traced political and constitutional ones. It was all very well to make obeisance to the life of the people; it was another matter to connect the general statement meaningfully to the peace movement or temperance.

Intellectual history illustrated the dilemma of the scholars who sought to treat a theme in social context. Merle Curti neglected to probe the inner development of ideas which he explained by reference to economic forces, but did not examine those either because they were outside his field and he could only take them for granted. On the other hand, Ralph H. Gabriel gave a more satisfactory account of the ideas he took more seriously than Curti, but to the neglect of the context. Ironically, in the decades between the wars the most important contributions to intellectual history in the United States came from Arthur O. Lovejoy and Perry Miller, the one trained in philosophy, the other in literature.[53]

War was a more serious diversion in 1941 than it had been in 1917. As earlier, it interrupted careers, shifted interests back to

[52] Marcus L. Hansen, *Atlantic Migration* (Cambridge, 1940), and *Immigrant in American History* (Cambridge, 1941); T. C. Blegen, *Norwegian Migration to America* (Northfield, Minn., 1931–40); George M. Stephenson, *Religious Aspects of Swedish Immigration* (Chicago, 1932); W. E. B. DuBois, *Black Reconstruction* (New York, 1935); Rudolph J. Vecoli, "European Americans: From Immigrants to Ethnics," in William H. Cartwright and Richard L. Watson, Jr., *Reinterpretation of American History* (Washington, 1973), 82 ff.

[53] Merle E. Curti, *Growth of American Thought* (New York, 1943); Ralph H. Gabriel, *Course of American Democratic Thought* (New York, 1940); Robert A. Skotheim, *American Intellectual Histories and Historians* (Princeton, 1966). Henry S. Commager, *American Mind* (New York, 1950), unsuccessfully applied the same methods to the 1890s.

diplomacy, military history, and politics, and directed attention to the present and the immediate past—all tendencies damaging to the development of the discipline. The war also left long-term aftereffects, some of which did not surface until decades later.

The return of peace in 1945 did not bring with it a return to stability. The fragile professional structures developed since the 1880s could not withstand the gusts of change, unpredictable in direction and often concealing in frothy first appearances more somber underlying currents.

The profession had always been vulnerable. Realistically viewed, it did not aim to produce original creative scholars, but rather to supply the thousands of teachers with the cachet of the Ph.D. that the hundreds of collegiate institutions and advanced secondary schools demanded. As creative scholarship, there was something pathetic about the Ph.D. dissertation, laboriously compiled, meticulous in its apparatus, factually accurate but intellectually arid, and generally marking the end rather than the beginning of a writing career. William James had long before 1945 made that clear. But from the point of view of American education, it was no mean attainment that so large a proportion of teachers should at least once in their lives have learned through this exercise the values of precision, of balanced judgment, and of openmindedness. If such exercises produced in addition occasional contributions to knowledge, they more than served their purpose.

The qualities evoked by training toward those ends were not, however, such as in themselves produced original scholarship. The ability to raise meaningful and unexpected questions, to exercise critical judgment in arriving at broad conclusions, and to discover relationships between the experiences of the present and the data of the past were not discouraged by the graduate schools and the profession in general; they were simply, and in the nature of the case almost inevitably, overlooked. The exceptional writer who maintained his creativity did not encounter the opposition of his colleagues and teachers, but, more discouraging, their apathy. No aspect of the system prepared it to absorb the changes it encountered after 1945.

The explosion in higher education immediately increased the numbers of historians. Supply followed demand. The proportion of young people satisfied to leave high school for a job dropped and the size of the total age group rose. Classrooms bulged and textbook sales soared. New institutions of higher education appeared and old ones expanded or sprouted branches. Suddenly a scarcity of staff! Teaching positions, impossible to find in the 1930s, hard to get in the 1940s and still scarce in the 1950s, went begging in the 1960s. Desperate administrators courted any plausible candidate, and scores of universities undertook to grind out doctorates with the greatest of speed, encouraged to do so by the awareness that a graduate school was a nice reservoir of cheap labor; its docile students instructed undergraduates at low cost and moved on before they learned to make demands. The fellowship programs of the Ford Foundation and of the federal government in the effort immediately to multiply the number of scholarly centers of excellence made it profitable for students to go where there were neither libraries in which to work nor faculty capable of educating them.

The discontinuities in control, training, and experience had disastrous, although at first hidden, consequences. For a time, more was better—more books, more journals, more essays, more monographs, more crowds at the convention.[54] Then came the reckoning. Not only did deflation in the 1970s leave scores of would-be historians without jobs, which was tragic enough, but the subsequent contraction was as senseless as the previous expansion had been, following as it did the classic tactic of craft unions and tight professional associations which limited access to protect the interests of entrenched incumbents, however incompetent. The old informal control network was too weak to stay the decay; and cautious compromisers permitted the conversion of the learned societies into politically oriented interest groups feebly trying to further the immediate interests of a heterogeneous membership. The policies of reviewing media and of program committees spread the plums, and also the mediocrity, at the expense of standards.

The broadening subject matters also had a deceptive appear-

---

[54] The self-congratulatory tone of contemporary appraisals illustrated the exuberance of the decade. See, e.g., Cartwright and Watson, *Reinterpretation of American History*. Timothy Paul Donovan, *Historical Thought in America Postwar Patterns* (Norman, Okla., 1973), evaded these problems in a mechanical categorization of rhetorical statements by historians.

ance. Stimulated by foundation and government support, whole new fields opened up, notably in Asian, Middle Eastern, and African history. But the more traditional non-American areas grew weak. Ancient and Medieval history suffered from the declining ability of Americans to use languages other than their own, as ultimately also did Renaissance and modern European history. The presence in the United States of a corps of refugees and the entry into the profession of some of their children for a time concealed the true gravity of the situation. But the difficulty of finding competent scholars in European history stood in ironic contrast to the more general job scarcity in 1977.

Loss of contact with the older centers of learning across the Atlantic also hurt. First, totalitarian assaults on the universities, then the war, and then its aftermath stifled historical studies there. With faculties dispersed, students in uniform, and many libraries in ruins, the break in continuity of teaching and research was even more drastic than in the United States. The Old World became dependent upon the New for financial and intellectual aid, in the reconstruction of the curriculum as of buildings. Foundations and exchange programs supported by the United States government influenced both the place of history in the university and the shift in emphasis from the premodern to the more recent past and from politics and diplomacy to social and intellectual development.

When European scholarship revived in the 1960s, it moved in new directions. Emancipated from the traditional schools, young scholars, who had nevertheless benefited from the old training, sought new subjects and new interpretations. A tortuous process of modernizing Marxism bore some fruitful results; and social history attracted energetic investigators in the VIe Section of the École Pratique des Hautes Études, among the contributors to *Past and Present,* and elsewhere. But in the absence of continuity of contact with the United States, few Europeans were aware that an earlier transatlantic generation had already explored the strange territories they invaded. Ironically, too, Americans who did England and France in the 1960s were so specialized that they were unaware of the extent to which E. P. Thompson and Fernand Braudel traversed conceptual grounds long since entered by colleagues who did the United States.

Growth in numbers encouraged further fragmentation and

further dispersal of efforts. To expect mastery of the whole of American history from a scholar trained to burrow in a tight corner was excessive; to dream as well of an acquaintance with the French or Roman past was absurd. Specialization by country or region and by a contracted time interval was not enough. The specifications for teaching and research called as well for a focus on a social or demographical or family or urban or ethnic subfield. The manifestos made plausible cases for littleness: for the city apart from the region, for the suburb apart from the city, for medicine apart from science, for technology apart from economics, for entrepreneurship apart from business, and for leisure apart from society—and presumably for popular healing apart from medicine, and sport apart from leisure, and baseball apart from sport. Lost in the process was the ability to describe the whole game while dealing with only the shortstop.[55]

Too often those who perceived the difficulty, in the attempt to escape blundered into narrowing corridors. A variety of regional fields appeared, among them American studies, in an effort to break loose from the shackles of petrified subjects. Interdisciplinary and comparative studies launched to surmount barriers before long became specialties on their own account. Often the enthusiasm of the first promoters and the fact that they had themselves been trained in some older branches of learning yielded valuable results and original insights. At the hands of F. O. Mathiessen, the marriage of history and literature produced a book which brought neglected aspects of a whole period into focus. Henry Nash Smith went beyond earlier efforts to study public opinion and propaganda and used a wide variety of materials to examine popular attitudes toward the West. But the followers were not as successful and the words—image, myth, and symbol—

---

[55] E.g., Eric E. Lampard, "American Historians and the Study of Urbanization," *American Historical Review*, LXVII (October 1961) , 49 ff.; Stephan A. Thernstrom, "Reflections on the New Urban History," in Felix Gilbert and Stephen R. Graubard, *Historical Studies Today* (New York, 1972) , 320 ff.; Charles E. Rosenberg, "Medical Profession, Medical Practice and the History of Medicine," in Edwin Clarke, ed., *Modern Methods in the History of Medicine* (London, 1971) , 22; Marie B. Hall, "History of Science and History of Medicine," *ibid.*, 157 ff.; David E. Harrell, Jr., *All Things Are Possible: The Healing & Charismatic Revivals in Modern America* (Bloomington, Ind., 1975) : Marshall Smelser, *Life That Ruth Built* (New York, 1975) ; Ronald L. Numbers, *Prophetess of Health: A Study of Ellen G. White* (New York, 1976) .

fluttering through the pages without precision, as often clouded as illuminated issues. It was rarely more than a decade before the apparatus of courses, programs, societies, conventions, and journals hardened the new subfields into molds as rigid as the old—and narrower.[56]

Offsetting the negative trends of the postwar period were positive stimuli that permitted creative individuals to compose works of solid and enduring value. The furious years after 1941 effectively dissolved the faith in progress and, for a time at least, the belief in a unique American mission. In the aftermath of Hiroshima and of exposure of the European concentration camps, only the most stubborn optimists continued to mumble the old phrases about the inevitability of human improvement. With the spread of totalitarian Communism after 1945, the United States no longer stood, either for its allies or for its enemies, in the vanguard of human history. The wave of the future lapped in another direction.

With the rhetoric stripped away, the materials of social history were more visible than they had been to writers of earlier generations. Moreover, the expansion of the profession had the beneficial side effect of opening positions to historians of diverse economic, cultural, and ethnic backgrounds; the loss of cohesiveness permitted a gain in the variety of experiences scholars of the 1960s and 1970s brought to their work. The impressive monographs they produced did not add up to the corpus of a school, as did those of the contributors to *Annales* in France; but significant books and articles on religion, science, ethnic life, class, the city, regionalism, the family, and education widened the view of the development of American culture. Moreover, some at least of those studies located their particular subjects within a context broad enough to consider the way of life and the common assumptions of the people. As important, they provided a basis for apply-

---

[56] Tremaine McDowell, *American Studies* (Minneapolis, 1958); Richard M. Dorson, *Birth of American Studies* (Bloomington, Ind., 1977); Giles B. Gunn, *F. O. Mathiessen* (Seattle, 1975); Henry Nash Smith, *Virgin Land* (Cambridge, 1950); Richard W. B. Lewis, *American Adam* (Chicago, 1955); John W. Ward, *Andrew Jackson: Symbol for an Age* (New York, 1955); Marvin Meyers, *Jacksonian Persuasion, Politics and Belief* (Stanford, 1957); Charles L. Sanford, *Quest for Paradise* (Urban, Ill., 1961); William Taylor, *Cavalier and Yankee* (New York, 1961); Cushing Strout, *American Image of the Old World* (New York, 1963); Leo Marx, *Machine in the Garden* (New York, 1964).

ing fresh understandings to the materials of political, intellectual, and regional history, and transformed those once-traditional fields.[57]

The lack of schools of the European sort was in part the result of the vast scale and the heterogeneity of American higher education. With so much space, every Ph.D. swam on his own, if he wished. Then again, departmental university organization limited the power of individual professors over their students and offset to some extent the dependency of apprentice to master. But, in addition, the unideological character of the discipline in the United States long inhibited the formation of such groups. In the first efforts to impart a political spin to scholarship the seekers after partisanship had to dream up a nonexistent category—the "consensus" school—by jumbling together authors of the most disparate sorts. Tossed into the chaotic winds of scholarly discourse, that misleading term soon attained the status of a cliché that took the place of thought.[58]

In the 1960s external events generated a drift toward self-conscious identification by radicals as New Left historians. The civil rights movement, the Vietnam war, student protest, and gen-

[57] Robert Kelley, "Ideology and Political Culture from Jefferson to Nixon," *American Historical Review*, LXXXII (June 1977), 531 ff., surveys the literature; Allan G. Bogue, "United States: The 'New Political History,'" *Journal of Contemporary History*, III (January 1968), 5 ff., is more aware of continuities with the work of the previous generation and, therefore, more measured in its enthusiasm. For other variants, see Charles S. Sydnor, *Gentlemen Freeholders: Political Practices in Washington's Virginia* (Chapel Hill, N.C., 1952); Bernard Bailyn, "Politics and Social Structure in Virginia," in James Morton Smith, ed., *Seventeenth-Century America* (Chapel Hill, N.C., 1959), 90 ff. Among the important regional works were James C. Malin, *Grassland of North America* (Lawrence, Kans., 1947); F. L. Owsley, *Plain Folk of the Old South* (Baton Rouge, La., 1949); and W. H. Stephenson and E. M. Coulter, eds., *History of the South*, 10 vols. (Baton Rouge, La., 1948). Edward C. Kirkland, *Men, Cities, and Transportation*, 2 vols. (Cambridge, 1948), located an important strand in economic history in its social context.

[58] John Higham, "Cult of the 'American Consensus'; Homogenizing Our History," *Commentary*, XXVII (February 1959), 93 ff., and "Beyond Consensus: The Historian as Moral Critic," *American Historical Review*, LXVII (April 1962), 609 ff. The essays in Jacques le Goff and Pierre Nora, *Faire de l'histoire*, 2 vols. (Paris, 1974), are interesting in themselves, but show no awareness of work in the United States or indeed anywhere outside France. See also Bernard Bailyn, "Review Article, French Historical Method," *Journal of Economic History*, XXXVII (December 1977), 1028 ff.

eral rebelliousness against all authority coincided with the uncontrolled expansion of the universities and created a situation in which dissidence easily bubbled up all over. In history as in politics generally, the New Left was heterogenous in composition and in ability, incoherent in objectives and in methodology, and more prone to manifestos and proclamations than to practical results. But those who rallied around the unfurled banner shared a common predicament and unwittingly arrived at a common posture. Insisting upon making the world absolutely and immediately perfect, they could not pin their hopes on any existing Communist regime, party, or platform—certainly not the old discredited Stalinism, nor the bureaucratic Brezhnevism of their own day, nor yet the Maoism of Richard Nixon's host. A few could cling doggedly to the vision of an as yet nonexistent communism with a human face. In the absence of any positive intellectual refuge, others retreated to the defensive shield of thoroughgoing anti-Amerikanism.

The posture was plausible so long as those who took it abstained from asking why the country they assailed was so awful, as bad as, nay worse, than any other. Unfortunately, the writing of history called for some explanation, and in the tortuous attempt to provide it, the New Left wiggled into a pattern of thought of the most Orthodox character—without knowing it. Marxism was intellectually too demanding and its dialectical argument too rigorous to make its case. But it required no proof to assert that the United States had engaged in "a remarkably consistent effort to turn back the revolutionary wave which has swept across large parts of Asia and Africa and has threatened a number of countries in South America and Europe. In this counterrevolutionary campaign our government consistently allies itself with authoritarian regimes of the right, justifying that policy on the ground that the various revolutionary movements are inhospitable to Western democracy (and capitalism)."[59] For New Left convenience, imperialism preempted a good part of the past, and before that a record of conquest, and all along exploitation and victimization by a people dedicated to racism and violence. Not only the Vietnamese, but also the Cubans and Puerto Ricans, and the Mexicans, and the

---

[59] Leo Marx, "Comments," *American Historical Review*, LXXXII (June 1977), 599. This particular vision goes back to David Horowitz, *Free World Colossus* (New York, 1965).

Africans, and lo, the poor Indians!—to say nothing of the women always. Thus, the return to the concept of uniqueness and mission —only now inverted, with the saints of yore become Satanic.[60]

Only a few dissenting historians of the 1970s fixed their attention upon the actual life of the people; and some of them did not have the regard for accuracy of detail of the Puritan who wrote under the scrutiny of a vigilant deity. But the most important difference was the absence of an equivalent of the sense of cosmogony which had given meaning to the world of the seventeenth-century writers. Marxism did not supply the want, for in its scriptures the United States was the most advanced presocialist society, politically and socially as well as economically.[61]

Such gaps did not at the moment seem disturbing. Problems of historical knowledge had never seriously troubled Americans. Although Becker and Beard had shown some concern with the questions of epistemology raised by philosophers, they and the few others interested usually confined their thoughts on these matters to inaugural proclamations and farewell addresses, a circumstance which persistently misled critics, more given to reading programmatic statements than solid monographs. Nor had the concepts of progress, of cycles, and of race often affected what historians wrote. To the extent that they approached their subjects with a pragmatic temperament and with disciplined methods, their efforts could be productive, to whatever interpretation they adhered.[62]

Political differences were likely to be temporary. More durable

---

[60] Barton J. Bernstein, ed., *Towards a New Past: Dissenting Essays in American History* (New York, 1968) ; Gerda Lerner, "New Approaches to the Study of Women in American History," *Journal of Social History*, III (Fall 1969) , 53 ff.; and Alfred F. Young, *American Revolution: Explorations in the History of American Radicalism* (Dekalb, Ill., 1976) , are representative. Irwin Unger, "The 'New Left,' and American History," *American Historical Review*, LXXII (July 1967) , 1237 ff.; and David H. Donald, "Radical Historians on the Move," *New York Times Book Review*, July 19, 1970, are critical. See also Edward N. Saveth, "A Decade of American Historiography: The 1960s," in Cartwright and Watson, *Reinterpretation of American History*, 17 ff.; "Revisionism," *Time*, February 2, 1970, pp. 14 ff.; Clifford Solway, "Turning History Upside Down," *Saturday Review*, June 20, 1970, pp. 13 ff.

[61] Not until 1929, and thereafter only intermittently, did Stalin reverse the judgment of Marx, Engels, and Lenin. See V. I. Lenin, *Collected Works* (Moscow, 1966) , XXXVI, 214 ff.; Theodore Draper, *American Communism and Soviet Russia* (New York, 1960) , 409 ff.

[62] See Chapter 4 at note 8; Chapter 5 at note 10.

were those that sprang from eroded critical standards and from specialization. The continued quest for additional techniques and for insights borrowed from other disciplines created subgroups immersed in problems of their own, particularly when the trend operated in the context of hoary American attitudes that discounted the importance of interpretative theory and blunted the edge of criticism.

# 4

## *Theories of Historical Interpretation*

IN AMERICA as in Europe the Enlightenment turned attention away from traditional interpretations of the past and ultimately prepared the ground for more scientific ones. The escape from old dogmas was far from complete, and historians never entirely liberated themselves from inherited bias, but increasingly their subject appeared a distinct form of writing, no longer to be contained within a religious framework. Free of dependence on theology, history became a form of knowledge worth possessing for its own sake and a discipline governed by reasonable rules.[1]

The miraculous and providential ways of understanding the past disappeared, not so much through brutal attacks, as in Thomas Paine's *Age of Reason,* but more important in a slow, subtle alteration which made the extraordinary manifestations of God's hand less relevant than the continuing processes of the world of nature. The events of the past transpired within a regular order. Not that every occurrence was entirely rational, but even irrational and superstitious phenomena were open to understanding by the human mind because natural laws governed all.

The altered point of view required historians to examine evidence by procedures analogous to those which prevailed in other fields of knowledge. Already in the seventeenth century Jean Mabillon had subjected venerable documents to careful scrutiny and Pierre Bayle had urged the critical questioning of authority. David Hume's insistence that belief in miracles yield to the canons of evidence (1739) pushed to an extreme the concessions of more pious writers like Thomas Woolson, who had already explained

---

[1] Oscar Handlin et al., *Harvard Guide to American History* (Cambridge, 1954), 15 ff.

that the Scriptures dealt not with actual events but with parables (1727), or Bishop Butler, whose *Analogy* (1736) argued that these were but imperfectly understood manifestations of the true law of nature.[2]

Assaults upon authority continued in the nineteenth century. Geology and astronomy then extended the accepted time span, which had set creation of the universe at 3947 B.C., and thereby finally destroyed the ancient chronology derived from the Scriptures. Moreover, the plurality of human experiences, once perceived, required a far more complex pattern of historical explanation than had satisfied earlier generations. The old continuities—from the classical-biblical era in the eastern Mediterranean down to modern Europe and thence to the United States—could not withstand the discoveries of a prehistoric past and of other civilizations elsewhere in the world.[3]

As the overpowering grip of authority relaxed, the relation of factual detail to more general propositions took on a new appearance. The littlest incidents were not mere illustrations of some large truth vouched for by church or tradition, but things in themselves validated by accurate recording. Accumulation of tiny bits of information could soften if not resolve the differences about authorized truths over which men and states had done bloody battle for hundreds of years. Old documents, properly verified and analyzed, provided disputacious monarchs and prelates an alternative to the sword. So, back in the seventeenth and eighteenth centuries such diverse thinkers as Samuel Pufendorf and Gottfried von Leibniz had felt the need to set their ideas in historical context; and J. J. Moser was but the most prominent of the German lawyers who sensed a relation between the law and the times which an objective pursuit of the truth could illuminate. Mastery of the sources counted more than immersal in a system.[4]

2 Leslie Stephens, *History of English Thought in the Eighteenth Century*, 2 vols. (London, 1876), I, 293 ff., 309 ff.

3 Peter Hanns Reill, *German Enlightenment and the Rise of Historicism* (Berkeley, 1975), 75 ff.; Charles E. Gillispie, *Genesis and Geology* (Cambridge, 1951); Francis C. Haber, *Age of the World, Moses to Darwin* (Baltimore, 1959), 187 ff.; and, in general, Ernst Cassirer, *Philosophie der Aufklärung* (Tübingen, 1932; Princeton, 1951), ch. 5.

4 Reill, *German Enlightenment*, 14 ff.; Reinhard Rürup, *Johann Jacob Moser* (Wiesbaden, 1965), 110 ff.; Erwin Schömbs, *Das Staatsrecht Johann Jakob Mosers* (Berlin, 1968), 196 ff. For precedents among sixteenth-century French legalists, see George Huppert, *Idea of Perfect History* (Urbana, Ill., 1970).

The altered perspective in which fact stood to truth offered the hope of an end to the oceans of blood spilled in war and inquisition to uphold one theological position or another. Moslem and Christian, Protestant and Catholic could afford to tolerate the large doctrinal differences over which they disagreed, so long as they could discuss upon equal terms the independently verifiable details. Objectivity, which became the universal goal of historians, did not require them to abjure faith or allegiance; it did demand that they approach the facts through a search for evidence also available to those of other faiths or allegiances.

Awareness of the value of objectivity persuaded nineteenth-century Europeans of the worth of critical, factual precision and especially of the necessity of distinguishing actuality from myth. Important strands in nineteenth-century philosophy and history no doubt lent themselves to the propagation of new myths revolving about the state or nation or folk; but Hegel and Ranke, whose writings nurtured some of those tendencies, nonetheless never ceased to urge the importance of a careful scrutiny of the facts. Meanwhile, the higher criticism subjected even the Scriptures to persistent scholarly attention; and the Darwinian emphasis upon development cast doubt on all rigid or formal systems of belief which left no room for evolution through time.[5]

In the United States the example of Europe justified a rough-and-ready pragmatism and emphasis on factual objectivity. Knowledge of the past was accessible through patient and objective study and required only industry, the suppression of personal opinion, and the systematic exercise of detachment. James Ford Rhodes believed that impartiality, the surrender of all preconceived notions, diligence, and accuracy were sufficient to make a historian. So long as this attitude prevailed, broad comprehensive theories of history had little direct or conscious effect on the way Americans wrote.[6]

Yet the facts did not quite interpret themselves. However determined the chronicler and however stark the narrative, the mere process of inclusion and exclusion and the simplest narrative links

5 Franklin L. Ford, "Ranke: Setting the Story Straight," Massachusetts Historical Society, *Proceedings*, LXXXVII (1975), 57 ff.; George C. Iggers, *German Conception of History* (Middletown, Conn., 1968), 63 ff.

6 James Ford Rhodes, "History," American Historical Association, *Annual Report, 1899*, I, 60, 61.

required at the very least some judgment of what was important and that in turn implied a conception of causation, even when vague and imprecise. Removal of the guiding hand of Providence from the day-to-day affairs of men, and even from the long sweep of the past, did not end but only altered and concealed the need for the operation of some active agency to explain what had happened, and why.[7]

In the United States, even more than in Europe, theory entered unobtrusively in the guise of the preconceptions within which historians interpreted their own experience and that of other people. The personal desire for a comprehensible past exposed the unwitting writer to a bold explanation of why he had arrived where he was. "In the lives of our ancestors we become parties concerned; and when we behold them braving the horrors of the desert, and surmounting every difficulty from the burning climate, thick forest, and savage neighbors, we admire their courage and are astonished at their perseverance. We are pleased with every danger they escape, and wish to see even the most minute events, relating to the rise and progress of their little communities, placed before us in the most full and conspicuous light." When Alexander Hewatt published those lines in 1779 he was hardly aware that hidden in the words "rise and progress" was a theory as yet unrecognized, though it conformed to the long-held view of the past implied in the concept of mission.[8]

In Europe the starting point of the theory of inevitable progress was elsewhere—in tedious academic disputes over the relative merits of ancient and modern authors, in romantic visions of the personality liberated to self-expression by casting off the shackles of the past, and in the desperate need to explain the shattering changes in the continent that approached a climax in the last decade of the eighteenth century. Then Condorcet in France and William Godwin in England read in all clarity a natural law in history as certain as that of Isaac Newton in physics: the condition of man had improved steadily in the past and would continue to do so in the future. The nineteenth century locked that certainty

[7] Reill, *German Enlightenment,* 100 ff.

[8] Alexander Hewatt, *Historical Account of the Rise and Progress of the Colonies of South Carolina and Georgia* (London, 1779) , I, 2.

into the framework of hard science. Auguste Comte and Herbert Spencer explained all human development as the ascent to ever higher stages. And a succession of influential histories published within a few years of each other—by Henry Thomas Buckle and William E. H. Lecky in England, by Hippolyte A. Taine in France, and by John William Draper in the United States—demonstrated the advance from barbarism to civilization. The conviction endured well into the twentieth century, when Karl Jaspers described the goal of history as the civilization of man and the restoration of his primal unity.[9]

Americans simply appropriated the law of progress and applied it to the United States. Citizens of the newest of nations, bred in the belief in their own destined mission, did not find it hard to think of themselves as moving in the vanguard of human development, particularly since many a foreigner, for his own reasons, was ready so to identify them. Insofar as any broad interpretation served them at all, American historians reverted to some variant of the idea of progress.

In both the Old World and the New a strain of pessimism was a necessary concomitant of the overriding optimism of the late eighteenth century; and both the dark and the light aspects of change passed on to the heirs of the Enlightenment. People who moved without fixed guidelines toward an unknown destination could not help wondering from time to time how good that glowing future would be; and the personal and social costs of progress left some dissenters in doubt about its beneficence. The nostalgic reminiscences of local-color novels, short stories, and poetry celebrated the peculiar characteristics of places that had been prosperous, happy, and virtuous before they had yielded to the spoiling effects of change. Americans, in addition, knew that a penalty of being a pilgrim people was the obligation to meet severe standards of performance; the brightest angels had the farthest to fall. The Jeremiad tone, never far beneath the surface, left an uneasy sense

[9] J. B. Bury, *Idea of Progress* (London, 1920); Henry Thomas Buckle, *History of Civilization in England*, 2 vols. (London, 1857–61), I, 204–206; William E. H. Lecky, *History of the Rise and Influence of the Spirit of Rationalism in Europe* (London, 1865); Hippolyte A. Taine, *Histoire de la littérature anglais* (Paris, 1863–64); John William Draper, *History of the Intellectual Development of Europe* (New York, 1863); Karl Jaspers, *Origin and Goal of History* (Zurich, 1949), trans. Michael Bullock (London, 1953), xv, 261 ff.

of the ever-present danger of declension. Like Bradford, almost three centuries earlier, Mark Twain ascribed the country's fall from grace to a hunger for wealth. Just when the great civilization completed its youth—strong, pure, clean, ambitious, impressionable—California and Jay Gould drew it into temptation. What was true of the present and future, could also have been true of the past.[10]

Progress, however, was the dominant theme. By way of John Stuart Mill and Herbert Spencer, such popularizers as John Fiske repudiated all metaphysical thinking as vestiges of an outmoded past and assimilated the evolutionary concept to a vision of the steady upward advance of mankind. James Harvey Robinson's *New History* affirmed the certainty of advance. In 1927 few Americans disputed Charles A. Beard's assertion that belief in progress—the continual improvement in the lot of mankind on this earth "by the attainment of knowledge and the subjugation of the material world to the requirements of human welfare"— was "the most dynamic social theory" in the history of thought. Until the twentieth century no apostle of degeneration attracted a following in the United States, and the theme had no influence on the writing of history.[11]

At most, doubters of the rule of progress escaped by some theory of cycles, waves, or oscillations. Once they got over his hostility to Christianity, a few Americans read Edward Gibbon with interest and speculated about the rise and fall of civilizations in terms of the experience of Rome. Others knew about, even if they did not read, Montesquieu's essay on its greatness and decline. The inference usually drawn, however, was that modern nations, and particularly the United States, were avoiding the old errors. Indeed, with only a little ingenuity the fall of ancient states became a necessary preliminary to the westward passage of the course of empire and its ultimate transfiguration in the New World, which

[10] See Chapter 3, n. 39; also Henry Vyverberg, *Historical Pessimism in the French Enlightenment* (Cambridge, 1958), 62 ff., 122 ff., 155 ff.; Mario Praz, *Romantic Agony*, trans. Angus Davidson (London, 1970); Bernard DeVoto, ed., *Mark Twain in Eruption* (New York, 1940), 68 ff., 77 ff. On the inversion of progress, see Robert Nisbet, *Sociology as an Art Form* (New York, 1976), 115 ff.

[11] Charles A. Beard, *Rise of American Civilization*, 2 vols. (New York, 1927), I, 443; Milton Berman, *John Fiske* (Cambridge, 1961), 205 ff.; James H. Robinson, *New History* (New York, 1912), 247, 251, 252.

happily escaped even the Malthusian dangers of unbearable population growth. "The earth," Henry George knew, was "the tomb of the dead empires, no less than of dead men." Every civilization, in its own time as vigorous as his own, had "of itself come to a stop," so that people who had "built great temples and mighty cities, turned rivers and pierced mountains" declined into "a remnant of squalid barbarians" without even "the memory of what their ancestors had done." That awareness did not, however, drain away faith that by appropriate corrective measures his society could escape the downfall of its predecessors.[12]

Such assurances never totally quieted apprehension that the world might be speeding toward catastrophe. The dizzying discoveries of nineteenth-century science destroyed the boundaries of time and space, altered the nature of matter, and stripped man of his uniqueness in nature. The limitless possibilities of the future—for disaster or beatitude—drew attention to the vastness of a past whose amplitude was only recently undreamed of. The implications of Darwinian evolution reached back as well as ahead, as did the frightful pivot on which all turned—the chance mutations by which whole species perished or thrived.

Cyclical ideas applied to history could express either the hopes of optimists or the fears of pessimists. Clarence King made recurrent catastrophes essential elements in evolution, while Brooks Adams developed a rigid law of civilization and decay. Henry Adams, tantalized by images from Gibbon, pondered the significance of modernity and wondered "whether the American people knew where they were driving." Despair set in as he saw the complex chaos created by the dynamo supplant the simple order of which the virgin had been the symbol, and he at last escaped in a vision of accelerating depletion of energy. The very long time span within which twentieth-century writers about the past exercised their imaginations enabled H. G. Wells to outline the resolutely upward march of mankind toward perfection; and Carl Becker encapsulated a gloomy outlook on his own times in a scheme which pointed toward a roseate but remote future. The same extended time frame, by contrast, made room for the gloom-

12 Henry George, *Progress and Poverty* (1879; New York, 1929), 485; William Graham Sumner, *Folkways* (Boston, 1907), 100 ff., 604; James G. Brooks, "Our Own Country," *Knickerbocker*, V (May 1835), 416 ff.

ier, more sophisticated cyclical theories of Oswald Spengler, P. A. Sorokin, and A. J. Toynbee.[13]

Despite the popularity in the United States of authors who articulated the prevalent apocalyptic fear of cataclysm, their works did not affect directly the mode in which historians wrote. The logic was simple. If the broad theories were true and the iron necessities of progress or of the cycle ruled, then the details did not matter. Rome would fall whether Nero fiddled or not; the United States would expand to the Pacific whether or not Jefferson bought Louisiana. By the same token, the validity of the generalization did not depend upon the little undulations on the way. Facts added or clarified about Nero and Jefferson would not alter the explanation of the inevitable process of rise and fall. The historian, strapped into his seat on the roller-coaster, could only take the ups and downs as they came; descriptions of the view on the way threw no light on the destination to which the rails led. And since what happened en route and why most interested the historian, flashy information about the facilities at the terminus was useful only to calm occasional queasy feelings in the stomach.

Historians who shied away from the sweep of grand cycles could, however, neatly spread along the slopes of a curve particular regularities perceived in the past, thereby avoiding the necessity of further probing. Changes in styles of art thus fell into place as alternations of classical and romantic impulses. The economy moved in waves of prosperity and depression. Radicals and conservatives succeeded one another in the control of power. The interpretations could be tautological: when one period closed, another began; and one phenomenon could ride piggyback upon another, as with the ups and downs of prejudice and the business cycle. To get beyond the obvious required different sets of questions about the concomitants and consequences of move-

13 Clarence King, *Catastrophism and the Evolution of Environment* (New Haven [?], 1877) ; Brooks Adams, *Law of Civilization and Decay* (New York, 1895) ; H. G. Wells, *Outline of History,* 2 vols. (London, 1919–20) ; Henry Adams, *Education of Henry Adams* (New York, 1931) , 231, 498 ff., and *Letters,* 2 vols. (Boston, 1930–38) , II, 235; William B. Jordy, *Henry Adams, Scientific Historian* (New Haven, 1952) ; Henry Wasser, *Scientific Thought of Henry Adams* (Thessaloniki, 1956) ; Timothy Paul Donovan, *Henry Adams and Brooks Adams* (Norman, Okla., 1961) ; Frederic C. Jaher, *Doubters and Dissenters: Cataclysmic Thought in America* (New York, 1964) ; Carl Becker, *Progress and Poverty* (1936; New York, 1949) .

ment in one direction or another and about the phasing of re-
verses in trend. Once those questions emerged, the effort to answer
usually drained the concept of the cycle of importance.[14]

More generally, cyclical theories like faith in progress were sub-
stitutes for explanation and permitted the evasion of the deeper
problems. To plot the course of the straight line, loop, or spiral
across time in itself furnished no key to what motive power
dragged men and societies along it. For Europeans the issue bore
weighty philosophical implications. Americans, who thought in
more practical terms and who in any case believed in the uniqueness of their own country, rarely considered seriously the systematic regularities in the way societies or civilizations developed.

In Europe thinkers who approached the past as philosophers
rather than as historians defined the basic terms of discourse. From
his predecessors, the pivotal continental writer, Johann Gottfried
Herder, derived some sense of the importance of ideas—from
Schiller's standing theme of the people's struggle for freedom,
from Goethe's celebration of life as the expression of a profound
inner urge. Herder sought a universal explanation for the development of civilization and found it in ideas, by which he referred
to the complex of national character, religion, and culture.
Thence through Wilhelm von Humboldt and Leopold von Ranke
ideas served influential German historians as instruments for organizing and explaining the multitude of events they laboriously
assembled. National history was largely an unfolding of ideas in
that sense and bore some correspondence to the writings of American expounders of mission who, however, were rarely as conscious
of the philosophic significance of their assumptions.[15]

In Germany the belief that the idea was an autonomous force
in history acquired a philosophical foundation in Georg W. F.
Hegel's *Phänomenologie des Geistes* (1807) and in his later
treatise on logic. According to Hegel, the idea fulfilled itself in

14 See Chapter 14.

15 W. H. Bruford, *Culture and Society in Classical Weimar* (Cambridge, 1962),
184 ff., 264 ff.; Iggers, *German Conception of History*, 34 ff., 133.

time by passage through successive dialectic stages. The term "dialectic," since Aristotle, had referred to a form of argument in which the disputant advanced the opposite of a proposition in the expectation that contradiction would expose the way to a resolution. Hegel applied the concept of thesis, antithesis, and synthesis to the process by which ideas, and the superstructure of institutions which rested upon them, had changed in the past. The idea, that is, the embodiment of the complete and final product of the reason of each age, always evoked its contrariety as thinkers probed its deeper meaning. The resulting conflict led to conciliation by discovery of a higher formulation, which in turn resumed the process until the attainment of the ultimate or absolute or transcendent Idea of True Being.

Historians could trace the dialectic process by piercing through surface events to the idea behind them. By doing so they could make out the higher logic of the past, for the idea transformed the material circumstances which were the apparent stuff of history. Ranke and his followers rejected the Hegelian dialectic, which nevertheless continued to undergird all interpretations that stressed the influence of ideas on history.

These views reached the United States first through French and English intermediaries, then by direct exposure to German books and universities. Emerson and the transcendentalists assimilated the philosophical implications quickly, and the views of Hegel and the idealists dominated American academic teaching through much of the second half of the nineteenth century. But historians felt the effects more slowly; cultural and linguistic distance from Europe was too great to permit a profound effect of theory on Americans who wrote and read history.[16]

Abstractions had little influence upon practitioners in the United States other than occasionally to inflate the vocabulary of references to progress and mission. Apart from introductory flourishes, the sober, scholarly pages of nineteenth-century histories displayed no signs of indebtedness to philosophy. George Bancroft, who had actually studied in Germany enough to know Hegelian idealism at first hand and to espouse it, made the moving forces of his great history the ideas of freedom and democracy working themselves out through time under New World condi-

[16] Henry A. Pochmann, *German Culture in America* (Madison, Wisc., 1957), 198 ff., 257 ff.

tions. But in the actual exposition of his volumes, history unfolded less often through a dialectical process than in a continuing
conflict of ideas with environment.

The debt to German idealism was more substantial later in the
century, particularly in the cases of Hermann von Holst, and
J. W. Burgess—the one born in Europe, the other educated there.
Both scholars attempted to show the strong and continuing influence of the idea of union on American constitutional development. But even they were as much conscious of the problems of
Civil War and Reconstruction through which they had lived as
they were of the abstractions they accepted.

It was easier to slip into casual use of the verbal offshoots of
German idealism than rigorously to work out the relation to
events. In Europe efforts along these lines continued—some of
them fruitful, notably those of Wilhelm Dilthey. As against the
thinkers who tried to unify all the knowledge of an era in a metaphysical weltanschauung, Dilthey sought as a historian to locate
in a period's varied forms of expression some unifying shared
understanding, that is, the thoughts many minds were thinking
at the same time. As a philosopher he developed a *Lebensphilosophie* to describe the psychology of that understanding. But respected as he was in the Old World, Dilthey remained unknown
in the United States. Nor were Americans responsive to Karl
Lamprecht's alternative approach, which examined the social
environment for the psychological forces that produced a collective spiritual (*seelischer*) condition.[17] The closest approximation
came in Daniel Boorstin's sketch of the common body of assumptions that related the intellectuals of a period. But that stimulating effort, the source of which was in American studies, took for
granted rather than considered the questions of causation—why?
and therefore?[18]

[17] Hans-Georg Gadamer, *Wahrheit und Methode* (Tübingen, 1960), 205 ff.;
Georg Misch, "Lebensphilosophie und Phänomenologie," *Philosophischer Anzeiger*,
III (1929), 285 ff., 405 ff., IV (1930), 195 ff., 293 ff., 294 ff.; Hajo Holborn, "Wilhelm
Dilthey and the Critique of Historical Reason," *Journal of the History of Ideas*, XI
(January 1950), 93 ff.; Karl Lamprecht, *Kulturhistorische Methode* (Berlin, 1900).

[18] Daniel Boorstin, *Lost World of Thomas Jefferson* (New York, 1948). Stow
Persons, *American Minds* (New York, 1958), vii, is less successful; and Henry
Steele Commager, *American Mind* (New Haven, 1950), still less.

Another nineteenth-century tradition of historical interpretation also derived from Hegel. Karl Marx accepted the logic of the dialectic; he, too, argued that the conflict of thesis and antithesis and their resolution through synthesis explained the events of history. But, for the Hegelian idea Marx substituted the system of production. The developing economy was the dynamic element in the dialectic process; it defined the structure of classes, the interests and interrelationships of which determined all changes in the superstructure of society, intellect, government, and religion.

Marxian historical materialism proceeded from the general position to a more specific analysis of modern history: out of the ancient mode of production had emerged the characteristic medieval society of noble lord and serf; that in turn evolved into capitalism, the inner contradictions of which were leading to classless socialism. Progress came in a linear fashion; at each stage the victors in the conflict of classes, by exploitation of their inferiors, arrayed the forces which would take command at the subsequent stage.

In Europe, Marxism was enormously stimulating, and not only because it provided an intellectual tool for the socialist parties gaining strength after 1880. In addition, historical materialism significantly affected the content and treatment of written history. Responses to Engels' early call for study of the conditions of the laboring classes resulted in significant monographs, as did efforts to discover an economic component in familiar political stories. Before 1917 socialist historians, though often disputatious, recognized no obligation to dogmatic conformity and therefore responded freely to the material, although emphasis varied according to national tradition. More generally the stimulus of Marxist criticism exposed the drawbacks of treatments of diplomacy or religion or politics in isolation from economics. It thus unsettled, although it did not end, the rigid formalism of institutional academic history.[19]

Americans shied away from Marxism. It did not conform to their own perceptions of their past, and it stood outside the European university circles most respected in the United States.

[19] David McLellan, *Karl Marx: His Life and Thought* (New York, 1973), 144, 161 ff.

Above all, dialectical materialism in the New World lacked the political and philosophical bases that sustained it in the Old. Socialist parties appeared alien and were weak and given to splintering so that they supported no vigorous intellectual life. And by the time Americans staged their own revolt against formalism, an alternative, indigenous philosophical mode had supplanted Hegelianism.[20]

Two aspects of Marxist theory attracted American historians, although not in any systematic fashion. The concept of a substructure and a superstructure, of forces operating in society to penetrate institutional lines, conformed to the long-standing urge to describe the development of the whole people. And the feature of historical materialism that emphasized class conflict had a rough congruence with the recognition of clashes of interest in government which went back at least to the Tenth Federalist and to which populists and progressives at the turn of the century gave immediate importance. But the desire to link politics or culture with economics or to explain why merchants and farmers fought one another did not make Marxists of turn-of-the-century scholars. Those attentive to the philosophical implications of their work had drifted away from Hegelianism toward another way of regarding the problems of logic and knowledge.

Charles S. Peirce, William James, and John Dewey addressed, in the first instance, the question of how to make ideas clear, and the focus of their attention remained on the reasoning process. In place of the contrarieties of the dialectic they set the orderly trial and error of the succession of experiments which arrived at ever-closer approximations of the truth. Development came by increments rather than by resolution of the clash of opposites; transposed to the social realm, that meant by progressive improvement rather than by the resolution of conflict between opposing forces. Although pragmatism did not gain the ascendancy in academic philosophical circles, it was in accord with current views of progress and therefore supported, and provided a vocabulary for, influential groups of historians.[21]

20 Friedrich Engels to Sorge, March 18, 1893, *Science and Society*, II (Summer 1939) , 371.

21 See the summation in William James, *Meaning of Truth* (1909) , *Works*, ed. Frederick H. Burkhardt and Fredson Bowers (Cambridge, 1975) .

Their task was to test against the data produced by their research the propositions formulated by the social sciences. But in the United States economics, government, and sociology were also detached from or hostile to Marxism. Their buried roots reached back to eighteenth-century moral philosophy, and, although a century of growth gave them altogether new shapes, they were still remote from Marxism. Even socialists like Richard Ely and radical reformers like John R. Commons found in the past a record of gradual improvement rather than the dialectic of historical materialism.

Insofar as they looked for testable propositions to the social sciences, therefore, historians in the United States followed paths that drew them away from the dialectic as a mode of analysis. The American economist who wrote about the economic interpretation treated a concept quite different from that of the Marxists, as did Beard, who used the words in two influential titles. For them, as for the New Historians in general, the term "economic interpretation" applied to efforts to uncover the personal or class interests behind politics—to a kind of retrospective muckracking.[22]

Charles A. Beard was the most popular exponent of the position in the quarter-century after 1910. *An Economic Interpretation of the Constitution* (1913), though methodologically faulty and riddled with error, excited its readers. It seemed to attack a venerated institution, and it described the financial interests of the Founders of the Republic. Beard was far from being a Marxist in his critique, however; he emphasized the individual rather than the class position of those who held government bonds and devoted little attention to the basic structure of the economy or of the society. His study of Jeffersonian democracy was more consistent as an analysis, but the strength of his work lay in its conformity with the temper of the times.[23]

The thrill of exposé, which also enlivened the debunking biographies of the 1920s, earned popularity among general readers.

22 Edwin R. A. Seligman, *Economic Interpretation of History* (New York, 1907); Arthur M. Schlesinger, *New Viewpoints in American History* (New York, 1922), 47 ff.; Robinson, *New History,* 50, 51.

23 Lee Benson, *Turner and Beard: American Historical Writing Reconsidered* (Glencoe, Ill., 1960), 151 ff.; Forrest McDonald, *We the People* (Chicago, 1958), and "Charles A. Beard," in Marcus Cunliffe and Robin W. Winks, eds., *Pastmasters* (New York, 1969), 110 ff.

But the economic interpretation, in the American sense, tended to oversimplify complex issues by reducing all explanations to greed; in place of historical necessity it set the willful acts of conspiratorial individuals. More important, it did not compensate for the interpretive weakness of writers who also wished to sustain programs of progressive reform. For the insistence that self-interest or group advantage accounted for past political action made it difficult to explain the crowded halls of the liberal Valhalla. A consistent economic interpretation would have implied that the staunch fighters for freedom from Roger Williams to Abraham Lincoln—and, indeed, at the moment, the very champions of direct election of senators and of the income tax—also acted out some impulse to self-advantage, and thus deserved no more moral approval than the robber baron or slaveowner. Later, in fact, status anxiety and the quest for power would provide just such reductionist explanations of abolitionists and reformers. But then the question came uncomfortably close to home: was the historian, too, simply a justifier of his own or his group's interest?

Americans showed no such awareness of the problem's complexity as troubled their European counterparts. Friedrich Meinecke, for instance, also considered ideas the vital force in history, but he labored subtly to explain their development as they operated against the impulses to passion and power in the social and economic world.[24]

In the United States scholars and journalists, untroubled by these niceties, continued to produce simple Manichean books in which class or personal interests motivated the propertied and conservative, while altruistic, rational understanding lay behind the deeds and thoughts of progressives and reformers. If only the good guys had the courage and determination to stand up to the bad, the drama would move toward its satisfying happy curtain. The oblique view dramatically distorted the treatment of ideas. Merle Curti thus assumed that good ideas flourished when they answered a need perceived by reasonable reformers, waned when the need no longer was urgent; bad ideas simply rationalized the

[24] Ari Hoogenboom, *Outlawing the Spoils: A History of the Civil Service Reform Movement, 1865–1883* (Urbana, Ill., 1961), thus described the reformists not as disinterested altruists, but as people who pursued their own objectives. See also Carlo Antoni, *From History to Sociology: The Transition in German Historical Thinking*, trans. Hayden V. White (Detroit, 1959), 93.

self-interest of people who obstructed progress. Few such authors were aware that they had reverted to an earlier version of human development as the unfolding of the idea of progress.[25]

Historians more given to introspection and aware of the intellectual dilemma struggled in the 1920s to wiggle loose from it. They, too, generally arrived at some idealist destination in the effort to extricate themselves from the tangles created by concern with their own objectivity. It was possible to float a considerable distance on some currents of the decade's European thought. Benedetto Croce, for instance, drawing heavily upon Hegelian idealism, argued that all history was contemporaneous and existed only in the mind of the historian, who was therefore less a scientist than a creative artist, a position which R. G. Collingwood later pushed even farther by giving thought the primary role in all human development. Being disappeared; all was becoming. Meanwhile Karl Mannheim, Franz Boas, and other sociologists and anthropologists explained that all ideas, as well as all moral and aesthetic values, were relative to the social situation of those who held them, and that each culture produced a version of the truth valid for itself.[26]

These notions, which resonated with sources reaching back to Montesquieu, tempted historians concerned with the social implications of their work. In a loose and unsystematic way some scholars fused social and cultural relativism with the image of a past that was the product of the thinker's mind and arrived at a new definition of pragmatism. Pragmatism ceased to be what it had been for the founding philosophers: a method for approaching the truth. It became instead a justification for treating as truth what worked or was useful. James Harvey Robinson, although eager to exploit the past for the benefit of the present, had shied away from that position. But Carl L. Becker, recurrently on

25 For example, John Chamberlain, *Farewell to Reform: The Rise, Life, and Decay of the Progressive Mind in America* (New York, 1932); Merle E. Curti, *Growth of American Thought* (New York, 1943), and *Probing Our Past* (New York, 1955), 72, and *Human Nature in American Historical Thought* (Columbia, Mo., 1970); Robert A. Skotheim, *American Intellectual History and Historians* (Princeton, 1966), 169.

26 R. G. Collingwood, *Idea of History* (New York, 1946); Benedetto Croce, *History as the Story of Liberty*, trans. Sylvia Sprigge (London, 1941), 54, 315 ff.; Edward A. Purcell, Jr., *Crisis of Democratic Theory* (Lexington, Ky., 1973), 210 ff.; Marvin Harris, *Rise of Anthropological Theory* (New York, 1968), 163 ff., 290 ff.

the verge of despair, followed the sound of Croce's pipe and concluded that since subjective interpretations were inescapable, they ought to serve desirable ends. Every man could be his own historian, because history was "a social instrument, helpful in getting the world's work more effectively done."[27]

Charles A. Beard's more complex intellectual hegira led from a kind of economic determinism to a kind of extreme idealism. He did not dissent from the common assumption of the 1920s that "History, if it is to be a science, must not be so written as to teach any particular national, party, religious or economic doctrine." Indeed Beard argued that scholarship had its own imperatives. "To say that science exists merely to serve the instant need of things . . . is to betray a fatal ignorance of inexorable movements in thought . . . Pure scholarship, of course, is a matter of degree . . . but it is an ideal which must be kept before us. Without the results which flow from the disinterested quest for the truth for its own sake, the social practitioner could scarcely rise above the plain of the astrologer." He nevertheless surrendered all hope of objectivity, which he described as a "noble dream." Historical understanding was necessarily subjective, unavoidably in accord with personal interests and values. The historian, therefore, had to make a basic commitment as "an act of faith" and write in accordance with it. Beard's commitment was in the direction of social change conceived as moving toward "collectivist democracy."[28]

A world frequently veering in course made cruel demands upon the agility as well as upon the faith of the historian. Toward the close of the difficult decade of the 1930s Beard noted wistfully his

[27] Carl L. Becker, "Mr. Wells and the New History" (1921), *Everyman His Own Historian* (New York, 1935), 169 ff., and "What are Historical Facts?" (1926), in Phil L. Snyder, ed., *Detachment and the Writing of History* (Ithaca, N.Y., 1958), 41 ff. See also Ralph H. Bowen, *"The Heavenly City: A Too-ingenious Paradox,"* in Raymond O. Rockwood, ed., *Carl Becker's Heavenly City Revisited* (Ithaca, N.Y., 1958), 141 ff.; Chester M. Destler, "Crocean Origin of Becker's Historical Relativism," *History and Theory,* IX (1970), 335 ff.; Hayden V. White, "Croce and Becker," *ibid.,* X (1971), 222 ff.; Ernest Nagel, *Structure of Science* (New York, 1961), 579 ff. James Harvey Robinson, *Mind in the Making* (New York, 1921), 13, 14, states his position. See also Chapter 17 at note 9.

[28] Edward P. Cheyney, *Law in History and Other Essays* (New York, 1927), 161; Charles A. Beard, *Charter for the Social Sciences* (New York, 1932), 2–3, 6, and "Written History as an Act of Faith," *American Historical Review,* XXXIX (January 1934), 219 ff., and "That Noble Dream," *ibid.,* XLI (October 1935), 74 ff., and *Nature of the Social Sciences* (New York, 1934).

deepened "respect for the facts of experience and association."
It was "still true, as was said long ago, 'no documents, no history.' " Although ideas constantly changed, knowledge was still
"to be obtained by the methods of bibliography, scrutiny, authen-
tication, and verification." At about the same time, *America in
Midpassage* moved forward the story told in *The Rise of American Civilization*. The concluding chapter of the later work summarized the history of the nation in terms largely familiar to
readers of the earlier. From John Wise and Thomas Paine
through Thomas Jefferson and Abraham Lincoln a broad stream
of thought had furnished the dynamic by which humanistic democracy countered the cold and fatalistic views of the defenders
of property. As the Beards wrote, that stream of thought approached its apotheosis in Franklin Delano Roosevelt.[29]

But already as the book appeared in print, changing circumstances called for altered views. Fear lest the future prove not as
progressive as it should led in *The Republic* to reconsidera-
tion of the worth of the Constitution and of the judiciary as
bulwarks of liberty; and a nagging worry about the dangers of
involvement in foreign wars crowded Beard into a narrow nationalism to justify isolation. *The American Spirit* (1942) focused
on the idea of civilization; the struggle of human beings in the
world for individual and social perfection—for the good, the true,
the beautiful—against ignorance, disease, the harshness of physical
nature, and the forces of barbarism had assumed "unique features
in origins, substance, and development" in the United States.[30]

Not long thereafter, the Beards's *Basic History* completely reversed the perspective of *The Rise of American Civilization*,
stressing the unifying instead of the divisive elements in the nation's past. To explain why Americans were pressed unenthusi-
astically into two disastrous foreign wars, the authors discerned a
radical perversion at the start of the twentieth century. A breach
with historical continentalism diverted attention away from internal development and, under the influence of giddy minds
(which inexplicably gained control), involved the country in

29 Charles A. Beard and Alfred Vagts, "Currents of Thought in Historiography,"
*American Historical Review*, XLII (April 1937), 482; Charles A. and Mary R.
Beard, *America in Midpassage*, 2 vols. (New York, 1939), II, 941, 948.

30 Charles A. Beard, *The Republic* (New York, 1943); Charles A. and Mary R.
Beard, *The American Spirit* (New York, 1942), 672.

foreign quarrels. To establish that perversion the *Basic History* made nationalism the consistent theme of the centuries down to 1890. As the American spirit matured, despite the abortive revolt of 1861, it kept interests centered at home and consolidated the resources of the continent with the tools of industrialism. An undefined élan from the beginning distinguished these people from others. The ideas of 1776 and the nineteenth-century humanitarian strivings—abolition, women's rights, prison reform, universal education—which to the Beards epitomized the concept of civilization, ceased to be international in character and became local, as did the continent's economic life and the Republic's diplomacy.

As a result, the narrative acquired a curious causelessness. The theme of the Beards's writing until then had been the conflict of interests between the agrarian and mercantile elements in American life. Now unity of national character overshadowed the diversity of class and interest. The very chapter headings illustrated the difference between *The Rise of American Civilization* and this work: "Independence and Civil Conflict" became "Independence Completed by Revolution"; "Populism and Reaction" became "Constitutional Government in the United States"; "Agricultural Imperialism in the Balance of Power" became "The Revolutionary Generation in Charge of the Federal Government"; and "The Second American Revolution: The Conflict of Agrarian Planters against Industrial Capitalists," became "National Unity Sealed in an Armed Contest."[31]

The desire to make history useful was hostile to any consistent pattern of historical interpretation. When radical scholars bent their arguments to changing political needs, they lost the ability to follow through on any coherent scheme of thought. The consequences became apparent when destalinization began to free the pens of writers in the Old World. First in Eastern Europe, then in the West, efforts to unshackle Marxism picked up lines of investigation dropped decades earlier by Antonio Gramsci, Walter Benjamin, and Georg Lukás. The philosopher Alexandre Kojève, the economist François Perroux, and the historian of ideas

31 Oscar Handlin, "Pitfalls of History," *Partisan Review*, XI (Fall 1944), 466 ff.

Lucien Goldmann, although still deferring to the authority of the traditional masters, wrote interesting studies, often especially relevant to America, of the relation of the productive system to communal forms, to ideology, to culture, and to the conditions of the people.[32]

In the United States, by contrast, few historians had sufficient grasp of theory to guide a meaningful radical approach to the past. Eugene Genovese, in the effort to get out from behind the bars of a deterministic dialectic materialism inapplicable to his subject, fastened upon Gramsci's stray references to ideology. These, however, failed to support the material loaded upon them, even apart from the problems created by a confusing mistranslation.[33] Other, less-sensitive radicals slipped uncomplainingly into the straightjacket of terms like "finance capitalism." Still others abandoned all effort at systematic interpretation and danced their way about the data in a visionary haze. In the riot of gaudy impressions, one writer identified Emerson, Thoreau, and Brownson as disciples of Marxism, which, another explained, rested not on the dialectic or the class struggle but "upon the classical and Old Testament distinction between good and evil." In the confusion, even Genovese at one point despaired of defining Marxism.[34]

[32] For example, Lucien Goldmann, *Human Sciences & Philosophy*, trans. Hayden V. White and Robert Anchor (London, 1969) , 86 ff., and *Recherches dialectiques* (Paris, 1959) , 64 ff.; Pierre Vilar, "Histoire marxiste," in Jacques LeGoff and Pierre Nora, eds., *Faire de l'histoire*, 2 vols. (Paris, 1974) , I, 169 ff.; Antonio Gramsci, *Selections from the Prison Notebooks*, trans. Quintin Hoare and Geoffrey N. Smith (New York, 1971) , 277 ff.; Georg Lukács, *History and Class Consciousness: Studies in Marxist Dialectics* (Cambridge, 1971) , 223 ff. There is a simple but not particularly enlightening application of Gramsci's linkage between economic forces and ideology in Raimondo Luraghi, *Stati Uniti* (Turin, 1974) .

[33] Gramsci's fugitive statements are difficult to interpret. In the effort to apply the concept of cultural hegemony to the slaveholding South, Genevose translates *blocco storico* as "historical bloc," which is plausible but does not convey the sense of the original, which is of a switching or transfer point, as in "una cabina di blocco apparati centrali elettrici," which implies an interplay rather than fusion of cultural and economic forces. See Eugene D. Genovese, "Marxian Interpretation of the Slave South," in Barton J. Bernstein, ed., *Towards a New Past: Dissenting Essays in American History* (New York, 1968) , 98; Antonio Gramsci, *Materialismo storico* (Turin, 1949) , II, 49, and *Selections from the Prison Notebooks*, 345; *Dizionario enciclopedico italiano* (Rome, 1955) , II, 335; Salvatore Battaglia, *Grande dizionario della lingua italiana* (Turin, 1961) , II, 269.

[34] The quotation is from William Appleman Williams, *Great Evasion* (Chicago, 1968) , 173. David Herreshoff, *American Disciples of Marx* (Detroit, 1967) , coopts Emerson and Thoreau. Theodore Roszak, *Making of a Counter Culture* (Garden

Most commonly, polemic urgencies focused energies on the diplomacy leading to the cold war and on the development of American imperialism. The term "imperialism," as used by such liberal critics as John A. Hobson, and particularly as used by V. I. Lenin and refined by Varga and Mendelsohn, had a precise meaning describing a stage in the general evolution of capitalism. Radical historians in the United States reduced it to a term of invective. Had they been interested in imperialism as Lenin defined it, they would have examined the flow of international investment, particularly in the quarter-century before 1917, instead of the flow of rhetoric in those years of leisurely oratory. Analysis of capital movements in the early twentieth century would have revealed that the dollars went not from more to less developed areas, but the reverse, not into unstable countries susceptible to colonial control, but into places with strong local governments that could be relied upon to maintain orderly conditions of doing business.[35]

The alternative actually followed was to redefine the term, so that as used by careless writers it signified the precise opposite of what it did both at the time and in Marxist theory. For many radical historians of the 1960s and 1970s imperialism meant the world system of free trade, exactly the system desired by John Bright, John Stuart Mill, and William E. Gladstone, the archfoes of nineteenth-century imperialism, as well as by their American counterparts.[36]

---

City, N.Y., 1969), is a sample. Genovese, "Marxian Interpretations," 115, 122, shows bewilderment. Gabriel Kolko, *Triumph of Conservatism: A Reinterpretation of American History, 1900–1916* (New York, 1963), and *Main Currents in Modern American History* (New York, 1976); and James Weinstein, *Corporate Ideal in the Liberal State 1900–1918* (Boston, 1968), define finance capitalism as the master of government, dictating the major economic legislation of the progressive era. See also Chapter 13.

[35] Eugen Varga and Lev A. Mendelsohn, eds., *New Data for V. I. Lenin's "Imperialism, the Highest Stage of Capitalism"* (London, 1939), attempts to document the Leninist position; and V. G. Kiernan, *Marxism and Imperialism* (London, 1974), ch. I, is a sensible radical view of the Marxist approach. For more inclusive data and a sounder interpretation, see D. K. Fieldhouse, *Economics and Empire, 1830–1914* (London, 1973); and Oscar Handlin, *One World* (Oxford, 1973).

[36] For a particularly muddled use of the term, see Ernest N. Paolino, *Foundations of the American Empire: William Henry Seward and U.S. Foreign Policy* (Ithaca, N.Y., 1973). Walter LaFeber, *New Empire: An Interpretation of American Expansion, 1860–1898* (Ithaca, N.Y., 1963), viii, wisely abstains from use of the word, although it errs in assuming that commercial expansionism was a product of the

Perhaps the author's absolute command of his words entitles
him to bestow on them any meaning he chooses; but when imperialism is indistinguishable from free trade, and William H.
Seward from William G. Sumner, the power to communicate
evaporates and with it the capacity for systematic or consequential
thought.[37]

⤜⤛

Most American historians avoided the pitfalls of theory. They
escaped the dangers of oversimplification by abjuring allegiance
to any comprehensive scheme for understanding the past. Although they thereby ran the risk of overlooking the broader significance of the subjects they treated, they remained eclectic when
it came to interpretation. From a variety of nineteenth-century
explanatory themes, each selected the strands from which to
fashion the nets appropriate to the task of containing a particular
cluster of facts.

Well back in the world of Thomas Jefferson, Americans who
had read Montesquieu and Robertson had ascribed human change
to the influence of the natural universe. People were the "logical
results of the environment," Edward Eggleston wrote as a matter of
course in 1890. A selective reading of Henry T. Buckle and of
Taine had confirmed those views, which entered into the formulation of F. J. Turner's propositions on the influence of the frontier
and of sections; and appeared also in the later work of Walter P.
Webb and James C. Malin. But historians backed away from more

---

late nineteenth century, rather than a concept as old as the Republic. See also
David L. T. Knudson, "Note on Walter LaFeber, Captain Mahan, and the Use
of Historical Sources," *Pacific Historical Review*, XL (November 1971), 519 ff.;
Felix Gilbert, *To the Farewell Address* (Princeton, 1961), 50 ff., 69 ff. Marilyn B.
Young, "Economic Expansion, 1870–1900," in Bernstein, *Towards a New Past*, 176
ff., and *Rhetoric of Empire, American China Policy, 1895–1901* (Cambridge, 1968),
recognizes the difference between rhetoric and actuality; as does Paul A. Varg,
*Making of a Myth: The United States and China, 1897–1912* (East Lansing, Mich.,
1968). Broader views of the issue include Milton Plesur, *America's Outward Thrust*
(DeKalb, Ill., 1971); Paul S. Holbo, "Economics, Emotion and Expansion," in
H. Wayne Morgan, ed., *Gilded Age*, 2d ed. (Syracuse, 1970), 199 ff.; and John A. S.
Grenville and George B. Young, *Politics, Strategy and American Diplomacy* (New
Haven, 1966).

[37] William Appleman Williams, *Tragedy of American Diplomacy* (Cleveland,
1959), and *Roots of the American Empire* (New York, 1969). See also Chapter 6.

extreme statements on the effect of climate and topography by the geologist Nathaniel S. Shaler and the geographer Ellsworth Huntington.[38]

Spinoffs from reflections upon biological evolution tempted historians, and particularly in the form transmitted by anthropologists. If mankind had passed through successive stages of improvement in the past, then the differences among races discernible at any given moment were the results of variations in the speed with which they advanced along the course. The superior were swifter, the inferior lagged. Bancroft had no doubt that the Anglo-Saxons were the fleetest. But he still believed in the unity of all the sons of Adam—others in time could catch up. Europeans, among them Taine, also referred to race in a loose general way, sometimes meaning any group with common lineage, like the nobility.[39]

Darwinism imparted a deeper meaning to race by describing the mechanism through which distinct species evolved, so that the distance between the fittest and less fit would ever widen rather than contract; and geneticists later demonstrated the practical consequences. Anthropologists, already busy classifying the various species of man, concluded that heredity was binding in the transmission of social characteristics and that racial qualities, passing from generation to generation, determined the course of human history.

In the closing decades of the nineteenth century J. A. Gobineau, Edouard Drumont, H. S. Chamberlain, and other European theorists based systems of historical interpretation on race; and the notion had obvious attractions in the United States, then troubled by the results of the failure of Reconstruction and by the conse-

---

[38] Edward Eggleston, "Formative Influences," *Forum*, X (November 1890) , 286. See also Chapter 3 at note 47; James C. Malin, *Contriving Brain and the Skillful Hand in the United States* (Lawrence, Kans. [1955]) ; Nathaniel S. Shaler, *Nature and Man in America* (New York, 1891) ; Ellen C. Semple, *American History and Its Geographic Conditions* (Boston, 1903) ; Ellsworth Huntington, *Civilization and Climate* (New Haven, 1924) . More recent, more sophisticated treatments which take account of reciprocal human influences include E. Le Roy Ladurie, *Histoire et climat* (Paris, 1968) ; and Teresa Dunin-Wasowicz, "Climate as a Factor Affecting the Human Environment in the Middle Ages," *Journal of European Economic History*, IV (Winter 1975) , 691 ff.

[39] For Bancroft see Chapter 7 at note 21.

quences of large-scale immigration from Eastern and Southern Europe and from the Orient. Reputable anthropologists and sociologists found merit in these theories, and Madison Grant's *Passing of the Great Race* restated them for a popular audience. Yet, despite the prestige of the biological and social sciences, historians were prudent. Under the influence of John H. Dunning and U. B. Phillips the view of black racial inferiority long distorted the writing of Southern history; and slighting references to Jews, Catholics, and immigrants crept into otherwise respectable writings. But deference to the factual record generally restrained all but the most prejudiced historians. Hesitancy in embracing theory, in this instance, served them well and helped them also steer clear of other forms of biologism.[40]

A commitment to the inviolable fact qualified the acceptance of all monolithic explanatory schemes—racial, geographic, materialistic, or idealistic. So long as historians committed to their science did not bend the provable fact, they had something of value to say apart from interpretation: Phillips, despite his racism; Malin, despite his ecology; LaFeber and Kolko, despite their abuse of the terms "imperialism" and "finance capitalism."[41] Their deficiencies as overall interpretations did not drain the single-factor theories of the capacity for furnishing specific insights to the prudent scholar.

The actual tasks of the historians in practice created a mind set hostile to the determinism built into all monolithic explanations. Be the pronouncements of essays, lectures, and prefaces as broad as rhetoric could make them, when it came to the details the scholar encountered another order of experience. The boxes of note cards, the pile of Xeroxes, the stack of printouts were reminders of hours spent in assembling innumerable little pieces which in themselves had little connection with the big picture on the box. Laboring to get the bits in place, the honest players, respecting the integrity of each jagged edge, again and again came upon unexpected fragments.

40 Madison Grant, *Passing of the Great Race* (New York, 1918) ; U. B. Phillips, *American Negro Slavery* (New York, 1929) ; Thomas F. Gossett, *Race* (Dallas, 1963) , 253 ff.; Kenneth M. Ludmerer, *Genetics and American Society* (Baltimore, 1972) , 45 ff. For the biologism hidden in psychoanalytic approaches, see Chapter 10 at note 33.

41 For the consequences of bending the facts, see Chapter 6.

In the long run the American colonies would gain independence and expand to the Pacific and divide in Civil War and then, united, grab the Philippines. In the long run. But the historian analyzing the American Revolution or the Louisiana Purchase or the dispute over slavery or the venture into imperialism treated events of a different order, some but not all of which matched parts of the big picture. Whig politics explained the sluggishness of English commanders, but a storm across a Virginia stream was a factor in the defeat at Yorktown. To satisfy the needs of the Old West, Jefferson wished to buy commercial rights at New Orleans, but a frozen Dutch harbor persuaded Napoleon to sell Louisiana. These incidents were not accidental; meteorologists could explain why the wind rose or the ice spread. But the historian needed more: some way of accounting for the wind rising or the ice freezing at the precise moment which gave them significance. Yet the chains of causes and effects that produced the wind or ice were entirely distinct from those which created the military, diplomatic, or political context.

The historians of the 1970s could not explain the convergence as marvelous occurrences which revealed the workings of the hand of God, for, having insisted that human development was the orderly product of forces operating implacably over long periods of time, they excluded discontinuous external interventions from the understanding of the past. For the same reason they could not concede a determining effect to the shape of Cleopatra's nose or to an explosion on the *U.S.S. Princeton.* Nor could they find refuge in the happy insistence that if not then, well later, if not Jefferson or Napoleon or Lenin or Hitler or Washington, then someone similar who bore a different name. Nor would it do to write off accident as that of which "we do not yet perceive the causes," in the assurance that some as-yet-unprobed law of history accounted for all events and ruled out all voluntary human action. These propositions, which explained nothing since they could neither be proven nor disproven, provided no help to historians concerned with the particularity of persons and moments.[42]

42 Thomas Hobbes, *Elements of Philosophy*, ed. F. J. E. Woodbridge, *Selections* (New York, 1930), 102; J. B. Bury, "Cleopatra's Nose," *Selected Essays* (Cambridge, 1930), 60 ff.; Oscar Handlin, *Chance or Destiny: Turning Points in American History* (Boston, 1955). See also Edward P. Cheyney, *Law in History and Other*

The scholar struggling to lock together the curiously shaped fragments could not fail to be aware that no interpretive theory could supply better than a provisional, partial picture for guidance. The focal length of no lens could take in the totality of the past. And the contingent elements, products of the convergence of distinct chains of cause and effect, complicated the task by introducing the possibility that the pieces to be fitted together acquired their edges in entirely different cutting processes.

The frustration of philosophers and novelists who turned to history to know the truth emanated from the polarity they recognized between the way of the hedgehog and the way of the fox. Like Tolstoy, they wished to know the one big truth and found themselves forced to know many.[43] The frustration of scientists who turned to history to know the truth emanated from the insistence upon forging precise links of Cause and Effect, $C_1$, $C_2$, $C_3$ . . . $= E$. They, too, sought the one big truth and found many.[44]

Vast panoramic dreams beguile the historian too, and aspirations to be that transcendental eyeball, mastering the whole by taking all in and giving all order. But in the waking hours he must return to the note cards and the tyranny of intractable facts.

Yet there he finds mastery of another sort, not of a whole universe or even of a whole mountain, but of the fragment he examines in its totality. Within its limited ambit he finds exposed all life's amplitude; and therein, too, the operations of numerous forces the intersection of which are open to his eyes. He will know his own valley the better for being conscious of its place in the range; and theoretical images may call his attention to the particular features within his regard. He may even long to fit his own piece into some larger whole. No harm to it, unless the dizzying image or the giddiness of the longing betray him into bending the pieces and falsifying the evidence, thereby destroying the ultimate worth of his efforts.

*Essays* (New York, 1927) , 7; Isaiah Berlin, *Historical Inevitability* (London, 1954) ; and G. J. Renier, *History: Its Purpose and Method* (Boston, 1950) , 221 ff.

[43] Isaiah Berlin, *Hedgehog and the Fox: An Essay on Tolstoy's View of History* (London, 1953) .

[44] Peter D. McClelland, *Causal Explanation and Model Building in History, Economics and the New Economic History* (Ithaca, N.Y., 1975) , 146 ff.

# 5
## *Historical Criticism*

CRITICISM IS THE LIFEBLOOD of science, of literature, of thought itself. The scholar, writer, thinker—an individual—launches ideas into a void, but lacks the means to estimate the accuracy of their course. Only the external reference points of comments emanating from other minds make possible the judgments, how far the flight, how true the aim. Those condemned to isolation turn inward and end up talking to themselves.[1]

Criticism is no less vital to the community, which in its absence either will sink into dreary veneration of a few respected old books, or will, generation after generation, repeat the errors of its predecessors, making each day the fresh start of the return to the tread-mill and mistaking energy expended for distance advanced. The historian and the audience alike require a reliable process of evaluation to assess the merits of books and articles and preserve the vitality of the discipline. Unhappily, while the need in the 1970s is as great as ever before, it has never been more poorly served.

The need affects both the general and the professional reader as well as the producer of history. A nation of 210,000,000 can in-dulge a variety of tastes, so that despite the battering from the electronic media there remain significant numbers who turn the pages of books for entertainment, edification, and enlightenment; even one in a hundred thousand yields a substantial quotient. Con-

[1] Oscar Handlin et al., *Harvard Guide to American History* (Cambridge, 1954), 22 ff.

111

fronted by the paperback racks, by the bookclub lists, by the book-store piles and the library shelves, the would-be reader has immense freedom of choice; yet subtle contraints shape the choice.[2]

To be read, the work of history first must find its way into print, an imperative which subjects it to a succession of decisions that are, in their nature, absurd. Print is a medium which will convey any message, and the book is a container which will enclose any contents. In most areas of a rational economy the producer adapts the container to the object vended: the manufacturer makes shoes or shirts or sugar cakes, which he encloses in the appropriate receptacles. The publisher, by contrast, is in the position of the box-maker who stuffs within his covers history, novels, detective stories, juveniles, how-to's, medicine, science fiction, poetry, journalism, religion, or whatever else may come to hand—and markets all with very much the same procedures. Necessarily, one consideration is paramount: what will sell.

Each publishing house would prefer to emit good books rather than bad ones, and each struggles to evaluate quality, a difficult task because no cluster of editors can be knowledgeable in all fields and authors' credentials are notoriously unreliable. The opinions of outside experts are tricky—their knowledge may not really run very deep or they may be prejudiced either in defense of or in opposition to accepted views—and their judgments more often serve as straws in the marketing wind than as firm appraisals of quality. Then, often the issue of freedom of expression intrudes. The interpretation may be wrong, the research shoddy, and the facts inaccurate, but the point of view deserves a hearing. On the other hand, a work impeccable in execution might just as well remain in manuscript or microform if it will find no buyers.

Now and again a publisher will deviate from the logic of these calculations. But even firms which do not have to display their balance sheets to conglomerates, even the presses of universities and learned societies, maneuver within the confines of the same limiting considerations. The decision whether to print or not to print pivots on the sales estimate. And, increasingly, inventory con-

2 The comments that follow arise from the experience of editing hundreds of books, of advising three commercial publishers, of long association with a university press, of some years of monthly reviewing for a national magazine, and of involvement in the management of a television station.

trols and warehousing economics define sales as those transacted within three or four years of publication date.

However, sales estimates in this as in other types of mass marketing have all the reliability of roulette, so that the player bends every effort to make the most of the odds. Correct or lucky guesses about the gusts of fashion are essential: blacks and women had no chance in 1957; in 1977 they were in, but perhaps on the way out. And choice of the good subject means little unless the treatment will catch attention by newsworthiness, that is, by confirming or contradicting a widely held belief, but in either case by doing so dramatically enough to compete against other boxes claiming the limited share of media time and space. The historian does not suffer to the same degree as the novelist from the pressure of an audience which demands that one be—not seem—outrageous, extreme, independent, anarchical.[3] But similar expectations hold to some degree for all the titles in the line. A book must be interesting, that is, so contrived as to attract the reader, or at least the purchaser, who is assumed not to be interested.

The initial decision to print opens into a sequence of others revolving about the question of whether the volume in process will be a book or an important book. The answer determines the size of the press run, whether stores will stock it or not, whether it will have a chance for a real book club adoption, the character of promotion and advertising, the prospect for appearance on the Today show, and the likelihood of gaining space in newspapers and magazines. Well before the work is bound, opinion will have taken form in the *Kirkus Review* and *Publishers Weekly*, circulated among booksellers and libraries, and space will have been allocated in the important daily and periodical reviewing media. Those judgments are usually more important than the ultimate contents of the reviews which are sometimes written by knowledgeable critics; for to be noticed at all is more important than the quality of the notice. An important book will find its way into libraries and become a contender for prizes; others, however meritorious, pass silently from the printer to the remainder dealer.

These procedures which shape the choices in history made by

---

3 W. J. Weatherby, *Squaring Off* (New York, 1977), 27, 55, 210.

general readers are no more absurd than those which influence
clothes or hair styles or other tastes in consumer expenditure. But
they are no less so. And they also shape the choices made by professional historians.

The professional is not much better off than any other consumer of books. Indeed, outside his own field the scholar is like any
other reader; and specialization year by year narrows the definition of fields, so that, apart from the collegial courtesy that inhibits
invasions of someone else's turf, only the bold feel, and only the
exceptional are, competent to judge the adequacy of work away
from their own little realm of expertise.

All specialists begin as generalists and often retain through life
the impressions implanted by a high school or college text. More
recent word on 1832 or 1848 or 1870 is not likely to reach the researcher on the eighteenth century. In the absence of continuing,
time-consuming criticism of the literature, old and new, scholars
stagger around under the burden of an assortment of half-remem-
bered wares of dubious worth. Their minds are likely to remain
puerile in the sense defined by C. S. Peirce—never having matured,
yet having lost the originality of youth.[4]

A generation ago a test, not particularly well designed, nevertheless revealed the abysmally low standard of criticism of the
time. Asked to choose the significant works of the three preceding
decades, a sample of historians showed no ability to recognize titles
other than those which had received general, as distinguished from
scholarly, acclaim.[5] There are no grounds for belief that the situation has improved in the intervening years. So long as historians
are unwilling or unable to exercise the critical faculty, considerations of enduring value, much less those of truth, receive less attention than those of the commercial marketplace.

The scholarly journals which should restore the balance fail to
do so. Generally they follow in the wake of the popular media in
deciding what is important, and they find increasing difficulty in
locating reviewers. Established scholars are reluctant to spend time

4 Charles Sanders Peirce, *Collected Papers* (Cambridge, 1960) , V, 57.

5 John Walton Caughey, "Historians' Choice: Results of a Poll on Recently
Published American History and Biography," *Mississippi Valley Historical Review*,
XXXIX (June 1952) , 289 ff.

or risk friendships on these unpaid chores. They hesitate to waste their artillery on the little fish who occasionally swim into their ponds; and they know that an incautious comment might some day cost one of their graduate students a job. Moreover, most journals are publications of membership organizations and tend to spread the favors about with no assurances of competence. But then, even the most conscientious editor of the scholarly as of the popular review, swamped by the massive outpouring of print, is hard put to differentiate between what deserves attention and what does not, between what is good or what is not. The misfortune is not so much that poor books escape without the criticism they deserve, but that good ones languish unnoticed and unrecognized, their authors unlikely again to accept the travail of stillborn parturition.[6]

Every historian must, therefore, be his own reviewer and assimilate into his own fund of knowledge the old works of enduring value as well as the new. That demands the application of rigorous standards of critical evaluation and assessment. Not many know how to do so.

An act of criticism calls upon the same mental processes as an act of creation. Properly to judge a work is to recapitulate, although not necessarily to repeat the steps in making it. The same pitfalls lie in the path of the unwary critic and the unwary creator.

No historian but is occasionally tempted to await inspiration from the grand theme which will in itself extend talent and spread words across the pages. They wait in vain who do not get seasonably to the archives.

No reviewer but is tempted to set aside the nit-picking chore and ascend to the empyrean of pure discussion of interpretations. Such exercises afford the opportunity for display both of intellect and of tolerance. Since every scholar has a right to his own point of view, and there is more than one side to every question, criti-

---

[6] Thus, E.N. Paolino's faulty *Foundations of the American Empire* received no criticism of consequence. See *American Historical Review*, LXXX (April 1975) , 508; *Journal of Southern History*, XL (August 1974) , 495. By contrast, Daniel H. Calhoun, *Intelligence of a People* (Princeton, 1973) , failed to receive the attention it deserved. See also Chapter 6 at note 11.

cism is a matter of placing the work scrutinized in its appropriate category. It is then possible simply to decide what a book is by the school to which it belongs.

An example. In the country's most important historical journal a critic complains that an author "is not self-conscious and his book is not exciting." A promising volume by a promising young scholar is thus written off for its lack of an explicit model of paradigmatic change in belief systems. Neither the reviewer nor the reviewed are personally known to this writer/reader, who, nevertheless, finds the grounds of criticism interesting, not so much because the very concept of paradigm has already been modified by the historian of science who first enunciated it and from whom it was borrowed, but also because that line of comment exemplifies the assumption that every statement is relevant and valid only in the context of its purpose.[7]

The impulse to categorize a book and discuss its interpretation does not get to the heart of the critical problem. Rather it asks of a work that it fit in. The leading question becomes: does it say what the reviewer (reader) wishes it to say? High marks go to those which do, that is, to those which utter the commonplace or spread the accepted myths of the moment. Lofty discussion of paradigms evades the discomfort of factual criticism, which thereupon becomes a pursuit unworthy of scholars. Exposure of a shoddy performance meets the angry retort that it did not discuss the interpretation—as if any interpretation could stand upon legs of putty. And a critic who ventures to examine the footnotes of well-regarded works is rebuffed for audacity in blowing the whistle on their deceptions.

Yet the first and, sometimes, the sufficient test of the worth of a book is accuracy of detail. A quotation which described color, hair, and lips as the distinguishing features by which "the hand of nature" branded the African "with a perpetual mark of disgrace" certainly seemed to express William Lloyd Garrison's racial ideas. But a critic, reaching beyond the tertiary and secondary sources to the *Liberator,* whence the quotation came, could fill in the ellipsis points and discover that Garrison actually explained that the

7 Jay Mechling, review of Edward A. Purcell, Jr., "Crisis of Democratic Theory," *American Historical Review,* LXXX (April 1975), 473. See also Thomas Kuhn, *Structure of Scientific Revolutions,* 2d ed. (Chicago, 1970), 174 ff.

identification of their physical characteristics with slavery made blacks seem contemptible; that ignorance and degradation associated with bondage created prejudice against the personal appearance of the Negroes and impeded efforts to improve their condition.[8] Quite another matter!

Every type of determinism also blunts the edge of historical criticism. No marshaling of evidence can prove or disprove general statements of inevitability. The play of words used to describe the appearance and disappearance of empires, the growth and decay of cities, the influence of climate and population tease the imagination, create suggestive images, and call to mind interesting analogies. The glacial power of the vast vision glides across discrepancies in the known record and smooths all in its way. The reader cannot say no: what happened had to happen, in small matters as well as large. Where the Mohawk and Hudson break through the mountains to join ocean and lakes, there the nation's largest city sprang, had to spring. There is no denying the Dutch traders and Indian trappers, the Erie Canal and the water-level railroad, the great steamships of the 1920s and the jets of the 1970s; and a comparison comes to mind with Antwerp at the mouth of the Rhine. So that even the critic who recalls—why not New Orleans on the Mississippi?—and who wonders about the capital to exploit the position or the power that shaped routes and rates can still get no handle on the basic affirmation. New York did outdistance Boston, Philadelphia, and its other rivals; and geography was a factor in the victory, along with economics and politics, so that the assertion that one force was less evitable than the others calls for a judgment beyond history. So, too, with the assertion that international monetary trends, not Jackson's removal of the bank deposits, led to the panic of 1837. And so, too, with the assessment of the parts played in the decline of Rome by hay, homosexuality, and Christianity.[9]

Individuals and accidents influence but slightly the evolution of

---

[8] Lawrence J. Friedman, *Inventors of the Promised Land* (New York, 1975), 235, cites Nathaniel Weyl and William Marina, *American Statesmen on Slavery and the Negro* (New Rochelle, N.Y., 1971), 158, who cite Leon F. Litwack, *North of Slavery: The Negro in the Free States, 1790–1860* (Chicago, 1961), 224. The source is *Liberator,* January 22, 1831, p. 14. See also Chapter 6.

[9] Robert G. Albion, *Rise of New York Port* (New York, 1939); Peter Temin, *Jacksonian Economy* (New York, 1969).

such ponderous institutions as the monogamous family, the yeoman farm, the Congregational church, or the democratic republic; and developments over very long periods—industrialization, immigration, rationalism, and romanticism—change direction only slightly in response to specific incidents along their course. The writer and reader may treat these impersonal forces as inevitable or may regard their convergence in any particular trend as the result of some unpredictable contingency or may consider them not as necessary but as probable outcomes of the element of regularity present in nature. The choice will spring not from the evidence alone but also from what reader and writer wish to believe about their own situation. "You *choose* to assume that the will is free," wrote Henry Adams to William James in 1882. "Good! Reason proves that the Will cannot be free. Equally good." So it will ever be. Historical criticism may illuminate or illustrate the choice; but judgment of its correctness lies in another realm, properly that of metaphysics.[10]

Truth in the abstract and how to know it also fall outside the historian's competence. However interesting and relevant the subtler problems of epistemology may be, they do not respond to his particular scholarly skills. Leaving to the philosophers resolution of issues which rarely have a direct bearing on his own work, he need only accept in a very general way the affirmation that truth is the correspondence of a representation with its object.[11]

Questions of inference introduce more complex considerations. The historian cannot avoid them entirely, since any selection and ordering of data involves some inferences about the relation among them. The writer must infer, the critic appraise, the inferences of others, but in a fashion different from that of the logician.[12]

Philosophers, even those who have not gone so far as to confine

10 Harold D. Cater, ed., *Henry Adams and His Friends* (Boston, 1947), 121. See also Maurice Mandelbaum, *Problem of Historical Knowledge* (New York, 1938), 27; Ernest Nagel, *Structure of Science* (New York, 1961), 592 ff.; Isaiah Berlin, *Historical Inevitability* (London, 1954); Morton White, *Foundations of Historical Knowledge* (New York, 1965), 273 ff.; Edward P. Cheyney, *Law in History* (New York, 1927), 7. For relations to analytical sciences and pseudo-sciences, see Chapter 10.

11 Peirce, *Collected Papers*, V, 390; Chapter 17.

12 Nagel, *Structure of Science*, 547 ff.

their attention to symbols for classes and propositions, deal with abstractions. Inference for them is a procedure of reasoning from correctly defined terms. By contrast, inference enters into the work of the historian as he organizes the evidence of activities in which irrational, unpredictable elements play a large part. He cannot allow the organization to take a form contrary to reason unless his is a tale told by an idiot; but neither can he cram his evidence into a mold previously defined by abstract or formal rules. Contradiction, non-sequitur, and abrupt discontinuities that appear in the evidence must remain there, however offensive they may be to the requirements of logic in exposition. By the same token, the rules of coincidence, consistency, and correlation that govern the logic embraced in mathematics are only suggestive for the historian. The two great musicians of the early eighteenth century, Bach and Handel, were born in the same year; the two chief authors of the Declaration of Independence, Adams and Jefferson, died, to the day, exactly fifty years after they signed the document; Abraham Lincoln expired on Good Friday, and as many unexplained circumstances surrounded his assassination as did that of John F. Kennedy. Defiance of probability is a commonplace of the record. Yet, however unreasonable the plea of coincidence may be, the historian cannot leap the gap, or infer a connection, in the absence of evidence. Who yields to the temptation to do so will discover anywhere the operations of an unseen hand or of a hidden conspiracy.[13]

Paradoxically, where the evidence allows, the historian must accept the hazard of guessing, recalling the injunction of a logician: "We often derive from observation strong intimations of truth, without being able to specify what were the circumstances we had observed which conveyed those intimations."[14]

In guessing, as in other forms of historical inference, whether in writing or in criticism, the reference point is always the evidence.

[13] See Lloyd Lewis, *Myths after Lincoln* (New York, 1929), 109 ff.; Otto Eisenschiml, *Why Was Lincoln Murdered?* (Boston, 1937), and *In the Shadow of Lincoln's Death* (New York, 1940); Leo Sauvage, *Oswald Affair* (Cleveland, 1966).

[14] Charles S. Peirce, "Guessing" (1907), *Collected Papers*, VII, 34.

The writer and the critic ask the identical question: how do I (how does he) know? The answer lies in scrutiny of the evidence.

It is not enough to judge a work by the density of the footnotes on its pages. The crowded titles of those unleaded lines may present the proof, offer a guide to replication of the process which led the author to his conclusions. But not always. And the reader will not be able to decide without reference to the sources and without comprehension of their contents. He therefore requires an understanding of the types of evidence and their limitations.

Everything made or recalled is evidence. Surviving objects and imprints on memory spread before the curious surveyor the material for reconstructing the past whence they came. Scarcity, the problem of students of earlier times, rarely troubles those of modern eras. For the medievalist access to a specific manuscript may be essential; his colleague treating the nineteenth century has trouble keeping his head above an abundance of documents, many redundant.

The historian regarding this vast jumble assesses it by the twofold tests of form and nature. Questions of form or outward characteristics have received the greatest attention in the manuals of traditional historiography.[15] The shard, clay tablet, coin of gold, page of parchment, vellum, or paper, the ink, and the tool of bronze, stone, or iron yield a sense of date and place of making. Since no such object came into existence but through a human act, each was the product of some person's purpose somewhere at some point in time—all knowable. The historian of the United States depends less than his colleagues on the skills of paleography, epigraphy, sphragistics, and diplomatics; nevertheless, he must know something about techniques for detecting forgeries and testing authenticity. Correct decipherment, transcription, and translation are not as difficult as for earlier eras, which require subtle differentiation of the words describing color and complex computation of the value of coins and of the equivalents of ancient

15 Ernst Bernheim, *Lehrbuch der historischen Methode und der Geschichtsphilosophie,* 6th ed. (Leipzig, 1908) ; C. V. Langlois and Charles Seignobos, *Introduction to the Study of History,* trans. G. G. Berry (New York, 1904) ; G. J. Renier, *History: Its Purpose and Method* (Boston, 1950) , 106 ff. For an outstanding example of American heuristic criticism, see A. P. Middletown and Douglass Adair, "Mystery of the Horn Papers," *William and Mary Quarterly,* IV (October 1947) , 409 ff.

weights and measures.[16] Yet similar problems do vex the historian who refers to colonial currency or to the banknotes of the Jacksonian period or who wonders whether the Indians actually spoke the words that miscellaneous intermediaries ascribed to them.[17]

The question "evidence of what?" introduces more troublesome considerations. The scholar, having applied all the tests of form so that he is sure that the page of print or script is what it purports to be must, nevertheless, also assess its reliability as evidence, distinguish the document composed to deceive from that composed to inform, decide delicate issues of competence and credibility, and balance off the weight given the contents by the trustworthiness of the recorded transactions, the artifacts, the testimony, and the rhetoric which are his sources.

The record of a transaction, on whatever material inscribed, offers the greatest margin of certainty. In a deed or bill of sale both the buyer and seller have an interest in accuracy in setting down date, place, terms. Other records bear the same attributes: a charter grants lands or privileges; a contract notes the terms of reciprocal undertakings; judges set their decisions down for the guidance of future courts as well as for the information of litigants; legislative bodies keep journals of the votes taken in the consideration of a bill and sometimes preserve minutes of debates.

All such documents (or tablets or stones) are evidence of what they record—an act performed, a word uttered—of that and no more. Serious qualifications limit their competence. Formalistic elements creep into phraseology used over and over again. A contract which reads "For one dollar and other valuable considerations . . ." is evidence of an agreement, but not of the sum involved—as were the peppercorns or bushels of grain many a grantee promised the King. Moreover, unspoken understandings sometimes permit falsification. *The Congressional Record* is not evidence of what was said on the floor of the House or Senate, because speakers freely edit or alter their remarks before printing and even insert, as if delivered, comments never actually made. The Dred

[16] For example, Eliyahu Ashtor, "Volume of Levantine Trade in the Later Middle Ages," *Journal of European Economic History,* IV (Winter 1975) , 573 ff.

[17] Lawrence H. Leder, ed., *Livingston Indian Records, 1666–1723* (Gettysburg, 1956) , 9–10.

Scott Decision notes the outcome of the slave's suit; but the majority opinion errs in its interpretation of citizenship and of the history of slavery.

Hence the limited utility of the conventional distinction between primary sources—those contemporary with an event—and secondary—later reconstructions. Every source is primary with respect to the moment at which it was made or written; and none is reliable except for matters of which it provides the record.

Government documents are particularly susceptible to misuse for, having begun originally as repositories of records and to some extent still serving that end, they acquired a credibility as official. They no longer always deserve to be taken on faith. The very act of organizing an archive to serve a state purpose may introduce a bias; and published collections are subject to censorship. In addition, in the nineteenth century and increasingly thereafter government reports came to include a vast amount of miscellaneous material of uneven dependability. The historian cannot treat the products of the Government Printing Office or of the National Archives as all of a sort, but must distinguish among contents of various types. Hearings before congressional committees and regulatory commissions contain statements which, though accurately transcribed, are wildly erroneus; and shoddy research deserves no more credance when performed by the staff or consultants of a government agency and published under its seal than when done privately. It means nothing to speak of the findings of the Dillingham or Kefauver or Kerner committees without knowing who did the finding. The numbers churned forth at taxpayers' expense call for, but rarely receive, the same critical scrutiny as all other statistics.[18]

The historian deals constantly with artifacts made for some purpose other than that of preserving a record. Human activity leaves behind an enormous residue of materials which, descending through time, preserved by chance or design, becomes available for

18 Chapter 8 at note 5; Oscar Handlin, *Race and Nationality in American Life* (Boston, 1957), 97 ff.; Special [Senate] Committee to Investigate Organized Crime in Interstate Commerce, *Report* (Washington, 1951); *Report of the Advisory Commission on Civil Disorders* (Washington, 1968).

sorting and sifting. Of this category it may be said in general that since the objects were made, there is a knowable place and date of their making and a purpose which, if not always known, may usually be inferred. But they differ from records of transactions in that accuracy may not always be in the interest of the maker.

Historians are most accustomed to the use of written communications. A letter or an exchange of correspondence conveys information—not always the truth or the whole truth—but enough so that read in context it is evidence not only of its own contents but also of the writer and of the recipient and of the relationship between them.

But ephemera, the relics of daily life, are also eloquent. Posters, broadsides, flyers, handbills, leaflets, and pamphlets say much about the society and culture from which they emanate. These bits of paper did not appear spontaneously, but were made by someone for some reason, produced for an immediate purpose. The printer of an advertisement or handbill aimed to inform or deceive, to entertain or persuade, to convert or impress a specific, particular audience; his handiwork, therefore, mirrored some aspect of daily life.

Students of ancient history long since learned to employ material artifacts to complement and correct literary sources. Garments, tools, jewels, weapons, and utensils, as well as works of art and other archaeological discoveries, expand a record in which words are meager—and do so by precise rules of evidence. Abundance complicates the task in modern history, particularly when objects flow in mass from factories. On the other hand, finding aids help not only those later prepared by museums but also contemporary listings originally intended for some other purpose; catalogues of mail order houses and department stores or household inventories in the records of estates describe and price goods in a fashion which illuminates the lives of the people who used them.[19]

Far greater hazards attend the use of the testimony of a witness, whether written or spoken, whether instantaneous with the event or recalled years later. The observer announces, "I was there and

[19] For example, Ramsay Macmullen, <i>Roman Government's Response to Crisis</i> (New Haven, 1976), 229–243; Michael Grant, <i>Roman History from Coins</i> (Cambridge, 1958); Chapter 9 at note 12.

this I saw." He may have been a bystander with only limited opportunity to see; or a participant with a stake in acceptance of his
own version of the event; or a traveling passerby regarding an imperfectly perceived landscape; or a dupe; or a swindler. The accounts are all evidence, all fallible, none acceptable on the face
of it.

The historian applies familiar helpful tests. Is the witness competent and in a position to observe? The skilled diagnostician,
whose detailed clinical reports deserve full credibility, is no more
dependable than other men in describing a street accident or a
foreign social system. Whether their accounts are informative or
misleading depends not only on the integrity of the travelers but
also on their motives, on the persons encountered, on the places
visited and the season of the voyage. Of such, and other, witnesses
the scholar must ask: Is the statement direct or hearsay, fresh or
remembered, after how long? To what extent is correction necessary for bias arising from prejudice, class- or self-interest, patriotism, religion, and personal passion? The sum of answers is still not
wholly adequate to a judgment of the worth of the evidence.[20]

The issue of credibility remains. For centuries—at least since
David Hume's essay on miracles (1748) —historians have learned
that the respectability of the witness is no guarantee of accuracy.
Wa-Sha-Quon-Asin, the Iroquois known as Grey Owl and a highly
regarded, popular lecturer and writer, proves, at his death in 1938,
to have been Archie Belaney, born an Englishman. Errors of perception plague the best-intentioned and worthiest as well as the
blatant prevaricators. Mrs. Alvester Williams of Las Vegas lost two
hundred pounds instantly, by "God's reducing plan." Her "body
could be seen shrinking visibly, as she sat in the service. Many
people commented on this."[21] Joseph Smith's encounter with the
angels and the experience of Mary Baker Eddy challenge the critic

[20] George W. Pierson, *Tocqueville and Beaumont in America* (New York, 1938);
Robert W. Fogel and Stanley L. Engerman, *Time on the Cross* (Boston, 1974), I,
170 ff.

[21] David E. Harrell, Jr., *All Things Are Possible: The Healing and Charismatic
Revivals in Modern America* (Bloomington, Ind., 1975), 198; Lovat Dickson,
*Wilderness Man* (New York, 1973); Peirce, *Collected Papers*, VII, 90.

by their earnestness. Not even the painstaking procedures for canonization in the Catholic Church will persuade unbelieving scholars. The historian struggles to balance the probabilities, but cannot be certain even as between the contradictory narratives of two witnesses equally well positioned. But, then, neither is the concordance of two or more different stories a warrant of accuracy, for the same circumstances which lead one witness into error are likely to deceive others. In any case, the too-perfect account, like the too-perfect alibi may be more suspect than that less likely by its imperfections to have been invented. So also, the more plausible, easy version of a text may be less authentic than that with imperfections acquired in the process of survival.

Then there is the dog which did not bark. What the witness did not observe may be more important than what he did, just as what the commander in battle did not know may be more important than what he did. Lapses in perception must enter into the judgment of the testimony's credibility.[22]

In the real world distortions creep into the evidence, sometimes out of the intent to deceive, sometimes out of willingness, for the most altruistic of purposes, not to falsify but to bend the testimony, to convert the second- or thirdhand account into direct observation, or to improve upon an incident seen, the statement heard. A generation of historians accepted the words attributed to Woodrow Wilson on the eve of the war declaration in 1917, as they did those attributed to Bartolomeo Vanzetti while in jail in 1927. The likelihood is that neither was accurate.[23]

The witness manifests his fallibility even in the privacy of a diary. Unintentional errors crept into the accounts kept by Puritans who knew that the lines they wrote were subject to the scrutiny of an angry God. But more deliberate distortions tempt writers who expect their pages to edify posterity—their heirs or a wider public—and who think that no one is watching. Autobiographies

22 Thus, Sidney and Beatrice Webb, *Soviet Communism* (London, 1935), II, overlooked the great famine in the Ukraine. Garrett Mattingly, *Armada* (Boston, 1959), 318 ff., gives a fine analysis of the importance of what a commander did not know.

23 Jerold S. Auerbach, "Woodrow Wilson's 'Prediction' to Frank Cobb," *Journal of American History*, LIV (December 1967), 608 ff.; David Felix, *Protest: Sacco-Vanzetti and the Intellectuals* (Bloomington, Ind., 1965), 178 ff.

written after the lapse of years, with the deliberate intention of forming an image or conveying an impression or retrospective justification, were even more open to mistakes resulting from faulty recollection, limited opportunity to observe, and ego-serving misinterpretations.

Often the circumstances of publication provide the autobiographer no incentive for getting the record straight, even if he is in a position to know the whole truth; an interesting story does better than an accurate one. The biographers of Jack London, for instance, are unaware of the extent to which accounts of his early life reflect the impression he wished to create when he first attracted public attention. When a ghostwriter stirs the brew, ingredients of uncertain origin add to the spiciness, not to the veracity. Readers moved by the *Autobiography* of Malcolm X have taken it at face value, unaware of the skillful hand in it of Alex Haley, a writer not particularly concerned with the line between fact and fiction. Other documents in the same genre—picaresque narratives of sex and violence among the lower classes—are also open to doubt and especially when contrasted with authentic accounts emanating from the same social sources.[24]

Twentieth-century technology added a new dimension to judgments of credibility by enabling any witness speaking into a machine to preserve words on tape.

Oral testimony and oral history of course antedated the written, and historians long since learned to avoid the nineteenth-century error of underestimating the reliability of such traditional sources. But the spool of tape erased the usual safeguards of veracity and thereby created a new set of difficulties.

The traditional oral account was face to face and, although subject to error, emerged under the constraints which tended toward

[24] London's story was incorporated in Irving Stone's novel *Sailor on Horseback* (Boston, 1938), and in Andrew Sinclair, *Jack* (New York, 1977), 243, 356. Peter Goldman, *Death and Life of Malcolm X* (New York, 1973), 407, accepts the *Autobiography* as "an authentic American classic." Piri Thomas, *Down These Mean Streets* (New York, 1967), falls into the same genre. Compare, by contrast, such authentic works as Ely Green, *Ely Too Black, Too White*, ed. E. N. and A. B. Chitty (Amherst, Mass., 1970); Theodora Kroeber, *Ishi in Two Worlds: A Biography of the Last Wild Indian in North America* (Berkeley, 1962); Rosalio Moisés, *Tall Candle: The Personal Chronicle of a Yaqui Indian* (Lincoln, Neb., 1971); Hamilton Holt, *Life Stories of Undistinguished Americans* (New York, 1906).

truth. Examination and cross-examination probed the story the witness told; and tribes chose as chroniclers men of probity and exceptional memory, whose narratives, often sustained by mnemonic devices, received frequent collective attention and correction which excluded the corruptions of liars and fools. The common stake in veracity of listeners and tellers under such circumstances preserved the integrity of the oral history for centuries. In contemporary society no analogous constraints hold the teller to the truth, and no oral tradition can make a prima-facie claim to accuracy. To depend on the recollections of aged folk about events or tales told seventy years or more earlier is to disregard the consequences of the incessant swirl of information in modern society.[25]

H. H. Bancroft and other local historians had early encouraged old-timers to write or dictate their reminiscences. But modern oral history took form after the Second World War. The first promoters, at Columbia University in 1948, aware of the dangers of distortion and mistakes, insisted that the interviewers be experts thoroughly familiar with the subject matter and with the documents bearing upon the career of the person questioned. Accounts transcribed in this fashion filled in gaps in the written record and sometimes illuminated the character of the speaker, for the moment of interview if not for the whole of a career.

But as the number of oral history enterprises multiplied, these cautionary procedures proved cumbersome in the eyes of the persons interviewed and time-consuming and expensive to the interviewer and to the sponsoring institution. All too often the tape recorder became an invitation to uninhibited reminiscence; the subject babbled on to his heart's content, while the interrogator adjusted the controls. The absence of documentary verification drained such accounts of almost all evidentiary value.[26]

The publishers' discovery of a market value to transcriptions of such narratives stimulated output. The unverified ramblings of an

25 Jan Vansina, *Oral Tradition: A Study in Historical Methodology*, trans. H. M. Wright (Chicago, 1965) ; Basil Davidson, *African Genius* (Boston, 1969) , 45 ff.; J. H. Parry, "Juan de Tovar and the History of the Indians," American Philosophical Society, *Proceedings*, CXXI (1977) , 317; Lawrence C. Goodwyn, "Populist Dreams and Negro Rights," *American Historical Review*, LXXVI (December 1971) , 1435 ff.

26 My own experience as a subject confirmed these doubts: Bruce M. Stave, *Making of Urban History* (Beverly, Hills, Calif., 1977) . See also Saul Benison, "Oral History," in Edwin Clarke, ed., *Modern Methods in the History of Medicine* (London, 1971) , 286 ff.

eighty-four-year-old sharecropper, edited and arranged by un-specified standards, sold well. Laborers, Indians, ethnics, former populists, and blacks had their turn at the tape, while journalists and talk-show personalities hastened to get their own transcripts into print. The smell of profit dissolved scruples about honor and honesty, as the turmoil over H. R. Haldeman's *Ends of Power* showed. All inhibitions fell away—about the fallibility of memory, about the innocent disposition of the narrator to tell the audience what it wished to hear, about the mental tricks of timing which altered what happened earlier in the light of what happened later. Even the barrier of language magically evaporated; Studs Terkel got the life story of an Italian waiter without understanding a word of the language.[27]

Here and there in the heaps of sound a nugget nestles; it is no mean task to separate it from the dross.

The problems of credibility are imposing. But the techniques of verification are simple, indeed traditional, if only historians were scrupulous in their use instead of accepting what seems con-venient to interpretation.

First, provenience. Whence comes the testimony and for what purpose is it offered? In 1831 a slave rebellion in Southampton County, Virginia, led by Nat Turner killed sixty whites, then was suppressed and its leader executed. Nat Turner's widely read con-fession gave the details of the conspiracy. The incident and the document shocked the slaveholding South, and news of it spread throughout the country. More than a century later it became the subject of William Styron's popular novel (1966), and that in turn opened into a bitter controversy about the character of the rebel and of the account.[28]

---

[27] Theodore Rosengarten, *All God's Dangers: The Life of Nate Shaw* (New York, 1974) ; [Louis] Studs Terkel, *Talking to Myself* (New York, 1977) , 20, 157. On the publishing aspects, see Carey Winfrey, "Haldeman's Book," *New York Times*, Feb. 17, 1978, p. A16.

[28] Thomas R. Gray, comp., *Confessions of Nat Turner* (Baltimore, 1831) ; John B. Duff and Peter M. Mitchell, eds., *Nat Turner Rebellion* (New York, 1971) ; John H. Clarke, *William Styron's Nat Turner* (Boston, 1968) ; Seymour L. Gross and Eileen Bender, "History, Politics and Literature: The Myth of Nat Turner," *American Quarterly*, XXIII (October 1971) , 487 ff.

The debate over the big questions of interpretation obscured a little question: how did the story of a convicted slave find its way into print? The book itself gave one answer. A white lawyer took down the narrative while Nat Turner awaited execution in Southampton County jail. Why? To provide a warning. To whom? Not to blacks, who were not encouraged to buy books, but to white Virginians. And what was the point of the warning? The danger of lax treatment, or permitting bondsmen to learn to read, of tolerating their meetings.

Conceivably an imprisoned slave would speak openly, candidly, and honestly to a representative of the master race. But surely in evaluating the evidence it is also necessary to recall that a state constitutional convention the year before had considered the issue of emancipation, that abolitionists were still active in the South and that free Negroes restively showed signs of an effort to improve their status, so that the document as printed actually served the interests of those who wished to preserve and increase the severity of slavery.

Second, the stake of the witness in his testmony. Clearly an accomplice, once seized, has an interest in collaborating with the authorities against his partners in crime to soften his own punishment. Less clear, but equally true, men and women under conditions of stress and eager to extricate themselves from trouble may not be able to distinguish fact from fancy. Many a report of conspiracy requires careful scrutiny and validation from other sources; and most will almost certainly be riddled with error. Without carefully picking the details over, without ample allowance for falsification, the historian will not know whether Denmark Vesey or Lee Harvey Oswald committed or planned their acts of violence alone or in concert with others.[29]

Finally, concordance. Is this testimony in accord with the other evidence? The agreement of several witnesses is not enough, for they may have spoken in collusion or, more likely, may have had the same distorted, limited view of the incident. But confirmation from different types of evidence is more persuasive. The observations of violence by occasional foreign travelers through the

[29] Richard Wade, "Vesey Plot," *Journal of Southern History,* XXX (May 1964), 143 ff.; John Lofton, *Insurrection in South Carolina* (Yellow Springs, Ohio, 1964), 259, n. 18.

Southwestern frontier in themselves carry little presumptive
weight—too few, too prejudiced, not well informed. The corroboration of Americans passing through the same places adds something,
but not much—better informed, more, but also subject to bias.
But contemporary debates about dueling, accounts of specific
fights, the details of the early lives of Andrew Jackson and Thomas
Hart Benton—all these bits of different types of evidence, conform-
ing to that of the witnesses, strengthen and sustain one another
enough to reduce the margin of uncertainty to an acceptable level.

Rhetoric, the evidence most frequently used by historians, is
also the most difficult to assess. The expressive employment of
language survives in many forms: oratory, to which the Greek term
originally applied; but also written essays and editorials, the pre-
ambles of statutes and other state papers, arguments (scientific,
philosophical, historical) , insofar as they are expounded in words
rather than in symbols, and also fiction, whether conveyed in print
or on the stage or motion picture screen, or by radio and television, over the air or by cable.[30]
Rarely is it difficult to verify place and date of composition.
Authorship presents more problems, not so much in the case of the
anonymous work—although many a critic has devoted years of ingenious effort to tracking such down—but in the case of the
amanuensis. The statesman writes or dictates, the secretary trans-
cribes. In writing, the executive may search out his own data or
have assistants do so; or they may pull the material together in
preliminary memoranda; or write up drafts; or compose the
speech. The historians must ask; how much was Roger Taney's
and Edward Livingston's in Andrew Jackson's farewell and nullifi-
cation addresses, how much Sam Rosenman in F.D.R., how much
Max Perkins in Tom Wolfe? Every writer knows, or should know,
how the process of composition influences content.[31]

[30] R. S. Roberts, "Use of Literary and Documentary Evidence in the History of
Medicine," in Clarke, *Modern Methods in the History of Medicine*, 36 ff.

[31] Carla H. Hay, "Benjamin Franklin, James Burgh, and the Authorship of 'The
Colonist's Advocate' Letters," *William and Mary Quarterly*, XXXII (January 1975) ,
111 ff.; James C. Curtis, *Andrew Jackson* (Boston, 1976) , 130, 145; Samuel I. Rosenman, *Working with Roosevelt* (New York, 1952) ; Samuel B. Hand, "Rosenman,

Perplexity also follows the contemplation of purpose. Words deployed may march off to a goal other than that of the ostensible title. The presidential message that accompanies a veto aims as often to stir up public opinion as to let Congress know the fate of the bill. Published books inform their readers but also advance the careers or earn royalties or propagate the beliefs of their authors. Judgments of these works as evidence must take account of, and compensate for, distortions emanating from varied intentions.

Such judgments are essential. It is difficult enough to read a plain word, so difficult it deserves a whole chapter. But often the word manipulator intends the meaning not to be plain, sometimes even arranges his sentences to deceive, and not infrequently is himself deceived.

Honest Abe Lincoln would not tell a lie. Now a New York editor, influential pest, demands to know what the President will do about slavery. Lincoln need not answer; other matters in plenty occupy his thoughts. But he does answer: a bitter war is bringing grief to homes throughout the land; above all, he must end the suffering; if freeing the blacks will bring peace closer, he is for it, if tolerating bondage will do so, he is for that. True? The historian knows what the correspondent did not; at that very moment, in Lincoln's desk lay the Emancipation Proclamation. He had long before decided for freedom.

What then were the purpose and meaning of the letter to Greeley? The decision once made, the calculation was clear. The rebel South would remain unappeased until crushed by force; Northern abolitionists would snipe at the President, but tag along with him on emancipation, if for no other reason than lack of an alternative. To be won over were the loyal slaveholders of the border states, and the Democrats who might draw votes in 1864 from people ready to fight for the Union but not for the "niggers." The letter thus had a purpose and meaning different from those which appeared on the surface; it laid the groundwork for the argument that emancipation would come not as an end in itself but as a means to preserve the Union.[32]

---

Thucydides and the New Deal," *Journal of American History*, LV (September 1968), 334 ff.; Andrew Turnbull, *Thomas Wolfe* (New York, 1969), 194 ff.

[32] John Hope Franklin, *Emancipation Proclamation* (Garden City, N.Y., 1963), 26 ff.

Timing and tactics make it likely that Lincoln knew exactly what he was doing. But more usually the words spoken or written carry connotations of which the authors are only imperfectly aware. In January 1940 Franklin Delano Roosevelt asks Congress to "look ahead and see the effect on our future generations if world trade is controlled by any nation or group of nations" through military force. This was not an expression of solicitude for American commercial interests, but rather an effort, along with similar references to freedom of the press and of religion, to provide a realistic cloak for F.D.R.'s pro-British policy.[33] George Baer and John D. Rockefeller have God's word for it that they and not their workers know best how to employ the fortunes of which they are custodians. Are they literally attentive to messages from on high; or do they choose phrases which will justify their robber-barondoms; or do they play out roles of which they are themselves scarcely aware but which require the enunciation of almost ritual language? When a hardheaded businessman demonstrates the profitability of round-the-world integrated transportations systems in 1910, he is putting into the only terms he regards as acceptable a wildly romantic vision. Lawyers' briefs emanate not only from the statute and case books, not only from political theory, but also from prejudice, personal and class interest, and large disinterested ideals. Marginal men, attempting to describe Africans, Indians, or immigrants for a larger audience make delicate choices of words as well as of substance.[34]

On the other hand, the detailed accounts by reformers and sociologists of the condition of paupers, criminals, or prostitutes, the descriptions by educators and missionaries of the savage or noble barbarians, the reports by anthropologists on head shapes and of geneticists on Germ-Plasm mingle with observations that may be almost clinical, language that reflects their own fears and fantasies. On the popular level, too, phrases repeated as ritual and

---

[33] Franklin Delano Roosevelt, *Public Papers and Addresses* (New York, 1941), IX, 4.

[34] See Philip D. Curtin, ed., *Africa Remembered: Narratives by West Africans from the Era of the Slave Trade* (Madison, Wisc., 1967); Charles A. Eastman (Ohiyesa), *Indian Boyhood* (New York, 1902), and *From the Deep Woods to Civilization* (Boston, 1916).

ideas and images accepted as conventional may or may not correspond to or be in accord with personal beliefs.[35]

Properly deployed, all is evidence—of something. And the
proper means of utilizing rhetoric are not more complex than
those for using other types of evidence. Respect for the integrity
of the text requires a careful and precise reading, in which
the scholar stands apart, maintains the absolute inviolability of
the quotation marks, and refrains from injecting himself into the
lines as written or spoken. Understanding the purpose and the
context will assist in interpretation, as will judgment of the extent
to which words correspond to action. Above all, the rhetoric must
fit in with the other survivals of the people who uttered it: the
testimony of observers, artifacts in all their variety, and the records
of their transactions. The more abundant the evidence and the
more various, the firmer the structure composed from it. For, although none are sufficient and free of fault, one type will offset the
weaknesses of another, so that all taken together are stronger than
the sum of the parts.

The failure to locate rhetorical statements in their appropriate
contexts is fatal to the dramatic thesis of Foucault's *Madness and
Civilization*. Passages from literary texts and impressions of various
works of art supply the material for his argument that madness is
a function of the civilization which defines it. More specifically,
in the transition from the classical era to that of the Enlightenment, unreason regarded as the extreme of reason evoked a great
fear that only development of institutions of confinement could
quiet. Foucault recognized that the leprosaria which later housed
the lunatics stood empty not because society ceased to define the
disease but because hygenic and medical factors had reduced its incidence. Critical reviewers might have suggested that madness,
just so, increased not in people's perceptions but in actuality as
the result of forces Foucault does not treat, while the altered environment of the eighteenth and nineteenth centuries (also outside his range) transformed the public consequences of behavior.
The Enlightenment somehow accommodated many types of unreason and showed no disposition to clap into institutions the vic-

---

[35] See, e.g., Margaret Meade and Rhoda Métraux, "Image of the Scientist among
High-School Students," *Science*, CXXVI (Aug. 30, 1957) , 384 ff.

tims of enthusiasm (Masonry and Mesmerism, Quietism and Pietism, Quakerism and Shakerism) , unless incapable of functioning outside the walls. Integration of texts with context, of words with events, alone could have opened a way to the understanding of change.[36]

✢

The historian faces more complex problems when the evidence comes to him either prepackaged, so that he must pull it apart, or in fragments, so that he must reconstruct it before using.

Newspapers are the most familiar of the forms of bundled-up data, although much of what applies to them would apply also to movies and television tapes.

It is ludicrous to consider the newspaper as a type of evidence. It is a medium or vehicle that assembles various types of evidence —advertisements and market reports which record transactions effected or putative; the testimony of reporters; the rhetoric of editorials, commentators, and letter-writers; and such artifacts as appear in comics, cartoons, and photographs. The historian must treat each according to its own nature. In some periods the press was political, tied to a particular party so that rhetoric spilled over into the narrative of events; at other times the egos or greed or ambition of powerful editors and publishers dominated; still again, commercial sensationalism ruled or the imperatives of action and exposé. Scholars must compensate for the resulting distortions.

But they must also know how the quality of the medium influences its content. Its essence lies in its periodicalness, in the fixed intervals between its issues. The newspaper appears daily; between deadlines it must find enough, just enough and no more, information, opinion, and other items of interest to fill the columns each time; because readers support it by buying out of habit, it cannot allow their attention to flag. News, therefore—what is each day printed—only roughly corresponds to the historian's judgment of

[36] Michel Foucault, *Madness and Civilization: A History of Insanity in the Age of Reason*, trans. Richard Howard (New York, 1965) , 109, 199 ff. The whole subject has been inadequately treated. See Henri Brunschwig, *Enlightenment and Romanticism in Eighteenth-Century Prussia*, trans. Frank Jellinek (Chicago, 1974) , 164 ff., 181 ff.; Mario Praz, *Romantic Agony*, trans. Angus Davidson, 2d ed. (London, 1951) .

importance, once the day has passed. When the wires are busy, the fall of a throne will earn no attention; when all is quiet, reporters are out looking for a dog to bite.

The obligations of the deadline affect style and content. Accuracy suffers from haste of composition; immediacy obscures the long-term context of events; and the journalist perforce depends upon observation, handouts, and interviews, with only rarely the opportunity to look back and reflect. The deficiencies of the medium, rather than any left-leaning bias, accounted for the extraordinary failure of the press during the Vietnam war.[37]

Extraneous forces also affect the quality of this evidence. No American newspaper in the 1930s adequately described what went on in any totalitarian country; the news from Berlin, Moscow, and Rome was either false or incomplete. The postwar performance was no better. The stories Harrison Salisbury wired from the U.S.S.R. as a correspondent in the 1950s differed markedly from the contents of the books he wrote after he left that country. Aside from understandable limitations on the ability of the reporter to observe and to ask questions, aside from the overt official censorship, an additional inhibition governs the journalist: the consciousness that offense to the government may result in his expulsion. The press is dependable only to the extent that it is free; what it prints under duress is mostly worthless as evidence, except insofar as it is evidence of that duress.[38]

Disentanglement of the intricate contents of the newspaper is therefore essential but difficult. The lead paragraph of the *Times* story on the Pentagon Papers was somewhat less accurate than the story taken as a whole; and the article left an impression somewhat different from that gained in a reading of the original document. The text as printed was accurate; but it was not an official record, only a secondary compilation by a team of unskilled historians. The circumstance of the printing was itself news—which buried the original factual content under piles of commentary and left

---

37 S. L. A. Marshall, "Press Failure in Vietnam," *New Leader*, XLIX (Oct. 10, 1966), 3 ff.; Peter Braestrup, *Big Story* (Boulder, Colo., 1977). In general, see Lucy M. Salmon, *Newspaper and the Historian* (New York, 1923).

38 Mark Vishniak, "Salisbury Re-Viewed," *New Leader*, XXXVII (Oct. 18, 1954), 16 ff.

the historian the Herculean job of sorting those particular issues into their component parts.[39]

∽

The reverse intellectual process is even more agonizing. The elusive evidence is not prepackaged, but scattered. The march of armies, the heedlessness of nature, the misjudgment or carelessness of men and women have broken, torn, discarded, and misplaced the bits and pieces the historian cherishes. He must reconstruct what was once a whole, what now exists only in fragments.

Humility is the prime requisite. The cracks in the vase will yield to no restorer's art. No researcher will encompass all the sought-for data. Many things he will wish to know will ever escape him—the smells of the early modern city, the sounds of the forest primeval, the unwritten decisions in the councils of vanquished people—all irretrievably gone. The record will remain partial and incomplete. But complete enough to supply the honest workman what he needs.

The problem is to provide the linkages; shard, print or paper, the evidence is only a bit of something larger; the historian connects one bit with others. How?

In the good old certitude days, the manuals supplied an easy answer: synthesis. Having assembled and verified all the facts, the historian arranged them in order of relevance, after which a process akin to the scientist's induction caused the generalization or interpretation to bloom.[40]

Others put it another way. The historian, as social scientist, brought to his heaps of data a testable hypothesis derived from economic, political, or some other body of analytical theory and then matched the specifics to the stated proposition, which provided a ready-made principle of organization. The facts in that happy world proved or disproved the theory; in return, the theory filled in the gaps in the evidence.[41]

Neither solution satisfied. Arrangement of the data could not

[39] *New York Times*, June 13, 1971.

[40] Langlois and Seignobos, *Introduction to the Study of History*, 211 ff.

[41] Samuel P. Hays, "Systematic Social History," in George A. Billias and Gerald N. Grob, *American History* (New York, 1971), 315 ff.

precede the act of synthesis; for the bits would not of themselves fall into place, but required some principle of organization which already anticipated the interpretation. The processes of periodization, of classification, and of distinguishing the particular from the general were not reflective responses to the data; they required the active interposition of the historian. And the relation of facts to theory, though symbiotic, was disjunctive; coexistence but not helotism was the rule. Just as no single particular could prove or disprove a general theory, so no theory required the justification of, or could account for, or substitute for, or supply a surrogate for an individual instance. Social scientists themselves thought in a different way. Usually the best of them, like Marx, Pareto, and Weber, found their stimulus not in discovery of a fact but in a negative critique of an accepted proposition.[42]

Nor could entrenched myths fill the gap for the historian; for, although the propositions people wished to believe about themselves were data worthy of study, they were inherently hostile to the literal record. Henry Ford declared that history was bunk because it diminished the past he had come to venerate. Mayor Bill Thompson and his followers refused categorically to accept the degradation of the heroes of American history. And the Scopes trial was a confused and inchoate protest against the science which detracted from the dignity of man by denigrating his past. Whatever the value of myths in illuminating the consciousness of those who hold them, they cannot take the place of facts.

The process of reconstruction follows different, grubbier, more detailed forms, always conditioned by the imperative of respect for the known fact, always guided by the obligation to keep the record straight. Putting the story together begins not in contemplation of a theory but in an encounter with the evidence.

Chronology provides a simple but much disregarded law: The event which happened later cannot be the cause of that which happened earlier. The industrial revolution cannot be responsible for New England transcendentalism; William Ellery Channing

---

[42] David McLellan, *Karl Marx: His Life and Thought* (New York, 1973), 60; Raymond Aron, *Main Currents in Sociological Thought*, trans. Richard Howard and Helen Weaver (New York, 1967), II, 169 ff. On periodization, see Gerald N. Grob, "Reconstruction: An American Morality Play," in Billias and Grob, *American History*, 191 ff.

was preaching, Emerson orating, and Thoreau brooding before the railroad and the factory altered the region. Vietnam cannot explain the disaffection of college youth; Mario Savio attacked Berkeley in 1964, and rebellion, with and without cause, goes back at least to the death of James Dean in 1958.[43]

There can be no such certainty about extrapolation. From that which is known and verified, scholars in many fields infer that which is not known, projecting a continuation of uniformities or trends from the one into the other. The anonymous author sometimes gives himself away by stylistic habits and patterns of exposition. The archaeologist matches up the bits of clay and sees the shape of the amphora; a few lines give the clues to the whole design. A prudent editor can safely supply missing words in torn eighteenth-century manuscripts and expand abbreviations. Having examined many jars and read many letters, the archaeologist and editor can edge over from the known to the unknown with a low probability of error. In an extended correspondence it is often possible to judge what was in a missing letter from those which preceded and followed it, but not always. A risk remains: Jno. may be Jonathan rather than John; and a tear in a letter of 1788 after *Con* may remove *stitution* or *vention* or *gress*. The risk grows greater with the size of the gap. Each decision is individual and the product of an informed appraisal of the hazards of stretching out as against the impotence of accepting ignorance.

The mode of inference employed in extrapolation bears a resemblance to that in thinking by analogy, that is, in reasoning that objects, events, and personalities which agree in many respects may agree in some others. The match among phenomena need not be as precise as if the social scientist were stating a law. Verification of the proposition: *a strong president has trouble with Congress* would require examination of all the country's chief executives, categorization of those who were weak and those who were strong, and analysis of all the instances which did or did not conform. It requires no such procedure to find an analogy to the difficulties of Franklin D. Roosevelt in those of Woodrow Wilson. The analogy imposes no such burden of proof upon the historian

---

[43] For the United States, see, e.g., Caroline F. Ware, *Cultural Approach to History* (New York, 1940), 252 ff.; for generational change in Britain, Bruce Mazlish, *James and John Stuart Mill* (New York, 1975), 7 ff. See also Chapter 12.

seeking to amplify evidence as it does upon the scientist in quest of a law.

Comparison as a mode of defining uniformities serves a function for the historian different from that it serves for the scientist. The latter seeks as many instances as required to establish the regularities that will support a general statement of probability. But the condition of doing so is an antecedent, even if hypothetical, theory to validate judgments about which instances to compare and how many. The objective is proof of the proposition. With varying degrees of success, political scientists and sociologists—and, to a lesser extent, economists—employ that method of analysis.[44] The drawbacks from their point of view are acceptable: approach from a predefined theory and dependence upon secondary sources. Max Weber exemplified the strength and weakness of the comparative approach; the flashes of insight of this scrupulous and learned scholar never added up to a coherent theory of society and did not offset frequent failures of detail.[45]

Comparison helps the historian define not laws but questions. By eschewing the grand intentions he avoids the practical problem of what and how much to compare and the logical issue, troubling since John Stuart Mill, of whether the procedure implies an unprovable uniformity of nature. The historian begins with no such broad concerns but with a bit of evidence: the record shows many business corporations chartered in Massachusetts before 1800. To the usual query—why?—there is a usual answer—to meet the needs of developing industry. Now comparison enters: manufacturing

[44] For example, S. M. Lipset, *First New Nation* (New York, 1963), and *Revolution and Counter-Revolution* (Garden City, N.Y., 1970); Orlando Patterson, "Slavery," *Annual Review of Sociology*, III (1977), 407 ff.; Louis M. Hartz, *Founding of New Societies* (New York, 1964); Crane Brinton, *Anatomy of Revolution* (New York, 1938); R. B. Merriman, *Six Contemporaneous Revolutions* (Oxford, 1938); Barrington Moore, *Social Origins of Dictatorship and Democracy* (Boston, 1966). By contrast, Robert R. Palmer, *Age of the Democratic Revolution*, 2 vols. (Princeton, 1959, 1964), is less an exercise in comparison than an effort to treat aspects of European and American history as a whole. See also C. Vann Woodward, ed., *Comparative Approach to American History* (New York, 1968); William H. Sewell, Jr., "Marc Bloch and the Logic of Comparative History," *History and Theory*, VI (1967), 208 ff.

[45] Arthur Mitzman, *Iron Cage: An Historical Interpretation of Max Weber* (New York, 1970), stresses the personal and family factors which shaped Weber's ideas. See also Neil J. Smelser, *Comparative Methods in the Social Sciences* (Englewood Cliffs, N.J., 1976), 115 ff.

grew more rapidly in England, France, the Netherlands, and the German states than in the United States, yet without the accompanying increase in the number of corporations. The comparison does not in itself provide an answer; instead it suggests that there was something wrong with the question as usually framed and points to a need for reexamining the meaning of corporation and of industry.[46]

Comparative history is thus not a discrete field or even a distinct method of inquiry. Comparison is a necessary precaution, instinctive or deliberate, taken by every historian to validate the questions asked of the evidence within the enclosed boundaries of every investigation. It may arise among countries or regions; among national, nonnational, and supranational groups; among social classes, states, or cities; and across eons of time—so long as its function is not to give answers but to raise questions.

One final tool is useful in putting the pieces together: corroboration at the interface. At the moment of the event's occurence the set was whole; every character, every object, every physical feature was in place, perfect. The surviving piece, found and identified, may be partial and incomplete, but must fit; and precisely. Any little sawing or chiseling at the edge will destroy its utility entirely. The problem of fit may be specific or general; the detail of when and where must be correct, but also the match of large trends —the exact date and text of the halfway covenant, but also the relation of social to theological change. Better to leave the evidence dangling intact in space than to do it violence.[47]

～

It is difficult enough, and achievement enough, to get the record straight. To have put the evidence in order, that is, to have brought it as close as possible to correspondence with the occur-

[46] Oscar and Mary Handlin, "Origins of the American Business Corporation," *Journal of Economic History*, V (May 1945), 1 ff., and *Commonwealth* (Cambridge, 1969), 87 ff. See also the way MacMullen, *Roman Government's Response to Crisis*, 203–204, compares Roman and Turkish bureaucracies.

[47] Although Mandelbaum, *Problem of Historical Knowledge*, 274 ff., argues that the components of history do not form a completely interrelated set, the historian must deal with the evidence as if amputating reality. See Gaetano Salvemini, *Historian and Scientist* (Cambridge, 1939), 60; Herbert Lüthy, "What's the Point of History?" *Journal of Contemporary History*, III (January 1968), 4.

rence in the past, should be sufficient reward for the historian. Properly speaking, that is the task most appropriate to this scholarly discipline.

But whoever becomes familiar with the evidence through struggling with it becomes aware of its incompleteness and inadequacy; and particularly of the yawning distance between the physical survivals and the living human beings they represent. The ink spread across the page emanated from the pen of a man or woman who once breathed and walked, then shared a common mortality and very likely also the common experiences of greed, pain, and love. So the sensitive historian longs, if he can, while allowing the characters to parade across the stage in the costumes of their assigned roles, also to find and reveal the inner impulses that directed them in a drama at least part of which was ad-libbed.

Then, too, not all the lines spoken survived as evidence. In the 1960s polemical references to the "inarticulate" smudged the outlines of this issue. The inarticulate, then suddenly discovered, turned out to be the lower social classes—seamen, vagabonds, brigands, and peasants—as if somehow they were less given to speech than their social superiors—capitalists, craftsmen, or warriors. The record does not at all support the truth of this condescending proposition. An unsympathetic chronicler described the American masters of money and industry as "all of them typically 'great silent men,'" sitting in silence with nothing to say and no time for thought.[48] Differences in the likelihood that evidence will survive may vary with family stability and spatial mobility, but there is no proof whatever that the gift of language or the power of expression is more abundant in some groups than in others. Some people are more literate than others; but that skill is not in itself an indication of articulateness; the clerk who spends his days at the copydesk is not more capable of expressing himself than the peasant bent to the plow.

Only a minority of men and women anywhere, anytime, are articulate in the sense that they are able to put their thoughts and emotions into language they themselves phrase. Most men and women, being neither orators nor poets, listen and repeat, communicate through formulistic phrases bred into their culture. Of

[48] Matthew Josephson, *Robber Barons* (New York, 1934), 336.

course they feel and believe and reason deeply, sincerely, and truly; but they are inarticulate in the sense that they express themselves in borrowed language.[49]

The historian cannot, therefore, safely confine his attention to the members of the cast—intellectuals, preachers, lawyers—who compose their own lines. He must regard also the merchants and peasants, the artisans and paupers, whose role is significant and sometimes decisive, but who utter phrases which may or may not express their inner thoughts and emotions. The people of the latter category cannot be known by their words alone, as perhaps those of the former can.

Historians have long struggled to reach across time and somehow penetrate the hearts and minds of the inarticulate, describing and naming their efforts variously. Herder wrote of *Einfühlung* (the process of feeling into) and Dilthey of *Erlebnis* (reliving) which later led to *Bedeutung* (signification or comprehension). Empathy is the more appropriate term, the imaginative projection of the scholar's consciousness into that of his subject.

The feat has dangers and, not least, that of identification, whereby the scholar projects his consciousness not into but onto his subjects, so that instead of putting himself in their place, he puts them in his; instead of thinking and feeling as they did, he bestows his thoughts and emotions upon them.

A widely read essay illustrates the perils of the process by falling victim to them. The point of departure is one of the "inarticulate," William Widger, a revolutionary seaman held in a British prison. The approach, borrowed from a study of obedience by a social psychologist, interprets the low percentage of defection (7 to 8 percent) as an index of loyalty to the Revolution. And the point ultimately reached is the assertion that these lower-class types were not only nationalists but also egalitarian collectivists and thus different from their own individualistic and hierarchical leaders.[50]

A return to the point of departure reveals that the author has not tried to reconstruct the thoughts of William Widger and the

---

[49] Eric A. Havelock, *Preface to Plato* (Cambridge, 1963), 138 ff., discusses formulaic styles of expression.

[50] Jesse Lemisch, "Listening to the 'Inarticulate' William Widger's Dream and the Loyalties of American Revolutionary Seamen in British Prisons," *Journal of Social History*, III (Fall 1969), 1 ff., 26.

imprisoned seamen, but has imposed upon them the radical ideas of 1969. Widger, who later became master of a ship of his own, is not quite inarticulate. He reads the newspapers and he keeps a diary, which shows some command of language the comprehension of which calls for no abstract psychological theory. About some matters he writes eloquently, indeed passionately—for instance, about a dream of his wife's infidelity. He is expressive enough when his thoughts turn to his country's independence, as in the account of a speech by Charles Fox or in the prayer composed for an end to Britain's tyrannical power. About other subjects Widger is matter of fact: receipt of cash subsistence payments, negotiation with guards, attempts at escape. An eighteenth-century fighting man takes these in stride. He notes without indignation defections, desertions, and betrayals, real and rumored, by Henry Middleton, the Vermonters, Pennsylvanians, French, Germans, Swedes, Marylanders, and others. No reflection of a more modern index of loyalty here. Above all, there is no tone of egalitarian collectivism. Widger invariably attaches deferential titles to the names referred to; he shows no resentment of the fact that the officers celebrated in their own ward on hearing of the Yorktown victory; and it is high praise for an English commissioner that "he appeared very Much like a Gentleman."[51] None of which is at all surprising to the scholar who wishes to understand this man not as a proto-revolutionary but as an American seaman of the 1770s.

Nor can the scholar, turning to the other end of the social scale, probe the wishes and interests of capitalists of the 1890s by conjuring up a "business community" knowable by statements from intellectuals or politicians. It takes a delicate weighing of deeds as well as of rhetoric and a sensitive distillation from the mass of words of those repeated from the past, of those shared with other Americans, of those derived from common regional or religious heritages, and of those personal and idiosyncratic to assay the residue properly ascribed to class and status.[52]

51 William Hammond Bowden, ed., "Diary of William Widger of Marblehead, Kept at Mill Prison, England, 1781," *Essex Institute, Historical Collections,* LXXIII (October 1937), 314, 318, 322, 332, 337, 347; LXXIV (January 1938), 23, 27, 36, 38, 145.

52 Walter La Feber *New Empire* (Ithaca, N.Y., 1963), 19, 62 ff., 150; Chapter 4 at note 36.

The modern historian who wishes to know an eighteenth-century peasant or a nineteenth-century factory worker or a seventeenth-century merchant or a prince, general, pauper, or slave at any time must take a leap of the imagination—but to his subjects, for they can never know what he does, think like him, perhaps even feel like him. Hence the need for empathy, for the effort to reexperience what they did. Hence the danger of identification, of the assumption that they could be some earlier version of a later type.

The evidence in all its variety is both a stimulus and guide to empathy; each shred, a survival of the human being who made it, calls for understanding. And, in response, the power of empathy imparts a synergistic quality to the evidence so that the inert parts, once assembled as a whole, spring to life.

The historian writing, reading, engages in an act of criticism; for he is ever appraising the evidence. Who fails as critic fails also as creator.

Composition, like criticism, is a continuing process—the literary record of an encounter with the evidence. There is no precise point at which research ends and writing begins. From the first setting of words on paper through the repeated revisions which shape the sentence to the facts, the struggle to approach the truth suggests—demands—more, better, and purer material. And the setting of the ultimate line brings with it the certitude not of being right, but of having exhausted the evidence.

The twentieth-century historian can, however, draw support from an instrument not so frequently available to his predecessors. It is a virtue of entry into a field in which others have labored that it affords an opportunity for an operation akin to triangulation. Those others made their own surveys in various corners and from various baselines, each subject to his own errors and to the limitations of his own perspective. Their accounts, available, critically read, are rough guides to the later writer who, knowing the earlier distortions of particular angles of vision, can begin to estimate his own by checking his reckonings against theirs.

# 6

## *An Instance of Criticism*

A SLOW LEARNER, I encountered late in life the expectation that books be reviewed, not on their own merit, but as representatives of a school and as statements of a thesis. Had I known in advance that William Appleman Williams' *Contours of American History* carried with it a heavy charge of political significance, I might have hesitated to tangle with it. Perhaps not, because I believed then that a reviewer ought not to pick and choose among the offerings, but should respond to the requests of respected editors.

I had not, until 1961, read any of this author's writings. In reviewing his book, therefore, I could not altogether exclude the possibility that he intended it as an elaborate hoax, that Williams had been enjoying himself by ingeniously pulling the legs of his colleagues.

Scattered through the volume were uproariously funny passages. The discussion of Poe, for instance, seemed surely to have been designed as a satire upon certain forms of infantile social criticism that had occasionally appeared in the 1930s: "*The Pit and the Pendulum* is perhaps the most subtle yet devastating fictional attack on laissez faire ever written . . . Captured and imprisoned by the rulers of a system that demands absolute ideological conformity, Poe's protagonist holds to his own values through extended interrogation, a trial, and a series of rigorous ideological lectures. The experience, relates the hero, 'conveyed to my soul the idea of a *revolution*' as the only way to deal with such a society . . . Only the fortuitous arrival of a conquering general rescues him: he is saved by armed resistance, and by forces of a foreign revolution at that. Just as a description and critique of laissez faire, the story would be a classic" (p. 273). It

145

takes a rereading of Poe's story to appreciate the extent of the per-version. The idea of a *"revolution"* there is associated "with the burr of a mill-wheel," not with a way to deal with a society; and the system under attack proves to be that of the Inquisition in Toledo (Spain) not that of laissez faire in Toledo (Ohio) .[1]

Nor could sentences such as the following be construed as other than parodies of the literary striving of unskilled freshmen: "Considerably more taciturn and withdrawn than Shaftesbury, who wived several women and in other ways lived at the center of society, Locke was temperamentally inclined toward the intro-spection which served as one of his principal tools in exploring and analyzing the nature of man and society." Or: "Nevertheless, like the little girl with a curl in the middle of her forehead, these early Puritans had a kink in their ideology." Or: "political theory of that age was both an engine and a caboose of immediate ex-perience."

As plausible as such an explanation of the work might have been, it did not altogether convince this reviewer. Certainly large sections were altogether farcical. But they seemed not to be intentionally so, otherwise they would not have been interspersed with equally large, dull, and unhumorous ones. On balance, it seemed necessary to conclude that Williams was deadly in earnest in writing his book.

If that were indeed the case, then some alternative explanation was needed for why the book was as bad as it was. The frequent failures of information and errors in fact were not enough to account for the total disaster. The pervasive wrongheadedness that distorted every page must have had a more general source.

I concluded that Williams simply did not understand that he could not use words arbitrarily but had to fix them to concepts which conveyed meaning. In dealing with ideas, he neither ac-cepted the categories of his subjects nor devised consistent new ones of his own. He improvised as he went along and was, there-fore, altogether incoherent.

---

[1] Oscar Handlin, "Review of *Contours of American History*. By William Apple-man Williams (Cleveland, 1961) ," *Mississippi Valley Historical Review*, XLVIII (March 1962) , 743 ff. Marie Bonaparte, *Life and Works of Edgar Allan Poe*, trans. John Rodker (London, 1949) , 575 ff., offers another, although only slightly more convincing, interpretation of *The Pit and the Pendulum*.

What could he have meant, for example, by describing Locke's philosophy as one of "individualism"? Locke did not use the term, which did not even enter political theory until the nineteenth century; nor was this a philosophical classification within which he conventionally fell. Nor did Williams assign the word a precise definition that fitted Locke but also all the other cases to which it was applied. No form of rational discourse was possible on this basis.

Such key concepts as mercantilism, laissez faire, liberalism, Christianity, and socialism were tossed about in the same heedless and contradictory manner. As a result, it was possible to describe the American Revolution as provoked by the spread of laissez faire in the mother country. A cardinal principle of feudalism was "the very backbone of England's colonization" (pp. 56–57). Benjamin Franklin was as much a mercantilist as Herbert Hoover was a syndicalist. John Wise in 1710 and 1717 "went on to secularize" the equalitarian Christianity of George Whitefield—who was born in 1714 (pp. 101–102). John Taylor was a physiocrat whose ideas, first published in 1793, guided the agrarians in the Constitutional Convention of 1787 (p. 151). On the other hand, Jefferson was "more than half an American mercantilist. His entire career can be understood as the attempt of a physiocrat to use mercantilist means to realize his feudal utopia" (pp. 154–155). Lincoln, however, was an exponent of laissez faire (pp. 295–296); but then "the first principles of laissez faire justified regulation, even demanded it" (pp. 308–309).

At the time I believed that was enough. This much it seemed could be said for the book: it was original. There had never been anything like it before.

I was mistaken. It was not enough. Even when chided for the inability to recognize a seminal work, I did not understand the issue involved. I continued to write about the abysmal quality of a work of historical scholarship; whereas those who objected to the criticism defended a manifesto of the revisionist school critical of American foreign policy.

∽

The basic discussion, it appeared, turned about the origins of the Cold War. The official account—in my view, largely the accurate one—ascribed World War II to totalitarian aggression, tardily resisted by its victims. By that interpretation, the struggle continued after 1945 as a result of the efforts of the Soviet Union, the one surviving totalitarian power, to expand its control in Europe and Asia either by subversion or by aggression. The Cold War followed from the determination, again tardy, of the United States and its allies not to yield.

The revisionists, although differing among themselves in many details, challenged all or parts of this analysis. They argued that the United States, far from being on the defensive, was mostly to blame for the failure of postwar peace efforts. Out of the selfish desire to preserve an outmoded economic system by expanding markets in Europe and Asia, it either deliberately or through ignorance provoked the Russians who responded out of justified fear of encirclement or attack. Even when the fact of aggression was clear, as in Czechoslovakia or Korea, the U.S.S.R. had only defended itself against anticipated hostile action; and whether its suspicions were well or ill-grounded, the United States shared the blame for not allaying them.

I continued to believe that the evidence would dispose of the arguments. Since 1953 revelations from within of unquestionable authenticity had illuminated the character of the Communist world. Americans learned that the Hungarians and Czechs, at least, did not welcome their Russian masters, that Stalin's regime rivaled Hitler's in brutality, and that Mao was far from just the Chinese version of a Jeffersonian agrarian reformer.

Yet, in the same decades, the trickle of revisionist writings shifting the onus for the Cold War to the United States had swollen to a stream. The position was inherently absurd; it flew in the face of all the evidence; and it blandly disregarded everything learned about the Soviet Union after 1945. Nevertheless, William Appleman Williams continued to be cited with respect, and the revisionists persuaded a considerable segment of liberal opinion.

They did so not because any significant number of respectable and influential historians were crypto-Marxists, who, as Eugene Genovese charged, "protected their jobs and their families by eschewing the Marxist label while writing from a Marxian viewpoint." Rather, revisionism supplied a pseudo-historical basis for the wishful thinking of latter-day isolationists. The yearning to be neutral always exposed those who tended their own gardens to the temptation of justifying aggression lest otherwise they face the obligation to look beyond their own fences. Hence the desire to establish a moral parity in the postwar world between the United States and the Soviet Union—neither entirely good, neither entirely bad. When "anti-Communist" became a term of reproach on the editorial page of the *New York Times,* there was a market for books which demonstrated that the fault was in ourselves, that peace would have been within reach had we only wished it enough or had not McCarthyism blocked it.[2]

The publishing business and the reviewing media, both increasingly devoted to marketing sensation, stimulated the demand. In history, as in journalism, the exposé was the most saleable commodity. A sober work which, weighing the one side and the other, concluded that Stalin really presented a threat to world peace after 1945 and that American intentions were not aggressive would have been too close to the official line to be new; whether it was true or not hardly mattered.

Then, too, the pervasive anti-establishment sentiment of the American establishment inhibited any scrutiny of credentials. It was as unfashionable in a publishing house or a periodical as in a university or foundation to inquire into the qualifications of authors. In an open market, everyone was privileged to peddle his wares.

Above all, I knew that the disarray of the historical discipline prevented an appropriate assessment of the revisionist books. The flaccid acceptance of shoddy work had long been a scandal of scholarly and literary journals, which encouraged reviewers to focus on interpretations rather than on craftsmanship. To expose an error of fact was regarded as irrelevant nit-picking, a reflection upon the critic who grubbed about in footnotes rather than soaring with the ideas. No one wanted to play that role. It was much

2 Eugene D. Genovese, "Marxian Interpretations of the Slave South," in Barton J. Bernstein, ed., *Towards a New Past* (New York, 1968), 94. Treatments which equated an opposition to Communism with McCarthyism included Robert Griffiths and Athan Theoharis, *Spectre: Original Essays on the Cold War and the Origins of McCarthyism* (New York, 1974), 17, 70, 92 ff., 157; George Q. Flynn, "Review," *Journal of American History,* LXIV (December 1977), 829; Lewis M. Purifoy, *Harry Truman's China Policy* (New York, 1976).

easier to relax in reductionism: different points of view produced different interpretations. No need to judge which was valid. The alternative was much more difficult: to accept nothing on faith, to verify every assertion, and to check every footnote. Manifestly, the case argued on pure theory alone would not convert the unconvinced. But surely the organized examination of the evidence, line by line, note by note, would establish the truth. Only thus could the critic determine whether misstatements were the incidental slips to which every author was liable or whether they were components of a total process of distortion and falsification.

Nevertheless, I continued to hope that the passage of time would set the record straight, free the judgments of the future from the partisanship and distortion of contemporary passion, and demonstrate truth's capacity to triumph. Hence I welcomed Robert J. Maddox's scholarly evaluation of the revisionists. Maddox examined the books he criticized point by point and revealed errors which were not aberrations of detail but basic to the whole revisionist position.[3]

Maddox made the case. But it did not sink in. The revisionists did not recognize or explain away their distortions. Instead, they justified error by further abuse of the evidence and put at question the very integrity of history as a discipline. More puzzling, some uncommitted scholars attacked the critic for having raised such awkward questions.

These were not tempests in academic teapots. They were not likely immediately to influence the conduct of American diplomacy. But the revisionists and their defenders confused public opinion at a time when clarity on these issues was important; and they did serious damage to scholarship.

The reviewer in the *American Historical Review* greeted an earlier observation that the revisionist argument was "inherently absurd" with such incredulity as to betray an utter lack of understanding of its meaning. It is, therefore, necessary to begin a re-

[3] Robert J. Maddox, *New Left and the Origins of the Cold War* (Princeton, 1973). See also Joseph M. Siracusa, *New Left Diplomatic Histories and Historians* (Port Washington, N.Y., 1973).

capitulation of responses to Maddox's book by explaining what should have been clear on the face of it.[4]

What was absurd was not of course necessarily untrue. The attacks upon Maddox were absurd, nevertheless, they existed. It was hard to believe that historians would so betray their professional obligations; they did. The revisionist argument, although inherently absurd, could conceivably have been correct; but the burden of the proof rested upon those who advanced it.

Historians never formalized their rules of evidence as lawyers did, partly because those rules largely conformed to common sense, partly because no courts provided the sanctions to enforce them. However, most historians, in the abstract, accepted as tests of reliability the extent to which they received access to the documents, the character of the witnesses, and the congruence of the parts with the whole. By those tests the revisionist argument was absurd and should have borne the burden of proof, rather than receiving the invariable benefit of the doubt.

The revisionists wrote as if the availability of the evidence had no bearing on credibility. On the domestic scene, they conceded, concealment created the presumption that there was something to conceal; public exposure, that there was not. The archives of the United States for almost the whole of this period were open. Vast quantities of materials were published, and researchers were free to move through the collections, with exceptions few in number and unlikely to bear on foreign policy. There was no need to wonder at the indignation voiced at any gap in the record, any bit of paper withheld.

The relative mildness of complaints about Soviet practice was less troublesome than the unwillingness to draw inferences from it. The archives of the Soviet Union were shut tight. The handful of documents published were selected and edited by standards the validity of which was unknown. Foreign scholars had no access whatever to Soviet diplomatic records; and the fate of Russian historians like Aleksander Nekritsch, who innocently ventured to pry into these materials, quickly enlightened and frightened others. The issue was not what another government ought to have

4 *Freedom at Issue*, no. 15 (September–October 1972) , 2; Warren F. Kimball, "The Cold War Warmed Over," *American Historical Review*, LXXIX (October 1974) , 1135.

done. The issue was what inferences historians ought to have drawn from what was actually done. Given the difference in the availability of evidence, the balance of credibility lay with the revealing open party. Systematic concealment at the very least raised the suspicion that there was something to conceal in a foreign state as at home. It offered the historian no ground for casting the balance in every case of doubt toward the country which withheld evidence.[5]

One illustration will show the perverse treatment of the availability of evidence. Even if Russian dread of encirclement was ill-founded, it was often said, the United States had a special obligation to allay those fears. Of course there was no evidence that the Soviets were actually afraid of an attack from the West; we could hardly expect exposure to the public gaze of matters of such confidentiality. Of course the public and private utterances of American statesmen consistently stressed their defensive intentions; but we could hardly expect the Kremlin to believe them. Thus, Soviet secrecy and American openness both became grounds for casting the balance of doubt against the United States.

Furthermore, the revelations of a quarter-century demonstrated beyond any question the character of the Stalinist regime which held power in the Soviet Union through the whole period of the failure at peacemaking. Those who wished to read the signs knew something about that regime even in the 1930s and 1940s; only the willfully blind, after the Khruschevian revelations could fail to recognize that in its control of the instruments of state power and in its relationship to the liberties of the people, it shared traits with the totalitarianism of Germany and Italy. By contrast, whatever their shortcomings, Franklin Delano Roosevelt, Harry S Truman, and Dwight Eisenhower were not totalitarians. In judgments of intent, in interpretations of purpose, and in imputation of motives the qualitative ethical difference between them and the Soviet leader with whom they negotiated was absolute. In every decision about whom to believe, the burden of proof should have fallen upon those who chose Stalin.

5 Daniel Yergin, *Shattered Peace* (Boston, 1977), recognizes the deficiencies of Communist sources; nevertheless, he gives the benefit of the doubt to the Soviets and blames the conflict on the failures of American diplomats. For the tradition of Soviet falsification, see Chapter 3 at note 50.

Yet the revisionists distinguished on specious grounds between the Soviet and Nazi regimes; they either established a moral parity between the Soviets and the United States or they cast the balance of doubt in favor of the Soviet Union. Poor old Joe became a helpless victim of the bloodthirsty man from Independence.[6]

Above all, a third element should have entered the calculation. Were the known actions of the United States consistent with the hypothesis of unremitting hostility to the Soviet Union, or would that hostility have dictated an alternative scenario?

Suppose that concern with halting the spread of Soviet Communism had really been an important element in American diplomacy, what course would Franklin D. Roosevelt or Harry S Truman have followed? They would not have exploded the atom bomb in order to end the war swiftly and impress the Russians, as some revisionists alleged. Far from it! Had they really worried about the Communists they would have prolonged the war with Japan in 1945. The Mikado's army in Manchuria, still intact and in fighting condition, could have tangled with the Soviets in a bruising encounter that would have weakened both parties and left the supremacy of the United States and its nationalist allies in China unchallenged. The bomb would then have been an ace in the hole. Yet, there is no indication that the Americans ever considered that alternative. Instead, they sought an immediate

[6] See, e.g., Les K. Adler and Thomas G. Paterson, "Red Fascism: The Merger of Nazi Germany and Soviet Russia in the American Image of Totalitarianism, 1930's–1950's," *American Historical Review*, LXXV (April, December 1970), 1046 ff., and the discussion following, 2155 ff., LXXVI (April, June 1971), 575 ff., 856 ff. This confused essay treated the association of Soviet and Nazi totalitarianism as simply the product of American thinking, without seriously examining the actuality. Toward the end it admitted that totalitarian systems exhibited "undeniable similarities," but then retracted part of the concession in a footnote. In any case, throughout the essay spoke of "seemingly" similar methods of government, of "alleged" forced labor conditions in the Soviet Union, and of the Red Army "liberating" rather than conquering Eastern Europe. Thereby Adler and Paterson presented the Nazi-Soviet connection as entirely a product of American Cold-War perceptions rather than of common economic, social, and cultural origins. The conclusion was that there was no danger of aggression from the Soviets as there had been from the Nazis—if only the Cold Warriors had not frightened Stalin. In sniveling responses to critical comments on their article, the authors predictably called for a halt to "unproductive name-calling" and then went on to argue the legitimacy of discussing perceptions without discussing reality, as if one could explain why people sounded the alarm without asking whether the house was on fire or not. The responses also asserted that every distortion of the evidence in the original article was just a matter of interpretation. See also Aryeh L. Unger, *Totalitarian Party* (London, 1974).

end to the war and the utter destruction of Japanese power—either through a landing, whatever losses that would have entailed, or through the atomic strikes.

Even earlier the United States acted as if hardly conscious of the potential Communist danger. A deal with Japan was well within the realm of possibility, in 1941 and later, that would have protected American economic interests and created a powerful restraint upon Soviet expansion. No such arrangements were seriously contemplated. Nor, in the closing months of the war, in Europe or in Asia, did the United States push for strategic advantages where military power would have permitted. Americans failed to act as they should have acted had the fear of Communism or economic self-interest genuinely moved them. In the face of these blanks in the record it would take evidence of an incontrovertible character to prove that F.D.R. or Truman took the inadequate, hesitant steps they did out of the motives the revisionists ascribed to them.

〜

There was no such evidence. The show of proof mounted in revisionist books did not withstand Maddox's scrutiny.

The precise factual exposure revealed the gravity of the issue. In *The Tragedy of American Diplomacy* (1959), William Appleman Williams quoted Stalin's opening statement at the Potsdam Conference; Maddox showed that Stalin made no such speech and that the phrases attributed to him were drawn from later discussions on other subjects.[7] Gabriel Kolko's *The Politics of War* (1968) alleged that Truman "reneged on clear commitments" at Yalta in objecting to the Oder-Neisse Line for Poland; Maddox proved there were no such clear commitments.[8] Lloyd C. Gardner's *Architects of Illusion* (1970) used a *Fortune* poll to prove that the Potsdam Conference altered American views of Russia; Maddox pointed out that the magazine was already in print before the Conference ended.[9] Such instances, among many, were cited from the work of professionally trained historians.

[7] Robert J. Maddox, "Cold War Revisionism: Abusing History," *Freedom at Issue,* no. 15 (September–October 1972), 4; Maddox, *New Left,* 20.

[8] Maddox, "Cold War Revisionism," 6, 16; Maddox, *New Left,* 117 ff.

[9] Maddox, "Cold War Revisionism," 16; Maddox, *New Left,* 150, 151.

These were simple factual matters. Did Stalin say it or did he not? Was there a commitment or was there not? Did the conference influence the poll or not? Maddox maintained that these and other examples of fabrication of evidence were representative. But it was not really necessary that *he* should prove that. The burden of proof should not have rested on him. How many instances of dishonesty were needed to raise the issue of integrity? The burden of proof should have fallen on those caught out in error.

The response of the revisionists was significant. They held to their positions of course, but neither explained away nor apologized for the errors. In a variety of ways they brazened it out, arguing that the errors were not errors at all, that the fact rewritten was closer to the truth than the plain meaning of the document. Williams, although not followed by the others, even invented the term "seriatim quotation" to describe the technique of choosing odds and ends of words to communicate the *Weltanschauung* of a protagonist, claiming thus to be able to reveal what a speaker or writer really meant, as distinguished from what was actually said or written.[10] Why quibble over the quotation marks, when the technique provided direct access to Stalin's mind?

The bluff worked. Trigger-happy journalists like Ronald Steel in the *New York Review of Books* bought the whole works. "Maybe . . . the revisionist view can be sustained only by distorting the historical record. But maybe such distortions, even where they can be demonstrated, do not undercut the central revisionist argument about the origins of the cold war." After all, "Many of Maddox's examples of distortion turn out, on closer inspection, to be questions of interpretation."[11] If one could conveniently forget where the burden of proof lay, all interpretations were created equal; one took a choice by preference or predisposition.

Some historians were just as gullible. Ideologically committed writers like Ronald Radosh in the *Nation* simply parroted the revisionist defense.[12] More distressing was the response of the

10 From the response by W. A. Williams in *New York Times Book Review*, June 17, 1973, 7.

11 *New York Review of Books*, June 14, 1973, 34.

12 *Nation*, CCXVII, July 16, 1973, 55 ff.

middle-ground diplomatic historians, writing in the media which should have set the standards of performance in the discipline. Naturally academics are timid; they shy away from controversy, particularly from nasty quarrels that might raise questions about the integrity of their colleagues. Still, the discomfiture Maddox created was significant, and even more so was the justification—a denial that the mere facts, the hard evidence, were decisive. Scholars who were themselves not revisionists displayed a preference for the discussion of free-floating interpretations and chided Maddox for his grubby concern with literal accuracy. Generally these critics pointed out that, while the evidence may have been inconvenient, the revisionists had a right to impose on it what meaning they wished to accord with their total world-view.

Some years earlier Christopher Lasch had astounded me by casually making this his defense when caught out in the fakery of a quotation. In the intervening years the position had become commonplace. It was no longer necessary to prove anything by the mobilization of evidence. Strong intuitive feelings could impose meaning upon the data.

From this distorted point of view, any challenge to anyone's strong feelings was an act of aggression. Hence the inverted logic by which respected historians shifted the blame to Maddox and away from those he attacked. The correctness or incorrectness of statements and the proper or improper use of evidence were trivial issues. Live and let live. Since each could do his own thing, no matter how outrageous, anyone who challenged another was disruptive.

The *American Historical Review,* official publication of the American Historical Association, stated the establishment doctrine. A long, opaque article by Warren F. Kimball preached the academic cover-up. Not that the revisionists were correct; but it was incorrect to attack them. On the specific points, concession. "There is no question that Williams strings together series of quotations on certain subjects without telling the reader when, where, and why they were said." That was not nice and reduced "the scholarly usefulness of the book." On the other hand, "intellectual history—for that is what Williams writes—simply cannot be judged in that way." The "key to true and useful intellectual history—as opposed to mere literary history—is the intuitive ordering of facts and ideas. No one is obliged to accept the interpretation that follows, but disagreement does not justify name-calling."[13] So much for footnotes and quotation marks! In the end it all became a matter of interpretation. In a touching plea for a return to the genteel tradition, Kimball explained that everyone had a good thing going, if only all would refrain from splattering each other's wash.[14]

This was the ultimate betrayal of the discipline. It was not only since Ranke that historians had insisted that there could be no good interpretation that did not rest on solid fact; way back with Cicero, they knew the first law: never to dare utter an untruth. Now truth and untruth became matters of choice; and fact yielded to intuition. Did not the members of the American Historical Association, in annual convention assembled, gravely listen to Professor James B. Parsons' prescription for research on President James K. Polk (1795–1849): retire to an antebellum mansion in rural Tennessee, adopt Polk's life-style, "ride horseback through the countryside and have an occasional drug experience."[15]

The intellectual flabbiness that tolerated this foolishness and rewarded other nonsense—whether expressed in revisionism or in other subjects—reached a danger point in the 1970s. Every profession that claims immunity from outside interference and freedom of expression for its members must recognize self-regulating, self-corrective procedures to catch out the crooks, plagiarists, and fools. History is no more free of knaves than other fields. No science is devoid of the cooked-up experiment, the misallocated funds, the blunders that are products of stupidity. The important question is: what is done when the fault is discovered? I confess to having yielded to the tendency, if not to cover up at least to remain silent—out of human sympathy with the culprit, out of

13 Kimball, "Cold War Warmed Over," 1128.

14 Kimball, "Cold War Warmed Over," 1135. See also the report of the joint committee of the American Historical Association and the Organization of American Historians, on another issue, which denied that it could presume to pass upon any historian's scholarly credentials; Organization of American Historians, *Newsletter*, V (January 1978).

15 Israel Shanker, "Drugs as a Key to the Past," *New York Times*, Dec. 20, 1971.

the empathy shared by all residents of glass houses. No more. In the end, the integrity of the discipline demands exposure.

In the 1970s rigorous criticism was more urgent than ever before. It was then difficult to overestimate the spread of sheer ignorance and the deterioration of skills, as the numbers of practitioners of history had expanded in the previous decade. I do not wish to be misunderstood. I do not have in mind only the fading away of the techniques traditionally associated with the historian's craft—the knowledge of languages, diplomatics, paleography, and the like. Nor do I refer to the spreading darkness which hides the factual terrain outside the particular little speciality into which ever more dig themselves. I have in mind rather an ignorance more pervasive and more ominous. There were people teaching in major universities, training other teachers, who were functionally illiterate, who simply did not know how to read or to write ordinary English. Criticism in this market was deemed an unfair labor practice.[16]

The increase in the numbers and in the heterogeneity of the background, training, and interest of the practitioners shifted the orientation of their organizations, which increasingly emphasized not the pursuit of common scholarly objectives but the accommodation of conflicting interests and points of view. The American Historical Association and the Organization of American Historians did not fall before the onslaught of the countercultural rebels in 1968 and 1969 as did some other "learned societies." The leaders possessed stamina enough to beat off the assaults. But having won in open battle, they yielded ground in subsequent negotiations. After the 1968 Democratic National Convention the A.H.A. did not give in to the radical demand that it punish Mayor Daley and candidate Hubert Humphrey by removing its next annual convention from Chicago. That would take sides in politics! But it nonpolitically shifted the site to New York on the ground that some participants wished it. Thereafter it adjusted to the presence of an increasingly diverse membership by making

[16] See the comment by John Higham, *Mississippi Valley Historical Review*, XLIX (September 1962), 407, 408.

its motto, "Don't rock the boat" and channeling its activities toward more jobs, more grants. It was no coincidence that the issue of the *Review* which carried the Kimball article bore on its cover a *New Yorker* cartoon. The journal, once a staid scholarly publication, had for some time enlivened its pages with illustrations appropriate to the tastes of the least of its members.

Yet, professions which refused to take a stand on the standards of practice left themselves vulnerable to malpractice suits and to even less acceptable forms of consumer retribution. Fortunately, in the 1970s Americans were too involved with other issues to inquire what intuitions passed for history in the schools and publications they supported.

The delinquency of the reputable historians poisoned public opinion. The summer of 1975 brought a nice example. "After 25 Years—the Parallel" dealt with the outbreak of war in Korea. The author of this *New York Times Magazine* article was Gaddis Smith, Professor of American diplomatic history at Yale; no revisionist he, but in his own work a competent and conscientious scholar. The most prominent illustration showed John Foster Dulles inspecting the 38th parallel. The caption asked: "Did his visit trigger the North Korean invasion a week later?"[17]

The question may have been injected by an overzealous Timesman. Smith went no farther than to suggest that the North Koreans may have been "acting pre-emptively—striking before a reversal of American policy, presaged perhaps by Dulles's visit, made attack too dangerous." But careful readers found that the author actually had "no doubt that the North Koreans attacked first"; he knew, as the North Koreans did, that the United States had denied South Korea tanks, planes, and heavy artillery, while the Russians had shown no such restraint in dealing with their ally. Smith knew, too, as many citizens did from the newspapers and as the Russians knew from their spies in the British embassy, that Korea lay outside the United States defense perimeter. In any case, nothing that happened the week before could have set in motion the elaborately planned, carefully equipped invasion.

Why, then, in the absence of a scintilla of evidence, suggest the benefit of the doubt for the Communists? This was a cheap ges-

17 *New York Times Magazine*, June 22, 1975, 18.

ture for the revisionists—on the one hand; but on the other, all sinned a little and should have tried a bit more. Truman, Acheson, Kim Il Sung, Stalin, Mao—a little blame here, a little there, all spread evenly, with only one hard villainous lump.

Who?

Syngman Rhee, "a premature cold-warrior," a conservative, that is, educated in the United States, who won the free elections held in the South in 1948 after the Northerners booted out the United Nations Commission established to supervise a nationwide poll. Rhee's shortcoming was that of Mikhailovich, Chiang, Diem, Thieu, and others who refused to commit suicide for the convenience of American historians.[18] It was no surprise to find Professor Smith conclude with a plea for a neutral Korea, in which the Southern lambs nestle up to the well-known nationalist lions from the North. A good digestion solves the problems, past and present.

The straight revisionist argument persuaded only a minority of historians, although it provided just the juicy material journalists and fiction writers needed.[19] But the unwillingness of scholars to expose the argument for what it was, gave it respectability, permitted it to edge into textbooks as an alternative interpretation, and stifled the capacity for criticism. In the residual mush people discovered an excuse for believing that somehow the whole foreign policy mess should have been managed so as not to bother them. If only the cold warriors and anti-Communists had not spoiled it all . . .

More important, the polarization of discussion—as if the only alternatives were along the revisionist and official lines—prevented historians from examining another, more responsible explanation of the origins of the Cold War, one supported not by intuition but by evidence. A novelist with integrity enough to value the truth restated that explanation in 1975 and thereby alienated many American intellectuals. Aleksander I. Solzhenitsyn and

18 By 1978 Menachem Begin was being added to the list (*Boston Globe*, Feb. 4, 1978, p. 4).

19 For example, Charles L. Mee, *Meeting at Potsdam* (New York, 1975); Morris Dickstein, *Gates of Eden: American Culture in the Sixties* (New York, 1977), 25, 282, 283. See also Daniel J. Fuller and T. Michael Ruddy, "Myth in Progress," *American Studies*, XVIII (Fall 1977), 99 ff.

thousands of enslaved Europeans knew that "World War III began immediately after World War II: The seeds were planted as that war ended, and it first saw the light of day at Yalta in 1945, as the cowardly pens of Roosevelt and Churchill, anxious to celebrate their victory with a litany of concessions, signed away Estonia, Latvia, Lithuania, Moldavia, Mongolia, condemned to death or to concentration camps millions of Soviet citizens, created an ineffectual United Nations Assembly, and finally abandoned Yugoslavia, Albania, Poland, Bulgaria, Rumania, Czechoslovakia, Hungary, and East Germany."[20]

Americans could ill-afford to allow glaring revisionist intuitions blind them to the lengthening roster of places abandoned to slavery in the 1970s. Historians could ill-afford to remain silent while corruption spread through their discipline. Meanwhile, imperturbable, indefatigable William Appleman Williams continued to set fantasy in print to the bafflement of librarians who still gave his books nonfiction classifications.[21]

[20] Aleksander I. Solzhenitsyn, "The Big Losers in the Third World War," *New York Times,* June 22, 1975, sec. 4.

[21] For example, William Appleman Williams, *America Confronts a Revolutionary World, 1776–1976* (New York, 1976).

# Dealing with the Evidence

THE MODERATELY ATTENTIVE reader will by now have made the acquaintance of a character referred to as "the historian." It will surprise few to learn that the designation was an unobtrusive way of avoiding excessive use of the first-person singular pronoun.

Nevertheless, I readily confess that idiosyncratic elements conditioned the way in which I, and no doubt others, wrote history. Before turning to the more specific problems of dealing with the evidence, therefore, I recall the particular circumstances of training and apprenticeship that shaped my own views. Since those are not likely to be replicated in the future, they need an explanation, the interest of which will not be merely autobiographical.

For the past decade or more, graduate students have yielded only too easily to the pressures toward premature and excessive specialization. By contrast, although I knew that I would be a historian at the age of eight, it was not until well along in my career that I felt the obligation to choose among subspecialties. I came to Harvard in 1934 to do graduate work in medieval history, but took seminars with William L. Langer and Arthur M. Schlesinger because I assumed that a professional historian should be familiar with more than a narrow segment of a single field. Later the pull of external forces led me to the modern history of the United States, but to this day I retain an interest in scutage and nineteenth-century Morocco. As it happened, too, the subject about which I wrote my dissertation had an international dimension which forced me, or so I thought, to look beyond the borders of the United States for sources and antecedents.

Furthermore, my first decade and more of teaching deprived me of the opportunity to specialize. As a tutor in history I was almost as likely to deal with an undergraduate working up a field in Greek as in modern history. I became involved in a project of the Social Science Research Council's Committee on Research in Economic History that was self-consciously interdisciplinary and that required me to develop a background in law, economics, and political theory. Before that task reached completion I put in spells as a member of the Psychology, Sociology, and Social Relations departments at Harvard. In the various roles those affiliations demanded I struggled to make connections between history and social science, not in rhetoric, but in teaching and examining students and in discussing common tasks with colleagues. Thereafter, for many years, on the instructional committees on undergraduate degrees in history and literature and on the graduate program in the History of American Civilization, I collaborated with colleagues in literature, philosophy, government, and fine arts.

I mention these experiences not to count the battle scars, but to explain the somewhat unusual vantage point from which I made the observations that follow. Necessarily, when I now read a word or count a number, when I look and listen, my perceptions cannot escape the effects of those experiences.

# 7

# *How to Read a Word*

FEW DISCOVERIES bewilder the teacher more than the revelation that students can more easily learn to read a book than a chapter, a chapter than a sentence, and a sentence than a word. Somehow the process of slogging through the pages conveys the general drift of an argument or of a story. Persistence yields vague impressions of what the whole is about. That plausible if passing acquaintance is necessarily imprecise and certainly inadequate for any critical understanding. Attention focused on the single word, by contrast, is not so easily satisfied. The reader either knows the meaning of "red" or "chair" or "strong," or he does not.

Yet words, even as simple as those in the lines above are slippery. The writer who wishes to use them carefully must maintain a grasp on them sufficiently firm so that they will convey his proper intention to whoever later encounters them. The reader has a corresponding difficulty in receiving and mastering them. A thrown ball which changes its shape in passage through the air frustrates the thrower, baffles the catcher.

The subject of words has always occupied philosophers as well as grammarians, poets, and critics. More recently, sociologists of knowledge and the students of linguistics have subjected it to their own forms of analysis, as have ethnographers and other anthropologists. Periodically, in the past half-century startling new theories have burst across the scholarly horizon: Ludwig Wittgenstein's proclamation of the world's incomprehensibility apart from language, Alfred Korzybski's manifesto against abstract terms: Noam Chomsky's discovery of innate syntactic structures; and the revelation of generative-transformational grammar. Certainly anyone concerned with the modes of conveying meaning in our society must have some understanding of the basic unit of language.[1]

Anyone of course includes the historian. His concern differs from that of other scholars. The intricacies of generative-transformational grammar need not involve him; and he may rarely be in a position to follow leads from sociolinguistics. But a discipline that treats utterances widely separated in time, space, and tongue, nonetheless requires of its practitioners a serious comprehension of the words that are its raw materials. Yet rare is the historian who uses words with precision or who reads them with understanding. Rare is the historian even conscious of the problem's existence much less prepared to deal with it.

All too frequently historians take pride in their emancipation from jargon. Unlike other scholars, they need no special language. Good old English is good enough for them. Take a solid declarative sentence: "The entrepreneur's quest for innovation and profit consciously or unconsciously influences his attitude toward the law." Anyone can understand that, for the words have plain meanings—as plain as black and white.

They should have had my homeroom teacher in P.S. 48—a man whom I hated with the intensity only an eleven-year-old can achieve, but from whom I nevertheless learned something, as I now understand.

Strategically situated, toward the front but on the right-hand side and therefore out of the direct line of vision of our overseer, who habitually and suspiciously looked toward the back and the doors, I escaped the scorn heaped upon his proximate targets. It was a time for filling out forms, and on this occasion among the spaces provided was one for race. I put down Jewish, as did most

[1] See I. A. Richards and C. K. Ogden, *Meaning of Meaning*, 3d ed. (New York, 1930) ; Zygmunt Adamczewski, "Being and Sense," in James M. Edie, *Phenomenology in America* (Chicago, 1967) , 48 ff.; Jonathan Culler, *Saussure* (Hassocks, Eng., 1976) ; Ernst Cassirer, *Philosophy of Symbolic Forms*, 2 vols. (New Haven, 1953) , I, 115 ff.; John R. Searle, *Speech Acts* (Cambridge, 1969) , 97 ff.; Peter Farb, *Word Play* (New York, 1974) . Robert D. King, *Historical Linguistics and Generative Grammar* (Englewood Cliffs, N.J., 1969) , is a simple introduction. L. G. Heller, *Communicational Analysis and Methodology for Historians* (New York, 1972) , is disappointing.

of my fellows, except for those who put down Italian or Syrian. Our ignorance, perceived in a glimpse at the very first card, justified the teacher's withering commentary that made the day memorable. As I hastily blotted over my own response, I learned that race meant color and not religion.

But I worried about which color until the information trickled along that we were all white. Meekly I accepted the designation, although I did not understand it. Examining my own hands, I would have said sort of orange-pink; and looking around the types I knew in class, I found none who matched the label white. I filed away another among the many incomprehensibilities of school.

Later of course I discovered that the meaning of white was not white but not-black. But even that was not free of ambiguity, for among the blacks I came to know were many shades of visage from deepest ebony to lightest chocolate. All of which led to the ultimate understanding that the words black and white as used in American society in the twentieth century referred not to colors but to social identifications.[2]

If such be the uncertainty in our own day, we can by no means take for granted the meanings other men and women at other times and places meant to convey by the use of familiar terms. Traced back through the centuries, those same words, black and white, retain their puzzling aspect. A sixteenth-century Englishman referring to skin color would less likely have used them than fair or pale and swarthy. Actually, black to begin with bore a meaning more like white as we know it than like black as we know it. It stemmed from *bleich*, the German descendent of which still means white or pale. Black, akin then to blank, implied a state of colorlessness, similar in a sense to the appearance of tin, the shade visible in some paintings of the time. Other European languages then also used two or more words: *negro/obscuro; nègre/obscur; svart/dunkel/mörk; schwarz/dunkel/dunkeles schwartz.* In German also the additional word, *der Russ* (soot) perhaps applied to a Slavic people considered dark (from whose designation the term slave derived). Curiously, colorlessness was also sometimes a char-

---

2 There is no historical evidence for the claim in Harmannus Hoetink, *Slavery and Race Relations in the Americas* (New York, 1973), 200 ff., that whiteness is a somatic norm linked with the ideal archetype of personal beauty.

acteristic of whiteness, although associated with brightness, glare, or light; and a whitesmith was one who worked with tin or who finished (as contrasted with one who forged) iron. Indeed color interested Shakespeare's contemporaries less than did tone, contrast, and character. In using the words black and white they more likely thought of the intensity of an image, of its darkness and lightness, than of its tint—a mode toward which, curiously, Malcolm X vaguely groped centuries later.[3]

In any case, the modern blackness of black and whiteness of white are products of history, rather than fixed elements of language. The historian runs a risk, therefore, in taking their connotation for granted, in assuming that "white and black connoted purity and filthiness, virginity and sin, virtue and baseness, beauty and ugliness, beneficence and evil, God and the devil." John Webster entitled his drama, *The White Devil* (1612), by which he meant hypocrisy; and a poem printed in South Carolina ran:

> Her eyes to suns, her skin to snow compare
> Her cheeks to roses and to jet her hair.[4]

In fact all colors, upon examination, prove to be indeterminate. On charts of the solar spectrum and of the colors derived from it yellows, browns, greens, and blues run together. Chrysolite green appears closer to pyrethrum yellow than to myrtle or marine green. The witness who saw red may have seen cerise, claret, carmine, vermilion, maroon, scarlet, or crimson—each quite different from the others.

⌒

Words which name colors generally serve as adjectives conveying an impression of the quality of the objects they modify—black girl, white man, red chair, green house. We use other adjectives

[3] C. F. E. Spurgeon, *Shakespeare's Imagery* (New York, 1935), 59, 66, 158; Peter Goldman, *Death and Life of Malcolm X* (New York, 1973), 6–7, 70. For the basic problems in optics and psychology, see C. A. Padgham, and J. E. Saunders, *Perception of Light and Colour* (London, 1975), 37 ff., 61 ff., 131 ff. See also Culler, *Saussure*, 24 ff.

[4] Winthrop D. Jordan, *White Over Black* (Chapel Hill, N.C., 1968), 7; *South Carolina Gazette*, July 12, 1735; also Bernard Lewis, "Race & Colour in Islam," *Encounter*, XXXV (August 1970), 20.

similarly; soft, hard, rich, poor, modern, radical, and conservative impart a sense of the characteristics of some thing, and their meaning hangs largely on the things they modify. Whether there really are essential characteristics of blackness, softness, richness, or radicalness is an interesting question, perhaps more interesting for logicians of the past than for those of the present. But the historian can evade those questions, since his purpose is instrumental, that is, to know in what senses earlier writers employed the word, to be consistent in his own use of it.[5]

The problem may be taxonomic; that is, it may involve classification. Perhaps not all the colors named green or the people described as rich belong in the same category. On the other hand, the problem may be one of perception. Color-blind persons will not distinguish green from red; and paupers will regard as rich the employed laborer seen as poor by his master. Or the problem may be one of inadequate analysis. A better understanding of physical optics and of the psychology of vision could perhaps explain the shadings of color; and a persuasive theory of social structure could more adequately define rich and poor. But these hypothetical issues are beyond the scope, competence, and immediate concern of the historian who has enough to do to keep straight the manner in which the words appeared in the evidence, the manner in which he manipulates them in his own exposition.

He has less difficulty with verbs, words which denote acts. Verbs describe movements—walk, sit, run, fly—or processes—make, employ, think. Of course they do not tell the historian everything he wishes to know: how far, how fast, to what destination; or employ whom, for how long, under what conditions? But the term of action is clear, has changed little over the centuries, and poses few of the problems adjectives do.

Historians need do little with verbs and with adjectives can do little but keep the usage in order. But the noun substantive, the word which gives a name to a thing (or person or a place), deserves their most careful attention. It can be a subject of historical study and understanding which will not only keep its usage straight, but will further analysis and add meaning to evidence. Here we see, as

[5] John Locke, *Essay Concerning Human Understanding* (1690), bk II, ch. XVIII, sec. 4; Morton White, *Science and Sentiment in America* (New York, 1972), 12.

Locke did, the imperfection and abuse of words. But here, too, are the greatest rewards for correcting imperfections and abuses.[6]

೬

Some common writing practices, intentionally or not, impede the apprehension of clear meaning. The reader often welcomes the flash of irony, the epigrammatic flourish, the hint of satire, the understated inflection, the overstated exaggeration—all those devices which stave off tedium. Let him also be ready to probe beneath the literary embellishment for the sense the words convey.

The use of a metaphor aims deliberately at imprecision. Sometimes the device covers up the honest inability to describe a complex phenomenon; or, it fudges or obscures an issue by a smoke screen of language. Sometimes it lends dramatic, even sensational, weight to an otherwise simple event.

Stretching for a catchy title, authors take leave of their subject matter and refer to a national "mind" or to "climate" of opinion or ideas, or to an "age" or to a "coming of age." William Bradford becomes a Caesar in the wilderness, Cotton Mather a pathetic Plutarch, and Calhoun the Marx of the master class. Often the fancy is harmless, but not when the result is to conflate the object of the metaphor with its source. The reader must wonder, as the author should have, whether a country has a mind as an individual does; whether an intellectual zone is similar to astrological or meteorological ones; whether a given time span is simply a convenience or implies a duration from a determinate beginning; whether the phenomenon referred to matures as an organic being does; whether Bradford was a soldier-dictator; whether the Puritan wrote as the Roman did; whether the slaveholder's views were similar or analogous to those of the theorist of revolution. For one author the age of revolution extends from 1789 to 1848, for another from 1760 to 1800; and Victoria reigned from 1837 to 1901, an interval long enough to justify application of her name to almost any modern development.[7]

6 Locke, *Essay*, bk III, chs. IX, X.

7 Random examples include: William M. Johnston, *Austrian Mind* (Berkeley, 1972) ; Stow Persons, *American Minds* (New York, 1958) ; Joseph Dorfman, *Economic Mind in American Civilization*, 3 vols. (New York, 1946) ; Rush Welter, *Mind of America, 1820–1860* (New York, 1975) ; David W. Noble, *Progressive Mind* (New

A desire to ornament the narrative accounts, too, for the temptation to fall back upon words like climax (a rhetorical arrangement of propositions in an ascending series or a change which indicates whether the result of disease will be recovery or death), turning point (a place at which direction alters), or watershed (the boundary line between one drainage area and another). These devices convey an abbreviated general sense of the intention of an author who considers more precision unnecessary or is incapable of achieving it. Here the danger lies in identifying metaphor with source and assuming that application of the term sufficiently explains the phenomenon. To refer to a decade (the 1890s) as a watershed in American ideas leaves a general sense that events before were different from those after but not how or why, or whether more so than in the decade before or the decade after.[8]

A heady sip of Freudianism, in one brand or another, converts the amiable metaphor into a symbol and, dissolving all sense of discipline, turns any text into a fun house where no word has a fixed connotation. If land is really mother-virgin and the lay of the land one continual rape, then the whole story is one of masculine penetration of the feminine wilderness. On the other hand, if the source was the river, as the continent's waterways beckoned Europeans, then the earliest acts of exploration were the primal events which set the imperial dialectic in motion. No doubt the twisted shapes reflected in the mirrors have a meaning but not one that corresponds to the outer world.[9]

York, 1970); Carl Becker, *Heavenly City of the Eighteenth-Century Philosophers* (New Haven, 1932); Hamilton Cravens, "American Science Comes of Age," *American Studies*, XVII (Spring 1976), 49 ff.; Peter Gay, *Loss of Mastery* (Berkeley, 1966), 26, 53; Richard Hofstadter, *American Political Tradition* (New York, 1948); Mark H. Haller, *Eugenics: Hereditarian Attitudes in American Thought* (New Brunswick, N.J., 1963), 5, 24, 51, 120, 145; Eric J. Hobsbawm, *Age of Revolution, 1789–1848* (Cleveland, 1962); Robert R. Palmer, *Age of the Democratic Revolution* (Princeton, 1964); Daniel W. Howe, ed., *Victorian America* (Philadelphia, 1976).

8 H. S. Commager, *American Mind* (New Haven, 1950). Walter T. K. Nugent, *Money and American Society, 1865–1880* (New York, 1968), finds a watershed in the 1870s.

9 Annette Kolodny, *Lay of the Land: Metaphor as Experience and History in American Life* (Chapel Hill, N.C., 1975); John Seelye, *Prophetic Waters: The River in Early American Life and Literature* (New York, 1977).

Other perils abound along the verbal shortcut which converts adjectives to nouns, that is, which transforms words describing the properties of things into things in themselves.

A few strokes at the typewriter keys and modern, poor, soft, become the modern, the poor, the soft, or modernity and modernization, poorness and softness, as if the qualifiers cease to modify and attain a reality and identity of their own. The reader again must ask whether the poor of 1760 are indeed the poor of 1960.[10]

To name a thing does not bring it into being. Coinage of a word is not the same as discovery or explanation of a thing. The exigencies of international politics after 1945 brought into being the terms "underdeveloped" and "Third World" both defined in opposition to what they were not, much as black and white had been. Underdeveloped assumed a nonexistent identity among those parts of the world which had not followed the same pattern of economic change as Europe and the United States had. It also assumed that all could and would follow along the same lines. The word, therefore, brought together, as if they were the same, entirely dissimilar societies—India, Syria, Morocco, Uganda, Uruguay, Mexico—all of which followed entirely distinct patterns of change, lands whose history, culture, and social structure had few common features. The term Third World assumed an identity among the countries not affiliated with either the Western or the Soviet blocs—and thereby threw together Saudi Arabia and the South Yemen, Tanzania and Indonesia.

Other terms of opposition are "non-Jew," as if there were some common element among all those not part of the group; and Protestant in the sense of practice in the United States, which applies to anyone not a Catholic or a Jew and thus counts as one Mormons, Baptists, and Unitarians. The reasons why these words come to name the things they do must interest the historian, who, however, must not assume that the subjects named thereby spring into being.

Practical exigencies do sometimes give currency to a word and then reality to that which it names, which makes the task of differentiation more difficult and more necessary. Thus, the unfolding

---

[10] Raymond A. Mohl, "History of the American City," in William H. Cartwright and Richard L. Watson, Jr., eds., *Reinterpretation of American History and Culture* (Washington, 1973), 183.

pattern of affirmative action programs in the United States in the 1960s and 1970s made a noun of "Spanish-speaking" as if there were an identity among the Puerto Ricans of New York, the Mexicans of Chicago, the Chicanos of Southern California, and the Hispanos of New Mexico and Arizona. So, too, the word African blanketed an immense continent with a heterogeneous population extending from Morocco to Mozambique and including people of many colors, but, significantly, excluding the only ones who called themselves Afrikaner. The historian who considers the actualities of the land mass to which the word Asian refers will use it only as a rough convenience.

And yet, sometimes to name a thing does reflect a genuine trend or does create a momentum that actually brings that named into being. The authors of the Declaration of Independence wrote of themselves as "one people," using a term which referred to no existing political or social actuality. Nevertheless, in a vague way they referred to a potential or impending reality, one so close to being that the very fact of naming it created a consciousness of its existence and converted the word into something more. So, too, a Harvard student adopted the word Albania, ordered a language and religion, and launched a campaign for statehood; the response in little more than a decade gave birth to a nation. Czechoslovakia and Yugoslavia offer interesting parallels.

Equally tricky is the flow of language that permits use of the identical name for different things or different names for identical things. Sir Thomas Smythe and Harry S Truman were both haberdashers, but the trade and the social rank of the one were quite different from those of the other. The influence of the attitude of Powderly's Knights established the use of the term labor to describe anyone who worked, despite the enormous differences among those thus covered.[11] City in London and Paris referred to both the whole and a particular part. But, then, the United States census long counted all places with more than 2,500 residents as if they were the same—thus putting New York and Los Angeles in a common category with New Milford and Los Alamos. And

[11] John R. Commons, et al., *History of Labour in the United States* (New York, 1918–35) ; Herbert Harris, *American Labor* (New Haven, 1938) ; F. R. Dulles, *Labor in America* (New York, 1949) ; Henry Pelling, *American Labor* (Chicago, 1960) ; Philip S. Foner, *Labor and the American Revolution* (Westport, Conn., 1976) .

historians continued blithely to write about the city and about urbanization as if they were a single thing and a single process.[12] On the other hand, they set propaganda apart from information— generally on the basis of disapproval and approval.

∽

A plausible escape from these problems is to define words by function. Surveying the immense variety of appearances a chair presents to the eye, it is tempting to conclude that a chair is to sit on, a definition with some clarity and operational utility, so long as it goes on to include enough other elements general to all, but not too many that exclude some. For instance, it will not do to include in the specification, fabrication of wood, because those made of steel or plastic are also chairs. And to exclude oriental divans and tree stumps which also serve for sitting, legs might have to enter the definition.[13]

However, even understanding a word by function will not in itself eliminate the need for differentiating among different things which bear the same name or for distinguishing mutations of subjects described by the same old frozen word. By the middle of the nineteenth century the developing law had given the word slave a precise meaning in the United States: the slave was an unfree laborer held with his offspring in perpetual bondage—legal property, entirely at the disposal of the master, and without personal rights. The word had not always or everywhere referred to the same status, although usually to the same function: work considered low or degraded. John Cotton, writing in Boston in 1650, mentioned Scots "sold for Slaves," but not in perpetuity, rather "for six, or seven, or eight years as we do our own." Englishmen

12 Thus, earnest studies of the effects of urbanization on fertility and mortality go astray when the most urban place in one sample proves to have a population of 403 and another sample, which finds little difference between urban and rural areas, notes incidentally that there does seem to be a difference between towns of more than 10,000 and those of less. See John Modell, "Family and Fertility on the Indiana Frontier, 1820," *American Quarterly*, XXIII (December 1971), 629; Maris A. Vinovskis, "Angels' Heads and Weeping Willows," American Antiquarian Society, *Proceedings*, LXXXVI (1976), 284. See also Richard C. Wade, "Agenda for Urban History," in George A. Billias and Gerald N. Grob, eds., *American History* (New York, 1971), 367 ff.; Mohl, "History of the American City," 165 ff.

13 Patricia E. Kane, *300 Years of American Seating Furniture* (Boston, 1976).

in the eighteenth century applied the word to servitude for a fixed term and small wages, a usage similar to the Russian, which recognized "limited service contracts" and even elite, high status slaves who held important bureaucratic and managerial positions. The confusion could be general. Marc Bloch showed how a casual eighteenth-century reference to a medieval "esclave de la glèbe" in the nineteenth century erroneously became fixed.[14]

The word slavery, at first general, narrowed in the hands of chartists, lawyers, and other rigidifiers. Other words passed through the reverse process, becoming more diffuse and altering their character with usage. Down to the eighteenth century the word corporation denoted a body politic or corporate, such as a municipality, a university, or a guild, which received the powers specified in its charter by the formal act of the sovereign. In the nineteenth century it applied widely and loosely to a form of business enterprise. The word monopoly, as its etymology shows, originally was an exclusive privilege granted by the sovereign; later it became control over the market by a single individual or group, however obtained; and still later it referred to arrangements among competitors allocating shares of the business. Privilege, once an ordinance, law, or decree in favor of some person, became the benefit emanating from a position of power, influence or prestige. Establishment and Elite, formerly status ascribed by government, came to apply to informal groupings, even to those based on merit and achievement. Injunction entered the law as a command to act; by the twentieth century it generally meant a command not to act. Family and community did not mean to a seventeenth-century Puritan what they did to his descendants or to the authors of the books which inspired him. All these words and a dictionary full of others are comprehensible to the writer and

[14] J. C. Hurd, *Law of Freedom and Bondage in the United States* (Boston, 1858); George P. Anderson, "Ebenezer Mackintosh," *Publications of the Colonial Society of Massachusetts*, XXVI (1924), 14; Richard Hakluyt, *Inducements* (1585), E. G. R. Taylor, ed., *Original Writings and Correspondence of the Two Richard Hakluyts* (London, 1935), II, 338; Edmund S. Morgan, *American Slavery, American Freedom* (New York, 1975), 324, 382; and review *American Historical Review*, LXXXI (October 1976), 958; Richard Hellie, "Recent Soviet Historiography on Medieval and Early Modern Slavery," *Russian Review*, XXXV (January 1976), 13, 18; Marc Bloch, *Slavery and Serfdom in the Middle Ages*, trans. William R. Beer (Berkeley, 1975), 179 ff.; Basil Davidson, *African Genius* (Boston, 1969), 214 ff.

reader who locate their function in time and trace the evolving institutions to which they apply.[15]

Maintaining control of a slippery noun is more complex when it denotes not a thing or an institution but an abstract concept, such as the word reason with which Locke grappled.[16] Even less than others are such nouns static, their meaning fixed and dependable. Sometimes derived from an adjective—redness, softness—they are subject to all the ambiguity of modifiers detached from the objects they modify. When adapted from a verb, the abstract noun loses some of the precision of its stem—to be into being, for instance.

However, since these words acquire their meaning from their employment, careful study will not only permit useful definition but will also illuminate the context. The history of a word traced in this fashion becomes akin to A. O. Lovejoy's history of an idea. By following the continuities, combinations, and transformations of such words as chain of being, empire, attitude, and property the scholar can clarify the concepts and the conditions of their use.[17]

Knowledge of the exact moment and circumstances of the coinage of a word is rare but yields a wealth of understanding. In drafting the text of the Declaration of Independence, Thomas

[15] For the variety of usages, see Oscar and Mary F. Handlin, "Origins of the American Business Corporation," *Journal of Economic History,* III (May 1945), 1 ff.; Robert Wiebe, *Search for Community* (New York, 1967); R. Jackson Wilson, *In Quest of Community* (New York, 1968); E. Digby Baltzell, ed., *Search for Community* (New York, 1968); Jean B. Quandt, *From the Small Town to the Great Community* (New Brunswick, N.J., 1970); Edward M. Cook, *Fathers of the Towns: Leadership and Community Structure in Eighteenth-Century New England* (Baltimore, 1976).

[16] Locke, *Essay,* bk IV, ch. XVII, sec. 1.

[17] A. O. Lovejoy, *Great Chain of Being* (Cambridge, 1950); Richard Koebner, *Empire* (Cambridge, 1961); Donald Fleming, "Attitude: The History of a Concept," *Perspectives in American History,* I (1967), 287 ff.; Richard McKeon, "Development of the Concept of Property," *Ethics,* XLVIII (April 1938), 297 ff. Charles A. Beard, *Idea of National Interest* (New York, 1934), gropes in the same direction. For the related concept of begriffe, see Hans-Georg Gadamer, *Wahrheit und Methode* (Tübingen, 1960), 361 ff. For Weberian ideal types, see Raymond Aron, *Main Currents in Sociological Thought,* trans. Richard Howard and Helen Weaver (New York, 1967), II, 197 ff.

Jefferson set about to enumerate the grievances of the subjects of George III as he had in the Virginia Constitution. But as he worked, the revolutionary perceived that the word "subject" was inappropriate to describe the residents of the new nation. He needed some other term to apply to the free men about to bring the republic into being. Reaching for the noun which came closest to expressing his understanding of the status of the colonists in rebellion, he inserted the word "citizen," vaguely connected in his mind with Roman antecedents. Later, during the French Revolution, the rebellious subjects of Louis XVI borrowed it and spread its usage throughout the world. So, too, James Madison, in the effort to describe the relationship of citizens to the state, hit upon the term "responsibility"; and the translator of Tocqueville made up "individualism" as an equivalent of the characteristic the French traveler discerned in the United States.[18]

Changes in meaning are revealing even under less specific circumstances of transition. Conscience, in the sense of a kind of knowledge which dictated obedience to a higher law than that of man, originally implied first, that such a higher law existed, and second, that men gained knowledge of it directly from God its promulgator with no human intermediaries. By the 1960s it meant any strong belief that justified individual defiance of the law. The word agrarian in the eighteenth and nineteenth centuries meant the forceful equalization of land ownership; in the twentieth century it came to mean simply rural or agricultural.[19]

Words are often weapons. There's the rub. Language, in its primitive uses, is a mode of action as well as, or rather than, an instrument of reflection; it also controls behavior, mobilizing men and women into deeds. It is not so much that people deliberately alter the meaning of words in order to sharpen their weapons, but that meanings change when words serve polemic or partisan pur-

[18] Thomas Jefferson, *Papers,* ed. Julian P. Boyd (Princeton, 1950) , I, 338, 357, 378, 418–420, 425, 428; Yehoshua Arieli, *Individualism and Nationalism in American Ideology* (Cambridge, 1964) , 183 ff. For the word "ideology," see John Adams to Thomas Jefferson, July 13, 1813, John Adams, *Works,* ed. Charles Francis Adams, 10 vols. (Boston, 1850–56) , X, 52.

[19] Thomas P. Govan, "Agrarian and Agrarianism: A Study in the Use and Abuse of Words," *Journal of Southern History,* XXX (February 1964) , 35 ff.; Michael G. Baylor, *Action and Person: Conscience in Late Scholasticism and the Young Luther* (Leiden, 1977) .

poses. Applied to the arrival of Europeans in America, discovery and settlement leave a connotation different from invasion or conquest, just as colonists and immigrants do. Only the precise location of each term in context will preserve clarity.

Revolution, the dictionary defines as a radical change in thought, science, or dress; or a fundamental change in political organization or in a government or constitution; or the overthrow or renunciation of one government to replace it by another. Thus far, the thought is consistent. But the dictionary also gives an earlier usage: the motion of a body round a center so that it returns to its original position. The idea of radical departure is manifestly not the same as the idea of recurrent return; indeed the two are conceptually opposed. Yet a single word applies to both. The seventeenth-century Puritans who fought the Stuarts and the American colonists who defied George III long believed that they struggled to restore ancient liberties invaded by the Crown. But, in the process they transformed the word and the reality into a movement toward an altogether new start, new society, new government.[20]

Race early in the nineteenth century meant any conventional description or division of mankind—a type or species. For French writers it meant simply lineage, as, for instance, that which distinguished the noble from the lowly born. Bancroft, who wrote about the virtues of the Anglo-Saxon race, also wrote about the "unity of the human race." At the end of the nineteenth century, however, the word bore a biological connotation and applied to inerradicable hereditary traits that divided mankind into unalterable species set off by immutable genetic characteristics. In the second half of the twentieth century in the United States the word more likely referred to anyone who denied the claims of blacks or minorities to compensatory treatment.[21]

20 Melvin J. Lasky, *Utopia and Revolution* (Chicago, 1977) ; Hannah Arendt, *On Revolution* (New York, 1963), 13 ff.; Bernard Bailyn, *Ideological Origins of the American Revolution* (Cambridge, 1967), 144 ff.

21 George Bancroft, *History of the United States*, 10 vols. (Boston, 1834–74), II, 326, 454; William Stanton, *The Leopard's Spots: Scientific Attitudes toward Race in America* (Chicago, 1960) ; Oscar Handlin, *Race and Nationality in American Life* (Boston, 1957) ; Ruth Benedict, *Race: Science and Politics* (New York, 1959) ; Robert Blauner, *Racial Oppression in America* (New York, 1972) ; William E. Alberts, *White Magic of Systemic Racism* (Somerville, Mass., 1977) ; Joel Kovel, *White Racism: A Psychohistory* (New York, 1970).

Polemic, partisan purposes obscure and distort the meaning of such words. By the end of the nineteenth century, for instance, the word socialism applied to a miscellaneous array of proposals to alter the political and social system. Utopian and scientific versions had flourished for decades; and, despite the efforts of the Socialist Party in the United States and elsewhere to cast all its members in the same homogeneous mold, diversity grew ever more complex. The term blanketed men and women who sought the ownership and control of means of production by the state; others who believed in cooperative and voluntary effort; and still others who sought regulatory reforms. On both sides of the Atlantic, it took in anti-Semites who parroted Marx's venomous words about the Jews, outright racists and worshipers of brute violence like Jack London or H. G. Wells, and gentle humanitarians, pacifists, and vegetarians. The pod that housed seeds of such variant types, after the First World War yielded a full crop of mutants: the Communist Party of the Soviet Union, the Social Democrats affiliated with the Second International, the National Socialists of Germany, and the Fascists of Italy. The common use of the word socialism, as well as the still more numerous and heterogeneous forms it took after 1945, indicated that all may have somewhere, sometime, somehow, sprouted from a single stem; but that, if so, the outcome was an array of spectacularly dissimilar fruits.[22]

The word democracy suffered changes fully as drastic. Claimed in the 1970s by regimes as different as those of East Germany, Denmark, North Korea, and Switzerland, it evolved through a curious, often paradoxical process. Americans of the 1770s, for whom it generally bore a negative connotation, disliked it when identified with the chaotic egalitarianism of other societies, although some approved when connected with equality in their own. They were all, nevertheless, more entitled to it than other claimants at the time and later. The meaning it conveyed in early nineteenth-century Virginia differed from that in Massachusetts or Nova

[22] On the word socialism, see Edward Bellamy to William D. Howells, June 17, 1888, *Harvard Library Bulletin,* XII (Autumn 1958), 370 ff.; also Ira Kipnis, *American Socialist Movement, 1897–1912* (New York, 1952); David A. Shannon, *Socialist Party of America* (New York, 1955), 43 ff.; Solomon F. Bloom, *Liberal in Two Worlds* (Washington, 1968), 93 ff.; David McLellan, *Karl Marx: His Life and Thought* (New York, 1973), 86, 184 ff.; Renzo De Felice, *Interpretations of Fascism,* trans. Brenda Huff Everett (Cambridge, 1977), ix, 178.

Scotia or Britain. And such terms as liberal, radical, conservative, and public are no simpler of comprehension.[23]

◡◡◠

It does not follow that anyone can impart any meaning to any word—not unless for the purpose of concealment. A rabbi in New York in the early twentieth century was not necessarily a student of the Torah; he might also be a politician who covered up for corrupt policemen. Commonly words of foreign derivation—argot, jargon, and other colloquialisms—serve those who do not wish others to understand.[24]

All arbitrary usages impede comprehension. If the magic of verbal manipulation can turn imperialism into free trade and convert colonialism into class or ethnic exploitation, the consequence is destruction of all basis for communication.[25] Each individual or, at best, each sect speaks its own language, incomprehensible to all but the elect. Moreover, unlimited license to make of words what the user wishes forecloses the possibility of describing changes in language that are not arbitrary, capricious, or accidental, but reflect the evolution of institutions or the refinement of concepts. Alterations in the meaning of corporation or citizen were not the products of whim or intellectual laziness, but corresponded to changes in the actuality to which the words referred; and looseness in usage blasts the possibility of reconstructing those changes.

A study of the context establishes a signification for words pre-

[23] Morton J. Horowitz, *Transformation of American Law* (Cambridge, 1977), xiv, does not grasp the difference. See Oscar and Mary F. Handlin, *Commonwealth: A Study of the Role of Government in the American Economy* (Cambridge, 1969), 203 ff., 229 ff.; Leonard W. Levy, *Law of the Commonwealth* (Cambridge, 1957), 307 ff. See also John B. Brebner, *Neutral Yankees of Nova Scotia* (New York, 1937), 207 ff.; Lewis Namier, *Structure of Politics at the Accession of George III* (London, 1963), 62 ff.; Charles S. Sydnor, *Gentlemen Freeholders: Political Practices in Washington's Virginia* (Chapel Hill, 1952), 126.

[24] Robert M. Fogelson, *Big-City Police* (Cambridge, 1977), 99; Ramon F. Adams, *Cowboy Lingo* (Boston, 1936), and *Western Words* (Norman, Okla., 1944), and *Language of the Railroader* (Norman, Okla., 1977); Howard W. Webb, Jr., "Development of a Style: the Lardner Idiom," *American Quarterly*, XII (Winter 1960), 482 ff.

[25] For example, Michael Hechter, *Internal Colonialism: The Celtic Fringe in British National Development* (Berkeley, 1975); Chapter 4 at note 35.

cise enough to permit the historian to understand to what they referred in the past, to how he may use them in the future. That approach rests upon evidence; it examines the way in which words actually served at the time and place of utterance, and it notes also whether they corresponded to things, evidence of which exists. Meaning, taken not at face value but understood from the use to which words were put, permits the scholar to trace their actual descent and their relevance to social reality.

~~o~~

It takes a whole book just to approach a definition of such an immensely complicated concept as liberty.[26] Many of the same problems cluster about a simpler, more direct yet as frequently abused concept: laissez faire. The word long current in Britain and on the continent of Europe as well as in the United States had an import in theory only tangentially related to its use in reality. Examination of a particular instance will reveal the discrepancy.

The idea of laissez faire maintained that an economy composed of self-seeking individuals and private business enterprises would function harmoniously so long as government refrained from interfering with it. Certainly rhetoric on both sides of the Atlantic abounded in references to the term throughout all of the nineteenth and much of the twentieth centuries. The evidence reveals that as long as the word was thus employed it bore no relation to practice, and that when it did begin to apply to actuality the concept passed through a drastic transformation.[27]

Acceptance of the idea in the abstract long nurtured the common misconception that ascribed a continuous laissez-faire bent to policy in the United States. The serious works of such careful scholars as John U. Nef thus referred to laissez faire as "part of our national heritage." Yet, in general, and specifically as applied to Massachusetts, the association was completely erroneous.[28]

Federalism was a frequent source of misunderstanding. But

[26] Oscar and Mary F. Handlin, *Dimensions of Liberty* (Cambridge, 1961).

[27] Oscar Handlin, "Laissez-Faire Thought in Massachusetts, 1790–1880," *Tasks of Economic History, 1943*, pp. 53 ff.

[28] John U. Nef, *The United States and Civilization* (Chicago, 1942), 319, 345; also Dorfman, *Economic Mind*, II, 512 ff.; Handlins, *Commonwealth*.

arguments which denied powers to the national government on the ground that they belonged to the states hardly betokened laissez faire. Nor were debates concerning the advisability or expediency of particular measures relevant; whether a board or a single commissioner should regulate banks did not involve the question of the appropriateness of doing so. The conception of laissez faire required the total abstention from interference with or participation in economic processes and the restriction of political functions to narrow police powers, mainly the protection of life and property.[29]

In the realm of the practical, in no period of Massachusetts history was this conception of the slightest consequence. From the very first organization of the Commonwealth in 1780, the state actively and vigorously engaged in all the economic affairs of the area, sometimes as participant, sometimes as regulator. Whatever the citizens thought or wrote, they did not act in accordance with the laissez-faire idea.

The rejection of that doctrine was not unconscious. Massachusetts people knew and appreciated the writings of the English liberals—Adam Smith and his successors, British and French. J. B. Say, for instance, had readers by 1820 and was translated a year later. For a long time close ties linked the leaders of the Manchester school and Bay State thinkers, who, however, never espoused the laissez-faire ideas.[30]

No large group or section of the state found those conceptions compatible with its interests. The merchants, the most powerful segment of the community, were throughout the period more than willing to foster interference from the government. They eagerly accepted bounties for their venturesome enterprises, monopolies for the turnpikes, bridges, and canals in which they invested, and inspection laws that guaranteed the security of their export markets.

[29] For the origin of the phrase, cf. August Oncken, *Die Maxime Laissez faire et Laissez passer, ihr Ursprung, ihr Werden* (Bern, 1886). A brief classical statement may be found in J. R. M'Culloch, *Discourse on the Rise, Progress, Peculiar Objects, and Importance, of Political Economy* (Edinburgh, 1824), 53 ff. See also Roberto Michels, *Introduzione alla storia delle dottrine economiche e politiche* (Bologna, 1932), 2–22; Edward R. Kittrell, " 'Laissez Faire' in English Classical Economics," *Journal of the History of Ideas*, XXVII (October–December 1966), 610 ff.

[30] E. R. A. Seligman, "Economists," *Cambridge History of American Literature*, 4 vols. (New York, 1921), IV, 431; Dorfman, *Economic Mind*, II.

At the beginning, it is true, they were dubious about protection. Some importers like Henry Lee always questioned the virtues of the tariff.[31] Until the 1820s, though, that issue affected the general run of traders little. In considering their commercial interests, they believed that the impost was a tax on consumers with little influence on their own profits safeguarded by drawbacks and rebates. As for manufacturing, artificial stimuli could have only a slight effect, and Massachusetts enterprises needed little assistance.[32] Frequently the merchants' attitude toward specific bills was political rather than economic. They supported the earliest tariff measures as part of Hamilton's general scheme; they opposed those of 1816 out of antipathy to the national administration. But they considered the merits of each bill in the light of immediate interests. Daniel Webster made this point bluntly in 1824: "There may be good reasons for favoring some of the provisions of the bill, and equally strong reasons for opposing others; and these provisions do not stand to each other in the relation of principal and incident." The same line of reasoning led him to vote against the Act of 1824 and for that of 1828. In both he wanted duties on woolen and cotton cloth; in both he opposed those on raw cotton, raw wool, molasses, tallow, hemp, and iron. The balance of advantages and disadvantages, not a general attitude toward protection or free trade, was decisive.[33]

In the 1830s expansion of trade with England convinced many that their interests as merchants required a protective tariff. In the free exchange of British manufactures for American staples Boston fell far behind New York, New Orleans, Philadelphia, and Baltimore; the Massachusetts city never acquired the direct communications with the South and the West which sustained the prosperity of her rivals. The niggardliness of her hinterland made Boston's trade, whether with Russia, the East Indies, China, the

---

[31] Henry Lee, *Report of a Committee of the Citizens of Boston and Vicinity* (Boston, 1827) ; J. T. Morse, Jr., *Memoir of Colonel Henry Lee* (Boston, 1905) , 114, 115.

[32] On the importance of drawbacks, see J. T. Austin in *North American Review,* XII (January 1821) , 61 ff. See also F. C. Gray, *ibid.,* X (April 1820) , 317 ff.; *ibid.,* XVII (July 1823) , 188 ff.; Edward Everett, *ibid.,* XIX (July 1824) , 223 ff.

[33] Speeches of April 1, 1824, and May 9, 1828, Daniel Webster, *Works* (Boston, 1853) , III, 95, 228 ff. See also F. W. Taussig, *Tariff History of the United States* (New York, 1923) , 72, 75, 101.

West Indies or the Mediterranean largely triangular. The essential problem of her merchants was how to import without exporting, how to build up a surplus of specie or London credits to serve their worldwide exchanges. Like their European contemporaries, Boston merchants recognized the existence of a fixed balance of trade in which imports always equaled exports. But they also believed, as A. H. Everett explained, that the United States "forms a sort of exception to the general rule." For American cotton was free of competition, its flow limited solely by the needs of the English market. A protective tariff on English imports would not affect the amount of cotton that crossed the Atlantic. Needing as much as before and prevented from paying entirely with their own products, the British would make up the difference by balancing American exports with specie or with credits on London. Sound or not, these doctrines carried weight in the countinghouses of Boston's State Street and pushed important elements in the mercantile community solidly behind the tariff.[34]

Protection was but one facet of the state's merchants' hostility to laissez faire. As exporters of specie in the normal course of trade, they needed a flexible but sound circulating medium, and they looked for strict control by the Commonwealth to keep the value of bank notes constant. Also as traders, eager for improved communications between the seaport and interior markets, they turned to the state for leadership in planning, for monopolies to encourage private enterprise, and for outright grants and guarantees. With B. R. Curtis they incredulously asked: "What people has ever doubted, that the building of roads and bridges was a subject not only fit for the action of government, but necessarily under its *exclusive control?*" And added: "We suppose no one will be so hardy as to attempt to make a distinction between a ferry and a canal, or a bridge and a railroad."[35]

[34] A. H. Everett, "American System," *North American Review*, XXXII (January 1831), 146; Amasa Walker, *Science of Wealth* (Boston, 1866), 327; Lee, *Report*, 155; Francis Bowen, *Principles of Political Economy Applied to . . . the American People* (Boston, 1856), 306 ff., 457 ff. For London credits, see Ralph W. Hidy, "Organization and Function of Anglo-American Merchant Bankers, 1815–1860," *Tasks of Economic History, 1941*, 59, 60. For the export of specie, see Willard Phillips, *North American Review*, IX (September 1819), 224 ff.

[35] B. R. Curtis, "Debts of the States," *North American Review*, LVIII (January 1844), 128, 129; see also Loammi Baldwin and Jared Sparks, *ibid.*, VIII (December 1818), 3 ff., XII (January 1821), 17, 18.

After the middle of the century, as the industrial stake of many merchants increased, their protectionist leanings grew more pronounced. Now they allied themselves with small manufacturers all over New England, whose demands for higher tariffs found ultimate expression in the writings of E. B. Bigelow. Merchants and industrialists generally worked together. But on the rare occasions when their interests diverged both groups looked to the state for assistance, as when financial stringency after the panic of 1857 turned many manufacturers against financial control by Boston merchants.[36] Even when it was to their interest, the owners of industry rarely troubled to invoke laissez-faire arguments. Thus, in opposing the ten-hour movement they argued from inexpediency rather than from theory—the relatively good conditions in the mills and the bad effect on business—while conceding that the state could act "if it should ever appear . . . that the social well-being of society were endangered." Abbott Lawrence expressed the general opinion of both merchants and industrialists that laissez faire was a transcendental philosophy, "not likely to be adopted by any government on the face of the globe."[37]

Equally unlikely to find in this source a pattern for state policy was the other large, politically conscious group, the yeoman farmers. They opposed bank regulation and monopolies which ran counter to their interests. When they reached power in 1843 they abolished the commission which had exerted a dampening influence upon the exuberant finance of some of the country houses. But agriculturists grounded their attitude toward banking in immediate expediency rather than in general theory and, where their own interests dictated, never hesitated to invoke the machinery of the state. For many years they fought for an agency to encourage farming by bounties, education, and other methods, and, at their insistence, many charters between 1792 and 1812 carried provisions for a fixed percentage of loans to the rural interest. The Massachusetts Society for the Promotion of Agriculture had administered state aid since 1792, helped by local societies. Always they

36 Erastus B. Bigelow, *Tariff Policy of England and the United States Contrasted* (Boston, 1877), and *Remarks on the Depressed Condition of Manufacturers in Massachusetts* (Boston, 1858).

37 *Mass. House Docs., 1845,* No. 50; *Mass. Senate Docs., 1846,* No. 81; Hamilton A. Hill, *Memoir of Abbott Lawrence* (Boston, 1884), 169.

were among the most active in getting government support for internal improvements that would benefit them.[38]

Other groups less committed to the status quo couched their ideas of change in terms of new state activities. Artisans and handicraftsmen displaced by new industrial techniques opposed corporate monopolies, but asked the legislature to enact a ten-hour law and to restrict immigration. And a developing proletariat in the new factories also sought help from the same source.[39] Finally, the movement for humanitarian reform in the two decades before the Civil War espoused causes which infringed upon economic matters and assumed that the government could act in such spheres.

The receptive ground for laissez-faire thought was thus thin indeed. Some reformers, like Amasa Walker, became free-traders on the score of their internationalism, and isolated figures like A. L. Perry of Williams College, a follower of Bastiat, held liberal doctrines to a greater or lesser extent, but they were clearly exotic, without influence on the thought or action of the state.[40] Willard Phillips, criticizing Henry Carey's *Political Economy,* summarized Massachusetts opinion when he argued that it was useless to attempt to delimit the sphere of the state, for every action of government affected the economy: "Is it not evident to every man, that a vast proportion of the legislation and administration of the laws, and the police regulations, have a prodigious effect, direct and indirect, upon productive activity? . . . Upon this subject we shall find the British economists most meagre and unsatisfactory. Only the newest and greenest legislators think of looking into their works for principles. The invocation of their authority excites the

[38] St. 1843, ch. 43, *Acts and Resolves* (Boston, 1845) , 26, 66; *Mass. Senate Docs., 1854,* No. 7, p. 10; Arthur B. Darling, *Political Changes in Massachusetts* (New Haven, 1925) , 253; Harry E. Miller, *Banking Theories in the United States before 1860* (Cambridge, 1927) , 148, 160, 161, 173; J. H. Lockwood, ed., *Western Massachusetts,* 4 vols. (New York, 1926) , I, 207 ff.

[39] Darling, *Political Changes in Massachusettes,* 198; Commons, *History of Labour,* I, 291 ff., 302 ff., 493 ff., 536 ff.; Seligman, "Economists," *Cambridge History of American Literature,* IV, 436 ff.

[40] Amasa Walker, *Science of Wealth,* viii, 5, 9, 70, 90 ff., 269 ff., 318, 403 ff., and *Nature and Uses of Money and Mixed Currency* (Boston, 1857) , 52, and *Suicidal Folly of the War-System* (Boston, 1863) ; Francis A. Walker, *Memoir of Hon. Amasa Walker, Ll.D.* (Boston, 1888) , 6, 8–12; Carroll Perry, *Professor of Life: A Sketch of Arthur Latham Perry* (Boston, 1923) , ch. 1.

smile of men experienced in affairs." And the cautious Governor Emory Washburn in his legislative message of 1854 concluded that there was an "intimate connection . . . between the administration of a government and the business prosperity of its citizens."[41]

༆

The Massachusetts economist Francis Bowen exemplified the state's complete rejection of laissez faire as a theory. Others went further than he. John Rae, for instance, who came to Boston to publish his *Statement of Some New Principles* . . . (1834) because he felt its intellectual milieu most receptive to his ideas, denied completely the identity established by Adam Smith between public and private interests and public and private wealth, and thus undermined the whole laissez-faire doctrine. But Bowen was more typical; he accepted the basic premises of the classical thinkers and rejected their laissez-faire implications.

Long editor of the *North American Review* and professor of political economy at Harvard, Bowen was a prolific writer on many subjects. His chief economic work, *Principles of Political Economy Applied to the Condition, the Resources, and the Institutions of the American People* (Boston, 1856), was first delivered as a series of popular lectures, and then published as a textbook, dedicated to Nathan Appleton, one of "the Merchant Princes of Boston." It passed through five editions in little more than a decade, and its basic argument remained unchanged in a complete rewriting in 1870. It thus represented accurately the dominant economic thinking of Massachusetts.[42]

Starting with the same fundamentals as the English writers, Bowen reached conclusions essentially different. With the most optimistic, he believed in a natural order, in "a wise and benevolent arrangement of Providence" that converted individual selfishness into public good. Consequently, he could, a priori and in theory, accept the whole liberal argument. Government action only marred the perfection of the natural order. The function of legislation was "not to meddle with the general laws of the uni-

41 *North American Review*, XLVII (July 1838), 89 ff.; *Mass. Senate Docs., 1854*, No. 3, p. 5.

42 Bowen, *Principles*, iii, vi.

verse," but "to remove all casual and unnatural impediments from
that path which society instinctively chooses for itself."[43]

Bowen, however, considered the abstract theory meaningless. It
acquired significance only in the application to the concrete, practical configuration of the entire economy. English ideas grew out
of English circumstances. "Such theories as those of Malthus upon
population, Ricardo upon rent and profits, Adam Smith upon
free trade, and McCulloch upon . . . the succession to property
. . . originated from experience in an anomalous state of society,
from observation of the laws of wealth as exemplified in their operation under very peculiar circumstances." An American system
had to tailor the general laws of wealth to American circumstances.[44]

In the application Bowen transformed the general laws. Thus,
the ideal system of free trade was impractical because imperfections in the law of nations required that each country be independent economically as well as politically and justified tariffs to
protect infant industries—an argument repeated endlessly by publicists. Also on the count of inconsistency with American conditions, Bowen rejected the Malthusian view on population, using
against it A. H. Everett's demonstration in *New Ideas on Population* (1823) that a rise in numbers led to greater division of labor
and therefore to greater abundance.[45] Bowen set aside Ricardo's
theory of rent on the familiar grounds that in the United States
increases in population brought frontier areas under cultivation
and led to lower prices for lands first settled. The theory of gluts
and crises passed through similar modifications, and a line of
reasoning that anticipated Francis Walker refuted the classical
concepts of a natural rate of wages at the subsistence level and of a
wage fund.[46]

These applications of general theory to American conditions

43 *Ibid.*, 20, 22, 23; *North American Review*, LXXII (April 1851) , 419.

44 Bowen, *Principles*, 13 ff., 522.

45 *Ibid.*, 24, 25, 131 ff., 457 ff.; *North American Review*, LXXII (April 1851) , 414;
also A. H. Everett, *ibid.*, XXX (January 1830) , 160 ff., XXXII (January 1831),
127 ff.; Willard Phillips, *Protection and Free Trade* (Boston, 1850) , Walker, *Science
of Wealth*, 452 ff.

46 Bowen, *Principles*, 164 ff., 193 ff., 271.

persuaded Bowen that, in practice, private and public interests were not identical and, therefore, that state interference was sometimes necessary. Consistently he belabored the point that laissez-faire doctrines fitted English circumstances; they could not apply unchanged to the United States. He convinced his contemporaries.[47]

The American experience, as exemplified in Massachusetts, differed from that of European countries at a similar economic level. Perhaps the well-known work exaggerated in affirming that after Waterloo: "Nothing remained which could possibly check the advent of laissez faire. Free competition became universal. The state renounced all rights of interference either with the organization of production or with the relations between masters and men." The old picture of bright and sturdy liberal ideas marching forth from Manchester to sweep English politics before them required considerable modification. But England did produce a consistent and well-developed body of laissez-faire thought from which, whatever the degree of their real influence, justifications for policy could be drawn. The United States had not even a von Thünen or a Bastiat.[48]

Laissez-faire theory in England and on the continent filled a need which did not exist in America. In the Old World a mass of obstructive practices and laws blocked swiftly moving economic developments. These obstacles and restrictions stemmed from the government and, under the general designation mercantilism, became the objective of a long campaign for liberalization. That is why it was always easier to say what laissez faire opposed than what

[47] *Ibid.,* vi, vii, 457 ff.

[48] Charles Gide and Charles Rist, *History of Economic Doctrines* (Boston, 1914), 170; Paul Mombert, *Geschichte der Nationalökonomie* (Jena, 1927), 277 ff., 307 ff.; Gerald Berkeley Hertz, *British Imperialism* (London, 1908), 123, and *Manchester Politician, 1750–1912* (London, 1912), 27 ff.; Kenneth O. Walker, "Classical Economists and the Factory Acts," *Journal of Economic History,* I (November 1941), 168 ff.; Wilson H. Coates, "Benthamism, Laissez Faire, and Collectivism," *Journal of the History of Ideas,* XI (June 1950), 357 ff.; Arthur J. Taylor, *Laissez-faire and State Intervention in Nineteenth Century Britain* (London, 1972); Colin J. Holmes, "Laissez-faire in Theory and Practice: Britain, 1800–1875," *Journal of European Economic History,* V (Winter 1976), 671 ff.

it favored. In America the practices and laws laissez faire fought
never existed, or were early eliminated. Some, like guild or manor-
ial restrictions, never survived transplantation to the New World;
the War of Independence liquidated others such as the acts of
trade and navigation; and still others, like primogeniture, entail,
and quitrents, yielded to revolutions within the new states.
Frontier conditions also stood in the way; thus, the Northwest
Ordinance of 1787 decided that the United States would have no
colonies for more than a century. Also the relative newness of the
country and the comparative swiftness of economic change inhibited legal formalism and rigidity in institutions. The corporation, for instance, was a much more flexible institution than in
England, and the laws of mills and roads were susceptible of innumerable adaptations to new circumstances. Laissez-faire thought
failed to develop because there was no place for it in the life of
Massachusetts as of the rest of the nation.[49]

The issue in the determination of American economic policy
throughout most of the nineteenth century was not whether the
government had or had not a role in the economy, but the character of its role, what agencies were to exercise it, who was to control it, and in whose interests it was to operate. Theory phrased in
terms of laissez faire was so thoroughly divorced from reality and
practice that it remained completely sterile.

The Massachusetts soil, however, already held the seeds which
after 1880 would yield the nourishment of these scorned ideas. Influential elements in the state no longer needed the intervention
of government and found state activities, once an aid, now a hin-
dance. A new phrasing of laissez faire justified their attitudes.

As the scope of business widened, former merchants became full-
fledged industrial capitalists and their interests became national
and international. In the field of transportation, for instance,
while the Commonwealth still poured its funds into the Hoosac
Tunnel in the vain attempt to wed its languishing seaport to the
Golden West, railroad men already preferred the New York route.
For the sake of secure profits the Boston and Albany Railroad
passed by an opportunity to control the New York Central. The

[49] Morton J. Horwitz, *Transformation of American Law* (Cambridge, 1977),
109 ff.; Handlins, *Commonwealth,* 203 ff.

struggle over the management of the tunnel through the Berk-shires and for control of the Boston, Hartford, and Erie Railroad showed the divergence between the objectives of the state and of those who owned the roads. On a wider scale, some industrialists like Edward Atkinson, eager to develop export markets in the 1870s, turned against restrictive tariffs and joined an embryonic free-trade movement, eventually organized formally in the Society for Political Education.[50]

No longer needing the state, business now used the laissez-faire argument in repelling attacks that mounted in bitterness after 1880. Criticism was not intellectual only; effective legislation, in Massachusetts at least, thrust the state into action. Restrictions on sweatshops drove the factory manufacture of ready-made clothing from Boston to New York in the 1890s. Such measures made con-verts to laissez-faire ideas among entrepreneurs convinced that the government would damage, not support, their interests.

Intellectual changes deepened laissez-faire feeling. The eco-nomic discipline passed through an abrupt transformation. As late as 1880 Cliffe Leslie had noted that economics in the United States was written largely by practical men interested in specific and im-mediate problems. After that date the science became increasingly academic, a trend marked by the establishment of numerous chairs in American colleges, by the founding of the American Economic Association in 1883, and by the publication of professional jour-nals. As the science grew professional and academic, economists lost their local ties. Dunbar, Carver, and Taussig were not Massa-chusetts men in the sense that Bowen, Phillips, or the Walkers had been. In addition, economists tended to play down the role of gov-ernment in order to take the political out of political economy.[51]

After the Civil War also the Darwinian concept of survival of the fittest and the new doctrines of marginal utility strengthened

[50] C. F. Adams' chapter in Justin Winsor, *Memorial History of Boston*, 4 vols. (Boston, 1881), IV, 111 ff., itself an example of the new attitude; also Edward C. Kirkland, *Charles Francis Adams, Jr.* (Cambridge, 1965), 34 ff.; G. S. Merriam, *Life and Times of Samuel Bowles* (New York, 1885), II, 103 ff.; Harold F. Williamson, *Edward Atkinson* (Boston, 1934), 37, 40 ff., 74 ff., 88, 148; F. B. Joyner, *David Ames Wells* (Cedar Rapids, Iowa, 1939), 147 ff.

[51] L. H. Haney, *History of Economic Thought* (New York, 1920), 614; Seligman, "Economists," *Cambridge History of American Literature*, IV, 441; Robert L. Church, "Economists Study Society," in Paul H. Buck, ed., *Social Sciences at Harvard* (Cam-bridge, 1965), 18 ff.; B. J. Loewenberg, "Darwinism Comes to America, 1859–1900," *Mississippi Valley Historical Review*, XXVIII (December 1941), 339 ff.

the theoretical foundation for laissez faire. The concept of the vigilant consumer seeking the ultimate measure of marginal utility replaced the classical concept of benevolently selfish producers competing against each other. As the century drew to a close, laissez faire was fast on the way to ideological dominance.[52]

The term had acquired fresh currency. Twentieth-century Americans, in Massachusetts and elsewhere, uttered it with respect and without the pejorative qualifications of their grandparents; the economic theory it denoted commanded wide assent. The effects on practice were, however, negligible. The tariff continued to rise and the scope of regulatory activity to broaden, so that the gap between theory and actuality widened.

A subtle change in emphasis made the discrepancy tolerable. All those exceptions argued so vigorously in the past by Bowen and others now fell into place as parts of a system within which the term laissez faire acquired a new meaning. By the end of the nineteenth century it no longer implied the total divorce of government from the economy, but only the abstention by the state from a directing role in the productive system. The police function, however, was broad enough to justify—in the name of laissez faire —a wide array of acts bearing on the economy. Politicians, businessmen, union members, and social workers still debated the appropriate course with regard to particular measures, but with a redefined meaning of laissez faire had accommodated the words to the practice of the society.

The experience of laissez faire was not unique. Other terms which denote abstract concepts have proven equally flexible and require equally cautious treatment.

Impatient with the deceptive medium of language, scholars who wish to express their thoughts clearly often long for a precise mode of communication. Those who reach for new knowledge stumble over flintlike and petrified words and, to escape, try to coin others

---

[52] Gaétan Pirou, *L'utilité marginale de C. Menger à J.-B. Clark* (Paris, 1938), 229 ff.; F. A. Fetter, "Amerika," in Hans Mayer, ed., *Die Wirtschaftstheorie der Gegenwart* (Vienna, 1927), I, 41 ff.

to convey their meaning. They run the risk in doing so that their audience will not understand, unless they carefully embed the invented words in a logical structure that contains its own definitions. An excess of such terms drains language of the power to communicate, reducing it to a jargon known only to the initiate, who talk only to themselves. The area of discussion thus screened off may indeed permit conceptual transactions of a subtlety and complexity only a few individuals can share. But privacy may also camouflage commonplace or erroneous or contradictory notions which in their nudity would appall any beholder.[53]

Historians generally are wise enough to refrain from the flight to neologism—first, because their communications draw on words used by others in the past, and, more important, because history does not provide them with the tools of analysis that permit other fields of knowledge to make their own definitions. Nevertheless, historians cannot entirely escape the use of jargon, if not their own, then that defined by others. "The entrepreneur's quest for innovation and profit consciously or unconsciously influences his attitude toward the law." That very simple sentence, when cited earlier in this chapter, may have appeared plain in meaning. But every word in it requires for full understanding a sense of its derivation in the social sciences. If there is one fault worse than using jargon needlessly, it is using jargon unwittingly.

The best of words, the most recently minted and most precisely defined, still retain an awkward plasticity of connotation that inconveniences the analytical scientist, who, therefore, prefers to replace them with symbols and formulae which mean what they mean—exactly. The procedure does render thinking more precise in some instances, but not in all; and the historian must learn to distinguish between the genuinely expressive and that which covers over deficiencies in thought. Numbers are among the symbols which represent quantity; their proper use demands a delicate understanding of their character. Other symbols represent sound; still others convey pictorial images. All require a consciousness of the problems of counting, looking, and listening and of the relation of those processes to other fields of knowledge.

[53] Stanislav Andreski, *Social Sciences as Sorcery* (London, 1972), 59 ff.; Chapter 10, note 43.

# 8

# *How to Count a Number*

THE ARRIVAL of the digital computer has carried the process of counting back to its binary origins.

Behind the hardware, embedded in the programs and shaping their products, lie problems of logic, different in order but of the same sort as those which confronted the men who, ages ago, recognized that two differed from one.

Although some logicians have argued in defense of threeness, essentially one and two exhaust the number concept. All else arises from the process of counting in series and from the combinations and relationships among the arrays of ones and twos.[1]

Historians accustomed to drawing their materials from words have until recently shied away from numbers; having trouble enough with the more familiar verbal symbols, they preferred not to tangle with the less familiar numerical ones. Yet tallies of various sorts survived in the evidence and persistently challenged the interpretive ingenuity of the scholars who uncovered them. The ancient actors recorded transactions that exchanged so much of one thing for so much of another; officials listed the amount of taxes levied and collected; the rosters of passengers on a ship or soldiers in a regiment added up to totals; and periodically surveys or inventories counted acres, heads, possessions.

The historian who used such numbers could usually assume

[1] Oscar Handlin et al., *Harvard Guide to American History* (Cambridge, 1954), 25 ff. Karl Menninger, *Number Words and Number Symbols,* trans. Paul Broneer (Cambridge, 1969), is a very enlightening introduction.

that they were valid, that is, that they were what they purported to be. The customs official noted the barrels landed and the duty paid, and the sums had to conform to those handed over to the collector and passed on to the treasury. Municipalities, banks, railroads, and other agencies that regularly handled money developed internal auditing systems to control transfers, so that the scholar could safely assume that the figures representing passenger miles traveled or checks cleared or taxes assessed closely corresponded to a reality.

With data of this sort the more important questions arose from the definition of the reality to which the figures corresponded. Certainly there were possibilities of error or of inadequacies in the tally or of mistakes in the record; certainly systematic fraud—in the customs houses, for instance—opened a gap between amounts collected and amounts reported. Above all, the source, by virtue of its own limitations, often showed only one among several relevant types of transactions: the barrels cleared through customs did not equal the number imported unless supplemented with information on those smuggled; the count of immigrants to the United States, 1820–1870, was not the same as that of passengers entering its seaports, for a good many arrivals in those years came overland from Canada and the maritime provinces; statistics of crime included only offenses known to the police. A comparison of the totals between one decade and another could be informative when the reality measured was the same, that is, when there was no change in the margin of error, fraud, and scope; but it could also reveal only a redefinition of the terms of counting.

The historian stands on familiar ground in coping with these issues. He deals with numbers as he does with other types of evidence: the document before him is the product of a person who, at a specific moment and place, had a reason for setting down a tally. Allowances for bias and for imperfections in the record are analogous to those called for in the account of a debate or a battle. The count is what it is, no more no less, and, properly appraised, is as serviceable as other observations are.

⁓

The accuracy of the observed data thus limits any use of numbers, no matter how sophisticated are the techniques for manipulating them.[2] The initial quality of the tally affects alike the validity of the simplest 2 plus 2 and the most complex computation of multiple regression. But the historian is particularly circumscribed in this respect. He cannot experiment, cannot, under most circumstances, gather his material at first hand; for the universe with which he deals has disappeared. He depends on ancient intermediaries and cannot improve the quality of the count. He must, therefore, carefully examine the validity and reliability of the measurements he uses, as other social scientists do. But, in addition, he must also respect the intractable character of the sources of his information, about which he can do little. The origins of sets of numbers are critical: those which emanate from a despotic regime, in which the incentive to falsification lurks all along the line from the tallyman to the supreme ruler, differ from those in an open society subject to repeated internal and external checks; those in literate organizations which value precision differ from those in bodies given to vagueness and generality. Population figures for Britain and the United States are of a totally different kind from those of Nigeria or China, so that per-capita comparisons have little meaning.

These considerations are particularly important to students of early American history, before the organization of state and federal governments. A substantial fund of quantitative data for the colonial era exists in the reports of officials, the administrative records of English and provincial authorities, tax lists, and parish records. Employed with care, such material may yield significant information. But it demands treatment with discrimination. Those who disregard its uncertain origins, its fragmentary nature, and its ambiguity are doomed to disastrous errors of interpretation.[3]

2 Oskar Morgenstern, *On the Accuracy of Economic Observations* (Princeton, 1950) ; Frank H. Knight, "Quantification: The Quest for Precision" and Jacob Viner, "Comments," in Louis Wirth, ed., *Eleven Twenty-Six* (Chicago, 1940) , 168 ff., 177 ff. See also Roger Lane, "Crime and Criminal Statistics in Nineteenth-Century Massachusetts," *Journal of Social History*, II (Winter 1968) , 156 ff.

3 Few quantitative studies were more often quoted than James A. Henretta, "Economic Development and Social Structure in Colonial Boston," *William and Mary Quarterly*, XXII (January 1965) , 75 ff., until it was demolished by G. B. Warden, "Inequality and Instability in Eighteenth-Century Boston," *Journal of Interdisciplinary History*, VI (Spring 1976) , 585 ff., which also disposed of Alan Kulikoff, "Progress of Inequality in Revolutionary Boston," *William and Mary Quarterly*, XXVIII

The fund of numerical data grew rapidly in the centuries after independence. As earlier, much of the accumulation was by agencies of government, the expanding social role of which showed itself in the development, elaboration, and refinement of techniques of collection and analysis. The change was particularly striking on the national level; by the twentieth century, the most important, best classified, and most readily available compilations emanated from Washington.

The earliest statistical work of the United States Government sprang out of the customs and census services. Duties on foreign imports were long the main source of federal revenue, and the Treasury Department regularly reported on them. Figures on foreign commerce and navigation became increasingly detailed and broader in scope in the nineteenth century especially after the creation of the Bureau of Foreign and Domestic Commerce. After 1875 some records of internal trade and finance supplemented these materials.

The Constitution required a decennial census for the purpose of fixing congressional representation; and the assignment originally went to United States marshals working under the direction of the State Department. The officials listed white males over and under age sixteen, white females, other free persons, and slaves. To population figures were added, in 1810, manufactures; in 1820, occupations; in 1840, mines, agriculture, commerce, illiteracy, insanity, and pensioners; in 1850, libraries, newspapers and periodicals, and criminals. The machinery and techniques of enumeration were not equal to these ambitious programs, and the results were correspondingly open to error. Not until 1830 did the marshals receive uniform printed schedules which provided them with at least a general guide; and political considerations undoubtedly severely distorted the count of 1840.[4]

The census of 1850 was the first to aspire to scientific accuracy. A central office in the new Interior Department then compiled and classified the raw data. Later, Francis Walker and other scholars tried to add precision to the count. But centralized con-

---

(July 1971), 375 ff., and Kenneth A. Lockridge, "Land, Population and the Evolution of New England Society, 1630–1790," *Past & Present*, XXXIX (April 1968), 62 ff.

4 William Stanton, *Leopard's Spots* (Chicago, 1960), 58 ff.

trol of supervisors and enumerators waited until 1880; the results for that year appeared in twenty-four volumes, five times as many as in any previous census. Machine tabulation appeared in 1890, and a permanent Census Bureau with its own staff in 1902. The Bureau broke up the decennial cycle by enumerations at more frequent intervals, such as the biennial census of manufactures. In 1906 it added a religious census and in 1940 began to use sampling techniques. Subsequent counts varied somewhat in coverage and in techniques. Errors of some consequence sometimes distorted the totals, but strict professional standards and relative freedom from political pressure gave the Bureau's work a high degree of credibility.[5]

The routine administration of government inexorably heaped up piles of numbers; the more numerous the agencies, the higher the piles. The reports of departments and regulatory bodies dealing with specific problems—agriculture, immigration, labor, conservation, public health—and of independent commissions on interstate commerce, trade, communications, and aviation contained masses of quantitative data generated by law enforcement, subsidy payments, investigation, and regulation. The Federal Reserve Board and Banks similarly collected material on finance. Special ad hoc inquiries by Congress through its committees, by administrative agencies, and by the courts from time to time also uncovered mines of numbers valuable because elicited by topical and controversial questions, but also correspondingly subject to bias.

*The Statistical Abstract of the United States,* issued annually by various agencies after 1878, contained general information on practically every subject for which government and certain other bodies collected data. Besides annual figures it included the most recent statistics assembled at longer intervals. In 1949 the Bureau of the Census issued a supplement, *Historical Statistics of the United States, 1789–1945,* a convenient compendium with helpful

[5] See Jacob S. Siegel, "Estimates of Coverage of Population," *Demography,* XI (February 1974), 1 ff.; A. J. Coale and N. W. Rives, Jr., "Statistical Reconstruction of the Black Population," *Population Index,* XXXIX (January 1973), 3 ff.; Ann Herbert Scott, *Census, U.S.A.* (New York, 1968), is a simple, uncritical history. For the British census, see E. A. Wrigley, ed., *Nineteenth Century Society: Essays in the Use of Quantitative Methods for the Study of Social Data* (Cambridge, 1972), 7 ff., 82 ff., 134, 311 ff.

notes on sources and their use, which it twice revised (1960, 1975).

⌒

State and municipal materials varied considerably in nomenclature, quantity, and quality. Early nineteenth-century registration laws compelled most jurisdictions to gather information on births, marriages, and deaths—the basis of all subsequent demographic studies. Local governments faced problems of taxation and representation that called for numerical data, especially when changes in political thought expanded their police and reform functions. Long before Washington felt the concern, city and state agencies collected information on public carriers, public health, education, industry, and the conditions of labor in response to demands for legislation and regulation. In addition, Massachusetts, New York, and Michigan for a time had more comprehensive censuses than the federal one. State agencies also served as the training ground for many statisticians who later commanded the federal government's expanding statistical apparatus. The Massachusetts Bureau of Labor Statistics, organized in 1869, earliest of many similar state bureaus, provided Carroll D. Wright with the experience he used in organizing the national department.[6]

Privately collected statistics met only private standards and varied accordingly. The American Iron and Steel Institute and other industrial and commercial organizations long gathered information on production and exchange. Reliable stock exchange records began early. Periodic reports in trade journals, like *Iron Age* or the *Publishers Weekly,* and in the business sections of newspapers made such material available. Chambers of commerce and boards of trade often gathered and published data. Private manuals, like Moody's and Standard and Poor, and periodicals of general business interest, like *Barron's,* conveniently drew together numbers gathered elsewhere. Farmer, labor, and professional associations—from the A.F. of L. and the C.I.O. to the American Medical Association—assembled counts of the number, distribution, and education of their members. Occasional studies

6 James R. Leiby, *Carroll Wright and Labor Reform* (Cambridge, 1960).

by advertising agencies like J. Walter Thompson touched on the problems of population and marketing. Insurance companies required data on fires, floods, and theft, as well as on mortality, health, and population. Early and late, reformers gathered the facts to prove their cases, as they argued in behalf of abolition, prohibition, suffrage, education, or eugenics.

Of a different order were fact-books or almanacs, often associated with newspapers. The *Tribune Almanac,* the *World Almanac,* and the *Information Please Almanac* were modern versions of the compilations of Tench Coxe, Pelatiah Webster, and Adam Seybert, as well as of registers like Niles and Hazard. In addition, many early gazetteers were repositories of miscellaneous information. Handled with care, all these works may be useful for the counts they report first- or secondhand.[7]

Other types of enumeration differ in their provenance and call for other precautions. Not all arrays of numbers trace or memorialize actual transactions; some are compiled contemporaneously or retrospectively for other reasons. The historian must understand the purposes that brought them into being and affected their character.

Statistics—the derivation of the word reveals the nature of such numbers and of the ways of treating them.

Statistics developed in early modern times as a form of applied political science. Conscientious legislators, monarchs, and administrators who dealt with the concrete problems of state needed information which they believed they could derive from the accumulation and systematic ordering of the numbers scattered through the documents that crossed their desks. Individuals and groups of subjects and citizens who sought to influence governmental decisions felt the same need. The appropriate figures, all hoped, would point to the appropriate policies. Often of course the figures deemed appropriate, then and later, were such as justified policies advocated for other reasons. Sometimes, indeed, the prudent historian discovers that policy considerations shaped the very mode of organizing and tabulating the data.

7 Handlin, *Harvard Guide,* 76 ff., 161 ff.

In the late seventeenth and early eighteenth centuries the Englishmen John Graunt and William Petty, among others, tried to convert the study of population into a quantitative science susceptible of theoretical abstraction. They still put considerable emphasis on practical utility, as did later writers on "political arithmetic"; but, in addition, the numbers themselves fascinated these scholars who aspired to develop a systematic understanding of the nature of numerical groupings. Through most of the nineteenth century, however, the major emphasis remained on the accumulation of data, medical and social as well as economic.[8]

Improvements in technique aimed primarily at making the material gathered as exhaustive and as wide in coverage as possible. The American Statistical Association, founded (1838) in emulation of its English counterpart by a group of Boston professional men led by Lemuel Shattuck, attracted a national constituency in the universities and in government service. Its *Journal* (1888–    ) and other publications reflected its members' interest in technical problems but also included miscellaneous quantitative series of high quality. Statistical research organizations later became more specialized. The National Bureau of Economic Research, the National Industrial Conference Board, and the Brookings Institution sponsored investigations into areas the government was slow to consider: for instance, the determination of national income, of employment, of the size of the labor force, and of productivity.

By then, however, statisticians had discovered the inadequacy of actual numbers and had embarked on a search for alternative modes of measurement more satisfactory for their purposes. In the eighteenth century efforts to compile series that would trace changes in prices ran afoul of the obstacle that the values of the money were themselves subject to sharp fluctuation, so that a rise in the cost of corn could reflect either scarcity of grain or abundance of cash. Before long, insurers learned that crude mortality rates could not tell them the odds of an individual's death unless

8 John Graunt, *Natural and Political Observations* (London, 1662), ed. Walter F. Willcox (Baltimore, 1939); Richard H. Shryock, "History of Quantification in Medical Science," in Harry Woolf, ed., *Quantification* (Indianapolis, 1961), 95 ff.; Paul F. Lazarsfeld, "Notes on the History of Quantification in Sociology," *ibid.,* 151 ff.; M. J. Cullen, *Statistical Movement in Early Victorian Britain* (New York, 1975), 38, 39, 64; Wrigley, *Nineteenth-Century Society,* 336 ff.

they knew the distribution of the population among age groups. Nor was it possible to predict the future trend of population from the birth rate without an indication of the percentage of women in the child-bearing cohort.

Life tables, which separated organized mortality experience by ages and laid the basis for calculating expectancy, involved little more than precise modes of counting and averaging. Similar refinements applied to fertility and marital status. But price computations exposed a problem that remained troubling for more than a century: how to find an average that would trace the changing relation of commodities to gold. The London *Economist* in 1869 began to track the prices of twenty-two items, and scholars thereafter wrestled with the issues involved in choosing the appropriate goods, in weighting them, and in finding the proper arithmetic or geometric mean. Ultimately dollars and cents proved intractable; instead, an index number pinned to a specific time provided an abstract reference point against which to measure changes in relative value. The index, though not an actual number, could be as valuable to the historian aware of its meaning as to the economist.

Representative, or relative, or average numbers replaced actual ones in many computations which sought to separate short- from long-term, primary from secondary reactions. Charles Dow thus expected to understand stock market fluctuations; and judgments which distinguished secular, cyclical, and seasonal trends from chance variations were basic to theories of growth and of the business cycle. Calculations of the Gross National Product, increasingly subtle after 1950, depended upon such abstractions; and diligent economists led by Simon S. Kuznets built up retrospective series of data that reached far back into the historian's territory.

The impressive precision of these statistics may tempt the incautious scholar to forget that they are abstractions which measure only what they purport to measure. The product, for instance, is the product which passes through the market. Fees paid a nursing home count; the identical service by the family does not. The commercial laundry, yes; the do-it-yourself laundromat, no. A change in the number up or down may reflect a change in output or an adjustment in the market's share. Or it may reflect an alteration in the index itself. The same caution applies to figures on unemployment, consumer prices, and corporate profits. Inadequate allowances for the shifting mix of market and non-market elements diminish the utility of efforts to push those indexes back in time.[9]

৵৹

While the economists and demographers led the way to use of abstract numbers, mathematicians and logicians explored the utility of partial ones.

The Belgian, L. A. J. Quetelet suggested the means of finding some order in a large, seemingly random universe. The title of his *Letters on the Application of Probabilities to the Moral and Political Sciences* (Brussels, 1846; London, 1849), stated an exciting proposition. It was not necessary to count every nose of a large population, only of a part large enough to permit an estimate of the whole. Later, Charles Sanders Peirce noted the utility of reasoning from samples; and empirically manufacturers of hats and shoes for mass markets learned that a few sizes would fit all heads and feet.[10]

A decisive shift came in the last quarter of the nineteenth century, when geneticists dealing with subjects that involved very large numbers began to work out sampling techniques with the aid of the calculus of probability. From their studies emerged increasingly dependable tests of reliability. Later, investigators in the field of public health, psychologists, and sociologists as well as advertisers, pollsters, and marketing specialists took up and developed the method.

Sampling is a process of reasoning from a part to the whole, but a process in which the reasoner selects the part by criteria designed

[9] See Martin S. Feldstein, "Economics of the New Unemployment," *Public Interest*, no. 33 (Fall 1973), 3 ff.; Michael R. Darby, "Three-and-a-Half Million U.S. Employees Have Been Mislaid," *Journal of Political Economy*, LXXXIV (February 1976), 1 ff.; Joseph J. Spengler, "On the Progress of Quantification in Economics," in Woolf, *Quantification*, 137 ff.; Peter Temin, *New Economic History* (Harmondsworth, 1973), 22 ff.

[10] Charles S. Peirce, "Illustrations of the Logic of Science. III. Doctrine of Chances," *Popular Science Monthly*, XII (March 1878), 604 ff. See also Wrigley, *Nineteenth-Century Society*, 146 ff.; Edwin G. Boring, "Beginning and Growth of Measurement in Science," in Woolf, *Quantification*, 109 ff.

to make it representative of the whole. Sometimes, however, only the part survives among the records of the past, so that the calculator must appraise its relation to the whole by an operation analagous to sampling, but also akin to extrapolation. Sellers imply buyers; figures on the volume of sales say something about the volume of purchases. On the basis of a well-rounded analytical theory, the ingenious statistician can expand fragments of information into reconstructed family data and into impressive series tracing changes in production, transportation, and money. The demographer or economist can run projections backward as well as forward and count such uncountables as illegal aliens.[11]

In the employment of the products of all these devices which enormously expand the available evidence, the historian can never afford to forget that they generate probable or abstract but not actual numbers. They rest on fragile factual underpinnings; and the web of theory which holds them in place is subject to frequent rearrangement. Above all, in treating unique events rather than a theoretical pattern, the margin of tolerance is narrower than that of the social scientists. The mesh of statistical probability is not fine enough to satisfy the requirements of historical probability. In dealing with the numbers of art, even more than with those of actuality, he must take account both of inner logic and of corresponding reality.

All meaningful arrays of numbers are kinds of counting. Every series, therefore, shows a distribution along a time or some other axis. The meaning lies in the display of a tendency to centrality or dispersion and in the correlations with, or variations among, one series and another or others. Regularities call for explanation: if money income goes up with the school years completed that points to a relationship between education and earning (either attendance adds to wealth; or those with wealth attend). Irregularities also call for explanation: the number of marriages for every thousand unmarried females dropped steadily after 1920, except between 1940 and 1950, when exceptional social circumstances prevailed. Swings or reversals in trend likewise suggest significant questions, as when Joseph Schumpeter adapted the

11 James K. Kindahl, "Estimation of Means and Totals from Finite Populations of Unknown Size," *Journal of the American Statistical Association,* LVII (March 1962), 61 ff.

waves Kondratieff had perceived in agriculture to the cycles in business activity. As the analysis of variance gained importance in every form of scientific analysis, the tools of regression, scaling, and factor comparison grew increasingly sophisticated, so that those who employed them sometimes ran the risk of forgetting their purpose.[12]

Not every correlation of deviation is meaningful. Some simply restate what is otherwise known. Others camouflage the unknown with the appearance of certainty.[13] And some, though plausible, remain unexplained—the relation of falling fertility and mortality rates to urbanization and industrialization, for instance. Only an effort at explanation will reveal whether the analogy implied by the appearance of parallelism is deceptive or conforms to some reality. The "number of persons accused of crime in France between 1826 and 1844 was, by a singular coincidence, about equal to the male deaths which took place in Paris during the same period."[14] Perhaps, or no doubt; but so what? A skilled student of linguistics moved on from the analysis of the frequency distribution of words and their constituent parts in the stream of speech to newspaper obituaries, concert programs, the size of cities, and migrations and discovered a generalized harmonic series expressible in a single equation and applicable to all. The historian must shrug off the obligations to explain these results.[15]

[12] Simon Kuznets, "Long Swings in the Growth of Population and in Related Economic Variables," American Philosophical Society, *Proceedings,* CII (1968), 25 ff.; Gaston Imbert, *Des Mouvements de longue durée Kondratieff,* 3 vols. (Aix-en-Provence, 1956), I, 2, 3. Most forms of content analysis depend on counting frequencies of words assumed to be identical, e.g., J. David Singer, *Quantitative International Politics* (New York, 1968); also Chapter 11 at note 44.

[13] For example, James K. Martin, *Men in Rebellion: Higher Governmental Leaders and the Coming of the American Revolution* (New Brunswick, N.J., 1973); Edward M. Cook, *Fathers of the Towns: Leadership and Community Structure in Eighteenth-Century New England* (Baltimore, 1976). See also Stanislav Andreski, *Social Sciences as Sorcery* (London, 1972), 123 ff.

[14] Henry Thomas Buckle, *History of Civilization in England* (New York, 1858), I, 19.

[15] George K. Zipf, "Generalized Harmonic Series as a Fundamental Principle of Social Organization," *Psychological Record,* IV (1940), 43 ff., and "Some Psychological Determinants of the Structure of Publications," *American Journal of Psychology,* LVIII (October 1945), 425 ff., and "Repetition of Words," *Journal of General Psychology,* XXXII (January 1945), 127 ff., and "On the Dynamic Structure of Concert-Programs," *Journal of Abnormal and Social Psychology,* XLI (January 1946), 25 ff.,

Tests of the utmost ingenuity confirm the statistical validity of measurement techniques; they are not good enough for the historian unless they conform to other evidence and demonstrate in answer to his question "what is being measured?" that they measure the real world.

⟨⟨⟨⟩⟩⟩

The computer transformed a realm grown increasingly abstract by bringing it back to the world of ones and twos. The long quest for a speedy way of counting and sorting had drifted into mechanical and electrical bypaths and gotten entangled with dreams of robotlike intelligence before the digital computer recognized the difference between ones and twos and thereby acquired the capacity to handle vast quantities of numbers, actual or abstract, with enormous rapidity and accuracy.

The computer eliminated the need for immense amounts of paper work. But it solved no intellectual problems. Although its pipe attracted numerous followers, especially those favored with generous foundation grants, it did not transform the practice of history. The questions of logic and of conformity to reality remained and, indeed, grew more urgent when raised with reference to large, total, inflexible systems. Manuals more often informed their readers how to do it than explained what was being done. Instead, to the extent that the excitement obscured underlying issues, the new hardware impeded understanding—which was the fault not of the computer but of those who misused it.[16]

*Time on the Cross,* the most widely read work in the genre, did not suffer from lack of attention.[17] Long before the book ap-

and $\frac{\text{``}P_1P_2}{D}$ Hypothesis" *Journal of Psychology,* XXII (July 1946), 3 ff., and $\frac{\text{``}P_1P_2}{D}$ Hypothesis," *American Sociological Review,* XI (December 1946), 677 ff., and "Frequency and Diversity of Business Establishments," *Journal of Psychology,* XXIV (July 1947), 139 ff., and "Hypothesis of the 'Minimum Equation,'" *American Sociological Review,* XII (December 1947), 627 ff., and *Human Behavior and the Principle of Least Effort* (Cambridge, 1949), 374 ff.

16 For example, Edward Shorter, *Historian and the Computer* (Englewood Cliffs, N.J., 1971); Roderick Floud, *Introduction to Quantitative Methods for Historians* (London, 1973); also Morton Rothstein, et al., "Quantification and American History," in Herbert J. Bass, ed., *State of American History* (Chicago, 1970), 304 ff.

17 Robert William Fogel and Stanley L. Engerman, *Time on the Cross: The Economics of American Negro Slavery,* 2 vols. (Boston, 1974); Oscar Handlin, "The Capacity of Quantitative History," *Perspectives in American History,* IX (1975), 7 ff.

peared it was the subject of nationwide discussion based on advance drafts and proofs broadcast throughout the land. Once published, the two volumes received prompt attention in the most important reviewing media and made the material for news stories in the country's most prestigious papers. Articles in support and rebuttal sprouted in the journals; and within the year of *Time*'s first appearance, conference after conference convened to pass judgment upon it.

Yet the hullabaloo obscured the significance of the book. Predictably, the Xerox blizzard subsided, the symposia tapes gathered dust, and newer fads edged *Time on the Cross* aside, unassimilated—which was a pity. This was an important work, not only for its conclusions about slavery but also for the method it exemplified. Both deserved serious consideration and did not get it because of near-fatal flaws in presentation and in publishing strategy.

Fogel and Engerman did not make it easy for historians to come to grips with *Time on the Cross*. By dividing it into two volumes—one a narrative, the other evidence—they sought to evade the problem of combining literary exposition and statistical data. In the event, they only compounded the difficulty. The arrangement demanded inordinate time and patience on the part of the reader who wished to check from the text to the notes, which were further laden with an elaborate pattern of cross-references. Furthermore, the distinction between narrative and evidence was by no means clear-cut, so that there was often no explaining what went where. As a result, it was extraordinarily difficult to associate the argument with the proof on which it rested. The rhetorical statements in Volume I were not precisely anchored in the data of Volume II and were sometimes significantly qualified and conditioned there. Yet, to have accepted or rejected the book on the basis of the narrative volume alone would have been a mistake; the task of assessment required constant reference, paragraph by paragraph, to the evidence proffered in Volume II. The time-consuming and difficult process of tracking down the sources uncovered serious gaps between the narrative and its evidence.

The elaborate promotional endeavors which preceded, accompanied, and followed publication compounded the difficulty of judgment. The publication strategy aimed to provoke controversy, and did so. Whatever gratification or pain the attendant furor brought the authors, it did not further dispassionate judgment. Many readers approached the book with opinions already formed, partisans for or against. Though the Fogel and Engerman sweatshirt worn by one youthful participant at the Rochester Conference (October 1974) went to an extreme, it manifested the team spirit that animated and distorted much of the subsequent discussion there. The mood of partisanship whipped up by the promotional efforts encouraged confrontation, not reflection; emphasis upon debating points, rather than considered judgments of very difficult problems.

The authors further fanned the flames of acrimony by stating their thesis in exaggerated and provocative terms. They trumpeted the book as a triumphant vindication of the pretensions of quantitative techniques and as a total revision of all previous interpretations of American slavery. On both accounts Fogel and Engerman were wrong and misleading.

It was late in the day for a crusade to persuade historians of the importance of quantitative techniques. All that was old hat in 1974. Historians objected not to the methodology, but to the wild claims made on its behalf and particularly to the assertion that its findings rested on a higher plane of reliability and certainty than those arrived at by other means (I, 10). The demand for absolute sovereignty weakened the more modest legitimate case.

"Unfortunately, many of the debates over the role of quantitative methods in history have been marred by a partisanship and dogmatism that are more appropriate to contending political ideologists than to scholars" (II, 10). The authors recognized the pitfall, then stumbled into it. Fogel and Engerman may have recalled the Williamstown Convention of 1957, when the quantifiers nailed their manifesto to the door; they did not recall the warning then sounded of the dangerous consequences of adopting an adversary posture toward other ways of knowing the past. Nor did they show evidence of having heeded the same caution voiced at the Mathematical Social Science Board meeting in Cambridge (1965), which launched the serious effort to support their enterprise. Instead, the cliometricians, unwilling to recognize the existence of other methods or the limitations of their own, displayed the zeal of a missionary sect guarding the one truth essential to salvation. And the more fervid their assertions of certainty, the less likely they were to win converts, particularly since bitter internecine squabbles belied the pretension to certain precise knowledge. The unfounded claim to having rewritten much of all economic history (I, 7) disposed the curious onlooker simply to write the whole lot off.

Thus, everybody else had been wrong on slavery. That misleading pose deprived *Time on the Cross* of much of the value it could have had. Fogel and Engerman began by asserting erroneously that a broad consensus in the understanding of slavery had gradually emerged by the midpoint of the twentieth century, repeated so often that it had the status of a traditional interpretation, taught in high schools and college classes across the nation (I, 3). On ten specific points the authors challenged the traditional interpretation. (There was some discrepancy in the counting for in II, 169, the refutation of the economic indictment of slavery ran to only five points.)

Who were the holders of the traditional interpretation thus laid low? In what texts did it appear and by what scholars was it espoused? Fogel and Engerman named no names. In fact, elsewhere (II, 168 ff.) they showed the great variety of viewpoints on these issues. A chapter on slavery in a typical 1967 American history college textbook displayed no resemblance whatever to the position they described.[18] Although some writers held some of the views enumerated, that was far from adding up to a coherent, traditional interpretation. Fogel and Engerman erected a straw man the more easily to demolish him: that tactic of controversy attracted attention; it did not win converts.

The result was calamitous for the evaluation of the book. The process of review, reflection, judgment, and assimilation of historical works is difficult enough when it proceeds leisurely, without passion, and extends over a long period. But in this case the exaggerations choked off the power of judgment. The fatuous rave review in the Sunday *New York Times* was no more adequate in assessing the work than the indignant denunciation in *Dædalus* or the bland summary in the *New York Review of Books*.[19] A few scholars took respectful exception to one point or another

18 Oscar Handlin, *History of the United States* (New York, 1967), I, 517 ff.

19 Peter Passell, *New York Times Book Review*, April 28, 1974, p. 4; David Brion Davis, "Slavery and the Post-World War II Historians," *Daedalus*, CIII (Spring 1974), 11 ff.; C. Vann Woodward, *New York Review of Books*, XXI (May 2, 1974), 3 ff.

of the argument; and the mathematical economists at once began to chip away at the evidence, providing, despite self-serving declarations of allegiance to the method, an ironic commentary on its claims to precision.[20]

Polarization of opinion prevented a clear definition of the historical problems raised by *Time on the Cross,* much less their resolution. Historians intimidated by the mathematics shied away from serious entanglement with the book and remained unaware, therefore, of the serious, subtle conceptual issues it raised.

This analysis begins with a paradigm. It is true that after publication Fogel and Engerman qualified the conclusion reached in the passage which follows. But the point is, nevertheless, central to much of their interpretation, and the reasons why they went astray are instructive.

They wished to refute the allegation that slave women were indifferent to their children and casual in sexual relations: "The distribution of the ages of mothers at the time of the birth of their first surviving child . . . contradicts the charge that black girls were frequently turned into mothers at such tender ages as twelve, thirteen, and fourteen. Not only was motherhood at age twelve virtually unknown, and motherhood in the early teens quite uncommon, but the average age at first birth was 22.5 (the median age was 20.8). Thus the high fertility rate of slave women was not the consequence of the wanton impregnation of very young unmarried women by either white or black men, but of the frequency of conception after the first birth. By far the great majority of slave children were borne by women who were not only quite mature, but who were already married" (I, 137).

On the basis of this finding, *Time on the Cross* proceeded to demolish the myth that sexual promiscuity destroyed the black family. Thence it was but a brief step to an idyllic portrait of

[20] David Rothman, "Slavery in a New Light," *New Leader,* May 27, 1974, pp. 7–9; John W. Blassingame, "Mathematics of Slavery," *Atlantic Monthly,* CCXXXIV (August 1974), 78; "Econometrics of Slavery: A Symposium," *Reviews in American History,* II (December 1974), 457 ff.; Paul A. David and Peter Temin, "Slavery: the Progressive Institution?" *Journal of Economic History,* XXXIV (June 1974), 379 ff.; "Symposium on Time on the Cross," *Explorations in Economic History,* XII (October 1975); Herbert G. Gutman, *Slavery and the Numbers Game* (Urbana, Ill., 1975); Paul A. David et al., *Reckoning with Slavery* (New York, 1976).

slave marriage performed in churches or in the big house under
the benevolent oversight of the masters (I, 128) .

An examination of the data on first births revealed the perils
in this easy progression. Fogel and Engerman wrestled manfully
with some of the statistical problems. They drew their data from
the probate records of fifty-four counties in eight Southern states
between 1775 and 1865 which enumerated 80,000 slaves. This was
a larger and probably more reliable fund of information than
any theretofore available, and its accumulation called for tremendous effort.

But questions about the validity of the sample remained. The
evidence presented revealed neither the number of family units
represented among the total of 80,000 individuals nor their chronological or geographical distribution, although it would make an
immense difference whether most of the cases clustered around
1780 in Virginia or around 1850 in Alabama. The aggregate,
alone given, could conceal variations of tremendous significance.

Such problems might yield to additions to, or refinement of,
the data. A serious question would remain. Did the age of birth
of the first surviving child measure either age of marriage or age
of first sexual experience? The early death of some offspring and
the sale of others before their names appeared in the probate
registers affected the answer to a degree not precisely quantifiable,
as did miscarriage and abortions, again in a number not count-
able. The result was certainly an upward bias in the stated average
of 22.5 years. And indeed the authors conceded to readers who
followed them into Volume II (114) that the average yielded
by data in the plantation records was for unexplained reasons a
year lower. Still other data, participants in the Rochester Conference heard, might bring the average down to eighteen—which
would make all the difference in the world.

Wherever the line was set, the question still remained: was 22.5
or 21.5 or 18 high or low? The authors recognized but did not
answer the question (II, 114, 115) . Figures from other societies
tended to be higher, which suggested that slave women gave birth
at a relatively early age; but all these comparisons were necessarily
inconclusive. What was quite certain was that the data they presented did not support the elaborate edifice Fogel and Engerman
erected upon it.

The bar chart (I, 138) which summarized their numbers suggested quite another conclusion. It called attention to the consistent preference in the discussion for reference to the average rather than to the median. Understandably, the authors selected the higher figure which supported their case better than the lower. The chart explained why the median was significantly below the average.

A substantial number of first births after the age of thirty pulled the average up. But the largest cohort of mothers (about 35 percent) encompassed ages at first birth between fifteen and nineteen, and some 5 percent more fell within the fifteen-and-under group. In the effort to recreate a picture of plantation life, the last figure was the most significant—that fully 5 percent of all surviving first births were to girls aged fifteen or less.

To scholars able to think realistically of the human relations under nineteenth-century American slavery, that was a number laden with meaning. To scholars willing to think imaginatively, it said much about the tensions generated by the peculiar institution. The number did not controvert any existing interpretation; perhaps, therefore, it was not sensational. But it fitted in, expanded the understanding of historical actuality.

To focus upon that number was to become aware that, despite their statistics, Fogel and Engerman were not wholly incorrect in their depiction of family life among the slaves. In their eagerness to shoot holes in the literary evidence, they misread it. Where did they find the stereotype of sexual promiscuity "published by many in both the abolitionist and slaveholding camps and accepted in traditional historiography" (I, 138)? *Uncle Tom's Cabin* celebrated the family ties among slaves, sustained under adverse conditions; and many an apologist justified Southern bondage by the extent to which it protected the family unit.[21]

Critics did point to the fear induced by the master-slave relationship and also to its corrosive human effects. And in that respect 5 percent was enough. How many rapes without redress, how many dangled inducements to acquiescence, how many mistresses to a master did it take to create fear and its attendant anxieties? Quantification may help approach the question. It does not provide the answer.

21 See also Herbert G. Gutman, *Black Family in Slavery and Freedom, 1750–1925* (New York, 1976).

✑

Fogel and Engerman went astray because they started from an adversary position, determined to use their data to create a new model rather than to amplify or modify the existing interpretations, which they incorrectly assumed formed a coherent, outmoded model. Time and time again valuable material went to waste because it was harnessed to the perverse intention of demonstrating the contrariety of quantitative as against conventional/traditional/narrative history.

Yet historians of whatever camp deal with essentially the same problems, so whoever confines himself to one type of evidence needlessly narrows his vision. The new computer-driven techniques extend the ability to mobilize and use large amounts of information. But in themselves they solve no problems; and precisely because their power is greater than those of the weapons earlier historians commanded, their use requires more care. Those who disregard any but their own experience will be condemned to mistakes others have learned to avoid.

The ancient practices of counting and measuring are basic to quantification as to much of history in general. Fogel and Engerman mastered the most ingenious statistical methods of how to and what; but they were unaware that historians, deliberately or reflexly, also had ways of knowing how and what to count and measure whenever they dealt with such aggregates as Americans, Southerners, planters, merchants, banks, or corporations. The particulars which fell within these categories were alike in some but not in all respects, and to determine what belonged together and what did not required sensitivity to variations of time and place. One would enumerate Texans among the citizens of the United States in 1870, not in 1780. Simple. By the same token, quantifiers should be conscious that roll-call votes do not test party loyalty, that mean household size may indicate nothing about family structure, and that shares of income need not reflect social class position.

✑

*What are we counting?* Slaves—80,000 from probate records, 1775–1865, and many thousands more from census schedules,

plantation accounts, and other sources spread across the South
in the same ninety years.

Do all those integers belong together in the sense that, for the
purpose the numbers serve, the apples and oranges have enough
in common to be counted together as fruit? We can trust that
Fogel and Engerman applied the appropriate statistical tests for
deviance by time and place, although it would have been nice
had some indication that they did so in either volume relieved us
of the necessity of resting on faith alone. But clearly they did not
apply the appropriate historical tests. They simply assumed that
a slave was a slave was a slave. Slavery, one of "the most long-lived
forms of economic and social organization," reached back to the
dawn of civilization (I, 13). If the institution described in
Thomas More's *Utopia* seemed identical with that which flourished in Mississippi in 1860 (I, 30), there could hardly be differences of consequence between that state and its neighbors or
that year and earlier ones.

Yet other sources—the statute books, the records of men's
thoughts, the traces of economic change—reveal that the slave of
1775 was not the same as the slave of 1860 in respects that affected
personal status, family life, and role in the productive system.
A few references to the legal system in *Time on the Cross* (I, 37,
52) might have been helpful, had they been properly used;
others (I, 118–119, 128 ff.) were fanciful.[22]

The occupational categories which framed much of the economic discussion (I, 38 ff.) were also faulty. "The common belief that all slaves were menial laborers is false," Fogel and
Engerman concluded. This central assertion rested on an analysis
which showed that "over 25 percent of males were managers,
professionals, craftsmen, and semiskilled workers," a level not far
out of line for that in the country as a whole. Slave society, therefore, did not eliminate, although it restricted, economic and
social mobility for blacks. Like free society, it offered people
positive incentives in the form of material rewards.

Again, openness to other evidence might have spared the authors serious errors. It was not only the numbers which informed
us of social mobility in the North, but also the literature of striv-

22 See also Chapter 7 at note 14.

ing and success. There was no equivalent among the slaves. Whether they expressed protest or resignation, the blacks before the Civil War uttered no sound of hope within the system.

Scrutiny of the data in *Time on the Cross* revealed, to begin with, that the occupational distribution of slaves in 1850 was compared with that in the whole country in 1870. The casual and unconvincing explanation for the gap across two long decades (II, 37) left dangling questions about possible distortions. Furthermore, the categories used were not current in 1850 nor did they really fit the variety of occupations of the time. Finally, the terms used in the bar chart (I, 39) were misleading, particularly when applied equally to the free and the unfree. More than 10 percent of the male slaves were artisans and craftsmen; somewhat less than 10 percent were semiskilled; and about 5 percent were managers or professionals. The slave artisans were carpenters and blacksmiths; but their status, whether on the plantation or for hire in town, was worlds removed from that of the property-owning, politically potent, free artisans. The semiskilled were house servants, gardeners, and coachmen who had few free equivalents. As for the managers and professionals—Volume II explained that those were mostly drivers and overseers. The ingeniously derived figure for black overseers was probably grossly exaggerated. But even accepted at face value, it emptied the category of meaning. Translated into real terms, Fogel and Engerman proved nothing whatever when they said that about 5 percent of slaves in 1850 were plantation taskmasters as compared with 30 percent of all males in 1870 who were doctors, lawyers, business executives, and clerks. Skill was irrelevant to status in 1850; there were numerous levels of proficiency in all occupations, and the lawyer did better than the carpenter by virtue not of knowledge or education but of elements not measured in the chart.

*What are we measuring?* To the point promptly. We do not measure weight by hat size. A 1971 Census Bureau profile emerges askew because it rests on country of birth or descent and therefore fails to recognize Jews and finds Russians and Poles in unexpected places. Comparisons of voting patterns that take no account of changes in units and issues, analyses of urban elites that throw

Philadelphia and Pittsburgh into the same category, and a break-down that joins Petersham, Rutland, and Stockbridge to Boston among the Massachusetts commercial-cosmopolitan towns of the 1780s will not be informative. On the other hand, tests for age and nativity as well as for occupation give meaning to patterns of wealthholding. The absence of those tests and of indications of who moved in and out of the unit measured calls all the numbers into question.[23]

So, too, in *Time on the Cross,* the index of railroad mileage per capital, 1860, in a table purporting to show relative levels of industrialization reads one hundred for the South, forty-three for Great Britain. It would be a mistake to take those measurements as proof of British backwardness; they prove only their own worthlessness. Arizona Territory in 1885 would rank even higher —with scarcely a factory in it.

The problem of establishing the validity of an index became even more complex to the extent that Fogel and Engerman were prisoners of a vocabulary fixed by the concepts of modern eco-nomics. Their readers could not be faulted for confusion when they themselves were unaware that the sense in which they em-ployed key words was not the same as that in common usage in 1974 or in 1860. Their discipline had changed drastically in the previous two generations. Gone were the days when terms like capital and wages had simple definitions, susceptible to easy quantification. Add the factors of human capital or nonpecuniary returns and try to put numbers on the value of education or Cali-fornia climate and the computations were bound to spin off in bewildering pyrotechnics. Those not thoroughly immersed in the process find it hard enough to link sophisticated current statistics to the external reality about them. The difficulties multiply when the process is pushed back into the past.

23 *U.S. News and World Report,* Aug. 9, 1971, p. 32; James T. Lemon and Gary B. Nash, "Distribution of Wealth in Eighteenth-Century America," *Journal of Social History,* II (Fall 1968), 1 ff.; Michael Rogin, "Progressivism and the California Electorate," *Journal of American History,* LV (September 1968), 297 ff.; John N. Ingham, "Rags to Riches Revisited," *ibid.,* LXIII (December 1976), 615 ff.; Van Beck Hall, *Politics Without Parties: Massachusetts, 1780–1791* (Pittsburgh, 1972), 10, 11. By contrast, Howard M. Gitelman, *Workingmen of Waltham* (Baltimore, 1974), 87 ff.; Lee Soltow, *Patterns of Wealthholding in Wisconsin since 1850* (Madison, Wisc., 1971), and *Men and Wealth in the United States, 1850–1870* (New Haven, 1975), 176, 179, take account of age.

⤟

*What is being measured?* That must be the guiding beacon in analysis of the concepts of efficiency and profit in *Time on the Cross.*

Fogel and Engerman asserted that Southern slave agriculture was more efficient than Northern family farming and that the slave field hand was harder-working and more efficient "than his white counterpart" (I, 5, 191 ff.). Leave out of account for the moment the question of whether there was a white counterpart of the slave field hand, for the answer woefully complicates the comparison. The authors really wished to prove that one system of agriculture was more efficient than the other.

The evidence appeared in Volume II (126 ff.) .[24] It would be a pity were readers, intimidated by the location in the Supplement and by the formidable appearance of the equations, to forgo the intellectual experience of absorbing this section. The awesome mastery of techniques, the ingenuity in marshaling the data, and the elegance of exposition made these the best-written pages in either volume.

Fogel and Engerman measured comparative efficiency by calculating a geometric index of total factor productivity for Southern relative to Northern agriculture. Lucidly and in specific detail, they explained the procedures followed, taking account of every difference which might distort the comparison, from the quality of the land to the constitution of the labor force. The result showed a substantial margin in favor of the slave system.

What had they measured? That is, what was the meaning of efficiency, when defined so that total factor productivity measured it? What quotient resulted from dividing the value of output by a denominator composed of weighted indexes representing the input of land, labor, and invested capital?

Ease into these questions by considering the case of oil. One less skilled than these authors, applying the formula to petroleum,

[24] A preliminary statement appeared in Robert W. Fogel and Stanley L. Engerman, "The Relative Efficiency of Slavery," *Explorations in Economic History,* VIII (Spring 1971) , 353 ff. The discussion of efficiency and profitability in this modern form was touched off by Alfred H. Conrad and John R. Meyer, *The Economics of Slavery and Other Studies in Econometric History* (Chicago, 1964) , 43 ff.

would find a striking rise in the efficiency of the oil industry between 1971 and 1974, for the value of output soared while the indexes of land, labor, and invested capital remained unchanged. The rise in efficiency had little to do with changes in the fields and refineries, but came from increasing demand in Europe, Japan, and the United States and from the action of a producers' cartel. Furthermore, the same formula would give a margin to Dubai over Texas for reasons also unrelated to the way in which either operated. The analogy is not inappropriate to the antebellum South; increased worldwide demand for cotton raised the price and, therefore, the value of output and, therefore, the productivity quotient. All those movements reflected less events on the plantation than in the mills of Old and New England and of Europe.

Fogel and Engerman were not so naive. They applied the formula not to productivity and efficiency but to comparative productivity and relative efficiency—to the relation of Southern to Northern performance. Presumably 1860, the year of their data, was not particularly favorable to the South (although the book presented no evidence on the issue), and no extraneous political events influenced price levels. True, the course of industrialization and of world trade favored cotton producers. Tough on the grain and livestock people that refrigeration and mechanization in baking and meat processing came later. It was an indication of efficiency that the South concentrated on the most advantageous crops, while the North let itself be stuck with the less advantageous ones.

But we are not so naive either. We know that in the real world choices were not that deliberate and options not that open. The efficiency Fogel and Engerman measured was abstract, which was not bad or wrong, but was different from the common understanding of the term.

Whence their meaning? The *Oxford English Dictionary* knows it not. *Nostrand's* does. In engineering, efficiency is defined as the ratio of output to input of energy or power in purely mechanical systems. Efficiency in that sense may apply to the economy considered as a purely mechanical system.

The *O.E.D.* does provide another definition, more in accord with current usage: "That nothing more powerfully promotes the efficiency of labour than an abundance of fertile land" (1863).

There the word means "fitness or power to accomplish, or success in accomplishing, the purpose intended." By that definition, Northern agriculture was far more efficient than Southern. *Time on the Cross* itself provided the explanation for the contradictory results yielded by the two definitions (II, 128). Its index of total factor productivity distinguished "those changes in output which are due to an increase in the efficiency of the productive process *per se* from those changes which are due merely to the fact that labor has been equipped with more land and capital than was previously the case." "Merely" told the story. For Fogel and Engerman efficiency was the residuum when land and capital were factored out. By contrast, in common usage efficiency was the application of improvements to the land and of more capital to enterprise.

*What are we measuring?* In the closed mechanical order of a forced labor system, total factor productivity does the job; it will tell us how well Gulag Archipelago functions. An open system which aims to minimize the human costs of production requires quite a different yardstick.[25]

The same discrepancy emerged from the discussion of the profitability of slavery. *Time on the Cross* treated profit, as modern economists generally did, as the rate of annual return on invested capital. That is what the book measured; and there could be no quarrel with its doing so.

Another, less constricted, definition was familiar to nineteenth-century Americans: "the pecuniary gain in any transaction; the amount by which value acquired exceeds value expended, the excess of returns over the outlay of capital." People who gave the term that loose meaning measured profit differently. They invested in land, factories, and securities in the expectation not of regular returns of rent or dividends but of swooping appreciations of capital. To use a later terminology, price-earnings ratios counted for less than the prospects of capital gains. And averages did not count at all. Merchants knew the perils and frequency of

---

25 Focus on the question of what is being measured will also reveal that the computations in Michael Paul Rogin, *Intellectuals and McCarthy* (Cambridge, 1967), 64 ff., 283 ff., are less elegant and more dubious.

bankruptcy; farmers were aware of the risk of foreclosure. That did not affect their estimate of the odds on the one big strike which was their objective. These were not jolly sanguine types, but men wracked by anxiety.

Again the question *What are we measuring?* Insofar as the authors wished to demonstrate the viability of slavery, to prove that it yielded enough return on capital so that the institution would not collapse of itself, the economist's definition of profit was valid; and Fogel and Engerman made their case.

But they attempted to do more. They wished to show that the Southern economy was not stagnant, but thriving and growing—as far along as or ahead of that of any other section—and precisely because of its superior, more profitable, labor system. Slavery was not dying in the United States from the end of the Revolution to 1810; nor was the regional economy in the doldrums between 1840 and 1860; nor were planters then becoming pessimistic about the future (I, 5, 6, 24). *Time on the Cross* aspired to destroy all these false impressions left, its authors believed, by earlier historians. In the effort to do so it blundered into a morass.

For the early period, to 1810, the expressed opinion of contemporaries was an imposing hurdle. So many of them kept saying that the institution was moribund, that the obstacles to its disappearance were social rather than economic, and that in time it would somehow vanish! The authors quoted no contrary views. Instead, they sought to prove that slavery flourished by showing that imports of blacks actually rose during the decades in question. They branded as erroneous the widely cited estimates of a decline in arrivals for the period, asserting that the numbers brought in between 1790 and 1810 were greater than in any previous span of equal duration.[26]

There was a gap in the reasoning. Imports might have risen, despite the prevailing view that slavery would ultimately disappear, for during those war years hazardous conditions of trade in the Caribbean might have persuaded African exporters to dump their blacks in the neutral American ports. In any case,

[26] The authors also attempted to demonstrate the profitability of slavery in the same period by indexes of slave prices and demand (I, 86 ff.) ; but their fragile data did not support the inferences drawn from them (II, 85 ff.) .

the argument was tenuous because there were no decent figures for landings. All attempts to quantify slave imports rested on a shaky basis, Fogel and Engerman acknowledged (II, 31). They inferred their conclusions from estimates of total population in the terminal years and from assumptions about the rate of natural increase—neither very secure.

For the period 1840–1860, the same method could not serve, for the authors wished to underplay the importance of the interregional slave trade then.[27] Nor could they explain away the evidence in politics and opinion of planter tension about the future. Instead they called upon an index of sanguinity which purported to chart the hopeful factors of the decades (I, 103 ff.). Basically they measured the solid foundation for profit and for the expectation of continuing returns responsible for the rapid increase of per-capita income. Slaveholders were prudent, calculating capitalists, not indifferent to their own best interests (I, 73); therefore, they had to be optimistic. The premise was that they held the economist's understanding of profit.

But the capitalists who opened up the China trade or built the Lowell mills or planned the transcontinental railroads were not prudent men and they did not calculate well. These wild romantics sought profit in the broad, not the narrow sense. So, too, did many planters, although the gains of which they dreamed differed from those of Northerners—running not to ships or machines but to more, ever more, territory: all of Mexico, the West to the Pacific, Cuba, Central America. So slavery was expansive all right—which was what Free Soil politicians charged throughout the 1850s. But that expansion was a sign not of economic growth but of stagnation. In the South the promise of profit in the broader sense lay not in improvement of productive processes but in addition of acres. No one tinkered with a cotton picker in these years; and the Virginian, Cyrus Hall McCormick went to Illinois to profit from his invention.

---

27 They underestimated the interregional movement of slaves (I, 48), because the survivor technique they used did not catch many of those traded, given the actual course of east-west transactions (II, 43). The argument that the decline of the urban slave population was the result of the bidding up of prices under the pressure of inelastic rural demand was probably correct (I, 102). See also Claudia Dale Goldin, *Urban Slavery in the American South* (Chicago, 1976), 76 ff.

❧

Much depends on how the data is used. As to quality, the quantitative material is not worse, but also not better, than any other. In assessing the level of their certainty, consider the extent to which the computer works from fragments, surrogates, and proxies, from whatever by accident survives from a past which did not keep or conserve appropriate records. For the internal slave trade there are risks in depending on information from New Orleans, when most of the bondsmen taken to Alabama, Mississippi, and Arkansas did not pass through that city; or in finding the ratio of slaves traded to population by projecting Maryland figures to the national level (I, 53); or in resting a judgment on how frequently slaves were bought for speculation upon inferences from the experience of nineteen plantations over a ninety-year period (I, 54). The margin of error in the observations of travelers can be no greater.[28]

Again and again we come back to the choice of adjectives. To show that the "destabilizing effects of the westward migration" (that is, of slaves traded down the River) on marriages were not "significantly greater among blacks than . . . among whites," an intricate and unconvincing analysis yields a figure of only about 2 percent destroyed (I, 49). Much or little? Only one slaveholder of twenty-two sold a slave a year (I, 53). Many or few? No matter how ingeniously the numbers are tortured, in the end the adjective chosen depends upon the ability to set the evidence in context, as historians should do with any other material.[29]

[28] Other instances: comparison of the "rate of expropriation" of "slave income" to the "modern tax rate on workers" (I, 56); derivation of estimates of slave diet by subtracting from total production an estimate for the overfed master (I, 109 ff.; II, 110 ff.); assumption of slaveholder farsightedness in statements about merit-based social mobility on the plantation.

[29] The key paragraph on slave marriages was held together by two "oftens," two "somes," a "sometimes," and a "many" (I, 128; also I, 146). The average of 0.7 whippings per hand per year on one plantation could as well read one whipping every 4.5 days; the statement that about one-half the hands were not whipped at all could also read that about one-half were (I, 45). The fact that only 9.9 percent of rural slaves were mulattoes in 1869 proved that the exploitation of black women was far from "ubiquitous" (I, 132). "Most planters shunned direct interference in the sexual practices of slaves" (I, 135). See also E. H. Hunt, "Railroad Social Saving," *American Economic Review*, LVII (September 1967), 909 ff.

✎

These deficiencies explain the inadequacy of the description of slavery in *Time on the Cross*. To their credit, the authors did understand that slavery was a system of forced labor and not a haphazard relationship of victimizers and victims. The best parts of the book throw light on the operations of that system. But Fogel and Engerman failed woefully to comprehend the ways in which forced differed from free labor; the only explicit discussion of the issue, tucked away in the Supplement (II, 155 ff.), was perfunctory and sadly wanting. On specific matters, as when they observed (I, 57) that the ownership of men was not incompatible with shifting labor requirements, they seemed unaware of the dynamic economic and social consequences of the opportunity to choose. They seemed unaware, that is, of the reason why thousands of well-fed slaves ran away to the North, while no miserable, underpaid, badly housed proletarian escaped to bondage in the South.

The discussion of such issues as family life and whipping gave no inkling of the pain slavery imprinted on the consciousness of black people. Human resilience is such that bondsmen, too, felt moments of triumph, achievement, and even joy, just as Ivan Denisovich found satisfaction in a job well done. But their situation circumscribed the lives of slaves, made them ever aware that they were black not white and that, therefore, all freedom was forbidden them. They understood no degrees to their lack of liberty. And if the authors believed that such calculations were not essential to a study of the economics of .American Negro slavery, that measured the narrowness of their view of economics.

✎

*Time on the Cross* deals with abstractions. Numbers, like other abstractions, acquire specificity when set in context; and this operation was out of the reach of Fogel and Engerman, strangers to the culture of history which might have helped them in the task.

They tried valiantly to get a handle on the literature, but the measure of their failure was the way in which they perceived that literature as a succession of schools supplanting one another. The material was intractable. The Phillips School, for instance, proved a conglomerate of ill-assorted scholars, which at one point took in Eugene Genovese and within a few pages both included and excluded L. C. Gray (I, 63–65). The comments on Gray elsewhere (II, 190) revealed the authors' inability to get hold of the issue. "Despite the high quality of the scholarship and the cogency of his critique of the main elements of the traditional interpretation of slavery, Gray's work was largely neglected by most historians of the South during the quarter century that followed its publication."[30]

Ponder the word "neglected." A year after publication the book was required reading in at least one college course; it received respectful reviews in the Journals; and in 1974 it was still a standard work on the subject. In what sense was it neglected? Perhaps in the sense that it aroused little controversy and no furious arguments. More likely, because it did not supplant what had been written before, did not dictate what was written later. Fogel and Engerman could not understand why earlier scholars continued to be read, why later ones did not either enlist under the Gray banner or set about refuting him. They were thinking, that is, of the expectations of economics, the most precise of the social sciences, in which the acceptance of a new model signals the rejection of the old.

Historians have no such expectations. Their discipline arrives at no established canon, no accepted, traditional interpretation. When a good new book comes along it does not simply supplant the good old ones that preceded it. It may correct their errors, add to their information, provide alternatives to their interpretations—that is, expand their meaning for a later generation. But they may, nevertheless, still be studied with profit. Perhaps the willingness to integrate quantitative with other materials at the expense of adherence to abstract models has kept political studies less daring than those in economics but also less exposed to error.[31]

[30] The reference was to Lewis C. Gray, *History of Agriculture in the Southern United States to 1860*, 2 vols. (Washington, 1933).

[31] Richard Jensen, "American Election Analysis," in Seymour M. Lipset, ed., *Politics and the Social Sciences* (New York, 1969), 226 ff.

It is in the nature of the materials with which he works that the historian requires not only the most modern tools of science but also a timeless adeptness at imagination. John Clapham once explained that the historian "will be modest in the presence of the economist," but that he will retain the pride of his craft so long as the tangled variety of human life attracts him and "even when his information is such that he can never hope to pick out with assurance the forces at work or measure exactly the changes brought about by the aggregate of them between dates $x$ and $y$," he will continue to study that tangle.[32]

Perhaps this is a poor time to make this point, a moment when the discipline of history is in disarray, when much of the work done in it is shoddy, and when almost anything goes. Ill-trained practitioners are so often the victims of ignorance, faulty thinking, nonsense from the softer social sciences, and propaganda, what difference does mastery of the numbers make? Can we expect those to read algebraic equations intelligently who can scarcely catch the meaning in a page of English prose?

On the other hand, perhaps this is a time when the point most needs making.

A less finicky writer might have borrowed from electrical engineering a more precise term for the title of an essay than that used here. Surely capacitance comes closest to my intention, "that property of a conductor which expresses its ability to keep the potential low for a given charge." When the power conveyed outruns the ability of the conductor to carry it, pretty sparks fly but the works are damaged.

Queasiness at the sound of the word leads me to a simpler term: capacity, as in the capacity of a river, that is, the power of receiving, containing, and carrying the maximum output of a stream. Quantitative methods, carrying along immense amounts of information, can turn the wheels of the historical understanding.[33] They can amplify analysis even if they do not overturn the accepted explanation. The same methods sweep down many an ob-

---

[32] Charles Wilson, "Transport as a Factor in the History of Economic Development," *Journal of European Economic History*, II (Fall 1973) , 334.

[33] Among the works which successfully integrate quantitative with other data are: Stephan A. Thernstrom, *Other Bostonians* (Cambridge, 1973) ; Robert R. Swierenga, *Acres for Cents: Delinquent Tax Auctions in Frontier Iowa* (Westport, Conn., 1976) .

vious craft overburdened with embellishment: when housing opportunities contract newlyweds are less likely to live independently than young families with children.[34] Out of control or too heavily charged, the same methods carry immense amounts of detritus, overpouring the shores and disordering the landscape.

[34] Howard P. Chudacoff, "New Branches on the Tree: Household Structure in Early Stages of the Family Cycle in Worcester, Massachusetts, 1860–1880," American Antiquarian Society, *Proceedings*, LXXXVI (1976) , 309.

# 9

## *Seeing and Hearing*

AMONG THE ARTIFACTS the historian encounters as evidence are numerous pictorial representations. Lascaux and Altamira and the Easter Islands sculptures, the pyramids in Egypt and the columns of Persepolis, remind us that man scratched and carved and built before he wrote and, doing so, left behind a vast heritage of visual materials. Modern survivals include drawings, paintings, photographs and motion pictures, statues and structures, roads and cities, all testimony to human thought and activity.

Sound is not stone, and vanishes with the wind. The historian cannot catch the voices which echoed in the past. Yet he cannot forget that no written language is identical with its spoken counterpart. The usage of words and structures of sentences, to say nothing of lilt, timbre, and accent, significantly affect the meaning conveyed. Nor can the student of former generations neglect the music made in singing, dancing, playing, and worshiping, some of which he can recover by examining formal systems of notation and, for the past century, various types of recordings.

The historian, therefore, must not only read. He must also look and listen.

But looking is not the same as seeing, and listening is not the same as hearing. Among the most difficult problems of the craft are those of how, by looking to see, by listening to hear.

⌒

No chronicler of the past can avoid making some approximation of the visual appearance of his subject matter. The image may never cross beyond the mind of the writer; still it is there. How to use it is of the first importance, and the abundance of material only complicates the problem.

Verbal descriptions are inadequate, although they may be all that is available and, therefore, indispensable. No pictorial representation can provide the image of a dark forest or the hold of a sailing vessel. The words of witnesses must supply the material for imaginative reconstruction.[1]

Those approximations, however, depend upon materials flawed in their very nature. A traveler sets down his description of buildings, people, monuments in the city through which he drives. However well-informed, competent, and accurate he is, his evidence passes through filters capable of distorting the picture conveyed. The vantage point of the transient often permits a view of a part rather than of the whole, at a narrow rather than wide angle, and at a speed conducive to blurring. On the other hand, the resident or familiar may attach to the object affective attitudes not intrinsic to it, but the product of his own experience. Furthermore, observers of both kinds must translate their perceptions into words, a considerable task even for the most skilled writers; and then the readers, decades or miles away, must decode the sentences and derive a visual image from them. Before accepting literally Richard Henry Dana's simple, eloquent, and precise paragraphs describing Santa Barbara and San Francisco bays, they must take account of the fact that he saw them after a voyage of 150 days in the first case, and twenty, in the second, on bright days in the stormy season.[2]

The same filters operate when the observer bears the credentials of critic. The historian, predisposed to verbal evidence, who reads about rather than looks at objects, becomes dependent upon secondhand impressions and is helpless when critics disagree or interpose their own extraneous judgments between the work and the viewer. The great advantage of Jakob Burckhardt, who began his career as a student of art, and of Johan Huizinga, who learned how to see, lay in their ability to look at rather than to read about.

Whether the object be a painting or photograph or mountain

1 For example, Sumner Powell, *Puritan Village* (Middletown, Conn., 1963), 76, 92, 108, 124.

2 Richard Henry Dana, *Two Years before the Mast* (1840; New York, 1909), 61 ff., 231.

or ink blot, the perceptions of viewers differ; this does not mean that all are equally correct, but does rule out reliance upon others. The indirect means of seeing must serve when the original has disappeared or is unavailable for direct inspection. But they do not substitute for the impression the knowledgeable historian gains from the original. Techniques of reproduction improved significantly in the three decades after 1945. Still no two-dimensional sheet can depict an object in the round or a building in its setting. No illustration does justice to the bust of Nefertiti or to the Viking ships in Oslo or to Duncan Phyfe's chairs. Indeed, the more adept the photographer, the more likely he is to intrude between object and viewer.[3]

Visual material in abundance survives as physical evidence. Even for the ancient civilizations, the explorations of archaeologists have uncovered a multitude of objects—entire cities, buildings, boats, armor, and tools—that speak eloquently about their makers. Modern data rests in Williamsburg, Sturbridge, Plymouth, and hundreds of other museums and reconstructions—as well as, for the most recent period, beneath the surface of still-functioning cities and towns. The massive quantities create problems of selection as well as of dating and anachronism and of interpretation.[4]

In some respects these materials yield readily to the conventional skills of the historian who can handle them almost as he does verbal documents. Issues of attribution—time, place, identity of creator—are much the same as those for page of type or holograph. The scholar can also make inferences about function, read the story told, grasp the message communicated, note the illustrations and representations provided, and even probe the hidden purposes of pictures and structures as he does of words and sentences. In other respects the nature of the visual evidence creates subtle challenges of a different order.

Whoever regards the columns that rise above the plain at Persepolis must wonder what function they served in the lives of the

---

[3] See Jules B. Davidoff, *Differences in Visual Perception* (New York, 1975).

[4] Oscar Handlin et al., *Harvard Guide to American History* (Cambridge, 1954), contains brief listings.

people who devoted immense energies to their creation. Without convincing answers about purpose, they remain puzzling reminders of the ingenuity and industry of man expended for unknown reasons. Other urban places—in Crete, Greece, and Rome—subject to longer study, are more eloquent. Their physical layout informs scholars about the lives of their ancient residents because each spatial and structural element acquired its physical character to serve a purpose.

Properly examined, the disposition of space in American places is fully as informative. The developing town plans of colonial Connecticut mark the transition from the defensive enclosures of a military post to tight communities living by a mixed agricultural and trading economy. The changes in the town plan of Philadelphia show the surrender of the initial concept of a closed homogeneous community in favor of one capable of expanding indefinitely at the periphery.[5]

Down through the nineteenth century the Atlantic coastal cities revealed in their iconography as well as in their physical layout the expectation that the primary approach to them would be by sea. That in turn reflected the economy as well as the practical experience of their residents. A Dutch watercolor of New Amsterdam in 1650 fixed the beholder's eye on the harbor, and for two centuries thereafter prints, engravings, and lithographs of New York held it there. In the same way the appearance of Pittsburgh, Chicago, Rochester, and St. Louis was a factor of their situation on rivers. In the twentieth century everywhere, access by water receded in importance and entry to the city shifted to highways. The result was evident in the aspects not only of relatively new communities like Los Angeles, Houston, and Dallas but also in the transformation of old ones like Chicago and New York.[6]

Smaller, more specialized, places also speak visually of their

[5] Anthony N. B. Garvan, *Architecture and Town Planning in Colonial Connecticut* (New Haven, 1951), and "Proprietary Philadelphia as Artifact," in Oscar Handlin and John Burchard, eds., *Historian and the City* (Cambridge, 1963), 177 ff.

[6] I. N. P. Stokes, *Iconography of Manhattan Island* (New York, 1895–1928); Walter Muir Whitehill, *Boston: A Topographical History* (Cambridge, 1959); Justin Winsor, *Memorial History of Boston*, 4 vols. (Boston, 1880–81), I; John E. Burchard, "Urban Aesthetic," *Annals*, CCCXIV (January 1957), 118; John A. Kouwenhoven, *Columbia Historical Portrait of New York* (Garden City, N.Y., 1953), 157 ff.

function. The locks and canals of the Merrimack River mill towns reveal the impact of the first phases of industrialization, just as the visionary designs of utopian communities illustrate the protests against it. A difference in the spread of structures shows which places responded to the railroad and which to the highway.[7]

The surviving evidence of every other sort exposes the function served. Buildings, or the floor plans for them, convey information about the use of space, posters about what they sold or argued, medals about what they commemorated. And understanding of the function opens an acquaintance with the clients, purchasers, and viewers who once commissioned, bought, occupied, or regarded the objects. The canvases of Yankee limners and the portraits of Paul Revere by John S. Copley and of Pat Lyon by John Neagle represent individuals but also speak of the situation of yeomen and artisans in the early Republic. Much of the sculpture and architecture of the same era served the personal and national pride of those who paid for them.[8]

It takes small skill as a viewer to follow the storytelling picture. The creators of such materials usually demanded little attention or understanding from their audiences. The plot lines, characters, and incidents left on the TV tape or movie film were intentionally simple, clear, and expressive, the stories they told as comprehensible as those of the easiest novel. The narratives in other pictorial types, ranging from contemporary comic books back through prints of Currier and Ives and the figures of John Rogers —indeed, as far back as the engravings of William Hogarth and the pages of the *New England Primer*—were equally free of complexity.[9]

[7] John Coolidge, *Mill and Mansion* (New York, 1942); Dolores Hayden, *Seven American Utopias* (Cambridge, 1976).

[8] Alan Burroughs, *Limners and Likenesses* (Cambridge, 1936); Jules D. Prown, *John Singleton Copley*, 2 vols. (Cambridge, 1966). Lillian B. Miller, *Patrons and Patriotism* (Chicago, 1966); and Neil Harris, *Artist in American Society* (New York, 1966), treat the social context, as Oliver W. Larkin, *Art and Life in America* (New York, 1949), does more generally.

[9] Stephen Becker, *Comic Art in America* (New York, 1959). On the European origins, see David Kunzle, *History of the Comic Strip* (Berkeley, 1973).

These materials bear a close relation to other visual messages intended to persuade. Sometimes the two genres look alike; the next episode in one comic strip is not much different from the breakfast-cereal sales talk in another. The television commercials and the advertisements in newspapers and magazines are as informative as, and often more skillfully devised than, the other material among which they are interspersed. The pictures in hortatory novels and pamphlets sometimes spoke more eloquently than the text. William H. Van Ingen's double frontispiece for Timothy Shay Arthur's *Ten Nights in a Bar-Room* stirred the emotions as much as the temperance tract did. The posters, medals, prints, and cartoons later assembled by private collectors and by museums and libraries were designed to convey an idea or sell a thing. Caricature, close enough to reality to be recognizable, yet susceptible to distortion and exaggeration for emphasis, reached back to the prerevolutionary period, attained the peak of its effectiveness in Thomas Nast's drawings for *Harper's Weekly* and in the satire of *Judge* and *Puck* in the 1890s, and survived in the daily press on into the twentieth century. Although political dictates never shaped the character of the cinema in the United States as they did in Eastern Europe, American directors had their own means of getting a message across, as in the portrayal of the bumbling capitalists who moved through the films of the 1930s.[10]

Every visual object is also an illustration of something. But the veracity of none is beyond question. Works purely of the imagination may have other uses; they show nothing of actuality. In the absence of any contemporary portraits of Christopher Columbus or John Harvard, there can be no way of knowing their appearance as there is of knowing John Smith's. The gap in the evidence is irreparable.

In general, the selective, scholarly regard will take no display at face value: will find more in one than its creator intended, in others will accept less than offered.

10 Richard L. Bushman, "Caricature and Satire in Old and New England before the American Revolution," Massachusetts Historical Society, *Proceedings*, LXXXVIII (1976), 19 ff.; Morton Keller, *Art and Politics of Thomas Nast* (New York, 1968); Mira and Antonin J. Liehm, *Most Important Art* (Berkeley, 1977).

Often particulars incidentally tucked in are revealing. Théodore de Bry's depiction of Lisbon Harbor shows clearly the structure and rigging of ships and the costume of merchants in the sixteenth century. John White's drawing of an Indian village (1590) says much about its agriculture and shelter. Van Ingen, in the effort to make his temperance sketches as persuasive as possible, loads them with realistic detail of furniture, buildings, clothing, and even manners.

Caution demands a check for anachronism and convention. Renaissance painters of biblical scenes described the landscape of Italy, not of Palestine; the gowns worn for sittings with Copley or Sargent were not those of ordinary domestic life; and no child ever looked like Charles Calvert as depicted by John Hesselius (1761).

Materials not incidental to a more general picture but deliberately intended as illustrations call for more caution still. In the immense repertory of photographs, paintings, and drawings of people and buildings, as well as of scenes which show or purport to show what existed or what happened, the design of the creator may distort the image. The historian must distinguish between the reality in the artist's mind and that outside it. John J. Audubon was a serious ornithologist and wished to show the birds he saw as they were (1833). But he was also a considerable artist. Above the St. Lawrence River he sketched a female greater cormorant and her brood, but later drew in a male to complete the composition. The gyrfalcons he painted to convey a sense of majestic, rapid flight; and in other pictures the spread of wings, the parted beak, and the position of the eyes imparted expression to his subjects.[11]

Portraits expose only part of the truth because they reflect the will of the painter or photographer as well as the physiognomy of the sitter. Mechanical constraints have some effect upon the product, as in the drape of sculpted costumes or the dark background of oil on canvas or the rigid posture of glass-plate images and daguerreotypes or the jerky motions of newsreels made with hand-cranked cameras. Conventions of composition also reduce the ac-

[11] John J. Audubon, *Birds of America*, 4 vols. (London, 1827–38); also Constance M. Rourke, *Audubon* (New York, 1936).

curacy of pictorial evidence. John Smibert's portraits, lavish in the display of cloth, wigs, and lace, all tend to look very much alike. The busts of Roman emperors, paintings, and other objects with religious connotations, and even photographs, may reveal the way in which the artists work as much as they do their subjects.[12]

Intention intruded into the work of photographers as of other artists. The newsreel was not a record of what happened, but the product of selection and editing. Edward Steichen's J. P. Morgan, although literally accurate, depicted a corsair; and a trick of light transformed the arm of a chair into a dagger pointed at the viewer. Jacob Riis used his lens in a campaign for tenement-house reform, just as Louis Hine used pictures in factories as part of a campaign to get rid of child labor. In fact, the presence of a photographer or TV camera crew could shape the character of the event—as in the weddings and riots of the 1960s. Filmstrips and motion pictures contrived for teaching or selling were even more suspect as illustrations.[13]

The historian must use these materials with care, but cannot overlook the value in them, sometimes quite independent of the artist's skill. Robert Earl's painting of Roger Sherman (c. 1787) and Joseph Wright's of John Jay (1786), a photograph of Jim Fisk in full braided uniform (1870) and one of Horace Greeley as presidential candidate (Napoleon Sarony, 1872), are simple, accurate, and expressive. Lincoln's image in the camera lens from 1846 until his death vividly reflected the changes in his character.[14]

Numerous details spring to life for the inquiring eye. A Russian traveler of 1811 paints in his notebook Philadelphians gaily eating oysters from a barrow at night, a solemn Baptist immersion ceremony, dancers making merry at a wayside inn to the music of a local fiddler, and the rickety stagecoach in which travelers jolt along the road to Trenton. George Caleb Bingham shows stump speaking (1854), and William Henry Bartlett (1838) and *Ballou's*

12 Martin W. Sandler, *This Was Connecticut* (Boston, 1977); Reese V. Jenkins, *Images and Enterprise* (Baltimore, 1975); Ramsay MacMullen, *Roman Government's Response to Crisis* (New Haven, 1976), 17 ff., 45.

13 Marc Ferro, "1917: History and Cinema," *Journal of Contemporary History*, III (October 1968), 45 ff.; Howard Gilette, Jr., "Film as Artifact," *American Studies*, XVIII (Fall 1977), 71 ff.; Zvi Dor-Ner, "How Television Reports Conflicts," *Nieman Reports*, XXI (Summer 1977), 23 ff.

14 Stefan Lorant, *Lincoln: His Life in Photographs* (New York, 1941).

*Monthly* (September 1865) reveal the operations of the Erie Canal at Lockport and of the inclined planes by which the Pennsylvania Railroad crosses the Alleghenies.[15]

Selectivity is essential and achievable only by integrating the visual with other evidence. The viewer must judge that the various types of fencing and the stumps in Patrick Campbell's engraving of a newly cleared farm (1793) are accurate, but that the dwelling is far too elaborate to be true; that Samuel B. Waugh's painting of Irish immigrants in New York (1855) is good for Castle Garden and the Battery, but not for the people and, therefore, not for what actually transpired.[16]

The work of the especially talented is both specially rewarding and specially dangerous. The perceptive eye of Edgar Degas painting the New Orleans cotton market (1873) noted the bespectacled face of a man feeling a sample, two others deep in negotiation, a fourth slouched over a newspaper, a fifth at work on the accounts, and several bystanders—each different. Mathew Brady's panoramic photos—of the Pennsylvania infantry at Camp Northumberland, of the seamen on the deck of a Union gunboat, and of the wounded after Chancellorsville (1863) —conveyed a vivid sense of people and place. And, although Hine conceived of himself as a reformer, he never lost a sense for the humanity of the ordinary people at whom he pointed the camera. On the other hand, the talented could inject more into a scene than was actually there. Russell Lee's photos of sharecroppers and WPA workers in Missouri and Oklahoma (1938, 1939) owed something to skillful posing, and Jack Delano's deserted farmhouse in Georgia (1941) was selective rather than typical. The fact that the Farm Security Administration commissioned them, along with Walker Evans and Dorothea Lange, to make a photographic record of rural depression did not diminish from the eloquence of their work, but did influence its character.

Conventions, or unarticulated understandings, also affect the distinctive representations of space that appear on maps. Histo-

15 Paul Svinin, *Picturesque United States of America, 1811–1813* (New York, 1930) .

16 Patrick Campbell, *Travels in the Interior Parts of North America* (Edinburgh, 1793) .

rians take for granted the difference in appearance between the globe and the two-dimensional depiction of part of it; but they rarely speculate about why north is always at the top of the page or what difference that arrangement makes in their own view of territorial relationships. Whoever tips a map containing the area 35° north to 10° south latitude, and 85° west to 60° east longitude, to put Charleston, South Carolina, at the top of the page, will discover a connection between the mainland and the West Indies once significant but entirely lost in the usual map.

Maps originally were not far different from other pictorial materials. Because they conveyed to the beholder a sense of where he stood in the world, the Mediterranean long was the most prominent orienting feature, with Jerusalem or Rome central, and sometimes with Gibraltar at the bottom. Maps grew more abstract and more usable with the development of long-distance trade and travel; the east-west horizontal axis became universal; and the English Channel became central to space as Greenwich did to time. These conventions did not, in themselves, create special difficulties for the historians. The failure to recognize and understand them did.[17]

The viewer must keep his guard up; visual material serves hidden as well as overt purposes. All too few have learned to look beyond the story it tells or the detail it illustrates at the object itself. A long, thoughtful analysis thus treats the themes and subject matter, that is, the contents, but not the pictorial elements of revolutionary iconography. But there is more to it than that, as the historians of art have explained in other connections. Each culture and each period has its own way of treating perspective, space, line, and color, reflecting its own world outlook.[18] The

17 See Samuel Y. Edgerton, *Renaissance Rediscovery of Linear Perspective* (New York, 1975), 91 ff.; Handlin, *Harvard Guide to American History*, 68 ff. See also Arthur H. Robinson and Barbara B. Petchenik, *Nature of Maps* (Chicago, 1976).

18 Michael Kammen, "From Liberty to Prosperity: Reflections upon the Role of Revolutionary Iconography in National Tradition," American Antiquarian Society, *Proceedings*, LXVI (1976), 237 ff. For excellent examples, see Fritz Saxl, "Veritas Filia Temporis," in Raymond Klibansky and H. J. Paton, eds., *Philosophy & History* (Oxford, 1936), 197 ff.; Erwin Panofsky, "Et in Arcadia Ego," *ibid.*, 223 ff.; E. H. Gombrich, *In Search of Cultural History* (Oxford, 1969), 30 ff.; Edgerton, *Renaissance Rediscovery of Linear Perspective*, 158 ff.

power of Paul Revere's engraving of the Boston Massacre (1770) depends not on its accuracy but on its composition: the scene boxed in by buildings as on a stage set within which the muskets of the rigid array of troops direct attention to the three prone bodies and to the fourth already being carried off.

Examples abound. Walker Evans' photos for the Farm Security Administration imposed order on subjects to emphasize their poverty. In the Moundville, Alabama, general store (1936) a coca-cola poster on the left offsets the calendar on the right, the piles of sacks in the foreground, the nearly stacked shelves in the background. A large cross rises in the graveyard of Bethlehem, Pennsylvania (1935), against a line of steel-mill chimneys, and as the eye passes from one to the other, it traverses the meager sod and a row of workers' homes. Dorothea Lange in Hall County, Texas (June 1937), achieves a sense of desolation by setting an abandoned tenant house far back, so that the parched furrows which occupy most of the picture seem to flow right by to the empty sky.[19]

A structure which looks like a small Greek temple in a medium-sized Midwestern town of 1900 would be deceptive, did not a plaque at its entrance identify a bank. No problem; a common form. Still, the historian must wonder why the architect who designed the building gave it that facade, why the banker wished it to appear that way and believed that appearance would impress his customers. American architecture is replete with evidence of this sort, ranging from Jefferson's interest in the classical revival to Trinity Church experiments in the Gothic (New York, 1846) and the Romanesque (Boston, 1872) to the extravagance and exuberance of Las Vegas. The Woolworth Building (Cass Gilbert, 1912), among New York City's tallest skyscrapers, bears a Gothic facade up where the passerby can hardly see it. Iranistan, P. T. Barnum's home in Bridgeport, Connecticut, thrust together shapes no less fantastic than those which later encased his circus wagons —but not really more fantastic than those of James C. Flood's country home or of Cornelius and George W. Vanderbilt's Breakers and Biltmore in Rhode Island and North Carolina. Similar, though more modest, fantasies ornamented many a humble car-

[19] See also Walker Evans, *American Photographs* (Garden City, N.Y., 1938).

penter-built cottage. In each case the function of the building was not shelter alone but expression of some personal meaning.[20]

Critics and philosophers, dealing usually with high art, have explored the relation between function and symbolic form, between ritual and mode of expression, and between reality and human consciousness of it.[21] These analyses, rich in insight, are suggestive also for the understanding of humbler graphic forms. Costume, paintings, sculpture, photographs, film, and tape clothe, record, portray, ornament, or narrate, just as architecture shelters; but, in addition, each may carry in its lines and colors a message its fabricator intentionally or unintentionally conveyed. Daniel Chester French's statue of John Harvard says nothing about the actual appearance of the seventeenth-century minister; it does reveal a nineteenth-century ideal type, just as successive portrayals of Columbus reveal the painters, not the navigator. The illustrations of Charles Dana Gibson, John Held, Jr., and J. C. Leyendecker reflect and also shape the tastes of viewers about fashion, the appropriate appearance of a man or woman abreast of the times.

All these judgments yield to the normal methods of historical inquiry, skillfully pursued, alertly used. The historian examines the evidence both as a thing in itself and in its social context. He asks what purpose it served and who commissioned it and why. He tries to discern how much in it is repetitive, how much new, how much deliberate, and how much the expression of unconscious desires and fears. In other words, he treats these materials much as he does verbal ones.

A swirl of words about the creation eases the task of understanding the form of an object. Great monuments, built over a considerable period, called forth heated discussion, as did the Statue

20 Neil Harris, "Housing the Rich," *Reviews in American History*, II (March 1974), 27 ff., makes a thoughtful comparison of prairie and New York row houses. Compare the ideological elements in Nazi architecture in Barbara Lane, *Architecture and Politics in Germany, 1918–1945* (Cambridge, 1968).

21 For approaches to the phenomenology of culture, see Ernst Cassirer, *Philosophy of Symbolic Forms*, trans. Ralph Manheim, preface Charles W. Hendel (New Haven, 1953), I, vii ff., 29 ff., 35 ff., 47 ff., and *Essay on Man* (New Haven, 1944), 137 ff.; Susanne K. Langer, *Feeling and Form* (New York, 1953); R. G. Collingwood, *Principles of Art* (Oxford, 1938), 128 ff.; 206 ff.; Herbert Read, *Art and Society* (London, 1945), 48 ff.; Yrjö Hirn, *Sacred Shrine* (1909; Boston, 1957).

of Liberty and the Brooklyn Bridge; and the rhetoric supplements, tests, and verifies the visual impression. Other works conform in a general way to contemporary views; Thomas Cole's *Titan's Goblet* or *Course of Empire* (1836) and Albert Bierstadt's *Valley of the Yosemite* (1864) depict the vague understanding of the American landscape painters then shared with patrons. Sometimes the patrons themselves attempted to explain their tastes. The stereotypes which blur the human image of occupational or ethnic groups on the popular stage and in the movies summarize the previous visions of the audience and, therefore, persist. Still again, function furthers explanation: in the lithograph, twelve drawings beneath a great eye and the motto "United We Stand Divided We Fall" illustrate the obligations of brotherhood and the dignity of the job—membership certificate, United Mine Workers (1889). The shapes of clipper ships and automobiles owe something, but not everything, to use in transportation.[22]

Sometimes no suggestive linkages appear; the artist himself does not know what considerations framed his vision. A sensitive viewer can attach broad and perhaps correct meanings to a comic strip or motion picture.[23] But as these judgments slip toward the subjective, they depart from the evidence and are in danger of losing touch with the criteria for truth and falsity.[24] It is tempting then to fall back upon Lévi-Strauss, Freud, or Marx, and in the absence of data to limp along on the crutches of anthropological or psychological theories of myth or symbol. There are hazards in resting too much weight on those fragile structures, and whoever relies upon them must inspect the object carefully enough to avoid the

22 Oscar Handlin, *Statue of Liberty* (New York, 1971); Alan Trachtenberg, *Brooklyn Bridge: Fact and Symbol* (New York, 1965); Donald A. Ringe, "Painting as Poem in the Hudson River Aesthetic," *American Quarterly*, XII (Spring 1960), 71 ff.; Arthur O. Lovejoy, "First Gothic Revival," *Essays in the History of Ideas* (New York, 1960), 136 ff. For stereotypes, see Buck Rainey, "'Reel' Cowboy," in Charles W. Harris and Buck Rainey, eds., *Cowboy* (Norman, Okla., 1976), 17 ff.; Chapter 16 at note 23.

23 See, e.g., François Truffaut, *Hitchcock* (New York, 1966); E. E. Cummings, Introduction to George Herriman, *Krazy Kat* (New York, 1946); Gilbert Seldes, *Seven Lively Arts* (New York, 1924), 41 ff.

24 Compare the impressions of individual cities in Burchard, "Urban Aesthetic," 112, 127.

kind of disastrous error that follows upon the failure to distinguish a bosom from a cloak.[25]

The difficulty in knowing not only what the physical world was but also how it appeared to the artist arises in any effort to go beyond the understanding of the words and probe the thinking of a novelist, poet, or dramatist. But there the analyst at least operates through the same medium as the creator. By contrast, when it comes to visual materials, the necessity of translating sights into words enormously complicates the problems.

Whoever inspects the designs painted onto Easter eggs, the characters in Western movies and comic books, the cut of women's skirts, the layout of space advertisements, or the shape of upholstered furniture looks at the products not of individuals but of collectivities. One need not embrace any particular interpretation of folk art to recognize the timelessness and repetitive quality of these objects. It is difficult and perhaps unnecessary to fix a particular date for their creation or to associate forms and designs transmitted by habit with particular external incidents. The meaning lies rather in the elements, including inertia, which dispose the collectivity to cling to or alter its inherited images. In pursuit of that meaning the historian, the sharpness of whose tools depend upon dating and association, labors at a great disadvantage.[26]

The artist, although a special kind of person, more readily yields to historical analysis. He or she was born in a specific year, died in another, and completed each work in still others. Family, places of residence, education, and responses to external constraints, pressures, and stimuli are all susceptible to study.

But artists also have exceptional scope within which to focus their expressive intentions. Commanding a skill that is out of the

25 Otis A. Pease, "Review of Stuart Ewen, Captains of Consciousness," *American Historical Review*, LXXXII (October 1977), 1093. See also Chapter 7 at note 9. Paul Monaco, *Cinema and Society: France and Germany during the Twenties* (New York, 1976), is reductionist and disappointing.

26 See Chapter 10 at note 30.

ordinary, they are not as bound by culture and society as are other people—or as is even the gifted user of words. Uninhibited by the requirements of translation, artists put their observations directly into visual form, so that historians who know how to look at the product they create can see what they saw. To handle this material is difficult, and the results of interpreting it are necessarily tenuous —though rewarding if successful.

A single illustration will illuminate the problem.

What did people see when they looked at a great modern city? What visual image passed through their minds?

Verbal descriptions by travelers and residents provide some materials for an answer, but their limitations cry out for reference to the surviving visual data. Thousands of woodcuts, engravings, aquatints, lithographs, photographs, and paintings of urban places in the United States offer access to the images perceived at the moment and from the place of their creation. By fitting together the appropriate pieces from among this material, the historian may derive an image of the actual physical shape of the city—or of a city. But he will not thereby have arrived at an understanding of what the city appeared to be to its earlier viewers. Only the borrowed eyes of the artists of the time can bring him that.[27]

Artists in the United States inherited a convention. The President's House and Bunker Hill monument gave them little to go on when it came to imitating the palaces, fountains, and churches that provided subjects for the European engraver. But Americans could follow the practice of depicting an entire city as a whole. Whoever in the Old World saw Albi or Sion called up the vision of a place enclosed in walls and comprehensible within a single frame. Down well into the second half of the nineteenth century, Americans sought to capture the same image, retreating for vantage points across harbors and rivers to nearby heights. Even photography did not change the intention. As late as 1870 J. W. Black attempted to get a picture of the whole city of Boston onto a photographic plate. He succeeded quite well by ascending in a balloon to an altitude at which he got a substantial area in and yet still made out the topographical configuration, the layout of

[27] There is a useful collection of plans in John W. Reps, *Making of Urban America* (Princeton, 1965).

streets, the wharves along the harbor, and some notable buildings. The emphasis on wholeness was not iconographic only, but conformed to the way in which citizens thought of their cities.

Later the focus narrowed. Population rose and boundaries expanded. Improved, high-speed lenses made possible aerial photographs which revealed the general layout and topography but could show specifics only in blown-up parts; details were visible only in a small area, with no view of the entirety. This was characteristic of twentieth-century urban experience; the residents of the city perceived only fragments rather than a whole community, except perhaps in the moments of ascent from the airport when the lines of light reaching through the darkness suggested the larger entity.[28]

Thus, toward the end of the nineteenth century the question acquired an altered character and became: what did Americans see when they looked at the part of the city within their range of vision?

In framing an answer, photographs have the utility of realism and in specifics are accurate. Pictures by Jacob Riis or Louis Hine portray city sights graphically. Early movies like the Chaplin shorts or Buster Keaton's *Coney Island* (1917), filmed before the withdrawal to California and the studio set, use the street as stage and get down what the camera saw. There is more manipulation in Erich von Stroheim's *Greed* (1925), in Josef von Sternberg's *Docks of New York* (1928), and in the Harold Lloyd comedies; but the urban images still predominate.

Yet photographs can mislead, for their very appearance of realism conceals the bias or the intention of the photographer. Riis and Hine are photopolemicists whose cameras argue causes. Their perspectives, the stationing of their lenses, and the impression they wish to impart condition the character of their pictures.

Elements of distortion also creep in when the picture is background for action or for the portrayal of character. In F. W

28 See, e.g., illustrations in Robert Sears, *Pictorial Description of the United States* (New York, 1852) ; Kouwenhoven, *Columbia Historical Portrait of New York*, 188 ff., 330 ff.; Moses King, *Photographic Views of New York* (Boston, 1895) , 5, 7. Compare also complaints about the inability to speak "of London as a whole" and about "the huge looseness of New York"—Henry James, *Essays in London and Elsewhere* (New York, 1893) , 27, and *American Scene* (1907) , ed. Leon Edel (Bloomington, Ind., 1968) , 116 ff.

Murnau's *Sunrise* (1927) the city street seems real, authentic, but actually is a huge set, its dimensions deliberately exaggerated to overwhelm by its very size the young man and woman just arrived from the country. The picture is eloquent, but the historian must seek the source of its eloquence elsewhere than in its conformity with reality. With the coming of sound and color after 1930, and with technological refinement of equipment, opportunities for manipulating the lens multiply; and with them the historian's problems of seeing. The candid camera catches the subject off guard, but diminishes the candor of the photographer who can select among a large number of shots, often thus emphasizing the individual rather than the place. For Walker Evans, Coney Island (1929), the Bronx (1933), and 42nd Street (1929) are faces and legs.[29]

For the half-century after 1880, therefore, the nonmechanical arts offer more informative impressions of the appearance of the city than do the mechanical. The painter also wishes to convey an opinion. Depictions on canvas are interpretive—but intentionally, deliberately, and openly so. Furthermore, the work of those decades, while still representational, is yet free enough of old conventions and inhibitions to allow open and impressionistic treatment of the subject.

In the 1880s emphasis falls upon the animation of the urban landscape, as in J. J. Fogerty's lithograph of New York's dry-goods district, which reveals a street jammed with horses and people in motion and communicates a sense of confusion and chaos, but also of life. But in the twentieth century, depictions of the city more often stress straight lines and rectilinear shapes, conveying an impression of rigid order and cold surfaces, so that whatever human beings appear seem held in the grip of streets and buildings. In *New York Pavements* (1924) Edward Hopper boxes everything off into precise squares, sidewalks and houses alike; and the squares enclose the black figures of people. His *Nighthawks* (1942) uses a similar arrangement of space to show personal isolation. In *Cliff Dwellers* (1925) by George Bellows the dark, shadowy buildings of the background confine the light colors of the children in

29 Helen Levitt, *Way of Seeing: Photographs of New York* (New York, 1965) ; Evans, *American Photographs*, 30, 32, 46, 90.

the foreground. The smallness of humans in these settings does not impress the painters as it does Murnau in *Sunrise*. They more often see the artificial and mechanical quality of life, a stark contrast with the animation earlier viewed. John Marin, drifting away from realism, loses sight of the human entirely in the fine thin lines of *Downtown New York* (1921) .[30]

Traffic occupies the streets of the city of the 1920s as of the 1880s, but now motorized, organized in straight lines, and stationary. The automobile has excluded the horse; the machine has stifled life. In Maurice Canton's *Farewell to Union Square* (1931) the cars kill the area as they advance in a rigid pattern dictated from elsewhere, themselves confined and constraining others. Rapid transit, elevated and subway, has the same impact. Charles Sheeler's *Church Street El* (1921) and John Sloan's *Sixth Avenue L* (1928) enclose the landscape in prisonlike girders which overshadow the humans; pictures of the subway crowd the riders into boxes.

Light takes on a new form, visible in the contrast between the flickering gaslights of the nineteenth century and the glare of twentieth-century electricity; the former move and cast shadows, the latter does not. Peggy Bacon's *City Lights,* like Charlie Chaplin's movie of the same name at about the same time, makes that glare contrived, even sinister. In Peter Blume's *Light of the World* (1932) the artificial glare attracts people who disregard the reality around them—home, others, indeed all that lives. The hints of light in Adolf Dehn's lithograph *Central Park at Night* (1934) emphasize the silhouette of the surrounding skyline. And in *Armistice Night in New York* (1918), which George Luks intended to be joyous, the yellow lights expose the drab masses and looming shapes of dark buildings.[31]

All efforts at real life are contrived. In Glenn Coleman's *In the Mirror* (1927) everything is reflected, nothing is viewed directly. The voluptuous curves of the roller coasters and the animation of the people at the amusement park in Reginald Marsh's paintings

30 Kouwenhoven, *Columbia Historical Portrait of New York,* 16, 17. Compare also the street in the German Expressionist cinema, Lotte H. Eisner, *Haunted Screen* (London, 1969), 251 ff.

31 On the spell of light and the world of shadows and mirrors, see also Eisner, *Haunted Screen,* 39 ff., 89 ff., 129 ff.

offer a stark contrast to the flat, linear life of the actual city. The same contrast takes another form in William Glackens' *Hammerstein's Roof Garden* (1901) ; and in John Sloan's *McSorley's Bar* (1912) the figures come forth from the shadows. The artist can display real men and women, moving, feeling, only on the stage or at nightclubs.

The paintings breathe nostalgia for the vestiges of nature in the city. DeThulstrup's drawing in *Harper's Weekly* (1891) of a popular concert in Tompkins Square and Maurice Prendergast's *Central Park* (1910) show the liveliness of the people in a setting that preserves a rural refuge within the city. Jerome Myers, *East Side Market,* and John Sloan, *Backyards* and *Washington Square* (1929), do the same. Rivers, as in George Bellows, *Floating Ice* (1910), though hemmed in, retain a sense of flow.

These perceptions of the paintings' contents are in accord with the other visual materials of the period. They conform also to much written about the city and by and about the artists. The evidence from canvas does not overturn that from paper, but amplifies and deepens its meaning.

The problems of hearing are similar to those of seeing, but more difficult. The sight may endure; the sound vanishes with the uttering.

In the nature of the case, efforts at reconstruction succeed only in part. Where the script of a drama or the notes of a score survive, the lines can be respoken, the song resung. The task is not simple. The ears best attuned to dialect set down approximate equivalents; too often the syllables form only a caricature of the language. The texts most carefully located in context reveal the importance of the physical structure of the Elizabethan theater to Shakespearean acting, of the assignment of female roles to boys or castrati in seventeenth-century opera, of the difference between earlier and later instruments, and of the latitude of phrasing permitted the performer. Even with account taken of these manageable factors, there remains the impossibility of recreating the specific audience, the specific circumstances, the specific setting. The sound of a hymn in a Massachusetts meetinghouse depends not on the tune or voices alone, but on the building, the sermon, the feel of the weather, and the mood of the worshipers which gave it resonance. And so, too, with the minstrels' melodies and the voice of the Swedish Nightingale and the jazz out of New Orleans or Chicago.[32]

It takes more than the availability of the notes to know these sounds. For more than a century cylinders, disks, and tape have preserved voices in speech and song. Useful anthologies of early American drama, the Library of Congress Archive of Folk Song, and the Smithsonian Institution's National Collection of Fine Arts (some of it transcribed by New World Records for the Recorded Anthology of American Music) put other materials within reach. But the historian must be able to lay hold of it.

Sound, like sight, has functions discernible from the context. Music becomes a mode of worship and, entwined with many forms of bodily motion, accompanies work, dance, and various types of play. Bound up with words or lyrics, the song tells a story or communicates emotions, often more expressively than words alone can in prose or poetry. Interesting analyses have begun to probe these uses and messages. But music, like the graphic and plastic arts, has its own character, not independent of, but apart from, the purpose served and the words or motions accompanied. And retrospective access to that character is even more difficult than in the case of painting, where the canvas survives.

Folk songs present the usual difficulties of dating and attribution, precisely because their singers believe them timeless and claim possession by inheritance. They tend thus to minimize the extent of borrowing and diffusion and to blot out the date of actual composition or appropriation. Southerners after the Civil War were unwilling or unable to recall the circumstances of the origin of "Dixie"; black jazz players were rarely conscious of the influence of the popular tunes of the whites.[33] On the other hand,

32 Notable efforts to reproduce dialect include: James Russell Lowell, *Bigelow Papers* (Cambridge, 1848) ; A. B. Longstreet, *Georgia Scenes* (Augusta, Ga., 1835) ; Henry Roth, *Call It Sleep* (Paterson, N.J., 1960) ; Finley Peter Dunne, *Mr. Dooley's Philosophy* (New York, 1900) . See also H. L. Mencken, *American Language* (New York, 1937) , 319 ff., and Eric A. Havelock, *Preface to Plato* (Cambridge, 1963) , 36 ff., 115 ff., on oral culture.

33 Hans Nathan, *Dan Emmett and the Rise of Early Negro Minstrelsy* (Norman, Okla., 1962) , 245 ff., 255 ff.; Chadwick Hansen, "Social Influences on Jazz Style," *American Quarterly*, XII (Winter 1960) , 493 ff.

such music circulates within a knowable collectivity, the tastes, attitudes, and interests of which are subject to examination and description. It may be difficult to judge just when a specific song heard in 1867 entered the slave repertory and what it owed to Africa, what to the crossing, and what to the South; but its association with the freedmen who remembered it is clear. So too with the spirituals and rag heard in the 1890s.[34]

Individuals, even creative ones, expose a graspable surface when they make contact with the society in which they operate. Performers, for instance, mediate between the composer and an audience, and to that extent they operate in a describable market susceptible of analysis. Responding to habits, manners, and choices which are more than personal, they become comprehensible. For, even though the particular qualities which account for the greatness of a soprano, pianist, or conductor are idiosyncratic, the greater part of their role involves interaction with intermediaries and with listeners who are also parts of the knowable collectivity.[35]

Much the same was true of the great majority of composers, who also operated within a definable market that shaped their compositions. Few in the United States felt the impulse to move beyond the expectations of their immediate audience. William Billings, an eighteenth-century Bostonian and a man of many trades, cheerfully turned out solemn or celebratory tunes for his townspeople, in a fashion followed by Stephen C. Foster, Mrs. H. H. A. Beach, and John Philip Sousa, among others. Since little in their music was original their work offered material mostly for studies in derivation—ethnic, religious, and social—and in the way it provided vocal symbols, for the listening participants. It has, however, been much more difficult to judge whether their music,

[34] Dena J. Epstein, *Sinful Tunes and Spirituals* (Urbana, Ill., 1977) ; W. E. B. DuBois, *Souls of Black Folk* (Chicago, 1903), 251 ff.; Lawrence W. Levine, *Black Culture and Black Consciousness* (New York, 1977), 190 ff.; William J. Schafer and Johannes Riedel, *Art of Ragtime* (Baton Rouge, 1973), 24 ff., 143 ff. See also Theodore C. Blegen, *Grass Roots History* (Minneapolis, 1947), 31 ff.

[35] Impressions by performers are useful but not altogether reliable; e.g., Henri Herz, *Mes voyages en Amérique* (Paris, 1866). William Weber, *Music and the Middle Classes: The Social Structure of Concert Life in London, Paris and Vienna* (London, 1975), is excellent despite the encumbrance of references to modernization. Lisa Appignanesi, *Cabaret* (New York, 1976), is a meager, disappointing text for nostalgic pictures. See also Collingwood, *Principles of Art*, 325 ff.

as such and apart from the lyrics, had anything to say either about the composers or the audience.[36]

The truly creative individuals and their work have largely eluded historical analysis, and perhaps will always remain a formidable mystery susceptible to criticism and appreciation, not to explanation. Attempts to derive from Marxist premises the conclusion that artistic forms "cannot stand higher than the society which brought them forth" falter at encounters with genius.[37] Seventeenth-century Spain and eighteenth-century Austria and nineteenth-century Russia have much to do with subjects and modes of expression, little to do with creativity. By reaching deeply into the world of Central Europe in the late eighteenth century, the scholar can understand the development of the opera, of the symphony, and of chamber music. He can learn a good deal about partronage, about the composition of audiences, about the roles of impressarios and librettists, about the beginnings of advertising and promotion, and about the penetration of Enlightenment ideas. But he will not thereby be able to explain the music of Mozart or what it tried to say; not, that is, without somehow achieving the miracle of entering the composer's mind and listening to the sounds take form there.

Much less than that usually satisfies historians. The ablest accounts deal with the circles in which the composers moved, as in the analysis of Mahler's relation to the Viennese Pernersdorfer circle, which attempts to link symbolist art and populist politics. But even that devotes more attention to the composer's metamusical cosmos than to the contents of his music.[38]

The history of music in the United States reveals only one composer of comparable merit. The unfortunate biography that treated him illustrated the danger of reducing the explanation of art to its social context. Frank R. Rossiter was factually wrong in

---

[36] David P. McKay and Richard Crawford, *William Billings of Boston* (Princeton, 1975). Jerome L. Rodnitzky, *Minstrels of the Dawn* (Chicago, 1976), misses an opportunity for analysis by taking his subjects at face value.

[37] Georg Lukács, *Historical Novel*, trans. Hannah and Stanley Mitchell (London, 1962), 348.

[38] William J. McGrath, *Dionysian Art and Populist Politics in Austria* (New Haven, 1974), 92 ff., 122 ff. Frederic Jameson, *Marxism and Form* (Princeton, 1971), 11 ff., 19 ff., summarizes T. W. Adorno, who is at once suggestive and perverse in adherence to the dialectic.

describing that context as, for instance, in supposing that in the United States music was tainted by suspicions of effeminacy. Nor did he take account of the alternatives the country offered dissident contemporaries in other arts. Most important, he did not explain why Ives's creativity flagged. The biographer could do so only by seeking the source of that creativity not in the social setting but in the composer's ways of handling melody, harmony, polyphony, sonority, and rhythm. Ives, who believed that interpretations were personal and emotional, to be recreated by the artist at each performance, stood more in need of such analysis than most; and the lack of it distorted Rossiter's account.[39]

Changes in the mode and substance of communication have compounded the difficulty of penetrating the mind of the artist, whether musician or painter, for students of the twentieth century. Alterations in the media of expression and in relations to the audience have been as radical as those which accompanied the diffusion of print and the replacement of the salon by the concert hall and museum. But, in addition to the intrusion of electronics, which depersonalized viewers and spectators, interior changes in the nature of what was seen and heard reduced the ability of the historian to look and listen.

American artists inherited a tradition that focused their attention on external reality. They produced objects for clients who dictated function and use and, to some extent, form and content. A family, guild, or church commissioned a painting because it wanted a portrait of one or several members or the depiction of a sacred scene for veneration. Music was for dance or worship; a mass accompanied a holy ritual, and the congregation which intoned a hymn addressed God. The links between the artist's creative act and his audience were social and cultural and, therefore, comprehensible to the historian.

The long-term tendency toward abstraction, down to the end

39 Frank R. Rossiter, *Charles Ives and His America* (New York, 1975) , 311 ff., 320. By contrast, see W. H. Mellers, "Music in the Melting Pot: Charles Ives and the Music of the Americas," *Scrutiny,* VII (March 1939) , 392 ff. On the situation of Frank Lloyd Wright, whose most productive years left him resentful of uncritical acceptance and thoughtless praise, see Robert C. Twombly, *Frank Lloyd Wright* (New York, 1973) , 97; Peter I. Abernathy, "Expatriate's Dream of Home," *American Studies,* XVIII (Fall 1977) , 46.

of the nineteenth century, still did not detach the artist from the context in which he worked. When painting became decorative and narrative it removed the power of the purchaser to dictate what faces and incidents would appear on the canvas. Subjects from classical mythology and history and landscapes and still life freed the artists' imagination. In time, Americans learned to value the faces of unknown sitters, certified as the compositions of Old Masters. So, too, a suite ceased, in the eighteenth century, to be accompaniment for a dance and evolved into a variety of purely auditory forms, as did much of the music composed with a deep religious content for the purpose of worship. By the nineteenth century the listener to a symphony, mass, or march heard the sounds alone, detached from their external function, that of the original creator or any other. In all the arts, color, line, shape, and tone alone mattered. The transformation, having gained strength in Europe, eventually affected the United States.

A more extreme phase began toward the end of the nineteenth century. Ever more often and more intensely the artist conceived himself in revolt against society—not only against the government and its established institutions, not only against the bourgeoisie and its conventions, but even more against the whole order, conceived as a vague encompassing constraint upon individual creativity. The attitude was not new; the ability to act upon it was. Painters, musicians, and sculptors not only insisted that they alone set their own values, choose their own subjects, and decide upon their own modes of treatment, as the romantics earlier had; but, seceding within autonomous communities, the later rebels actually did so.

By a variety of routes they arrived at a variety of types of modernism. In Europe the new forms of expressionism offered outlets to a generation of genius. But, though enormously stimulating, they pointed consistently in the direction of abstraction, isolating the image from its function and treating it as its own reality. Impressionism opened out into schools which moved undeviatingly away from representation in painting and sculpture. Musicians, having accepted the challenge of a story or program, quickly went on to the aspiration of conveying an idea. In time they came to play with pure tonal relationships, so that the sound of it became entirely subsidiary. After the middle of the twentieth century nonmusical music was beyond the comprehension of the listener, nonrepresentational art beyond that of the viewer.[40]

The queries—why a can of soup became a painting when transposed to canvas by Andy Warhol, or blotches of color by Jackson Pollock; or what made John Cage's arrangement of noises and silence music—received the identical answer: Art was what the artist said it was. There was always an element of illusion in art.[41] But not illusion alone; the will to communicate preserved threads that linked creator and audience.

With those threads severed, the historian examining this evidence can see only the intention of the artist and nothing of the context—except perhaps something about the market which tolerated and encouraged the output. Art under those circumstances is a subject for biography or criticism, not for history.

That broad tendency toward abstraction did not directly affect the popular or vernacular forms of visual or musical expression. While the comics lost the specificity of "Hogan's Alley" in the 1890s, the quest for the widest audience drew them toward more universality and comprehensibility. But the tendency toward artistic abstraction did have a counterpart in literature, and analagous problems arise in the use as evidence of modern poetry and fiction.

[40] Read, *Icon and Idea*, 39 ff., 130 ff.

[41] R. L. Gregory and E. H. Gombrich, *Illusion in Nature and Art* (London, 1973).

# 10

# History in a World of Knowledge

FIFTY YEARS AGO Harry Elmer Barnes stated the relation of history to its surrounding disciplines. In the nature of the case, he outlined a simple design with Comtean origins. History dealt with the time dimension of a subject—man in society—of which the social sciences provided the analytical theoretical descriptions. Simple chapter headings adequately served the needs of the day: geography, psychology, anthropology, history of science, economics, sociology, political science.

Although Barnes's book amounted largely to a vast compendium of names, its design conformed to the assumptions then current. History provided a field for experiments mobilizing the data from past experience to test theories evolved by the social sciences, each of which treated its own subject matter, just as chemistry, physics, and biology did. The organization of knowledge fitted, in the one case, the institutions of society, in the other, the properties of nature.[1]

The leading historians of the day confidently accepted the role thus assigned them. Carl L. Becker, somewhat skeptically, and Charles A. Beard, with wholehearted enthusiasm, endorsed the position; and the scholars active in writing social history did not dissent. The world of scholarship by 1925 had grown accustomed to thinking of itself in these comfortable terms of which the federal structure of the Social Science Research Council provided a reassuring example.[2]

---

[1] Harry Elmer Barnes, *New History and the Social Studies* (New York, 1925) .

[2] Carl L. Becker, "Review," *Saturday Review of Literature*, II (Aug. 15, 1925) , 38. For earlier statements, see James Harvey Robinson, *New History* (New York, 1912) ,

In the decades after 1925 the number of specialities multiplied, and the lines within and among them shifted. The conception of history as a social science, nevertheless, remained unchanged.

Yet the challenges to the basic assumptions of the social science scheme became more compelling decade by decade. It had always been clear that history's linkages reached beyond the area known as social sciences on into the territory known in the United States as the humanities. Affiliation with the American Council of Learned Societies quietly acknowledged the kinship, although scholars eager to demonstrate their usefulness rarely made much of that aspect of the subject.

Furthermore, the development of the social sciences after 1925 took an unexpected direction: they refused to remain coherent uniform disciplines and grew less rather than more coherent as each fragmented into divisions hardly comprehensible to practitioners across the internal boundaries. The prefixes sociology of— or economics of—could adhere to any human activity; and an anthropology department could shelter courses on myth and folklore, law and conflict resolution, art, and economic aspects of peasant societies, as well as on paleontology, primate anatomy, and archeology. As a result, some anthropologists and sociologists were closer to one another than to the colleagues of their own designations. Not infrequently social scientists reached out into altogether alien turf and within it faced challenges from marauding philosophers, physicians, biologists, geologists, and physicists. The disconcerting disposition to wander characterized techniques as well as subject matter; every group sheltered scholars who employed quantitative, behavioral, and theoretical methods to which the old divisions were scarcely relevant.[3]

The situation was not unlike that in the physical sciences, which also passed through drastic divisions and recombinations in re-

---

70 ff.; for later ones, Thomas C. Cochran, "Historical Use of the Social Sciences," *Inner Revolution* (New York, 1964), 19 ff.; Edward N. Saveth, ed., *American History and the Social Sciences* (New York, 1964); Chapter 3 at note 49. Richard Jensen, "History and the Political Scientist," in Seymour M. Lipset, ed., *Politics and the Social Sciences* (New York, 1969), 1 ff., is more sensible.

[3] For example, George E. Pugh, *Biological Origin of Human Values* (New York, 1977), by a physicist.

254     *Dealing with the Evidence*

sponse to new discoveries and fresh interpretations. The once stable field of biology shot splinters in all directions with the emergence of biochemistry and molecular biology, which required practitioners to establish links with chemistry, physics, and biophysics and had implications for genetics, pharmacology, immunology, and physiology—and, therefore, for medicine and agriculture, insofar as the two last-named were also sciences. The historian who recalls that demography, the designation for a well-established subject, is less than a century old will not be startled to discover in the 1977 Olms catalogue of scholarly books, between Hübschmann's *Armenische Grammatik* and Wilhelm von Humboldt's, *Über die Verschiedenheit des menschlichen Sprachbaues,* Wolfgang K. Hünig's *Strukturen des Comic Strip,* a volume of the Series Practica of Studia Semiotica. And indeed, Semiotics, recently greeted among the sciences, already has produced its share of discoveries. The standing strategy of modern scholarship, after all, defines every change as either a new synthesis or a new discovery—and evades the consequences by calling chaos growth.[4]

The fragility of all lines doomed to failure the efforts to impose coherence upon the social sciences whether by structural-functional sociologists in the 1950s or by behaviorist-oriented anthropologists in the 1970s, either by buttressing particular subjects or by providing a common language for all or some of them. These fields were not so much coherent organizations of a homogeneous subject matter as institutional arrangements within the academies which housed practitioners trained in a common fashion, communicating through journals of their own and recognizing the judgment of their peers. If historians turned their backs upon the theories of Immanuel Velikowsky or Erich Von Däniken, it was on the basis not of scrutiny of the evidence but of judgment by trusted experts in neighboring departments.[5]

---

[4] "Discoveries and Interpretations Studies in Contemporary Scholarship," *Daedalus,* CVI (Summer, Fall 1977) . See also Jonathan Culler, *Saussure* (Hassocks, Eng., 1976) , 90 ff. Thus, too, paralinguistics and glottology, tactile communication and olfactory signs.

[5] Talcott Parsons and Edward A. Shils, eds., *Toward a General Theory of Action* (Cambridge, 1951) ; "Social Sciences, One or Many," Louis Wirth, ed., *Eleven Twenty-Six* (Chicago, 1940) , 113 ff. The faith of Robert F. Berkhofer, Jr., *Behavioral Approach to Historical Analysis* (New York, 1969) , 27 ff., in a start from "basic theory" is misplaced.

♙

An understanding of the development of the social sciences would have spared Barnes's contemporaries the penalties of mistaken assumptions which all too frequently still bind historians a half-century later.

In the eighteenth century the world of knowledge recognized no such distinctions and accepted no such boundaries. The old scholastic organization of learning no longer held, except in the most backward universities, and the heirs of Bacon, Newton, and Bayle sought new organizing principles. Ephraim Chambers, Diderot, and the other Encyclopedists worried about arrangement—whether systematic or alphabetical—and about the desirable balance between assembling and systematizing information. But their basic premise was encyclopedic; that is, they assumed that a common subject matter, nature, and laws of universal validity unified all knowledge. After 1800 European theorists and, above all, Auguste Comte sought more refined definitions—especially after Herbert Spencer applied evolutionary ideas to the fields of learning. But the term "scientist" did not become common in England and the United States until mid-century and the modification "social" came still later.[6]

In the world of knowledge history always had an identity of its own, although in modern times local conditions shaped the scholarly development of the subject because concern with the past grew out of interests in law, politics, religion, philosophy, art, and literature, which varied from place to place. History entered the formal curricula of European universities through the establishment of individual professorships not linked in departments or affiliated to any equivalent of the social sciences. On the eve of the Second World War that remained everywhere the case.

In the United States, however, tardy development until the last quarter of the nineteenth century cast the universities within a departmental structure that recognized the autonomy of history but also its special affinity to politics and economics. The decisions

[6] Robert Collison, *Encyclopedias: Their History throughout the Ages*, 2d ed. (New York, 1966), 82 ff., 114 ff.; Robert Flint, *Philosophy as Scientia Scientiarum and a History of the Classification of the Sciences* (New York, 1904), 104 ff., 141 ff.

that established the trend reflected the bias of influential individuals, the desire to make the study of the past useful, and the pressures that arose from the association of scholarship with teaching.
The graduate faculties at Columbia and Chicago set history firmly
in the domain of the social scientists; and the other major institutions followed a pattern scarcely less rigid. Economists, political
scientists, and sociologists accepted the arrangement because many
of them then hoped to dip into the past for data; and the protag-
onists of the new history welcomed it as a way of making their subject useful and of providing it with a ready-made theoretical
framework.[7]

The drawbacks of the outcome hobbled the efforts of historians
to get on with their work. Dependence on the analyses of others
left many a generation behind; the obsolescence of information
acquired as undergraduates obliged them to retool when John M.
Keynes crowded out Alfred Marshall and John B. Clark or when
Talcott Parsons supplanted C. H. Cooley and Robert E. Park. It
took a good deal of confidence to judge rival claims rather than
drift along with the tides of fashion; or, for that matter, to affirm
that scholars like Arthur F. Bentley and Simon N. Patten suffered
undeserved neglect at the hands of their colleagues. The historian
who read German and French might well wonder why Max Weber
and Émile Durkheim were less well known in the United States of
the 1930s than the translated Vilfredo Pareto, but was rarely in
a position to raise a dissenting voice in an alien jurisdiction.

The situation in the social sciences produced other anomalies, as
in separating the study of history from natural alliances with the
classics, literature, and philosophy. A variety of interdepartmental
and interdisciplinary mechanisms corrected the more obvious distortions, but depended upon collegiate tolerance and the quirks
of individual friendship. Yet historians continued to embrace the
relationship with social science. None dared to challenge its claim
to utility or its pretension of predictive value, although abundant
evidence after 1940 raised doubts about the ability to forecast
population trends, swings in the business cycle, the incidence of
juvenile delinquency, or the results of elections. The alternative to
acquiescence was independence, and few were willing or able un-

---

[7] See Chapter 3 at note 27; Laurence R. Veysey, *Emergence of the American University* (Chicago, 1965) , 113 ff., 173 ff.

aided to formulate the organizing concepts which gave meaning to their results.[8]

⤳

The knowledge embraced in the disciplines known in the United States as social sciences is important. No scholar can dispense with it, any more than with that embraced in those known as humanities. But the historian cannot simply become possessor of a distinct chunk of information or of a particular tool chest of techniques, judged in advance to stand in a helpful relation to future research. He must immerse himself in a whole world of knowledge, within which boundaries are not precise and the configurations of which change constantly in response to winds of endlessly restless thought.

In that world most inhabitants know the particular plots they cultivate, as do the historians among them. But those gain an inestimable advantage who become familiar with its totality—with its varied parts and with their interrelations. The task is difficult. But excellence in scholarship is not easily come by.

Three kinds of experiences await the historian who ventures afield. Two are familiar. The usual critical skills will help evaluate works about the past not written by historians, and will help appraise the value of evidence of past research by practitioners in other subjects. To understand the theoretical structure of other fields of knowledge, however, demands sharp readjustments to unfamiliar ways of thinking.

In every area scholars in pursuit of knowledge and experts in the exercise of a skill have felt the call to chronicle past events within the scope of their competence. They write special, as distinguished from general or integral, history, work in the *historische Wissenschaften,* as distinct from the *Fach, "Geschichte."*[9] In some cases the need for retrospection grows out of intellectual curiosity: how did ancient predecessors build bridges or forge iron? In other cases the will to know responds to a desire to trace

---

[8] See, e.g., Sheldon and Eleanor Glueck, *Predicting Delinquency and Crime* (Cambridge, 1959); David S. Landes and Charles Tilly, *History as Social Science* (New York, 1971), 10 ff.

[9] Maurice Mandelbaum, *Anatomy of Historical Knowledge* (Baltimore, 1977), 12 ff.; R. H. Shryock, "Interplay of Social and Internal Factors in Modern Medicine," *Medicine in America* (Baltimore, 1966), 166 ff.

development back from the present, in the expectation that the habits or decisions of long ago will help explain current usages. More rarely, the attraction of history reflects the wish to avoid repeating the mistakes of the past—or even to learn from its achievements. In any case, physicians, attorneys, statesmen, architects, and critics have compiled histories of medicine, law, politics, art, literature, and music.

These books, in general, take an interior view of the subject. They accept its current premises as given and regard its development as inevitable, moving from past error to present truth. The historian, who cannot match the practitioners in familiarity with the subject, may find them enormously useful, but must avoid the temptation of being sucked into acceptance of their assumptions, to which the usual criteria of criticism must apply.

Those who write from within generally view their subject as whole, integral, and detached—a perspective framed by limitations of training and interest. However well-intentioned, they tend to see development unfolding from self-contained causes. If they make general references to external social forces, meaningless schematic associations take the place of explanation; frequently they arrive at the dead end of phrases like capitalism, the industrial revolution, the middle class, or urbanization. Rarely can these scholars look beyond the confines of their own particular subject to establish linkages in detail. It would demand a break with long-standing habits of thought to expect a physician to relate medicine to other forms of healing or an attorney to consider the law one of several ways of resolving disputes.

Furthermore, the prevailing doctrines of the moment narrow the vision of the insider. The very best of the economists of the 1960s was likely to understand the history of the productive system as the story of the penetration of society by market forces defined in terms of the analysis of the previous two decades; and was, therefore, likely to pay little attention to development of the infrastructure, the distribution and service sectors that acquired new significance in the 1970s.[10]

Practitioners committed to their own procedures and outlook tend to consider the past progress to a present destination. Their predecessors, held within a structure of outmoded beliefs, moved

[10] John Hicks, *Theory of Economic History* (Oxford, 1969) ; Chapter 17 at note 5.

along a path that pointed upward—and had to because knowledge, by its very nature, was cumulative. The same mode of regarding the past less readily fitted the arts. Few historians of music or literature considered nineteenth-century composers or poets superior to those of the seventeenth century. Yet even in those areas the ongoing liberation of the artist became a form of progress.

The historian equipped with the requisite knowledge can take a longer view. The outsider can escape the diversion exerted by immediate policy considerations and can discern age-old secular trends hidden in kaleidescopic changes in theory, as, for instance, the ancient controversy over heredity and environment concealed in many of the flips and flops of sociological, psychological, and anthropological theory in the half-century after 1925. The outsider also need not fall victim to the trap of linear progress, but can perceive, even in pure science, the wrong turn and the treadmill activity that expends enormous energy but gets nowhere, except perhaps in applying new terms to old problems.[11]

Above all, the historian who knows enough can demand, or can himself make, connections between one form of practice and another, as well as between politics and the productive system, between art and family life, between religion and technology. Gross, schematic formulas come easily to hand. The meaningful linkages, products of careful study and thought, are more difficult to establish and more rewarding. The historian readily concedes the superior expertness in the area of their competence of the specialists working from within, but must challenge errors of omission or commission in the linkage to the wider world of knowledge. It is not a denial of the competence of a great twentieth-century historian of painting to decide that he is wrong in defining Hegelianism so that it blankets Burckhardt and Huizinga.[12]

Historians stand in an entirely different relation to the world of knowledge when they confront the remnants of its activity in the

---

11 For an example of a wrong turn see the introduction by Leo M. Hurvich and Dorothea Jameson to Ewald Hering, *Outlines of a Theory of the Light Sense* (Cambridge, 1964). Thomas S. Kuhn, *Structure of Scientific Revolutions*, 2d ed. (Chicago, 1970), an ingenious but, even in its revised form, an unconvincing effort to juxtapose linear progress and occasional error, perceives the trap of relativism (everything correct for its time); but cannot escape it.

12 E. H. Gombrich, *In Search of Cultural History* (Oxford, 1969), 14 ff., 29.

past. Mountains of words on paper survive, generated by physicists and philosophers, physicians and economists, critics and chemists. The formal reports and treatises, the notes on experiments and sketches for buildings or paintings, the marginalia and the drafts of essays, all testify to human minds at work on definable problems. In reconstructions of the past they provide information for expanding the evidence vertically and horizontally. On the one hand, they throw light on the evolution of the modes of knowing and of expression through time; on the other, they illuminate the myriad aspects of the life of the period of which they are the residue.

In most cases the usual techniques are adequate for evaluating and interpreting this form of evidence. These, too, are records, judged by their location in time and place and by the characters of their authors, as letters and travel accounts are. The task becomes somewhat more complex when the document nestles within a shield of scientific conventions that reach for generality and impersonality and obscure its specificity. Historians of the United States encounter the problem most often in assessing the products of social research generated since the middle of the nineteenth century. The reader knowing something about the bias of travelers can compensate for distortions in the descriptions of society by Peter Kalm or Timothy Dwight; the adjustments are more difficult when it comes to evaluating the useful yet tricky evidence in *Middletown* or in a Harris poll.

The genre originated in philanthropic investigations of the health and welfare of the population touched off by the assumption that social factors influenced the incidence of disease. Occasional dramatic outbreaks, such as the cholera epidemic of 1849, emphasized the urgency of gathering data on the environment. The day-to-day concerns of physicians also produced a helpful body of reports; and some, like Lemuel Shattuck, extended the range of their investigations to housing, immigration, and the conditions of labor.[13]

The emergence, toward the end of the nineteenth century, of the organized study of social science increased the importance of

---

[13] G. Melvyn Howe, "Mapping of Disease of History," in Edwin Clarke, ed., *Modern Methods in the History of Medicine* (London, 1971), 335 ff.

such material. The influence of Lester Ward compelled some scholars to apply their generalizations to improve society. For them the city became a social laboratory, brimful of data, careful study of which would yield conclusions to enrich science and also to solve practical problems. The unsystematic observations of well-intentioned physicians and benevolent laymen had to give way, however, to carefully designed research and formal questionnaires.

In the 1890s a variety of students examined life in American cities, inspired to some degree by Charles Booth's study of London. Some, like Robert A. Woods's volumes on Boston, were the prod-ducts of settlement houses and of organizations dedicated to charity. Others, like Kate Claghorn's work on New York, treated minority groups. Still others, like the Pittsburgh Survey or the DeForest and Veiller tenement-house investigation, followed par-ticularly violent disorders or pressing social tensions. Mostly they dealt with the large cities, although smaller towns like Lawrence and Minneapolis, Kansas, and Springfield, Illinois, also received attention, with emphasis resting everywhere upon intemperance, housing, and malfunctioning institutions such as the family or the church. The appearance of community funds and the pressure for more scientific and more efficient philanthropy increased the num-ber of such studies, which bequeathed a valuable body of informa-tion to historians.

In the 1920s social scientists, less directly concerned with ameli-orating social conditions, shifted emphasis to surveys as sources of data for abstract generalizations. Back in the first decade of the twentieth century, J. M. Gillette and C. J. Bushnell had demon-strated how maps and statistical tables could serve as analytical devices. Students of the sociologists F. H. Giddings, R. E. Park, and C. J. Galpin examined the ecological contexts of many Ameri-can rural and urban communities, using an approach that was still primarily empirical, with the sources concrete and specific so that the reader could distinguish between the generalizations of the scientists and the observations of the investigator.

After 1929 the newer uses to which sociologists and social an-thropologists pushed the community survey complicated the prob-lems of the historian who sought to draw upon their data. These investigations accumulated significant material, much of it dealing with attitudes and habits not earlier studied in detail. But the means by which the researchers gathered their information and the purposes they intended it to serve deprived it of specificity and seriously diminished its usefulness. The investigators of the next half-century decisively subordinated empirical findings to theory. Some surveys developed or tested general propositions of social-structural stratification by analyzing the division into classes of the communities they examined, as in *Middletown* by R. S. and H. M. Lynd and in Lloyd Warner's Yankee City Series. W. F. Whyte's *Streetcorner Society* (1943) and David Riesman's *Lonely Crowd* (1950), among others, used the survey to develop typological theories about personality types and character structure, often taking as their points of departure the sociology of Émile Durkheim and Ferdinand Tönnies. Unlike the ecological works of the earlier part of the century, these surveys glanced by the specific place and the concrete data and focused upon the generalization. Since the test of their conclusions was not by replication but by conformity with a general theory, the presentations minimized reports of direct observations and concentrated on methodological procedures and abstract analysis.

Increasingly these works assumed the appearance of generality by obscuring the identity of the place described. The authors of *Middletown,* of *Deep South,* of the Yankee City Series, and of *Plainville* drew their data from specific towns, but insisted that they dealt with kinds of communities, so that the species was more significant than the individual instance. The justification that anonymity was the condition for securing the desired information was specious; earlier works had encountered no difficulties on this account. In any case, the practice diminished the utility of the survey products to historians who had no means of checking the worth of the data once the particularity of the subject disappeared. Scholars who ventured beyond the information supplied all too often discovered considerable distortions of the evidence.

The shift in character altered the techniques of the community study. Although the old formal questionnaires still served limited purposes, research also depended upon less structured methods. Following the practice of anthropologists, the investigator became a participant-observer, so that subjective elements intruded, nay often were welcomed. In that role the claim to be able to reconstruct the thinking of the host people was plausible; questions of veracity became less important than those of inner meaning. For instance, the truth or untruth of oral traditions was irrelevant.[14] In modern societies the open-ended interview, a directed conversation without defined questions or responses, sometimes yielded valuable insights but also lent an impressionistic quality to the data that limited its utility. Lloyd Warner carried this technique to the extreme in the use of "fictive" personalities or characters invented to embody previously defined social traits.

In the 1960s and 1970s the arrival of the tape recorder further loosened procedures. Immense globs of conversation found their way into print, often with little organization or sense of the criteria of selection. The historian dealing with those decades could not reject the evidence out of hand, for among the transcribed pages were passages of genuine value; and by then the pretense of anonymity and generality had all but disappeared. Yet the persistent tendencies toward theoretical abstraction and the orientation toward conclusions that would influence immediate social policy warned the scholar of the hazard of drawing indiscriminately upon such data. The safest course was to regard these in the same light as the descriptions of travelers—doubtful in their overall reliability, but likely to contain useful particular information and sometimes, the reflections of thoughtful observers.[15]

Modern community studies drew increasingly upon the developing techniques for measuring group attitudes quantitatively by means of public opinion polls. By the 1920s market analysis, the appraisal of the tastes and preferences of consumers, had demonstrated its commercial utility. The method then was simple: a question asked returned an answer. Polls of sorts also served the Departments of Agriculture and of Labor. The confused political

[14] Bernard L. Fontana, "American Indian Oral History," *History and Theory,* VIII (1969) , 370.

[15] Oscar Handlin, et al., *Harvard Guide to American History* (Cambridge, 1954) , 54 ff., contains complete citations of the works mentioned above. Later examples include: Oscar Lewis, *La Vida* (New York, 1966) ; Herbert J. Gans, *Urban Villagers* (New York, 1962) , and *Levittowners* (New York, 1967) ; and Robert Coles, *Children of Crisis* (Boston, 1967) . See also Maurice Stein, *Eclipse of Community* (Princeton, 1960) . For an extreme statement of social-science relativism, see Gunnar Myrdal, *Objectivity in Social Research* (New York, 1969) .

conditions of the decades after 1930 put a premium on the ability to predict political events; and after 1950 television-rating systems even more urgently called for accurate assessment of opinion.

All polls rested on sampling theory which had grown in subtlety of definition and application since its rough nineteenth-century beginnings. Down to 1936 the most important poll was that of the *Literary Digest,* based on a large number of mail interrogations from a list of automobile registrants and telephone subscribers. Thereafter, smaller, but more carefully selected, weighted, and, later, stratified, samples furnished the basis for the polls of George Gallup (American Institute of Public Opinion), of Elmo Roper, of Louis Harris, and of the National Opinion Research Center, among others. Furthermore, the pollers extended the area of their investigations from simple political preferences to the analysis of a wide range of social attitudes and examined intensively such particular groups as soldiers and factory workers. These data remained available, and potentially useful, to the cautious and critical historian. The exaggerated claims that the poller had introduced a "fourth stage" of democracy sometimes obscured the real value of such data. Although no poll could prove or disprove a historical interpretation, many added new types of evidence and illustrative material.[16]

The failure of the polls in 1948 showed that they could not predict the outcome of elections, and results in the next three decades were no more conclusive. A national sample of three thousand or so exposed the polls to errors of 3 or 4 percent, a margin often decisive in presidential contests.

Other technical considerations diminished reliability. The preconceptions that entered into construction of the sample, the phrasing of the text of the questions, the variability of the responses, the bias of the interviewers, and the nature of the rapport with the respondents seriously affected the results. More generally, pollers could not escape the inherent ambiguity of the situation and uncertainty about what they were measuring. The situation

16 Hadley Cantril, *Public Opinion* (Princeton, 1950) ; Handlin, *Harvard Guide,* 33 ff.; Melvin Small, ed., *Public Opinion and Historians* (Detroit, 1970). See also Mark Abrams, *Social Surveys and Social Action* (London, 1951) ; Paul F. Lazarsfeld, "Episode in the History of Social Research," in Donald Fleming and Bernard Bailyn, eds., *Intellectual Migration* (Cambridge, 1969), 270 ff.

was ambiguous because it confronted the subject with the unusual demands that he predict his own future actions or analyze his own attitudes. The responses could not be totally accurate when the respondents might themselves be incapable of forecasting or understanding their actions. The large percentage of "no answers" or "don't knows" in all polls, whether the product of lack of knowledge or apathy or unwillingness to answer, might substantially distort the conclusions. Finally, a large margin of indefiniteness obscured the meaning of "public opinion" and of "attitudes." Did a summing up of individual answers without weighting for intensity give a reliable picture of a whole? Were respondents simply parts of a homogeneous "public" rather than members of a variety of groups? If the sampling did take account of such groupings, was the actual poll redundant? The pollers themselves were aware of the gravity of these questions; historians could not afford to be less so.[17]

Most troublesome of the relationships of history to the world of knowledge is that involved in drawing upon other disciplines for concepts to help in the task of explanation. The relationship is unavoidable; connotations the origins of which lie embedded in science charge the very words used. Implicit in every step, from the recognition of evidence to its arrangement, ordering and interpretation, are assumptions about the nature of man, about his linkage to others in society, and about the universe he inhabits. Every scholar approaching a neat little problem, unless endowed with wisdom equivalent to the learning of all the ages, borrows from the accumulated store of knowledge about him. The danger arises not from the borrowing, but from unawareness of the source and from slavish dependence upon a narrow range of knowledge.

Hence the drawback in accepting the prearranged disciplinary lines defined for purposes of abstract analysis, which, of their very essence, separate out rather than integrate various aspects of experience. The student whose research deals with nineteenth-century New England merchants must of course know something about economics—of his or her day and of theirs—but also some-

17 Michael Wheeler, *Lies, Damn Lies, and Statistics* (New York, 1976).

thing of what anthropologists say about kinship and trade, what
lawyers say about contract, and what political scientists say about
the role of government. No one can arm himself in advance with
all these disciplines—and indeed with others that may also be relevant. But everyone can prepare to probe wherever necessary for
whatever may illuminate the evidence.

Much of what historians know about the individual human who
is their subject they derive from projections of their own experience, to which they add impressions derived from novels, dramas,
and movies. Some of what scholars know about motives, perceptions, and impulses originates in an understanding of biological
and psychological science. The rest—not as much as from experience but more than from science—comes from biography, a mode
akin to that of history, yet a separate kind of endeavor. The biographer uses evidence from the past but focuses upon the individual
and answers questions about personality and character that the historian usually does not ask.

Biography is thus a mode apart, although some historians either
practice it or mingle the two within the confines of a single book.
Plutarch, Suetonius, and Vasari are monuments of the ancient dignity of the form, which, though it passed through centuries of drastic transformation in Europe and in the United States, did not run
into apparent conflict with history until the intrusion of science
drove a cleavage between them.[18]

In 1834, when Jared Sparks conceived the notion of collecting
and publishing the biographies of the great Americans, no sign of
a division had yet appeared. Sparks was certain both that the task
was important and that the series he projected would find eager
readers. The continued popularity of Plutarch down to his own
day was evidence of the heavy literary interest in the lives of great
men. Moreover, biography had been a favorite device in American
literature. Cotton Mather had labored in the *Magnalia* to show the
operations of Providence; and within Sparks's lifetime Emerson
would demonstrate that "Representative Men" illustrated philosophical truths.

Literary conceptions of biography did not, however, satisfy

Sparks; his ambitions had a wider range. He wished to collect "the lives of all persons, who have been distinguished in America, from the date of its first discovery to the present time," because such a collection "would embrace a perfect history of the country." The assembled stories of the great figures of the past would contain the history "of its social and political progress, its arts, sciences, literature, and improvements of every kind; since these receive their impulse and direction from a comparatively few eminent individuals."[19]

The assumption that history was the sum of the biographies of a limited number of dominant individuals came easily to an age which conceived the hero as the center of society. The actions of lesser characters were only elements of a setting within which the greater operated; and other forces, if considered at all, were part of the background. The personages of history were either godlike figures like Washington or devilish ones like George III. These assumptions conformed to the current romantic conception of the hero as protagonist, a conception expressed in the same years in the striving characters who peopled American novels.

This conception of biography had scarcely changed fifty years later, in the 1890s, when J. T. Morse embarked upon the publication of the American Statesman Series. Many of the volumes in that series, taken individually, were high in merit. But the key to the project was the view that events were products of the simple will of single men whose achievements and failures summed up the history of the United States.

These biographies were already outmoded as they were published. Historians had by then developed quite another conception of the past. Since their discipline was a science which studied the operation of social laws, the exceptional individual held little interest for them; rather, they fixed their attention upon the large impersonal forces that brought political, social, and economic institutions into being. No statesman or soldier could substantially affect the course of the remote influences working themselves out in time. At most, biography could describe variations within a general pattern. The scholars of the early twentieth century, therefore, devoted themselves to such subjects as the frontier, constitu-

[19] Jared Sparks, *Library of American Biography* (Boston, 1830), I, iv.

tional government, and the town. Almost without exception the great historians of the period, Frederick Jackson Turner, Edward Channing, C. M. Andrews, and J. F. Jameson, shunned biography, as did their colleagues in European history.

Biography followed a separate course, largely shaped by writers who were not historians and who took as a model the English nineteenth-century "life and times." Such multivolumed monumental works as William F. Moneypenny and George E. Buckle's Disraeli and, later, Winston S. Churchill's Marlborough vastly impressed Americans and fortified a tradition set in the United States by James Parton and his contemporaries early in the nineteenth century.

Such books used the career of an individual as the framework within which to depict a whole era. By tracing a single life through its times, they aimed to convey an understanding both of the central character and of the events in which he participated or which he observed. Douglas S. Freeman's Lee and Washington, Carl Sandburg's Lincoln, Dumas Malone's Jefferson, and Frank B. Freidel's Franklin Delano Roosevelt were notable modern examples of the genre.

The form was attractive. It presented the historian with a ready-made outline for the organization of the subject's life, the details of which fell into comprehensible sectors marked out by birth, marriage, death, and the various stages of a career. The authors often could write about a character without moving away from the materials he himself left. The papers of prominent individuals, conveniently accumulated and easily exploited, simplified research, so that Allan Nevins did not have to wander far from such collections in his useful studies of Cleveland, Hewitt, Fish, and Rockefeller.

However, important defects marred such works, which too often left critical questions unanswered. Ease of execution had its costs. Writing out of a collection of personal papers, the biographer subtly acquired the point of view of his subject. Seeing all matters as they appeared to the central character, the author tended to become advocate and defender. The long biographies almost inevitably were partisan, in the sense that they took the side of the men whom they treated.

So, too, the ready-made organization was deceptive. The first volume of Arthur Link's Wilson touched on American historiography, collegiate education, state politics, and the national election of 1912. Wilson's involvement was, however, an arbitrary basis for treating all these subjects in a single book. In each case the author had to drop his account of the protagonist and develop the complex antecedents of the background against which the central character moved. On the other hand, there was never an opportunity to work out a subject whole. History, Princeton, and New Jersey were alike suspended in midair when the author's interest shifted with his subject to newer matters.

More important, the "Life and Times" was ambiguous on the question of the role of the individual in history. Such works usually proceeded doggedly on the assumption that the full assemblage of all the facts in a man's life would throw light on his times. Hence the tendency to spread over three, four, or five volumes, to the limits of publishers' tolerance.

Such books contained instructive sections. Freeman's Lee offered a splendid panorama of Civil War battles; and Brant's Madison an incisive analysis of the constitutional convention. But Freeman might as easily have written a military history of the Civil War; Brant, a constitutional history of the early republic.

Giganticism concealed the absence of a consistent theory of biography. At the center of action in these works moved a single individual about whom everything that happened revolved. Yet the historians, though turned to biography, accepted the primary importance of broad impersonal forces; they did not endow their characters with decisive heroic attributes, but treated them as products of their times. Madison did not create the Constitution; Lee did not lose the Civil War. But if Lee or Madison exerted no determining influence upon the outcome of events, what significance inhered in their lives, specifically and concretely? The proposition that Lee and Madison were typical in the sense that, if they had not been where they were, others like them would have taken their places, led into a determinism that deprived the individual of all significance. Few authors knew how to escape from that cul-de-sac.[20]

---

[20] The concept of "actor dispensability" restated but did not resolve the problem; Fred I. Greenstein, *Personality and Politics: Problems of Evidence, Inference, and Conceptualization* (Chicago, 1969), 40 ff.

For a time after the First World War some did not wish to escape. A market developed for debunking biography which aimed to expose the subject's foibles, weaknesses, and follies. W. E. Woodward's *Meet General Grant* (1928), one of the most popular, was representative of the school. Such books played upon the universal interest in gossip and attracted readers by the promise to reveal the failings of distinguished personalities. That there were no genuine heroes was their guiding premise; everyone shared the same faults. The incessant reiteration that there were no uncommon individuals by implication argued that each was unimportant, the product of chance and hardly conscious of impulses from external forces which moved him.

The disdain with which these authors treated their subjects was self-defeating. By denying the exceptional nature of those about whom they were written, these books destroyed their most important reason for being read. The same titillations could as well come from the daily gossip column or from contemporary naturalistic novels.

In any case, these works rested upon a flimsy foundation, emphasizing the trivial at the expense of the significant aspects of men's lives. For it takes no commitment to a romantic view of the hero to recognize that individuals act sometimes in an uncommon manner, which requires explanation.

The debunkers of the 1920s shared ground with psychological biographers who did focus upon the uncommon personality traits of their subjects. The success of such European practitioners of the art as Lytton Strachey, André Maurois, and Emil Ludwig influenced American imitators, as did the slow penetration into the United States of Freudian analytical concepts of the unconscious, nonrational elements in human behavior. The authors involved paid less attention to the analysis of historic events than to the development of individual personality; and they attempted to understand and describe character almost in detachment from its social setting.[21]

Few succeeded, although Harry Elmer Barnes enthusiastically

21 J. Z. Fullmer, "Medical Lives and Medical Letters," Clarke, *Modern Methods in the History of Medicine*, 185 ff.; Robert Partin, "Eminent Victorians and R. E. Lee," Central Mississippi Valley American Studies Association, *Journal*, II (Spring 1961), 48 ff.; Caroline F. Ware, ed., *Cultural Approach to History* (New York, 1940), 50.

hailed the union of Cleo and Freud. Occasional suggestive essays in the manner of Gamaliel Bradford mounted up to little; and the historians who tried their hands at the style were unfortunate. Competent scholars like Preserved Smith in his *Luther* and Ralph V. Harlow in his *Samuel Adams* had difficulty in applying the psychological theories to their data.[22]

At the root of the problem was the inability to impart authenticity to the analysis. It was all very well to accept the judgment of the psychologists about the crucial nature of the years of early childhood and of sex. But it was for those years, and those matters that historical records were most lacking. Scholars could speculate to their hearts' content about what Sam Adams might have felt toward his father and his wife; but the absence of documentary evidence drove them to vagueness or to guesswork, qualities which did not make for convincing writing. Not even men and women of letters whose writings *were* the record revealed enough of themselves to permit successful biographical analysis.[23]

To the extent that biographers attempted to wrestle with the inner development of their characters, they entered also into competition with fiction, but at a disadvantage—so long as scruples about evidence remained compelling. In the absence of evidence, the novelist and historian were on the same footing insofar as accuracy was concerned; and when it came to imagination, the former was less inhibited—and sometimes able to summon up the truer picture.

Nevertheless, twentieth-century biographers could not escape the temptation and the challenge; every aspect of the sensate culture about them, and many aspects of its science, drew them on to the assessment of the character of their subjects. More or less drastic and more or less fruitful efforts treated Woodrow Wilson,

[22] Harry Elmer Barnes, *History and Social Intelligence* (New York, 1926); Preserved Smith, "Luther's Early Development," *American Journal of Psychology*, XXIV (July 1913), 360 ff.; and, by contrast, his *Life and Letters of Martin Luther* (Boston, 1911), 8–13; Ralph V. Harlow, *Samuel Adams* (New York, 1923); John A. Garraty, "Preserved Smith, Ralph Volney Harlow, and Psychology," *Journal of the History of Ideas*, XV (June 1954), 456 ff.

[23] For example, Marie Bonaparte, *Life and Works of Edgar Allan Poe,* trans. John Rodker (London, 1949); Richard Lebeaux, *Young Man Thoreau* (Amherst, Mass., 1977), 5 ff. There is an excellent statement of the problem in Louis Fraiberg, *Psychoanalysis and American Literary Criticism* (Detroit, 1960).

Thaddeus Stevens, Charles Sumner, Benjamin Franklin, and Sir Henry Clinton.[24]

The breakthrough came in 1958 with the publication of Erik Erikson's *Young Man Luther*. Erikson, a distinguished psycho-analyst, reached toward biography both as a result of his own tortured personal life and as a means of explicating his theory of the life cycle in human development. His system, which left more room for external social, ideological, and cultural factors than did the Freudian, made *Luther* an immediate success. Taken up by the media, which popularized the term "identity crisis," it dribbled down in time to biographers to whom it provided a much-needed escape route. Back there in the inner life of the long since dead and gone, something had happened of the greatest importance, something of which no evidence survived. But if the analyst explained that all children on the way to becoming men and women passed through the same cycle, with its expected occurrences and their expected consequences, then those back there must also have done so. The absence of evidence thereupon ceased to close off descriptions of what happened or must have happened at age six or sixteen or in the privacy of the bed or closet.

But Erikson had not written as a historian. The pivotal event about which the interpretation of Luther's identity crisis turned may not even have happened. It did not matter to the analyst for whom it only illustrated a theory derived from other sources. Whether the young monk had actually fallen to the ground in the choir at Erfurt interested Erikson hardly at all; he wrote *as if* in order to criticize the views of others and to advance his own.[25] By

---

[24] A. L. and J. L. George, *Woodrow Wilson and Colonel House* (New York, 1956); Sigmund Freud and William C. Bullitt, *Thomas Woodrow Wilson* (Boston, 1967); Neville K. Meaney, "Arthur S. Link and Thomas Woodrow Wilson," *Journal of American Studies*, I (April 1967), 119 ff.; Fawn Brodie, *Thaddeus Stevens* (New York, 1959); David Donald, *Charles Sumner* (New York, 1964). More interesting efforts include Richard L. Bushman, "On the Uses of Psychology; Conflict and Conciliation in Benjamin Franklin," *History and Theory*, V (1966), 225 ff.; and Frederick Wyatt and William B. Willcox, "Sir Henry Clinton: A Psychological Exploration in History," *William and Mary Quarterly*, XVI (January 1959), 3 ff.

[25] Erik H. Erikson, *Young Man Luther* (New York, 1958), 23 ff.; Smith, "Luther's Early Development," 360 ff.; Lucien Febvre, *Martin Luther*, trans. Roberts Tapley (New York, 1929), 33 ff. See also Cushing Strout, "Ego Psychology and the Historian," *History and Theory*, VII (1968), 281; Robert Jay Lifton, "On Psychohistory," in Herbert J. Bass, ed., *State of American History* (Chicago, 1970), 282 ff.

contrast, the shift in interpretation between Preserved Smith's book on Luther and the article two years later turned about a specific bit of evidence.

The prospect of escape from the previous question—had the incident occurred or was it an invention of later detractors?—attracted historians, too, most notably in the thriving Hitler industry of the 1970s. With no one to defend the Führer, the way was open to spectacular speculation about his life; as also about Richard Nixon's. Venturesome biographers, with varying success, applied the same methods to other personages from the past.[26]

The danger in Erikson's procedure and in the wave of psychoanalyzing by followers less skilled than he lay in the substitution of a theoretically grounded formula for evidence. At the points at which the data ran out, the historian no longer confessed ignorance or maintained silence; he reached for a bit of clinical verbiage in a pretense of knowing. The effort was futile. Aside from the difficulty of choosing among competing and kaleidoscopically changing theories, borrowings from Erikson, Freud, Jung, or Adler added no force to what the analysts themselves wrote. Even when the borrowings did not degenerate into absurd reductionism, they stifled the imaginations of authors who allowed typology to obscure individual personality traits, and of readers who might otherwise have found their own way of filling in the empty spaces in the record.[27]

The fundamental mode of analysis is unavailable to the historian; the patient is not there to answer questions. The process of

---

26 Walter C. Langer, *Psychological Analysis of Adolf Hitler* (Washington, 1943), and *Mind of Adolf Hitler* (New York, 1972); Helm Stierlin, *Adolf Hitler* (New York, 1976); Rudolph Binion, *Hitler among the Germans* (New York, 1976); Robert G. L. Waite, *Psychopathic God: Adolf Hitler* (New York, 1977), 243. Of these Waite hews closest to the evidence. Friedländer, *Histoire et psychanalyse*, 87 ff. On Nixon, see David Abrahamsen, *Nixon vs. Nixon* (New York, 1977). Bruce Mazlish, *In Search of Nixon* (New York, 1972), 5, is more sensible and recognizes that psychohistory is not the same as psychotherapy of a patient, but floats away from the evidence. Lloyd de Mause and Henry Ebel, *Jimmy Carter and American Fantasy* (New York, 1977), is with-it gossip tagged with psychohistorical terms.

27 Friedländer, *Histoire et psychanalyse*, 21 ff., 61 ff.; Jack P. Greene, "Search for Identity: An Interpretation of the Meaning of Selected Patterns of Social Response in Eighteenth-Century America," *Journal of Social History*, III (Spring 1970), 189 ff., is an example of the pointless, but harmless, lacing of familiar material with Eriksonian identity crisis.

diagnosis is difficult enough for the skilled therapist, who can ask and listen after passing through a long apprenticeship and analysis, and who, even so, often yields to the impulse to pontificate. It is inapplicable by do-it-yourself practitioners to characters not subject to interrogation; and without it the psyche of the subject guards its secrets inviolably. Only where evidence exists, can theory complement it.[28]

Furthermore, the application of psychoanalytic theory to history rests upon the unexamined premise of the constancy, timelessness, and universality of human nature. The ability to communicate and empathize across the centuries and the continents—to feel with the characters in *Iphigenia in Aulis,* for instance—suggests the endurance of some traits. But changes in bodily structure, in the ages of menarche, puberty, and menopause, and the dramatic variations in the cultural components in the reactions to pain suggest considerable plasticity in others. The understanding of sexuality Freud derived from the study of middle-class Viennese at the opening of the twentieth century may not be valid for men and women of other times and places. In the absence of evidence, therefore, conjectures about Jefferson's relations with women must admit the possibility that his passions took forms other than those which seemed natural a hundred and fifty years later. The biographer knows that Washington married a widow, begot no children, drank wine liberally, and suffered from his teeth. But much remains unknown: about his relationship to his parents, about his virility, and about his body habits. The evidence permits some inferences, not others—no matter how liberal the recourse to contemporary theory.[29]

28 Friedländer, *Historie et psychoanalyse,* 11; Barnes, *New History and the Social Studies,* 225 ff.; Alain Besançon, "Psychoanalysis: Auxiliary Science or Historical Method?" *Journal of Contemporary History,* III (January 1968), 149 ff. For fast-triggered pronouncements, see, e.g., Meyer A. Zeligs, *Friendship and Fratricide: An Analysis of Whittaker Chambers and Alger Hiss* (New York, 1967); Carl Binger, *Revolutionary Doctor* (New York, 1966).

29 See Mark Zborowski, "Cultural Components in Responses to Pain," *Journal of Social Issues,* VIII (1952), 16 ff.; and, from another point of view, Thomas S. Szasz, *Pain and Pleasure,* 2d ed. (New York, 1975). Psychobiographies vary in quality: Emory Battis, *Saints and Sectaries* (Chapel Hill, N.C., 1962), does not succeed in linking Anne Hutchinson's problems to relations with her father; Fawn M. Brodie, *Thomas Jefferson* (New York, 1974), 205 ff., 229 ff., 467; and Michael Paul Rogin, *Fathers and Children: Andrew Jackson and the Subjugation*

And the psyche is not the whole of it. The Santa Ana wind, the mistral, the *föhn,* and the *ḥamsin* affect behavior in the present, perhaps in the past, so that atmospheric pressure might well have shaped reactions to crises. Somatic conditions also influence the acts, thoughts, and moods of men and women in ways once ascribed to the fluids or humors which coursed through their bodies or to the bumps which ornamented their craniums. Suffering from a chronic disease or deformity might very well affect the judgment and ideas of a ruler, soldier, philosopher, or merchant. Ingenious techniques of paleopathology sometimes provide a basis for informed guesses, but, given the primitive means of diagnosis and the vagueness of nomenclature through most of human history, there can be no certainty whatever about the physical state of the biographer's subject, any more than there can be about the psyche.

ॐ

Yet historians must assess the role of the individual.

Somehow the life of the single person adheres to some or many of the broad developments that shape society and culture. The biographer examines that relationship, observes the interplay between personal traits and impersonal forces, between the career of one and the destiny of the nation. Individuals no doubt exert but a slight impact on political, economic, and social institutions that develop over long periods. Dealing with industrialization or imperialism or changes in the treatment of disease, the historian cannot assign a causal role to Eli Whitney or Theodore Roosevelt or W. H. Welch. Neither can he regard men as automatons, responding blindly to currents over which they have no control. Whitney, Roosevelt, and Welch, although the products of the forces of their times, did have discernible influence upon the direction thereafter taken.

What is the nature of that influence?

The individual takes part in a drama that began long before the birth, that goes on long after the death, of any player. Entering

---

of the American Indian (New York, 1975), take leave of the evidence; James C. Curtis, *Andrew Jackson* (Boston, 1976), keeps a grip on it. See also Caroline F. Ware, ed., *Cultural Approach to History* (New York, 1940), 48; Dom David Knowles, *Historian and Character* (Cambridge, 1963), 7 ff.

for a brief turn on a scene already set, a stage already crowded, and with the action already in progress, each person confronts a situation that already exists, the product of long preparation. The search for a place reveals obstacles. The form in which the stage is set and the motions of others in response to directions given long ago limit the ability to move. Each one may or may not hear the prompter's instructions—or may imagine that he or she does so— and each may or may not apprehend the purpose of the whole.

But to some degree, all are free—to move, to alter the wandering of others, even to reshape bits of the set.

The individual arrives in a world in process, the product of untold centuries of development. Institutions that are the results of complex historic forces determine the situation.

But the situation does not determine the reaction to it. The response of any particular person depends to a considerable degree upon the traits brought to the situation, which some strive to alter in response to inner or outer promptings. Thus, whether any significantly affect the outcome cannot be known, since the end is not known; but some striving certainly affects the way in which movement toward the outcome proceeds.

The biographer lacks the means for the analysis of personality available to novelists or psychologists, but he can understand the situation the character encounters and can trace the individual's impact upon it. The proper subject of biography, therefore, is not the complete person or the complete society, but the point at which the two interact. There the situation and the individual illuminate one another.

The evidence for aggregates sometimes offers a readier link to theoretical knowledge than that for their components. Local records state the age of death of individuals, census schedules the number of children in a family. Any individual instance is so susceptible to idiosyncratic influences as to permit no useful generalization about mortality or fertility. But the totals for a whole community or even valid samples of them offer a basis for appraisals of life expectancy and birth rates and even of the factors which lengthen the one and raise the other, that is, for the fruitful interplay of demography with historical data.

For more than a century scholars speculated about the possibility of treating the aggregate itself as if endowed with an organic identity, or at least as if it were more than a statistical convenience and possessed attributes that molded the characters of its constituent elements. The persistent strength of forces inexplicable in purely rational terms, yet capable of moving, deluding, or inspiring large numbers of people, raised stubborn questions for scholars determined to understand the causes of events of every type. Having abandoned the belief that one system of faith was divine, the others the product of devilish error, students like Max Weber encountered the inescapable problem of explaining why not errant individuals but masses of men and women accepted a variety of gods; yielded to mesmerism, hypnotism, and faith healing; enlisted in crusades, lynchings, and revivals; and responded to demonic leaders. Reactions of such breadth and intensity possibly reflected the operations of a collective rather than individual psyche. In the twentieth century some, though not all, of this line of thought emanated from the disciplines of social anthropology and social psychology, particularly after the impact of behaviorist suggestions that human behavior paralleled that of other animals.[30]

The formulations of Gustave Le Bon and W. G. Sumner stressed the intractable nature of the crowd's thinking. Sumner argued that it was vain to imagine that any individuals could lift themselves apart from the characteristic mores, the ruling tendencies, of the groups to which they belonged. They might as well try to get themselves out of gravity or the pressure of the atmosphere. These views filtered into much of the writing about national character. Meanwhile, old fears about the dominance of the masses exercised Walter Lippmann and other intellectuals; and their concern mounted with the investigations by behaviorist psychologists of the means of manipulating the thought and behavior of large num-

---

[30] See, e.g., Hamilton Cravens and John C. Burnham, "Psychology and Evolutionary Naturalism in American Thought, 1890–1940," *American Quarterly*, XXIII (December 1971), 641 ff.; Maxwell G. Marwick, ed., *Witchcraft and Sorcery* (Hammondsworth, Eng., 1972); R. Trevor Davies, *Four Centuries of Witch Beliefs* (London, 1947); Alan D. Macfarlane, *Witchcraft in Tudor and Stuart England* (London, 1970); H. C. Eric Midelfort, *Witch Hunting in Southwestern Germany* (Stanford, 1972); E. William Monter, *Witchcraft in France and Switzerland* (Ithaca, N.Y., 1976); Paul Boyer and Stephen Nissenbaum, *Salem Possessed* (Cambridge, 1974); Norman Cohn, *Pursuit of the Millennium* (London, 1957); Keith Thomas, *Religion and the Decline of Magic* (London, 1971); Friedländer, *Histoire et psychoanalyse*, 126 ff.

bers. Jung's speculations about archetypal images and the collective unconscious also drifted westward, so that the ground was fertile after the Second World War for the transference of psychoanalytical concepts to historical data. The extreme outcome was Norman Brown's blithe effort to loosen "the grip of the dead hand of the past," so that "man would be ready to live instead of making history, to enjoy instead of paying back old scores and debts, and to enter that state of Being which was the goal of his Becoming."[31]

A more representative book revealed the dangers of the casual transference. Stanley M. Elkins explained the infantile personality of American blacks, recognizable in the Sambo personality, by the shocks of capture, transportation, and terror which detached slaves from their African culture. The argument depended entirely upon psychoanalytical theory and upon an analogy to the effects of confinement upon the inmates of German concentration camps; no evidence whatever linked these speculations to the black experience.[32]

In pursuing the analogy, Elkins accepted the literal accuracy of the observations by Dutch and Austrian social scientists trained in psychoanalysis about the behavior of their compatriots in the camps. He then transferred the diagnosis, without adequate extrapolation, to seventeenth-century Africans. In doing so, he lost sight of the immense difference in the previous cultural situations of the people involved. Men and women deeply rooted in an ordered universe, like that of the European immigrants, felt the trauma of detachment when forced away from home; but even they did not share identical experiences. And their responses may not have been at all relevant to people whose culture and personality were altogether different. Human beings who took en-

---

31 Norman O. Brown, *Life against Death: The Psychoanalytic Meaning of History* (Middletown, Conn., 1959). See also William Graham Sumner, *Folkways* (Boston, 1907), 98; Robert A. Nye, *Origins of Crowd Psychology* (London, 1975); Barnes, *New History and Social Studies*, 161 ff., 257; Friedländer, *Histoire et psychoanalyse*, 143 ff.; Stierlin, *Adolf Hitler*, 109 ff.; Paul Veyne, "L'histoire conceptualisante," in Jacques LeGoff and Pierre Nora, eds., *Faire de l'histoire*, 2 vols. (Paris, 1974), I, 75 ff. James D. Barber, *Presidential Character* (Englewood Cliffs, N.J., 1972), links the chief executive's office to distinctive personality types, but undogmatically and sensibly.

32 Stanley M. Elkins, *Slavery: A Problem in American Institutional and Intellectual Life* (Chicago, 1959). See also Ann J. Lane, ed., *Debate Over "Slavery"* (Urbana, Ill., 1971); Victoria Cuffel, "Classical Greek Concept of Slavery," *Journal of the History of Ideas*, XXVII (October–December 1966), 323 ff.

slavement as the manifestation of an incomprehensible fate, as in the ancient world, did not feel the identical shock; and there was no a priori reason for believing that the Africans experienced one reaction or the other. Above all, there was no evidence that the Sambo stereotype described all or a significant proportion of the plantation blacks, any more than the nineteenth-century Ike or Pat stereotype described the American Jew or Irishman.

The failure of the Elkins approach revealed the danger inherent in any facile grab for theory that took leave of the evidence. Again and again in the uneasy relationship of history to science this pitfall welcomed the unwary saunterer. For psychohistory was by no means the first or the only endeavor to provide a schematic explanation for the actions of men and women taken as an aggregate. The unhappy experience with all studies of ethnography, in its nineteenth-century as well as in its modern forms, reached in that direction, seeking as they did to explain the differences among groups by either inherent or external causes. Equally respectable lines of investigation led back, on the one hand, from the neurobiology and sociobiology of the 1970s through various geneticist schools and references to instinct to the racist speculators of the 1850s; and, on the other hand, from the contemporary anthropological concepts of culture and personality to the eighteenth-century Enlightenment environmentalists. The historian was never in a position to pass judgment on these rival claims to knowledge; and, therefore, was in peril the moment he took his ground on any one of them rather than on the evidence.[33]

Then, too, somatic factors affected the fate of aggregates as they did of individuals. The record showed the swathe cut by the black death in early modern Europe and the Middle East and by cholera in the nineteenth century. Endemic disorders like *bilharziasis* in Egypt and hookworm in the Southern United States shaped the character of whole peoples. And, though physicians and epidemiologists have not hesitated to diagnose these disorders, they have not always agreed. Whether or not they have, the historian is in no position to appraise their accuracy.[34]

[33] See Chapter 4 at note 40; E. O. Wilson, *Sociobiology* (Cambridge, 1975).

[34] See, e.g., Paul H. Buck, "Poor Whites of the Ante-Bellum South," *American Historical Review*, XXXI (October 1925), 41 ff.; Michael W. Dols, *Black Death in the Middle East* (Princeton, 1977). The impressively detailed economic, demo-

He does not have to do so, any more than he is obliged to concede the determinism of climatic, demographic, or biological theories. Whatever its ultimate cause, the disease, like changes in rainfall or the birthrate, exerted measurable effects upon the people it struck and upon the society they inhabited. There, where the evidence appears, lies the historian's proper task. If the diagnosis throws light upon the consequences, it will show up somewhere in the evidence; if not, its value is incidental. The same distinction applies to psychohistorical phenomena; interesting and curious they may be—but no more until they register in the data.[35]

⌒

In the end, the historian learns that an aggregate is not a magnified individual to which the scholar can attribute qualities similar to those of a single person. The aggregate is subject to study, but on its own terms. It acts, holds beliefs, and expresses opinions; and in doing so, it leaves behind records susceptible to understanding.

Twentieth-century scholars apply the term institution to the collectivities within which they sort out and interpret records. The term once implied establishment, ordination, or enactment by some superior power, so that, for example, the family was an institution in the sense that a divine ordinance governed it. But when an impersonal evolutionary process replaced the figure of the lawgiver, any cluster of social usages which offered a basis for organizing data about behavior and thought became known as an institution. The state is an institution, as is the economy, the family, and the church. But so, too, are the Congress and the Supreme Court, the factory and the family farm, primogeniture and monogamous marriage, and the parish and episcopate. Big ones bear little ones within them in almost infinite series.

To the scholar who studies it, each institution seems integral and self-contained, the product of a distinct evolution. And to

---

graphic, and environmental analysis in François Lebrun, *Les Hommes et la mort en Anjou* (Paris, 1971), 493 ff.; nevertheless fails to establish a link to collective psychology.

35 Ware, *Cultural Approach to History,* 49; Louis Chevalier, *Laboring Classes and Dangerous Classes in Paris,* trans. Frank Jellinek (New York, 1973), makes much of biological factors, but is nonetheless valuable.

some extent each is, otherwise the data would not fall within its confines with any degree of plausibility. Whoever examines the materials bearing upon the exercise of force in society discovers that much of it deals with the organization, control, and operation of government; that material, systematized and interpreted, becomes the stuff of political science. But a coherent segment of the data, at the same time, concerns the relations among the organs of the state and their effects upon the individual; and those become the subject of constitutional law. Another range of materials is the product of efforts to use government either to resolve disputes among individuals, or to punish them for actions defined as wrong. These attempts to do justice become the subjects of the study of law. Still other forms of violence appear altogether outside the boundaries regarded as legitimate—the acts of mobs, gangs, and bandits, for instance; and these become the subjects for sociologists.

Analysis of the institutions which shape the evidence of struggles to offset the transience of human experience reveals a similar morphology. Birth leads into a long period of dependence, during which the fledgling acquires the means of self-support and at the same time learns to conform to the standards of behavior and values of kin and larger group; establishes also sexual identity and the linkages preliminary to parenthood; and so is well on the way to death. In one sense, the rubric "family" can cover all these activities; but in another, the subheadings religion, health, education, and household are adequate for discreet sectors. The household itself, once identical with the economy, is now but a tiny bit of a complex network of transactions which produce, distribute, and consume goods and which furnish material to a variegated array of economists. On the other hand, economists have learned that education and skill become human capital and must enter their calculations.

Geographers and other scholars organize their material in spatial units, such as the region or metropolis, that cut across institutional lines and generate perceptive insights. To the extent that such investigations acquire a historical dimension, they must, however, abandon the insistence upon a static natural environment as a constant, a difficult task, particularly in the light of the concurrent obligation to establish an interface with economic, cultural, and social forms.[36]

The modern student of institutions of any sort aims to understand their present structure and to formulate about them statements of probability with predictive value for the future. The optimistic historians of the early twentieth century casually assumed that they could pluck those statements from the best authority and project them backward to explain the developments of the past. That happy formula never worked and is less than ever likely to do so, since the radical shift in orientation of the sciences after 1950.

Economists, sociologists, political scientists, and anthropologists were never oblivious to the distinction between their subjects and that of the experimental scientist. But, while recognizing the differences, they aimed in their own way to approximate the inductive procedures of which the controlled experiment was the ideal type. Careful observation tested the truth, or at least the usefulness, of the hypothesis and refined the existing body of theory.

The deficiencies of this understanding of the procedures of science seem first to have become apparent to physicists as they absorbed the massive changes in their discipline. They could not experiment in the usual sense with protons or electrons; and when they tried to imagine how those particles behaved within the atom, they did so by analogy with the solar system. As an aid to thinking, Niels Bohr tried to conceive a visual image of an atom, the structure of which he specified in functional equations relating to the characteristics of its constituent elements. Those equations he referred to as a model. The model was a tool of abstraction intended to help comprehend the reality of the atom.

From physics, the concept of the model spread to the other natural sciences and thence to economics and the other social sciences. Although the term differs in usage from discipline to discipline, it usually applies to a general proposition, the parameters of which

36 For example, Raymond D. Gastil, *Cultural Regions of the United States* (Seattle, 1975); Carl Frederick Kraenzel, *Great Plains in Transition* (Norman, Okla., 1955). Howard W. Odum and Harry E. Moore, *American Regionalism* (New York, 1938); Hans Kurath, ed., *Linguistic Atlas of New England* (Providence, 1939), and *Handbook of the Linguistic Geography of New England* (Providence, 1939), remain interesting, although they had little effect upon historians. See also David Harvey, *Explanation in Geography* (New York, 1969), 191 ff.; Chapter 9 at note 17.

are adjustable, one, therefore, not subject to the test of truth or usefulness in the way that a hypothesis was. The model adjusts to new data, until the point at which the formulas become so cumbersome as to call for reformulation.[37]

The historian, therefore, could no longer dip into a social science for a helpful natural law, or even for a clear statement of regularity or probability. A much more subtle, more abstract, line of goods had edged those wares off the shelf. Instead, the casual browser will find highly complex, rather tentative propositions which serve the analysis of their makers precisely because they are not ready-made for application to any concrete set of circumstances. Historians who still cling to the expectations of the Barnes generation and think they can simply apply theory to their subjects are doomed to frustration.

Some social scientists are aware of the limitations of approaches which extract a single area of experience out from the total context. Many a subtle analysis takes its point of departure in a confession of ignorance: "A recession started in 1929 due to some combination of factors which cannot be disentangled."[38] The model and the data are by no means as compatible as the practitioners of the "new economic history" believed. The pure economists in a variety of ways recognize the existence of "propensities" or "expectations" or "externalities," that is, of areas not governed by rationality and not measurable by usual equations. Forecasting experience has demonstrated that control of a few variables of production and consumption from among a vast and complex universe of forces bearing upon making and using yields only partial and qualified statements about what would happen if everything but the elements measured were to remain constant—which in actual life they never do. Indeed, soft causal path models must take account of latent, indirectly observed, variables. The inability to forecast changes in stock values, price movements, wage levels, and

---

[37] Roy Harrod, "What is a Model," J. N. Wolfe, ed., *Value, Capital and Growth* (Edinburgh, 1968), 173 ff. See also Peter D. McCelland, *Causal Explanation and Model Building in History, Economics and the New Economic History* (Ithaca, N.Y., 1975), 105 ff., 169 ff. Berkhofer, *Behavioral Approach to Historical Analysis,* 169 ff., oversimplifies.

[38] Peter Temin, *Did Monetary Forces Cause the Great Depression?* (New York, 1976).

birthrates has persuaded some economists and demographers to accept the persistence of stochastic, or random, processes, that is, processes which are, at best, guessable. The result subordinates the data to the theory which it never tests, only illustrates. Thus, the effort to develop large-scale simulation models entails a degree of imaginative abstraction so high as to make efforts at improving the estimated parameters pointless, so that speculations and guesses serve as well as correctness.[39]

This procedure is closed to the historian, who stands at a cross-over point and must somehow pull together the concrete data of the real world unencumbered by the abstractions which keep them apart. To do so, he or she must neither shrug off all theory as pointless vaporing nor accept a slavish dependence upon any single form. Whoever deals with the history of the suburb must take account of geographical as well as of quantitative and descriptive elements.[40]

The tail-chasing fact and theory ritual expends a good deal of energy, attracts attention, but gets nowhere. It was long ago apparent to historians that religion in the United States tended not to demand creedal allegiance but to encourage practices which integrated the population around shared values. A popular account in 1955 explained: "The basic unity of American religion is rooted in the underlying presuppositions, values, and ideals that together constitute the American Way of Life on its 'spiritual' side." Twelve years later a sociologist discovered "civil religion in America." The slight verbal change may or may not be theoretically significant; but it did not help, even if it did not hinder, the historian explaining the developing attitudes of the revolutionary period. Status anxiety, frontier homogeneity, and similar bor-

[39] Peter Temin, *New Economic History* (Harmondsworth, Eng., 1973), 8; Albert Fishlow and Robert Fogel, "Quantitative Economic History," *Journal of Economic History*, XXXI (March 1971), 15 ff. Compare Harvey Leibenstein, *Beyond Economic Man* (Cambridge, 1976); J. R. T. Hughes, "Wicksell on the Facts," Wolfe, *Value, Capital and Growth*, 223 ff. See also W. Brian Arthur and Geoffrey McNicall, "Large-Scale Simulation Models in Population and Development," *Population and Development Review*, I (December 1975), 260.

[40] Peter O. Muller, "Evolution of American Suburbs: A Geographical Interpretation," *Urbanism Past and Present*, no. 4 (Summer 1977), 1 ff.; Kenneth Jackson, "Suburbs," in Lee F. Schnore, ed., *New Urban History: Quantitative Explorations* (Princeton, 1975).

rowed concepts created more scholarly difficulties than they solved.[41]

Structuralism, which reaches for associations and contrarieties across immense reaches of time and space, making almost anything the same, analogous to, or the opposite of anything else, is inherently anti-historical in its tendency to wrench phenomena out of context. It subordinates data so thoroughly to theoretical structure as to leave the historian nothing to explain.[42]

The service of analysis lies not in furnishing scholars with aides in traversing the rough or empty spots in their information or in adding to the evidence, but in defining the key terms and concepts that common usage blurs. Profit, wages, labor, income, role, elite, and culture have entered the language of ordinary discourse. Still, the jargon-shy historian who uses them will think clearly only when aware of the meanings many years of scientific study attached to them. The prolonged controversy over the role of urban voters in Jacksonian democracy owed much of its vitality to the heedless use of undefined terms: laborers, workers, wage-earners, artisans, and mechanics. Many a study of the distribution of wealth has gone astray out of simple misunderstanding of the relation of age structure to social structure and the effects of that relation upon measurements of property-holding. Lack of a firm definition of class has permitted historians to take shelter behind borrowed terms—bureaucrats, functionaries, aristocrats, civil servants, professionals, white collar, middle class—and to evade the important questions: Is the figure of speech of a ladder an appropriate way to describe the social order? If so, are all the rungs an equal distance apart? Do the occupants of the highest control, or depend for support upon, those below?[43]

41 Will Herberg, *Protestant—Catholic—Jew* (Garden City, N.Y., 1955), 247; Sidney E. Mead, "From Denominationalism to Americanism," *Journal of Religion*, XXXVI (January 1956), 1 ff.; Robert Bellah, *Beyond Belief* (New York, 1970), 168 ff.; Catharine L. Albanese, *Sons of the Fathers: The Civil Religion of the American Revolution* (Philadelphia, 1976); Robert R. Dykstra, *Cattle Towns* (New York, 1968), app. A.

42 Lucien Goldmann, *Human Sciences & Philosophy*, trans. Hayden V. White and Robert Anchor (London, 1969), 12. See also Howard Gardner, *Quest for Mind: Piaget, Lévi-Strauss, and the Structuralist Movement* (New York, 1972), 222 ff.

43 Unawareness of these questions undermines the value of the hard work in studies of nineteenth-century classes—e.g., William Miller, "American Historians and the Business Elite," *Journal of Economic History*, IX (November 1949), 184 ff.,

Casual borrowings from contemporary usage have unanticipated implications. The term "modernization" appeared in a body of theory describing changes in one part of the world (traditional) induced by confrontation with the culture and technology of another (modern). The similarities, or apparent similarities, of shifts in nineteenth-century Britain or the United States could not have been products of the same process because they developed internally. Replacement of the pejorative "delinquency" by the neutral "deviance" reflected a transformation of attitudes about behavior in the 1960s as well as anthropological relativism and the rediscovery of Durkheim. Historians who project the concept of deviance back into earlier eras view all pre-1950 responses—progressive or conservative—as tainted with prejudice, stupidity, or self-interest. They do not, that is, concede the possibility of an alternative way of understanding the relation of individual behavior to the expectations of society. Since no theory of criminality or insanity, past or present, has proven its correctness by the tests of practical prediction or therapy, the historian has only the preference of his own prejudices for holding one or another. The historian is safe who accepts the concept of criminality as defined by the society under study. When the clumsy intrusion of the vague idea of deviance thrusts together criminality and art as deviance, the result is the absurd equation of artist and criminal. Meanwhile, important aspects of the subject without theoretical salience remain untreated—for instance, the role of homosexuals in the culture of the mid-twentieth-century America.[44]

---

and "Recruitment of the American Business Elite," *Quarterly Journal of Economics*, LXIV (May 1950), 242 ff.; Douglas T. Miller, *Jacksonian Aristocracy: Class and Democracy in New York, 1830–1860* (New York, 1967); Edward Pessen, *Jacksonian America* (Homewood, Ill., 1969), 39 ff. For the difficulty of ordering occupations, see E. A. Wrigley, ed., *Nineteenth-Century Society* (Cambridge, 1972), 191 ff. See also J. H. Hexter, "Myth of the Middle Class in Tudor England," *Reappraisals in History* (Evanston, Ill., 1962), 71 ff. On the workingmen, see, e.g., Arthur Schlesinger, Jr., *Age of Jackson* (Boston, 1945); Joseph Dorfman, "The Jackson Wage-Earner Thesis," *American Historical Review*, LIV (January 1949), 296 ff.; Richard B. Morris, "Andrew Jackson Strikebreaker," *ibid.*, LV (October 1949), 54 ff. On social structure, e.g., Edward M. Cook, Jr., *Fathers of the Towns* (Baltimore, 1976).

44 On modernization in general, see H. U. Wehler, *Modernisieurungstheorie und Geshichte* (Göttingen, 1975); Richard D. Brown, *Modernization: The Transformation of American Life, 1600–1865* (New York, 1976), 3 ff., and, as examples, Virginia Yans-McLaughlin, "Flexible Tradition: South Italian Immigrants Confront a

Such considerations remind the historian of other, older, ways of knowing, which modern science has not altogether displaced. The early nineteenth century still subsumed economics and political theory under the rubric "natural philosophy," which in turn was one of the branches of the larger body of learning, the essential procedure of which was correct reasoning from defined propositions. Human thought about the uses of power, about the nature of wealth, and about the structure of society antedated modern science, continued thereafter, and had something important to say even in the 1970s. Recourse to the accumulated reservoirs drawn from old wells will as often reward the historian as gulps from more recent pumping stations. The ideal regimen would utilize both.[45]

The modes of communication which join individuals in society have been the subjects of both philosophical and scientific analysis. Myth, folklore, and language have attracted the attention both of critics and anthropologists. Northrop Frye's analysis of popular romance and music opens into a suggestive eternal vision of the world. His analysis grows out of literary criticism—out of exercise of the techniques for reading a text, one offshoot of that branch of philosophy known as aesthetics. It is no less informative, although in a different way, from the results of other methods used by Edward Sapir or Claude Lévi-Strauss.[46]

New Work Experience," *Journal of Social History,* VII (Summer 1974) , 430; Patricia Branca, *Silent Sisterhood: Middle Class Women in the Victorian Home* (London, 1975) , 144 ff. On deviance, Howard S. Becker, *Outsiders* (New York, 1963) ; and E. Lemert, *Human Deviance* (Englewood Cliffs, N.J., 1972) , state the sociological theory, while Berkhofer, *Behavioral Approach to Historical Analysis,* 103 ff., summarizes the anthropological, and Kai T. Erikson, *Wayward Puritans* (New York, 1966) , illustrates it. Douglas Greenberg, *Crime in New York* (Ithaca, N.Y., 1977) , soberly adheres to the evidence; H. Bruce Franklin, *Literature from the American Prison* (New York, 1978) , fancifully takes leave of it in equating artist and cirminal. Distortion by lack of focus in context marks Michel Foucault, *Surveiller et punir* (Paris, 1975) , 261 ff., as it does that author's other works.

45 For eighteenth-century Scottish antecedents, see Gladys Bryson, *Man and Society* (Princeton, 1945) , 78 ff., 148 ff.

46 Northrop Frye, *Secular Scripture* (Cambridge, 1975) ; Claude Lévi-Strauss, *Savage Mind* (Chicago, 1966) , 21 ff. Berkhofer, *Behavioral Approach to Historical Analysis,* 123 ff., uncritically states his preference for the anthropological way. See also Richard M. Dorson, *British Folklorists* (Chicago, 1968) .

The historian and the critic approach the work of literature along different avenues. The former treats the poem, drama, or novel as documentation—a bit of evidence about the time and place of composition. E. P. Roe and Joseph Ingraham and Henry James are all the same in that regard—as are the commercial jingle and the symphony, the poster, and the painting. The critic seeks to fit the text to general statements variously defined (of goodness, beauty, truth). In the process he or she abstracts it from its local and temporal context. The ingenious historian will find interesting data about the Attic or Elizabethan worlds in Aeschylus or Shakespeare, but will also profit from insights valid beyond time and place into human emotions, motivations, and interrelations to which generations of comment offer a guide. Even the novels of Camus and Kafka and the plays of Genet, in which individual settings and characters rarely appear, address those matters.

The structured knowledge organized in science may further understanding of the family, power, and wealth, but so too will other forms of knowledge which have treated those subjects for millennia. It simply will not do to announce that the family was a neglected topic, which received serious attention only in the past few decades, or to imagine that a new topic was born when the Social Science Research Council appointed a committee on "biosocial foundations of parenting and offspring development." Efforts to understand the history of those problems antedate the doctorates of the current researchers.[47]

To uncover wisdom, old or new, is no easy task—that warning merits repetition. Historians who look beyond the statement of a theory may find flaws in its empirical foundation. For instance, Adorno's widely accepted propositions about authoritarian personality rested upon tests which incorrectly assumed that such traits appeared on the right but not on the left of the political

---

[47] "The Family," *Daedalus*, CVI (Spring 1977). But see, e.g., Bryson, *Man and Society*, 173 ff.; Ware, *Cultural Approach to History*, 93 ff.; David J. Rothman, "Note on the Study of the Colonial Family," *William and Mary Quarterly*, XXIII (October 1966), 627 ff.; Wrigley, *Nineteenth-Century Society*, 47 ff.; and compare the range of materials used in Jean-Louis Flandrin, *Amours paysannes amour et sexualité dans les compagnes de l'ancienne France (XVIᵉ–XIXᵉ siècle)* (Paris, 1975). Morroe Berger, *Real and Imagined Worlds* (Cambridge, 1977), seeks a truce in the battle of the two cultures, each in its place, but has difficulty defining the boundaries or establishing the greater reality of social science.

spectrum.[48] Historians who read carefully will sometimes discover that a veil of rhetoric supplants proof, as in Lévi-Strauss's figure of speech which compares magical thought to a shadow moving ahead of its owner.[49] Historians must keep track not only of changes within one body of knowledge but also of the effects on neighboring disciplines—for example, the import of transformational generative grammar in linguistics on cognitive psychology.[50]

Strong medicine; use with caution. The ultimate danger lies in judgment by the shape of the bottle; that is, the ingestion of a theory by its immediate external utility or political orientation or, as the fashion has it, by its place in the current paradigm or overlapping paradigms. The writer who rejects Freud in favor of Adler because the latter was consciously a socialist carries away from theory the same prejudices brought to it.[51]

One guide only will serve the historian: the extent to which the wisdom, whatever its source, illuminates the evidence. The anthropologist's interpretation of Seneca psychology throws light on Handsome Lake's written record; speculation about the effects of a wartime fatherless society conform to demographic factors which explain why Germany differed from England and France; and the symbolism attached to the Marian cult aids in understanding an important line of theological debate.[52]

[48] Gardner Murphy and Rensis Likert, *Public Opinion and the Individual* (New York, 1938), had found that anti-Jewish, anti-Negro, and anti-minority prejudices generally ran together in persons conservative on domestic and international issues in the 1930s. Theodor W. Adorno, Else Frenkel-Brunswik, Daniel J. Levinson, and R. Nevitt Sanford, *Authoritarian Personality* (New York, 1950), on the basis of a generalized F-Scale delineated a right-wing type without the means of testing whether the same type existed on the left. See Edward A. Shils, "Authoritarianism: 'Right' and 'Left,'" in Richard Christie and Marie Jahoda, eds., *Studies in the Scope and Method of "The Authoritarian Personality"* (Glencoe, Ill., 1954), 24 ff. Greenstein, *Personality and Politics*, 96 ff., recognizes the validity of the criticism, but tries unsuccessfully to rehabilitate the Adorno position.

[49] Lévi-Strauss, *Savage Mind*, 13; Edmund Leach, *Claude Lévi-Strauss* (New York, 1970).

[50] John Lyons, *Chomsky* (London, 1970), 83 ff.

[51] James M. Youngdale, *Populism: A Psycho-Historical Perspective* (Port Washington, N.Y., 1975), 58; Marvin Surkin and Alan Wolfe, eds., *End to Political Science* (New York, 1970), 7. For an extreme statement of social science practicality, see Gunnar Myrdal, *Objectivity in Social Research* (New York, 1969), 55 ff., 69, 72.

[52] For example, Anthony F. C. Wallace, *Death and Rebirth of the Seneca* (New York, 1970), and, to a lesser extent, *King of the Delawares: Teedyuscung* (Philadel-

In the maelstrom of data, theories, and ideas, the historian can cling to one secure point of orientation: the evidence. That, too, no doubt will sometimes sink beneath the rushing tide and hide beneath the creeping fog. But, though for moments lost to sight, the fact is always there. Men and women walked the earth—really did—and left behind the ineradicable traces of their residence—not imagined but actual. And though it takes a whole world of knowledge to know them, they are knowable.

phia, 1949); Peter Loewenberg, "Psychohistorical Origins of the Nazi Youth Cohort," *American Historical Review*, LXXVI (December 1971), 1457 ff.; Marina Warner, *Alone of All Her Sex* (New York, 1976).

# Persistent Themes and
# Hard Facts

EACH OF THE TEN chapters that have brought the reader to this point is an essay, as are the three which will conclude the book. The four immediately following are, however, monographs.

The difference is crucial. It revolves not about care of composition, accuracy in detail, strength of interpretation, or even about the depth of footnotes on the page. The difference involves, rather, two entirely separate modes of creation. The essay is a product of experience joined to scholarly thought: the historian, pondering a problem, conceives a solution and seeks the material to support and confirm it. The monograph, by contrast, is a product of research: the historian accumulates the evidence, often at first without a clear sense of its meaning; and the interpretation emerges later, from the process of wrestling with the data. Good essays draw together information and perhaps illuminate its meaning. Good monographs add to knowledge.

The chapters which follow illustrate four monographic modes of creation. The first was a product of simple curiosity. Frequent references in the 1770s to an obscure writer, clearly not a great politician or theorist, challenged the inquiring note-taker, yet did not seem worthy of investigation until years later, when the fragments of information began to fall together. Chapter 12 grew out of a single story, which seemed somehow not to fit the usual explanation of the relation of industrialization to culture. The next two followed upon discoveries of evidence that ran counter to persistent themes in American history. Each thus sprang from the obligation to face up to an ineluctable fact.

# 11

## Political Theory and Popular Thought

THE AMERICAN REVOLUTION is a classic subject, in the sense that it has always attracted the best minds among historians; and the body of writings about it are an important part of the heritage of the United States. Among the issues persistently raised are those of the national and the ideological qualities of the separation from Britain. The extent to which the rebellious colonists simply affirmed rights as Englishmen, the extent to which ideas, apart from interests, moved them—those matters troubled scholars who celebrated the bicentennial as they did those who celebrated the centennial.

In the twentieth century, moreover, those issues open into a question of penetration: how far into society did the philosophical subtleties that exercised bookish lawyers reach? Although numerous contributions in various forms have illuminated significant aspects of the problems, the account which follows, treating an obscure and ordinary individual, who nevertheless stood at an important strategic point in the transatlantic exchange of ideas, may throw additional light on them.[1]

In 1790 Thomas Jefferson advised Thomas Mann Randolph on the appropriate reading for a young man preparing for a career in the law. The Secretary of State recommended Adam Smith, Montesquieu (with reservations), Locke's "little book on Government," the *Federalist,* and James Burgh's *Political Disquisitions.*[2]

[1] Oscar and Mary F. Handlin, "James Burgh and American Revolutionary Theory," Massachusetts Historical Society, *Proceedings,* LXXIII (1961), 38 ff.

[2] Thomas Jefferson, *Writings,* eds. A. A. Lipscomb and A. L. Bergh (Washington, 1903), VIII, 31.

Jefferson was not alone in his respect for the last-named work. John Adams acquired two "invaluable" copies when it appeared in 1774 and felt close enough to its author to write him about the course of affairs in Massachusetts, as if Burgh would understand and sympathize.[3] The *Political Disquisitions,* printed in England in 1774 and reprinted in Philadelphia in 1775, had a widespread influence upon the revolutionary generation—not only upon the leaders, but even more upon the common folk. Its phrases were familiar in the town meetings of Western Massachusetts, for instance, for they not only made the colonists' stand against England comprehensible and justified, but they also explained, so that any ordinary man could understand, the relation of the individual to government.[4]

Burgh shone luminously for the Revolutionary generation, but briefly. He failed to glow thereafter in the galaxy of Adam Smith, Montesquieu, and Locke. In the nineteenth century his influence and even his memory faded. Later readers, venturing through his dense prose, found him an unsystematic thinker, able to quote readily from writers as diverse as Plato and Harrington, but by no means a Hume or Locke or Montesquieu.

Yet the question remains: what was the source of Burgh's appeal to the American revolutionary generation?

Conversant with the political ideas of his times, he used them to illustrate his dour view of the England he knew. His writings meandered over a wide range of contemporary problems. The decline of religious education, the debasement of manners, the need for improving rhetoric, the aggrandizement of the power of the Crown, corruption in voting, late marriages, insubordination of underlings—these were his subjects. In effect, he preached about the evils of his times; and that explains why Americans read him so avidly. He had value to people interested in the failings of eighteenth-century English society. Therein also lies his utility to the historian. Precisely because he could not embed his comments in a tight philosophical system or transcend the general assump-

3 John Adams, *Diary and Autobiography,* ed. L. H. Butterfield et al., 4 vols. (Cambridge, 1961), II, 182, 223; John Adams, *Works,* ed. Charles Francis Adams, 10 vols. (Boston, 1850–56), IX, 351, 352.

4 See, e.g., "Lenox Response" (1778), Massachusetts Archives, CLVI, 378; J. E. A. Smith, *History of Pittsfield (Berkshire County), Massachusetts, from the Year 1734 to the Year 1800* (Boston, 1869), 336.

tions of his times, he reflected sensitively important currents of contemporary opinion.

∽

James Burgh was a Scot, son of the minister of a parish in Perthshire, and a cousin of Dr. William Robertson the historian. Born in 1714, Burgh attended the University at Saint Andrews, where he hoped to prepare for the ministry in the Church of Scotland. When ill health interrupted his studies, he entered trade, where he lasted just long enough to lose a handsome fortune inherited from his eldest brother. At that point he decided to try his luck abroad and moved to England. In London he corrected proof for a well-known printer and supplemented his earnings by making indexes. After a year he became a teacher, serving in schools in Great Marlow and Enfield. None of these jobs was to his taste. "Being of a sociable disposition," he resented the confinement to the narrow round of boys' life.[5]

Burgh diverted himself in January 1745/46, by writing *Britain's Remembrancer,* a tract on the Scottish rebellion. Exhilarated by the reception of this first effort, he composed *Thoughts on Education* a year later. By then he was a confirmed author; in the next fifteen years he turned out a succession of books: *Directions, Prudential, Moral, Religious and Scientific,* pirated and sold as *Youth's Friendly Monitor; An Hymn to the Creator of the World; A Warning to Dram-Drinkers; The Dignity of Human Nature;* two pamphlets, *Political Speculations;* and *Rationale of Christianity; The Art of Speaking; Proposals . . . for an Association against the Iniquitous Practices of Engrossers; An Account of the . . . Cessares, a People of South America; Crito, or Essays on Various Subjects;* and *Political Disquisitions.* In addition, from time to time, he wrote on current political subjects for newspapers such as *The General Evening Post* (signed "The Free Enquirer," in 1753 and 1754) and the *Gazeteer* (around 1770, signed "Colonists Advocate" and "The Constitutionalist") .[6]

[5] *Biographia Britannica* ed. Andrew Kippis, 2d ed., 5 vols. (London, 1784) , III, 15; John Nichols, *Literary Anecdotes of the Eighteenth Century,* 9 vols. (London, 1778–93) , II, 264 ff.

[6] The following are the first editions of the works of James Burgh: *Britain's Rembrancer* (London, 1746) ; *Thoughts on Education* (London, 1747) ; *Directions, Prudential, Moral, Religious and Scientific* (London, 1750) ; *Hymn to the Creator*

Fame also permitted Burgh in 1747 to establish his own academy, first at Stoke Newington and then in adjacent Newington Green. He conducted this school until 1771, when he retired on account of ill health to a house at nearby Islington. As his own master, he could put into practice his theories of education. The immediate desiratum, to pull the country out of its morass, was the religious training of youth, not only for the present life but for the hereafter. Boys were to learn grammar, orthography, pointing (punctuation), Latin, Greek, accounts, and astronomy—and, above all, correct political principles. The school was to teach "the love of *liberty* and their *country*, and consequently the hatred of Popery, Tyranny, Persecution, Venality, and whatever else is against the interest of a free people." Its products would then understand "the proper medium betwixt an abject and slavish disposition in a people on the one side, and absolute licentiousness and a spirit of murmuring and complaining without reason against their governors, on the other." They would emerge with the conviction that "the true spirit of liberty is always corrected and restrained by a proper submission to government."[7]

At Newington Burgh at last found congenial neighbors. In the eighteenth century this was a pleasant suburban village to which the young bloods of London had been accustomed to resort for cakes and ale on May Day. It held less than a thousand inhabitants and attracted retired statesmen and merchants who desired a rural retreat with easy access to London. Here one could readily go for

---

*of the World* (London, 1750) ; *Warning to Dram-Drinkers* (London, 1751) ; *Dignity of Human Nature* (London, 1754) ; *Art of Speaking* (London, 1761) ; *Account of the First Settlement, Laws, Form of Government, and Police, of the Cessares, a People of South America* (London, 1764) ; *Proposals . . . for an Association against the Iniquitous Practices of Engrossers, Forestallers, Jobbers, &c., and for Reducing the Price of Provisions, Especially Butchers' Meat* (London, 1764) ; *Crito, or Essays on Various Subjects* (London, 1766–67) ; *Political Disquisitions* (London, 1774–75). In addition, Nichols, *Literary Anecdotes*, II, 265, mentions two pamphlets of which no copies have been found: *Political Speculations* (1758) and *Rationale of Christianity* (1760). Verner W. Crane, *Benjamin Franklin's Letters to the Press* (Chapel Hill, N.C., 1950), 285 ff., attributes the "Colonist's Advocate" series to Franklin. See also Chapter 5 at note 3.

7 Burgh, *Thoughts on Education,* 2, 7, 12.

an evening's diversion, and here one could recruit a wide company of friends.[8]

Newington Green had been noted for Dissent since the second half of the seventeenth century, when Charles Morton's Academy had begun to attract nonconforming parents and pupils to the area. Though no longer a "most rude wilderness" when Burgh moved there, Newington was still a charming rustic asylum from which critics could view, but not be sullied by, the corruptions of London.[9]

Burgh did not start in Newington unconnected. His Dissent had smoothed his career in London and in the various academies in which he had taught. Membership in a minority enabled him to move easily along a network of like-minded men that stretched from Scotland to London. Safely anchored by background, education, temperament, and habit within his own nonconformist group, he judiciously selected his connections with the outside world, the approval of which, in turn, reinforced his sense of earnestness and righteousness.

Burgh's circle quickly widened. In 1751 he dedicated his *Warning to Dram-Drinkers* to Stephen Hales, Clerk of Closet to the Princess Dowager and Chaplain to the Prince, and to Thomas Hayter, Bishop of Norwich and Preceptor of the young princes after the death of Frederick, Prince of Wales. He thereby gained entrée to the Princess Dowager's household, where he "met with a most gracious reception." The Princess herself "had much discourse" with him "on the subject of education and other topics," an event which Burgh must have ceaselessly related to his friends, for they remembered it well after his death. Joining, he believed, "all mankind in having the most profound regard and veneration" for the Princess Dowager, Burgh dedicated his *Dignity of Human Nature* to her. His intentions were simple: to urge the illustrious personage to continue her "pious cares in forming" her "lovely offspring to virtue and to glory." Burgh suggested that his book would be helpful, referring coyly to his early success and to his

8 Norman G. Brett-James, *Growth of Stuart London* (London, 1935), 51.

9 J. Lionel Tayler, *Little Corner of London (Newington Green)* (London, 1925), 15, 22 ff.; Roland Thomas, *Richard Price* (London, 1924), 30 ff.; Walter Besant, *London in the Eighteenth Century* (London, 1903), 170 ff.

repute among "persons in other parts of the world," who would not "fail to pay a peculiar regard to whatever comes from him."[10]

In Newington, Burgh fell into and helped build up a "happy company." A weekly supper club took turns meeting at his house and at those of Dr. Richard Price, who had arrived as minister in 1758, and Dr. Thomas Rogers. Joined by Mr. Thoresby, "the liberal and learned rector of Stoke Newington," this group was the nucleus of a widening circle. Here Joseph Priestley was brought to meet Dr. Price. Here Benjamin Franklin came when he was in England. Teas, friendly visits, and dignified conversation enlivened an earnest, pleasant, genteel, and godly existence. Years later Samuel Rogers recollected how Dr. Price, who lived next door, would drop by in his dressing gown to spend the evening. "He would talk and read the Bible to us, till he sent us to bed in a frame of mind as heavenly as his own."[11]

As the Newington group spread its connections, it took to meeting weekly at the London Coffee-House in Ludgate Hill. Here gathered a distinguished company, heterogeneous in interest, but drawn together by common assumptions and shared views and values which set them off from the scores of other clubs of London in this period. A selective ideological and social cement held together these clergymen, physicians, and other professionals. Others who drifted in and failed to adhere, quickly drifted out again. James Boswell regarded himself as a member soon after the publication of his book on Corsica; but interests other than the sober ones of the group cut his participation short.[12]

Their positions as outsiders in English society united those who continued to come. The growth of London had brought to the

---

10 *Biographia Britannica,* III, 15; Burgh, *Dignity of Human Nature,* iii, iv, vi.

11 P. W. Clayden, *Early Life of Samuel Rogers* (London, 1887), 8, 11; R. Ellis, *Samuel Rogers and His Circle* (London, 1910), 8; Verner W. Crane, "Club of Honest Whigs," *William and Mary Quarterly,* XXIII (April 1966), 215, 217 ff., 232. Benjamin Franklin, *Writings,* ed. A. H. Smyth (New York, 1905–07), IV, 220; Thomas, *Richard Price,* 38 ff.; Carl C. Cone, *Torchbearer of Freedom: The Influence of Richard Price* (Lexington, Ky., 1952), 53 ff.; John Towill Rutt, *Life and Correspondence of Joseph Priestley* (London, 1831), I, 55, 60 ff., 258, II, 109. See also J. H. Plumb, *England in the Eighteenth Century* (Harmondsworth, Eng., 1950), 133 ff.; Benjamin Franklin, *Papers,* ed. Leonard W. Labaree (New Haven, 1961), IV, 404.

12 Frank Brady and F. A. Pottle, *Boswell in Search of a Wife* (New Haven, 1956), 161, 167, 300.

metropolis a variety of men of talent—Welshmen like Price, Scots like Burgh and Sir John Pringle, Yorkshiremen like Priestley and Andrew Kippis, Quakers like Peter Collinson and John Fothergill, and provincials like Franklin. These men regarded the turmoil of life in the great city with mingled awe and distrust. In addition, some of them were teachers, and almost all of them were Dissenters, alienated from the established church and disposed to regard the society in which they lived critically. Their faith was science, education, and the application of the principles of correct reason to the problems of the day. Earnestly dedicated to doing right, they believed in the power of moderate common sense and knowledge to improve the lot of humanity.

And what a world they found about them in Georgian England and particularly in London! Across the Thames and to the westward, men of new wealth were building homes of unprecedented lavishness. There clubs of quite another sort flourished. Grocers made rich by speculation, nabobs come back from the colonies, gentry bored with life on their estates flocked to the capital and threw themselves into an unabashed quest for wealth and pleasure. Debauchery spread through the habits of new and old families: to gamble, to drink oneself into a stupor, to dally promiscuously with mistresses and lovers were accepted conventions of a society in which no one knew his place or station and in which obligations had no binding quality.

The corruption of morals extended to politics. Ministers of State and Members of Parliament shared the vices of those they represented. Government became an enormous speculative enterprise in which rival cliques and factions struggled for their own advantage. To the sober men of Newington, physically close to the sink of inquity yet spiritually remote from it, the first requisite of any change for the better was thorough moral regeneration of the whole country.[13]

The call for that rebirth rang through everything that Burgh wrote. His first work, *Britain's Remembrancer,* published toward the end of the rebellion in Scotland, had warned that God dis-

---

[13] M. Dorothy George, *London Life in the XVIIIth Century* (London, 1925), 27 ff.; Besant, *London in the Eighteenth Century,* 14, 308 ff., 345 ff., 360 ff., 399 ff., 455 ff.; Jay B. Botsford, *English Society in the Eighteenth Century* (New York, 1924), 68 ff., 128 ff., 162 ff., 243 ff.

tressed nations "for no other end than the punishment of guilt, and the moral improvement of mankind." Britain would disregard the handwriting on the wall only at the peril of utter ruin. In a single season it had faced a dearth of corn and a Popish pretender. Then it had escaped, but the country could not always expect mercy. It was time to mend its ways. Vice had infected not only the rich, but the entire nation, which was reeling toward the fate of other empires debilitated by luxury.

"*French* fopperies" and ostentation, lassitude and irreligion, gaming places and theaters distracted the people. No one did an honest day's work, and bankruptcies increased because young traders took more interest in living well than in paying their debts. But the prevalent unbelief made perjury a small matter. The casual disregard of oaths and the frequency of bribery resulted in "unhappy divisions." The rich got into financial difficulties; the inferior ranks, finding their affairs in disorder, became "dupes to the heads of factions" and joined "in the clamour against their governors." Thus, those "least qualified for finding fault" were "generally speaking, loudest in their complaints."

Only acceptance of a whole sequence of imperatives would save England: the clergy must lead the way to reform; the magistrates, in town and country, must enforce the laws guarding morals; wealthy traders must set an example of industry, sobriety, and economy; and, above all, education must form the minds of the young and imbue them with religion. These mild injunctions, "so much read and applauded by persons of a religious temper," carried the book "through five editions in little more than two years."[14]

Dismayed by "this thoughtless and voluptuous age," Burgh continued to write in the same moralistic vein. In 1754 his *Dignity of Human Nature* again recorded his forebodings and his suggestions for improvement. He despaired of the future, while a continual round "of idle and expensive amusements" filled up the bulk of people's time. The true dignity of human nature, he explained, encompassed the attributes of prudence, knowledge, virtue, and revealed religion. For the young, setting out in life, prudence or a turn of mind which induced a person to look forward and enabled

---

[14] *Biographia Britannica*, III, 14; Burgh, *Britain's Remembrancer*, reprinted in *Monitory Address to Great Britain* (Edinburgh, 1792), 260 ff., 272 ff., 278 ff. References throughout this chapter are to this edition.

him "to judge rightly of his behaviour" was "indispensably necessary." Too many, alas, were improvident. They spent before they
knew what they could earn or how many children they would have
to support. Speaking out of turn, venting singular opinions, satire,
boasting, and lying were forms of imprudence. Prudence, by contrast, called for circumspect behavior; there was no "more promising sign in a young person, than a readiness to hear the advice of
those" qualified by age and experience for mature judgment.

Method and regularity in business were essential. "Indefatigable
diligence, joined with frugality," permitted people of "the lowest
and most laborious stations in life" to rise and to relieve themselves from labor and anxiety in old age. A few shillings saved each
day mounted up; in thirty years they formed an enormous total,
particularly if put into "an advantageous trade." One should
neither borrow nor lend incautiously nor deal more than was
necessary with strangers. It was more important to be frugal of
time than of money, lest opportunities be lost. "Those pleasures
of life which cost the most" were the least satisfactory; balls, plays,
masquerades, gilt coaches, and powdered footmen could not compete with the "endearments of a faithful wife and innocent children" or "the study of virtue and religion." "Employing . . .
working people in improving barren grounds, . . . raising buildings for a continual increase of tenants upon a thriving estate,
. . . the encouragement of manufactures, and providing for the
poor"—these would "gain a country-gentleman more popularity,
than keeping open house the whole year round."

A prudent man had no need to deny himself "the moderate use
of such innocent amusements, as his fortune or leisure" allowed—
for instance, "reading, viz. history, lives, geography, and natural
philosophy; with a very little choice poetry; the conversation of
a few agreeable friends; and drawing," where there was a talent
for it. To these he could add "riding on horseback once or twice
in a week," where it could be done conveniently. Music, on the
other hand, was "never safely indulged." Desire for excelling in
it generally drew people into an expense of time and money,
above the worth of the accomplishment, "carried to the greatest
lengths."[15]

It was best to marry young, as soon as it was possible to support

15 Burgh, *Dignity of Human Nature,* iv, v ff., 2, 3 ff., 30, 32 ff.

a family. In London and other cities marriage, regarded "as the end of all the happiness of life," was unseasonably postponed, so a declining population enfeebled the country. Yet, entered into with prudence, marriage was the beginning of true pleasure, although it was well to seek not a woman with "the most exquisite beauty, the most sprightly wit, or the largest fortune," but rather one with common sense and good nature. Then the family would be able to sustain its responsibility for raising children to love school, work, and frugality, that is, to form "a rational creature."[16]

⌒⌐❍

Burgh's basic concern was thus with moral issues. But his environment and the temper of the times pushed him into political speculation. Some of the problems he discussed had implications for government; and the give-and-take of conversation at the club and of his correspondence with friends compelled him to deal with the role of the state in human affairs. However, his theories of politics emerged not from systematic analysis but from ad-hoc treatment of specific evils; and he revealed his general assumptions only incidentally in his utopian tract and in his polemical writings.

Selfishness produces licentiousness in society and venality and corruption in government. Extravagance impoverishes the wealthy and disorganizes the poor, so that all seek only their ends, heedless of the effects upon the social order. Agitators appear, concealing their true intentions beneath lofty slogans; for generally "a patriot is only a Courtier out of place, and a Courtier a Patriot in place." People become so contentious that even "the lowest of the mob . . . takes the liberty, over his cups, to rail at the legislators of his country."[17] Thus appear the unhappy divisions which are a curse upon England, for they destroy the whole fabric of society. The world cannot carry on "if children, apprentices, servants . . . spend time in disputing the commands of their superiors."[18]

Such license destroys liberty which "does not exclude restraint," but "only excludes unreasonable restraint." Reason must, after all,

---

[16] Burgh, *Dignity of Human Nature*, 50 ff.

[17] Burgh, *Britain's Remembrancer*, 278; Burgh, *Dignity of Human Nature*, 273.

[18] Burgh, *Thoughts on Education*, 12; Burgh, *Dignity of Human Nature*, 31, 274.

prevail over licentiousness, or "doing whatever the will, appetites and passions suggest." Since "true liberty desires only the freedom of doing what is agreeable to the dictates of reason and the rules of religion," men motivated by genuine love of country neither submit slavishly to their governors, nor complain without reason against them. "The design of all government" must allow "the governed the liberty of doing what, consistently with the *general* good, they may desire to do, and which only forbids their doing the contrary." Only thus can society be sure of that order which is an absolute necessity for the highest development of human dignity.[19]

The law determines "precisely how far *personal* liberty is compatible with the *general* good." And, since the object of government is the "securing the happiness of the whole," it follows that "the *consent* of the whole *people,* as far as it can be obtained, is indispensably *necessary* to every law, by which the whole *people* are to be bound." Subjects in a "free country" have the same rights as stockholders in a company.[20]

In an ideal state the whole populace, presented with a form of government, would make alterations and, by their approval, would express "their submission" and become "entitled to all the privileges of citizenship," eligible to vote and to hold office. Sober, industrious, and peaceable newcomers would be "permitted to subscribe the laws of the land," and would thereby become citizens. A religion which "sanctifies all manner of oppression and cruelty to protestants, and therefore must naturally prove destructive to every protestant state" necessarily excluded Papists from citizenship. Toleration was enough for them.

Well guided in exercising the power to vote, the citizens would set up a government with a hereditary executive of limited powers and with a senate elected for life, all subject to recall. Inspectors, also chosen by the people, would inquire into manners and conduct to preserve the virtue of the nation. This mixed form would "preserve a due balance, and keep a happy medium between the

[19] Burgh, *Thoughts on Education,* 12; Burgh, *Cessares,* 26 n.; Burgh, *Political Disquisitions,* I, 2 ff.

[20] Burgh, *Political Disquisitions,* I, 2 ff.; Burgh, *Crito,* I, 2.

tyranny of arbitrary monarchy, the factions of aristocracy, and the anarchy, licentiousness, and wild tumults of a democracy."[21]

There is no "perfect commonwealth," however. Only rarely have people formed "a constitution from the foundation"; and even the wisest governments have suffered from selfish or wicked pressures. Political establishments in practice usually consist of chance vestiges of older systems woven into new ones that obscure "the spirit of the constitution." To assert with David Hume, that whatever "is publicly allowed at any particular period, may be said to be constitutional at that period," is to beg the question. If the machinery of government operates so that the people have no share in power, they become "mere beasts of burden, instead of what they are, viz. the original of power, the object of government, and last resource."[22]

Yet few societies "have originally so principled" their constitutions that the people from whom power derives can themselves lay hold of it, "wield it as they please, and turn it, when necessary, against those to whom it was entrusted, and who have exerted it to the prejudice of its original proprietors." In England, Parliament "is constitutionally the last resort," and there is no provision for regular appeal to the people, who may be compelled "to take into their own hands the dangerous work of vindicating their liberties by force."[23]

To avoid a course that can only lead to anarchy and tyranny, the government must speak for the people. The British Constitution provides for "government by kings, lords, and commons." But actually, power is "vested in a *small* number of individuals," who link the legislative to the executive power. The Court influences elections and, through its ministers, placemen, and pensioners, prevents the Commons from representing the people. The Lords extend their power beyond their own house. Can the House of Commons, then, "be called even the shadow of a representation of the property of the people?" Only restoration of that body as a check on regal and ministerial tyranny would preserve the Con-

21 Burgh, *Cessares*, 16, 26, 27, 40, 48 ff.

22 Burgh, *Cessares*, 50; Burgh, *Political Disquistions*, I, v, 22, 23, 72.

23 Burgh, *Political Disquisitions*, I, 4, 6 ff.

stitution and enable the governed to express their consent. That would require revision of representation in Parliament, curtailment of the length of sessions, and elimination of corruption.[24]

Everybody should be represented, for everybody has "unalienable property . . . a personal liberty, a character, a right to his earnings, a right to a religious profession and worship according to his conscience." Even dependents on charity have wives and children "in whom they have a right." No doubt it is not feasible to allow the poor to vote; but many others, deserving of the privilege, remain unrepresented. Since only "a few beggarly boroughs" control elections, Parliament becomes a "juntocracy . . . or government by a minister and his crew," with the Court directing "the beggars whom to choose." Great parts of Middlesex, Kent, and Surrey and the inhabitants of Bristol, Liverpool, Manchester, Birmingham, and Ely have either inadequate representation or none at all; and "the overbalance of the power in the hands of the landed men" works to the disadvantage of the manufacturing and mercantile interest.[25]

An adequate plan would accord all forms of property "proportional weight and consequence" by giving each county that percentage of the 513 members proportionate to its "contribution to the public expence." Within the county, "men of large property" would "have more votes, than those, who have less to secure." Annual elections and the exclusion by rotation of placemen and pensioners would further make the Commons representative.[26]

Without such reforms the people will take power in their own hands; they will prefer the temporary evils of "dethroning a King, oversetting a government, or even massacring a court" to tyranny, "a permanent evil, distressing and debasing the human species from generation to generation, and deluging the world in a never ebbing sea of blood." And if, "headed by a spirit of an unusual boldness, they do rise like a whirlwind, and sweep away the combination against their liberties," they may give rise to new tyrants

[24] Burgh, *Political Disquisitions,* I, 24, 50, 386 ff., 406; III, 272, 310.

[25] Burgh, *Political Disquisitions,* I, 27, 36 ff., 49 ff., 53; "Constitutionalist," *Gazetteer and New Daily Advertiser* (London) , Feb. 28, 1770.

[26] Burgh, *Political Disquisitions,* I, 39, 49, 127.

who will "rivet on the unhappy people the very fetters they had just before knocked off."[27]

Avoidance of this fearsome eventuality justified almost any cost, for Burgh's intentions were far from revolutionary. His writings aimed to strengthen rather than to overturn the existing order; and so his English contemporaries interpreted them. His friends hoped that a reading of the *Political Disquisitions* would persuade the "men at the helm" to "remove those public evils" which the book exposed.[28]

"All sound patriots will avoid rousing the people, if redress can be any other way obtained." Therefore, Burgh does not propose recourse to force, but hopes "to apply the power of the people, guided, limited, and directed by men of property, who are interested in the security of their country . . . to prevent the application of the same power unrestrained, unlimited, and directed by mere caprice, or the spirit of party." The government might then "grant, voluntarily, and with a good grace, that redress, to which the people have an undoubted right, and which they see the people resolute to have."

A "grand national association for obtaining an independent parliament" would take an urgent first step to this end. Since more detailed plans might deter some from joining, it is best to leave the particulars "to the wisdom of succeeding times." Meanwhile, may the King of Kings "open the eyes of this unthinking people," to "send forth a spirit of wisdom, and of union, of submission to wise and just government, and of courage to resist oppression and tyranny," for "Thou art thyself the generous patron of liberty. Thy intention was, that man should be free."[29]

The perspective of Burgh's political ideas was entirely negative. When he reached for positive images he could only fasten on the reverse of what he saw about him; and such ideals he affixed to

27 Burgh, *Political Disquisitions*, III, 311, 312.

28 *Monthly Review* (London), L (1774), 109 ff., LI (1774), 344 ff., LIII (1775), 109 ff., 115; John Nichols, *Illustrations of the Literary History of the Eighteenth Century* (London, 1831), VI, 61. See also Herbert Butterfield, *George III, Lord North and the People, 1779–1780* (London, 1949), 259–266; Eugene C. Black, *Association* (Cambridge, 1963), 29.

29 Burgh, *Political Disquisitions*, III, 426, 428, 455, 457 ff.

places remote in either time or space. He made frequent though vague appeals to an earlier England, where order still rested on the "sober and regular manners of our fathers."[30]

Hence the special place of the colonies in the strategy of Burgh's argument. The colonists were mostly farmers, "wholly dependent on the produce of their lands, contented, and consequently happy," until taxed to gratify the *"voraciousness* of the *court-tools."* Against great odds, the Americans prospered. Their natural increase resulted from the "sobriety and temperate way of living, practised by the Dissenters retired to" the New World. The well-being of New England, Carolina, and Pennsylvania rested on "the education of their planters." Strict laws in New England disciplined the society; there "adultery, blasphemy, striking or cursing a parent, and perjury in matters of life and death" were capital offenses. Also the New Englanders took great care "of the morals of the Indians, . . . particularly to prevent drunkenness"—an ironic contrast that, to conditions in the mother country, where the government gained by the intoxication of the people. In the colonies Englishmen lived in the freedom that they earned by avoiding the vice and corruption of the Old World; the noble simplicity of their manners and their rusticity testified eloquently to their difference from the degradation of the Court and of London society. There the people kept up the right of instructing their legislators, while in England the decay of the constitution permitted the Members of Parliament to hold themselves unaccountable.[31]

The evils of English government became most apparent in relation to the colonies. The grievances of the Americans were evidence of the selfishness of courtiers, of the shortsightedness of placemen, and of the deficiencies of an unrepresentative Parliament. This outpost of liberty resisted the corruption of British Ministers, who "have opened a wound perhaps never more to be healed—all to get a few more *places* for their wretched dependents." Increased taxes only increased the opportunity to embezzle. "The iron rod of oppression" threatened to break "the free spirit of the colonists."[32]

---

[30] Burgh, *Britain's Remembrancer,* 273; Burgh, *Crito,* II, 71.

[31] Burgh, *Political Disquisitions,* I, 184, 204 ff.; II, 274, 311 ff.; III, 30, 31, 219.

[32] Burgh, *Political Disquisitions,* II, 274 ff., 276.

༄

The flattering image of themselves that Burgh held up to the Americans no doubt helped make his books popular. The provincials were pleased to learn that their society was better, purer, nobler than that of the mother country. His strictures upon the immorality of Ministers and Parliament added to the colonists' conviction in the righteousness of their own cause, and made it easier for them to condemn the villainy of their rulers. As the conflict passed the point of possible reconciliation, the Americans were quick to circulate Burgh's latest views and promptly reprinted the *Political Disquisitions* in Philadelphia. A list of "encouragers" revealed that the work was well launched and its contents known in advance. At the head of the roster of sponsors was "His Excellency, George Washington, Esq.; Generalissimo of all the Forces in America, and a Member of the Honorable, the American Continental Congress." Samuel Chase of Maryland, John Dickinson, Silas Deane, Christopher Gadsden, John Hancock, Thomas Jefferson, Thomas Mifflin, George Ross, Roger Sherman, John Sullivan, Charles Thomson, and James Wilson were among the other subscribers. John Adams set himself "to make the Disquisitions more known and attended to in several parts of America"; he wrote that they were "held in as high estimation by all" his friends as by himself.[33]

Approval in America increased the sensitivity of Burgh and his group to colonial opinion. Benjamin Franklin, Josiah Quincy, and other visitors served as channels of communication, and a steady stream of pamphlets and tracts flowed eastward across the Atlantic. Mutual esteem gave both parties to the exchange a feeling of strength and pushed them toward an ever more radical view of existing authority.[34]

The Americans found it helpful, in these years of intense political debate, to draw upon the armory of intellectual weapons Burgh

33 Burgh, *Political Disquisitions* (Philadelphia, 1775) , III, 3rd to 6th preliminary leaves; Adams, *Works,* IX, 351; Zoltán Haraszti, *John Adams and the Prophets of Progress* (Cambridge, 1952) , 302.

34 Burgh, *Political Disquisitions,* II, vii; Franklin, *Writings,* VI, 429 ff., VIII, 8 ff., 154, 451, 457; J. P. Agnew, *Richard Price and the American Revolution* (Urbana, Ill., 1949) , 2, 3.

put at their disposal. His books were immense grab bags, liberally loaded with quotations. Here appeared the honest whig views of the authors of *Cato's Letters,* the classic theories of Locke, Harrington, and Sydney, and the authority of Blackstone and Bolingbroke, as well as the ancient wisdom of Plato, Aristotle, and Cicero. Many colonists who never got to read the authors in the original were able to quote them with assurance by dipping into Burgh.

A significant congruence between Burgh's ideas on government and those the colonists had developed out of other sources in other ways enabled them to do so. The formulation at which the Scotsman arrived out of his criticism of English society bore striking resemblances to that which Americans reached by positive generalizations about the institutions that had in actuality evolved about them. The key concepts were similar in theoretical and in rhetorical expression; they differed profoundly in the practical meaning attached to them. Both the similarities and the differences are important.

Thus, Burgh, and in fact all the successors of Locke, spoke of the consent of the governed in terms analogous to those the revolutionary theorists used. But the context was by no means the same. The concept, for Burgh, was a means of exemplifying the shortcomings of parliamentary representation. To explain legislative corruption he had to account for the defects in the selection of members. He condemned the existing scheme because it failed to elicit the consent of the population; on that inadequacy rested his more general criticism of Parliament.

The consent of the governed thus became, for Burgh, the broad foundation of social order; it comprehended proper representation in the institutions of government, but also obedience to rulers, the respectful relationship of inferiors to superiors, and the acceptance of discipline. He could conceive of consent in an ideal form, as when the citizens of his utopia organized their state, or in a practical form, as in the projected national association to secure legislative reform. In either case, consent was a criterion against which to measure the disorderly behavior of the existing Parliament. Burgh could also envision a popular uprising when continued disregard of the need for consent demonstrated the lack of social order; Jamaica, Corsica, and possibly the American colonies were instances. But he could not conceive such an outcome in England.

These phrases were grist for the argumentative mills of the colonists as they debated the propriety of taxation without representation. An attack by an Englishman on an unrepresentative Parliament, which lacked consent, certainly supported their own position. In addition, the concept of consent was appropriate to their own position in a way that Burgh could not imagine. The emergence of government from an act of popular consent was for him a utopian abstraction; in the colonies it was a living reality. The national association was a visionary program for the future; in America the practice of association was a day-to-day actuality. What he described as an ideal on one side of the ocean, existed in fact on the other.

Furthermore, the revolutionaries wrenched the concept of consent out of the orderly context in which Burgh had located it. For him the corollary of consent had been obedience to established authority. But the Americans who defied the English laws moved toward another conclusion. The errors and injustices of Parliament proved the fallibility of all governments and the necessity of popular vigilance in defence of liberty. Consent thus became a continuous process by which the people passed upon the validity of the acts of their rulers. Grievances were by no means to be submitted to, but resisted by precisely such uprisings as Burgh dreaded in England.

Years later John Adams understood and feared the implications of his countrymen's idea of consent. He complained in 1789 that Mr. Burgh's *Political Disquisitions,* along with *Common Sense,* propagated among the people "a too ardent and unconsiderate pursuit of erroneous opinions of government." He had by then forgotten that the views to which he objected emanated not from Burgh but from what Americans made of him.[35]

A similar divergence appeared in the concept of the constitution. His most frequent use of the word trapped Burgh in a circu-

35 Adams, *Works,* IX, 558 ff. See also Oscar and Mary F. Handlin, *Dimensions of Liberty* (Cambridge, 1961), 225 ff., and *Popular Sources of Political Authority* (Cambridge, 1966).

lar argument. By the term "constitution" he usually meant the orderly machinery of government as it existed. But he also wished to show that Parliament's actions were bad and, therefore, against the spirit or intent of the constitution. Yet reform could come only from Parliament, the ultimate resort in determining what was constitutional. The people could do no more than plead for adherence to the true spirit of the constitution. Hence the association could only urge that King, Commons, and Lords each take its rightful place in the order of government.

Burgh also conceived of a constitution in another, more abstract, sense. In a new society, such as that of his utopia, the people could start afresh and frame a constitution of government. But that sense was by no means applicable to a settled society, where such efforts could only lead to violence, anarchy, and tyranny.

The revolutionaries readily accepted Burgh's criticism of parliamentary action as unconstitutional. But they did not apply the term "constitution" to the existing order of government, which was corrupt and venal and a device for filling the pockets of a few favorites at the expense of the rest of the population. To them the term meant something altogether new. They conceived of themselves in the position of the people of Cessares, starting afresh. The constitution was the written charter or agreement from which the government drew authority. The correction of abuses or deficiencies called not for gradual amendment from within the existing system, but for frequent new beginnings.[36]

Finally, there was a significant difference in the treatment of liberty. Burgh's specific discussion of rights and privileges hinged on criticisms of existing defects in government. Thus, the consideration of the inequity of parliamentary representation led into a definition of privilege as an unwarranted or dangerous preeminence, distinguished from a right. A discussion of prosecutions for libel led to an exposition of the liberty of speech and writing.

But Burgh also used liberty in a more general sense. "Since we are all brethren," his utopians explained, "and God has given to all men a natural right to liberty, we allow of no slavery among us; unless a person forfeits his freedom by his crimes." True liberty in this sense he equated with virtue and with the capacity for

[36] Handlin, *Dimensions of Liberty,* 254 ff.

doing what was good and reasonable. Hence it followed that in his own day liberty seemed "indeed to be bidding mankind farewell." Redemption could come, but only through education and the reform of manners which would restore virtue.[37]

Burgh's appeals for the restoration of liberty were always rhetorical, never related to the specific abuses of particular rights; the virtuous sufferers could only acquiesce until they persuaded Parliament of its unreasonableness. Thus, in the abstract, Burgh accorded even the dependent poor the right to vote. But in practice he could envision no orderly pattern of suffrage but one related to the amount of property.

The colonists never distinguished, as Burgh did, between abstract liberty and concrete liberties. Liberty, a general state, they equated with a natural inalienable right of man from which all specific rights derived or to which all were linked. They therefore set Burgh's attack on specific abuses in a totally different context, shaped by their own experience.[38]

Burgh formulated a few political propositions basically critical of the institutions under which he lived. In doing so he drew upon ideas that were widely current in his own times and particularly concentrated in the circle in which he moved. He thus acted as a conveyor between the speculative minds with which he had contact and his extensive body of readers.

These ideas had an impact in the colonies. Burgh's comments favorable to them and hostile to their enemies delighted the Americans who gobbled up his aphorisms, rhetoric, and occasional invective. Titillating slurs by an Englishman who called monarchs "worms" undoubtedly emboldened John Adams in references to the royal Ministers as "sharpers, gamblers, and horse-jockies."[39]

In addition, Burgh's writings communicated a set of general ideas about the nature of government. But the ideas did not sur-

[37] Burgh, *Cessares*, 83; Burgh, *Political Disquisitions*, III, 415.

[38] Handlin, *Dimensions of Liberty*, 58 ff.

[39] Adams, *Works*, IX, 351.

vive the crossing intact. The process of transmission adapted them to fit the context within which they would be embedded. The changes, often of the utmost importance, were nevertheless effected subtly and without notice. The concept of monarchy was a dramatic example. Burgh, like other eighteenth-century writers, could conceive of a utopian polity without a king. But no more than any other European writer of his time could he imagine that the actual government of his own country could function in an orderly manner without the Crown.

The colonists accepted no such discriminations between the ideal and the actual; royalty had no place in their own society. And whatever the abstract theories to which they adhered, Americans never seriously contemplated the possibility of anointing a king in the New World. It was the same with such concepts as consent, constitution, and liberty. Even when an American used the same words and adhered to the same formal principles as an Englishman, a novel situation transformed the meaning.

These distinctions have general relevance to the diffusion of ideas from one society to another. They also apply more specifically to the role of ideas in the revolutionary period. Regarded in the abstract, theories about the nature of the state are almost independent of time and place. But abstractions have rarely goaded men into action; in the application to concrete situations, ideas acquire a specificity that gives them historical significance.

It is possible to link Burgh, as Caroline Robbins has, with a general line of speculation derived from the Commonwealth period. Connections are also possible with economics writers of the late seventeenth century and with renaissance humanists. Indeed it is possible to draw the line much farther back, to Cicero and the Bible. But the full meaning of the Scottish schoolmaster's ideas is only revealed in the light of his moral revulsion from the social conditions of eighteenth-century London.[40]

[40] Caroline Robbins, *Eighteenth-Century Commonwealthman* (Cambridge, 1959), 363 ff.; George H. Sabine and Stanley B. Smith, *Marcus Tullius Cicero on the Commonwealth* (Columbus, Ohio, 1929), 39 ff., 51 ff.; Joyce Appleby, "Social Origins of American Revolutionary Ideology," *Journal of American History*, LXIV (March 1978), 935 ff.

So, too, it is possible to link the revolutionary currents of thought in the colonies with general lines of eighteenth-century political theory, as Americans frequently did. The revolutionary colonists had intimate links not only with the English group of which Burgh was a part, but also with like-minded Hollanders and Frenchmen. With reason, Jefferson once explained that the Declaration of Independence had not aimed "to find out new principles" or "to say things which had never been said before; but to place before mankind the common sense of the subject," which had largely been expressed "in conversation, in letters, printed essays, or in the elementary books of public right, as Aristotle, Cicero, Locke. Sidney, etc."[41] But it is misleading to interpret that statement, as Carl Becker and Robert Palmer did, to mean that the Declaration merely set forth ideas generally held in the Western world of the eighteenth century.[42] Jefferson's explanation proceeded to refer to the Declaration as "an expression of the American mind."[43] The document he drafted rested on broad principles that reached back as far as Aristotle; yet it was also distinctive—expressive of its own time and place.

James Burgh is an aid in making out the elements of distinctiveness. Precisely because he was not a great theorist, he reflected the attitudes of his particular environment. His situation located him as close to American thought as any European of his time; and the differences between his ideas and those of the colonists who read him illuminates the intellectual gulf that had opened between the thinking of the Old World and the New. The most refined modern measures of content analysis or of attention patterns will not note the distance, nor will the harvest of a bushel of quotations, because

41 Thomas Jefferson, *Writings,* ed. P. L. Ford, 10 vols. (New York, 1892–99), X, 343. See also [André] Morellet, *Memoires inédits de l'Abbé Morellet,* 2d ed. (Paris, 1882), 307 ff.; Richard Price, *Nadere Aanmerkingen over den Aart end de Waarde der burgerlyke Vryheid,* trans. Johan Derk van der Capellan (Leyden, 1777), 2, 30 ff., 43; Baron van der Capellan to Richard Price, Massachusetts Historical Society, *Proceedings,* 2d ser., XVII (1903), 313 ff.; Abraham J. van der Aa, *Biographisch Woordenboek der Nederlanden* (Haarlem, 1852–78), III, 148 ff.

42 Jefferson, Writings, ed. Ford, X, 343; R. R. Palmer, *Age of the Democratic Revolution* (Princeton, 1959), 213, 214; Carl L. Becker, *Declaration of Independence* (New York, 1940), 24–25; Benjamin F. Wright, *American Interpretations of Natural Law* (Cambridge, 1931), 98, 99.

43 Jefferson, *Writings,* ed. Ford, X, 343.

the same words served on both sides of the ocean. Only the juxta-position of ideas as actually used will trace their permutations.[44]

---

[44] See the review by Louis L. Tucker, *William and Mary Quarterly*, XXI (April 1964), 306. For futile efforts at quantification, see, e.g., Richard L. Merritt, "Colonists Discover America: Attention Patterns in the Colonial Press, 1735–1775," *William and Mary Quarterly*, XXI (April 1964), 271, and "Emergence of American Nationalism: A Quantitative Approach," *American Quarterly*, XVII (Summer 1965), 317 ff., and *Symbols of American Community, 1735–1775* (New Haven, 1966); Ole R. Holsti and Robert C. North, "Comparative Data from Content Analysis: Perceptions of Hostility and Economic Variables in the 1914 Crisis," in Richard L. Merritt and Stein Rokkan, eds., *Comparing Nations: The Use of Quantitative Data in Cross National Research* (New Haven, 1966), 169 ff.; Richard L. Merritt, "West Berlin—Center or Periphery?" *ibid.*, 321 ff.; Edwin Clarke, ed., *Modern Methods in the History of Medicine* (London, 1971), 258, 259. By contrast, the thoughtful analysis in Louis Galambos, *Public Image of Big Business in America* (Baltimore, 1975), 41 ff., though inconclusive, shows awareness of the problems. These problems are quite different from those raised in statistical analysis of a text to identify a single author, for which see Alvar Ellegård, *Statistical Method for Determining Authorship* (Göteborg, 1962); and Frederick Mosteller and David L. Wallace, "Inference in an Authorship Problem," *Journal of the American Statistical Association*, LVIII (June 1963), 275 ff.

# 12

## Man and Magic

A SIMPLE, satisfying way of thinking beguiled many a mid-twentieth-century historian. An industrial revolution in the eighteenth century had transformed the mode of production, had brought modern capitalism into being, and had disrupted traditional ways of making goods. In the new order great factories housed machines run by power and operated by working people who did not own their own tools and who, therefore, depended entirely upon the employer for their livelihood. The teeming cities failed to provide the laborers with decent habitations or an adequate standard of living and also cut them off from nature. The net effect was brooding discontent and a sense of alienation—the spiritual and ideological counterpart of economic exploitation. Thus, the crucial element defining American culture appeared between "1820 and 1875, in the midst of the transformation of the American economy into the most powerfully aggressive capitalist system in the world."[1]

One bit of evidence failed to fit this plausible scheme. The evidence was the observation of a perceptive writer, but an observation encased in a story.[2]

In 1854 Herman Melville was living in Berkshire County, Massachusetts. Bitterly disappointed at the failure of *Moby Dick*

---

[1] Ann Douglas, *Feminization of American Culture* (New York, 1977), 6; Leo Marx, *Machine in the Garden* (New York, 1964).

[2] Oscar Handlin, "Man and Magic: First Encounters with the Machine," *American Scholar*, XXXIII (Summer 1964), 408 ff.

and *Pierre,* he had tried unsuccessfully to secure a consular appointment. A somber mood undoubtedly influenced his work of this period. He wrote comparatively little; only a few short stories, and those not among his best. Yet one among them was a significant social document.[3]

In it Melville described a paper factory, such as existed in his neighborhood. The whole setting was dismal, in accord with the gloom of the author. The Devil's Dungeon Paper Mill occupied a large whitewashed building, "like some great white sepulchre." Passing through it, the narrator saw the "blank-looking" girls "pale with work," each a "tame minister" tending an "iron animal." "Machinery—that vaunted slave of humanity—here stood menially served by human beings."

At last the narrator stood before a great, new, $12,000 machine. "Something of awe now stole over me, as I gazed upon this *inflexible* iron animal . . . What made the thing I saw so specially terrible to me was the metallic necessity, the unbudging fatality which governed it." The dismay and foreboding of this account were far removed from the idyllic descriptions, common at the time, of the wonders of Lowell and of its cheerful ladies of the loom. Melville's personal sense of depression made him more acutely sensitive to certain human problems than his contemporaries and gave his observations special value (206, 207).

He could not, by any means, conceive the ingenious apparatus that became commonplace in the twentieth century. Yet already he confronted the machine with trepidation. Mechanization served humans and also threatened them. It did the work of hundreds, yet created profound social displacements. What his contemporaries admired, Melville dreaded; and his fears sprang from sources other than direct observation.

---

[3] Herman Melville, "Tartarus of Maids," *Apple-Tree Table and Other Sketches* (Princeton, 1922), 184 ff. Douglas, *Feminization,* 299, must classify this story "Freudian" rather than "Marxist" because it includes women, which her scheme excludes. Charles A. Fenton, " 'Bell-Tower': Melville and Technology," *American Literature,* XXIII (May 1951), 224 ff.; Marvin Fisher, "Melville's 'Bell-Tower': A Double Thrust," *American Quarterly,* XVIII (Summer 1966), 205 ff.; and "Melville's 'Tartarus': The Deflowering of New England," *ibid.,* XXIII (Spring 1971), 80, treat this and a related story as denunciations of industrialism. R. W. B. Lewis, *American Adam* (Chicago, 1955), 127 ff., does not deal directly with the story, but has a general relevance to Melville.

༄

The Massachusetts paper mills were neither very large nor particularly harsh in their treatment of employees. Dependence upon water power and upon proximity to raw materials kept them in the rural countryside. Melville's indictment, therefore, did not rest on the grounds of size, impersonality, or divorce from nature. Rather the factories depressed him because they harnessed those who labored there to a routine. The rows of girls stood before the machines like "so many mares haltered to the rack." They were totally controlled; and it was not right they should be so bound.[4]

Underlying that protest was an unexpressed grievance against the machine as such. Routine was not necessarily an undesirable circumstance of human life. In other contexts it brought the comfort of order and regularity. The husbandman bound to the cycle of his crops, the sailor who stood his appointed watches, did not consider the expected pattern debasing. But the mechanical routine differed from that established by the seasons or by the orbit of the sun because it took no account of human considerations, because it operated in an uncongenial setting, and because it detached man from the natural forces of life.

The iron animal enslaved those who served it. While it went its own way, the people bound to it ceased to be free. It limited wills, and, since it took no cognizance of moral considerations, it also limited the ability to choose good over evil.

The mechanical monster assumed a particularly frightening guise when installed in the factory, which organized labor in a novel manner. Here workers assembled in numbers so large that only some form of servitude offered a precedent for their management. An entrepreneur in 1820 who tried to conceive of how to mobilize a hundred people and bring them to act in coordination with the machine could fasten upon few previous models. He could imagine a military company, perhaps, or a ship's crew, a monastery or a poorhouse or a jail. The essential element by which each of these agglomerations coordinated many persons was

---

[4] The precise number of employees in the Coltsville Paper Mill when Melville lived in Pittsfield is unknown, but ten years later the new, much-expanded plant contained fifteen men and thirty women. See, J. E. A. Smith, *History of Pittsfield . . . 1800 to . . . 1876* (Springfield, Mass., 1876), 503 ff.; Lyman H. Weeks, *History of Paper-Manufacturing in the United States, 1690–1916* (New York, 1916), 180 ff., 196 ff.

a rigid code of discipline that curtailed individual freedom. It was no coincidence that the architecture of the early factories had much in common with that of barracks, military camps, and prisons. Hence the foreboding that the power of the machine in this setting would constrict personal liberties.

In the factories the machine exerted an unnatural effect upon the people who tended it. The routine of the farmer had been coordinate with the forces of the visible world around him, or at least it seemed so. The alternations of the seasons told him when to plant and when to reap; the rising and the setting sun told him when to begin his labors and when to rest. The machine disregarded all such considerations and operated at its own pace, winter and summer, day and night.

The new regime detached work from the other aspects of life. Melville's narrator asked why the operatives of whatever age were "indiscriminately called girls, never women." The answer was: "the fact of their being generally unmarried—that's the reason . . . For our factory here, we will have no married women; they are apt to be off-and-on too much. We want none but steady workers; twelve hours to the day, day after day, through the three hundred and sixty-five days." They were all maidens and would remain so (208, 209).

In time, married women would tend the machine, as well as men, boys, and girls. But the situation Melville found was nevertheless symbolic. Early efforts at paternalism in some places quickly faded, and workers confronted the enterprise alone in a relationship that was purely economic. All entered the dark, satanic mills as detached individuals. Within the gates they were not members of families or of groups but isolated integers, each with his own line on the payroll; nothing extraneous counted. During the working hours the laborers had no identity other than that established by the job. From being people who were parts of households, known by a whole community, they had been reduced to being servants of the machine. Hence the shock of such observers as Melville in the initial encounter with what was to come.

⤳

Throughout most of the nineteenth century such doubts agitated few but the intellectuals. Now and then artisans displaced by the machines expressed their resentment in Luddite riots and in political opposition toward great corporations. But the masses actually employed in the factories accepted the situation with equanimity. Often they suffered from difficult conditions of labor and from even more difficult conditions of life. But confidence in the human capacity to master the devices that humans had fabricated tempered their trials. They were sure that man could control and use the enormous power of the machines.[5]

The fact that the experience of factory labor was not altogether as discontinuous with the past as it seemed to outsiders sustained that belief. The physical setting, for example, was not totally different. The earliest factories appeared in the rural countryside, not far removed from the familiar landscape of open fields, streams, and woods. They used waterpower for a long time and thus gave the appearance of mills more complex than those familiar to every man, but essentially the same. Nor were the machines, whether of wood or iron, entirely strange. The waterwheels and the great drive shafts and pulleys that dominated these plants embodied no essential new principles. To onlookers they were impressive in their ingenuity and power, but the clearly visible manner of their operation seemed only to extend and improve devices long familiar to everyone.

The nineteenth century understood the factory in terms of widespread attitudes, particularly strong in the United States, but also characteristic of Western society as a whole. Modern man was a tinkerer who sought ever to avoid labor and to spare himself excessive strain. Generation after generation had searched for improvements toward that end; the first machines of the nineteenth century seemed to reward the quest. It was characteristic that one of the earliest American utopian works to conceive of invention as a way of liberating man from labor had a thoroughly rural setting. In Mary Griffith's *Three Hundred Years Hence* (1836), great machines, moved by some undescribed internal power, did all the work of agriculture.[6]

5 The effect of industrialization on the standard of living was the subject of a long, complex discussion; see R. M. Hartwell, "Standard of Living," *Economic History Review*, XVI (August 1963), 135 ff. On the other hand, the decline in mortality is incontestable, although opinions differ on the causes; see D. V. Glass and D. E. C. Eversley, *Population in History* (Chicago, 1965), 15 ff. In any case, the people who came to the factories and the cities showed by the willingness to migrate that they believed conditions improved by doing so.

6 Vernon L. Parrington, Jr., *American Dreams* (Providence, 1947), 18 ff.

Accordingly, Melville's contemporaries also regarded the machine as humanity's emancipator, as Étienne Cabet had suggested it would be in *Voyage en Icarie* (1839). In the series of great expositions that began at the Crystal Palace in London in 1851 and ran down through the end of the nineteenth century, the focal point was often the array of new machinery treated as symbolic of the age. The American Commissioners to the Paris Universal Exposition of 1867 published six volumes of observations on the inventions exhibited there. In the introduction to their report, Secretary of State William H. Seward explained that it was "through the universal language of the products of labor" that "artisans of all countries hold communication." Industrialization was "in the interests of the mass of the people," for it promoted "an appreciation of the true dignity of labor, and its paramount claims to consideration as the basis of national wealth and power." Far from fearing that the machine would debase man, Seward was confident that it would elevate him to new dignity.[7]

By and large, the nineteenth century clung to its optimism. Edward Bellamy, John Macnie, and the utopian novelists of the 1880s and 1890s had no doubt that the machine would liberate mankind through the abundance it created. They did not deny that it would also harness man to its service, but they welcomed the consequent routine, the regularity, and the order. Bellamy explained that the idea of *Looking Backward* came to him when he "recognized in the modern military system" the prototype of the Industrial Army that manned his utopia. The men of the year 2000 had "simply applied the principle of universal military service . . . to the labor question." The gains in efficiency and affluence that followed solved all the problems of freedom raised by doing so.[8]

H. G. Wells supplied a perfect encyclopedia of these hopes for the future. Beginning with his *Anticipations* (1902), a succession of roseate works showed the machine transforming and improving human life, which would evolve toward ever more centralized con-

[7] William P. Blake, ed., *Reports of the United States Commissioners to the Paris Universal Exposition, 1867*, 4 vols. (Washington, 1870), I, 3. See also Fred L. Polak, *Image of the Future*, 2 vols. (Leyden, 1961), I, 305; Christopher H. Johnson, *Utopian Communism in France* (Ithaca, N.Y., 1974), 51 ff.

[8] Parrington, *American Dreams*, 57 ff.; John F. Kasson, *Civilizing the Machine* (New York, 1976), 181 ff.

trol. One state, one language, and one ruling will would organize all men into efficient productive units. There would be no need at all for human labor as a source of energy. "Were our political and social and moral devices only as well contrived to their ends as a linotype machine . . . or an electric tram-car, there need now . . . be no appreciable toil in the world." Despite the anticipatory fears of those concerned with the future of man's spirit, in the last analysis there was faith that the machine remained a product of man and would obey his command.[9]

The hopes and the fears persisted beyond the turn of the century. People continued to expect the machine to compensate for the deficiencies of society and to resolve in the future the problems with which they could not deal in the present. Industrial plenitude that was a product of invention dominated *The Shape of Things to Come,* as H. G. Wells saw it (1933). Self-consciously the engineers assumed that they could not only make the machines run but manage society as well; and the technocrats envisioned a mechanical order, efficient, antiseptic, and capable of dealing with any contingency.

Yet doubts always offset the confidence. In the 1890s popular novels by William Morris and Ignatius Donnelly foresaw the factories leveled in cataclysmic civil war to make room for a restored bucolic society. Karel Čapek's *R.U.R.* in the 1920s created a sensation in its nightmare vision of a robot's universal that completely dominated humanity. In the next decade the greatest of the popular artists, René Clair and Charlie Chaplin, in *À nous la liberté* and *Modern Times,* expressed an identical protest: the assembly line made man its slave, repressed his emotions, and crushed his individuality. People could escape to freedom only by rebellion against the machine. In *Brave New World* (1932) and *1984* (1949), Aldous Huxley and George Orwell stood utopia on its head. The necessity for mobilizing large groups along military lines, which provided Bellamy with his Industrial Army, to these writers established a terrifying engine of oppression.[10]

9 H. G. Wells, *Modern Utopia* (New York, 1905), 102, and *In the Days of the Comet* (New York, 1906). See also, below, n. 21.

10 William Morris, *News from Nowhere* (1890; New York, 1966); Ignatius Donnelly, *Caesar's Column* (1891), ed. W. B. Rideout (Cambridge, 1960); Polak, *Image of the Future,* I, 357 ff.

Much in these protests had a familiar ring. To a considerable degree these artists repeated the criticisms Melville had made much earlier; to some extent their revulsion was the general response of the artist to the machine. Yet, many people indicated that they felt the threat increasingly menacing after 1900, the machine more dangerous to humanity than ever before.

The factory no longer counted its employees in the scores, but in the thousands; and larger numbers brought impersonality and rigid discipline to the plant. Individual identity diminished in importance. The analogy to the army became closer and more frightening. The manager had to account for the hordes that passed through the gates each morning and put their time to a precise, measured, profitable use. Before the turn of the century Frederick W. Taylor had outlined the principles of industrial engineering; and as the decades passed, strident demands for efficiency made technological innovation not only an end in itself but also a means of tightening control over the labor force. Enlightened enterprises recognized the importance of human relations; but they did so as means of raising efficiency, and the devices they used had the further effect of manipulating the lives of their employees.[11]

An altered environment increased the external pressures on personality. In the second half of the nineteenth century the factories had become urban, either through accretions of population around them or through shifts to metropolitan centers. In either case, the change compounded all the difficulties of industrial experience. The machine, the factory, and the city merged into a single entity, oppressive of man.

Finally, toward the end of the nineteenth century, the machine itself changed. Regarded from the perspective of the onlooker, the first indication of the transformation was visual. Visitors to factories built after 1900 no longer saw the drive shafts and the pulleys. Power passed through wires and tubes, often hidden, and the machine, covered up, gave the appearance of being self-contained and autonomous. It had ceased to be a comprehensible apparatus and had become an enclosed shape actuated from some hidden source to pour out products in an occult process.

11 See Milton J. Nadworny, *Scientific Management and the Unions* (Cambridge, 1955) ; Samuel Haber, *Efficiency and Uplift* (Chicago, 1964) .

Some of the changes in design were incidental to other purposes. The demands of safety, for instance, explained the shields that concealed the mechanism of operation. Other modifications were aesthetic, although even those related to the meaning the machine held for its viewers. An unbroken sheet of black metal seemed more pleasing to the eye than a complex of belting and gears because it conformed to the idea of the machine as self-contained.[12]

The application to industry of electricity broke even more drastically with previous human experience. Experiments with various manifestations of electricity reached back two hundred years, but it remained a mysterious force, somehow confused with galvanic magnetism, somehow related to the secret of life, but not popularly understood, not as comprehensible as water and steam power had been. Even after a multitude of appliances had brought it into every home, few persons could grasp how a current passing through a wire created light and sound or turned the wheels of great factories.

The gap between the machines and their users widened steadily. In the twentieth century it was no longer the tinkerer who was inventor. The innovations were less likely to be products of industrial experience than of a science that stood quite apart from the rest of life. The people who operated the machines understood neither the instruments they served nor the technical fund of knowledge that shaped the industrial process. The old fear that the "iron animal" would strip its slaves of their humanity deepened with the awareness that the machine itself was the product of a science that had become increasingly alien to the mass of people.

In Melville's day there had still been no sharp distinction between the scientists and others or between science and other kinds of learning. All knowledge was continuous and essentially of one sort, and it was accessible to anyone with the wit to seek it. Higher education was somewhat more formally organized than it had been in Franklin's Philadelphia, where a printer studied electricity; or a glazier, mathematics; or a politician, philosophy; or a farmer,

12 Kasson, *Civilizing the Machine,* 137 ff.; Siegfried Giedion, *Mechanization Takes Command* (New York, 1948) , interesting in detail and replete with suggestive insights, nevertheless slights the historical context.

botany. But the structural changes that isolated science from modern life had just begun.[13]

In the second half of the nineteenth century they proceeded rapidly and radically. Knowledge became specialized, professionalized, and institutionalized, and these interrelated tendencies created a closed body of skills and information not accessible to outsiders.

Specialization was the product of forces inside and outside science. The mere accumulation of data stored up in libraries and journals made it increasingly difficult for any individual to master more than a narrow sector of any field. It seemed to follow that the more limited the field, the more readily mastered; that, in itself, further encouraged specialization. In addition, the emphasis upon classification as the first step in all inductive learning persuaded scientists to mark out, and concentrate in, a distinctive and circumscribed area of research. Finally, the growing rigor of the tests for validation required constantly improved techniques, yet it was a rare individual who commanded more than one set. Science became the province of the expert who excelled in the one subject he knew thoroughly.

The result was a high degree of compartmentalization. C. P. Snow's discussion of the "Two Cultures" obscured the genuine issue. The problem was not so much the existence of two distinct —literary and scientific—cultures, but the fragmentation of all knowledge into a multitude of different disciplines, each familiar only to its initiates. A chemist was not much more able to discourse with an astronomer than with a sociologist, or an economist with an anthropologist than with a physicist. Overlapping techniques, language, and subject matter kept some lines of communication open, but each field was really known only to specialists in it.[14]

Specialization certainly contributed to the advances of modern science. But it also demanded such a high degree of competence that, in fact, it excluded the amateur and made the practice of science entirely professional. Learning now required a prescribed

[13] Compare Brooke Hindle, *David Rittenhouse* (Princeton, 1964) ; Edward Lurie, *Louis Agassiz* (Chicago, 1960) .

[14] C. P. Snow, *Two Cultures and the Scientific Revolution* (Cambridge, 1959) .

course of preparation; it imposed defined canons of judgment and validation; and it developed the esprit de corps of a coherent and united group.

Finally, specialization and professionalization tended to institutionalize science. Research became so expensive that no individual could buy his own telescopes, computers, or cyclotrons; it fell increasingly into forms established by government, business, universities, and foundations. This made the twentieth-century achievements possible, but at the same time cut scientists apart from other men and women.

Science, as a body of defined knowledge, had its own needs and set its own standards. But the population not served by science had needs of its own, which it satisfied through its own ways of knowing. Side by side with the official defined science there appeared a popular science, vague, undisciplined, unordered, and yet extremely influential. It touched upon the official science, but did not accept its limits. And it more adequately met the immediate requirements of the people.[15]

Popular science was not always less correct, by later standards, than official science. It would be hard to assert with confidence, for instance, that the faith healing, nature cures, and patent medicines of the 1890s were less effective than the ministrations of the graduates of recognized medical schools, or that the vision of the universe exposed in the Sunday supplement was less accurate than that of the physics textbook. By the tests of practice—of whether it worked—popular science did as well as the official science.

Popular science had deficiencies of quite another order. It formed part of no canon that marked out its boundaries or established order among its various parts. It consisted, rather, of discontinuous observations, often the projection of fantasy and wish fulfillment, and generally lacking coherence and consistency. Above all, it embraced no test of validity save experience. It was as easy to believe that there was another world within the crust of the earth as that there were other worlds in outer space. One took the little pills; the pain went away. One heard the knocking; the spirits were there. The observable connections between cause and

15 Oscar Handlin, "Science and Technology in Popular Culture," *Daedalus,* XCIV (Winter 1965) , 156 ff.

result were explanation enough. There was no need to comprehend the links between the two.

Popular science, in other words, was magic. The men and
women who moved into the highly complex and technically elaborate industrial society simply assimilated the phenomena about
them in terms of the one explanatory category they already knew,
that of magic.[16] And it was thus, too, that they understood the defined science of the laboratory and the university. The man who
pressed a button and saw the light appear, who turned a switch
and set the machine in motion, had not mastered electricity or
mechanics; the operations he performed made the limited kind of
sense that the other mysterious events of life did.

The machine, which was a product of science, was also magic,
understandable only in terms of *how* it worked, not of why. Hence
the lack of comprehension or of control; hence also the mixture of
dread and anticipation as in the past.

ᐟ⌒ᐟ

A modern version of one of the seminal human myths fore-
shadowed the complex relations among man, magic, and the
machine.[17]

Frankenstein, a dedicated young scientist, seeks knowledge to
help mankind. He discovers the secret of life through the study of
electricity, galvanism, and chemistry and applies his formula to
create a machine-monster.

The monster quickly proves to possess power superior to that
of the man. In the confrontation, the machine gives the orders:
"Slave, I before reasoned with you, but you have proved yourself
unworthy of my condescension. Remember that I have power . . .
I can make you so wretched that the light of day will be hateful to
you. You are my creator, but I am your master;—obey!" It is no

16 See also Keith Thomas, *Religion and the Decline of Magic* (London, 1971) ,
667 ff. For the view of magic as art, see R. G. Collingwood, *Principles of Art*
(Oxford, 1938) , 65 ff.

17 Karl Kerényi, *Prometheus* (Zurich, 1946) , 13 ff. On the general problem of
mythical forms and mythical consciousness, see also Ernst Cassirer, *Philosophy of
Symbolic Forms*, 3 vols. (New Haven, 1955) , II, 235 ff. Lévi-Strauss's depth analysis
of myths, whether valid or not, is ahistorical; see Philip Pettit, *Concept of Structuralism* (Berkeley, 1975) , 71 ff.

coincidence that the machine, which unmans the user, will seem
the master to many in modern society.[18]

Within the limits of the story the question properly rises: why
does the monster become the oppressive master? It was not evil to
begin with or created out of deliberate malice.

The machine speaks once more: "Once my fancy was soothed
with dreams of virtue, of fame and of enjoyment. Once I falsely
hoped to meet with beings who, pardoning my outward form
would love me for the excellent qualities I was capable of unfolding . . . I cannot believe that I am the same creature whose
thoughts were once filled with sublime and transcendent visions
of the beauty and majesty of goodness. But it is even so; the fallen
angel becomes a malignant devil."[19]

And it was even so that modern people continued to think of
the machine and of science—potentially good yet capable of per-
petrating a frightful catalogue of sins.

The question remains: why this ominous foreboding, which
antedated industrialization and was confirmed by it?

Mary Shelley recalled the circumstances under which the idea
came to her, in 1816, while she listened to her husband and Lord
Byron pass the long evenings in talk by the shores of Lake Leman.
Often their conversation turned to science, particularly to the
mystery of electricity and to experiments in creating life through
galvanism. A vision suddenly came to her of the dreadful "effect
of any human endeavour to mock the stupendous mechanism of
the Creator of the world." The impiety inherent in the magic of
which they spoke invited retribution.[20]

Mary Shelley gave her novel a subtitle: *The Modern Prometheus.* She was thus aware of the connection of her theme with the
ancient myth of the punishment visited upon the being who
robbed heaven of fire for the benefit of man. It was a theme that
her husband also treated and that had recurred for centuries and
would continue to recur in Western imaginative writing.

Even the most optimistic imaginations long continued to shud-

[18] Mary W. Shelley, *Frankenstein or the Modern Prometheus* (London, 1912),
178 ff. Emerson, too, feared that the machine would turn against its creator and
would unman the user; see Ralph Waldo Emerson, *Complete Works*, 12 vols. (Boston, 1903–04), V, 166 ff.

[19] Shelley, *Frankenstein*, 240.

[20] Shelley, *Frankenstein*, x, xi; Fenton, "Bell Tower," 222, 228.

der with that primeval fear. "This accursed science," exclaimed H. G. Wells, is "the very Devil . . . You tamper with it—and it offers you gifts. And directly you take them it knocks you to pieces in some unexpected way. Old passions and new weapons—now it upsets your religion, now it upsets your social ideas, now it whirls you off to desolation and misery!" The ability to work miracles leaves the world "smashed and utterly destroyed."[21]

In their first encounters with the machine some men, like Melville, already recognized it as a monstrous defiance of natural order and shuddered at the possible consequences. Their nineteenth-century contemporaries, however, were mostly dazzled by the enormous utility of the machine. Later, when it lost its familiarity and became identified with the magic of science, the old terror welled up; they would be punished for the use of that forbidden fire that was of such great service to them.

Analysis of a single, rather mediocre, story yields only a single, simple conclusion—and, that in itself, not a monumental one. But the suggestive discrepancy between the context Melville described and the later assumptions about the human effects of industrialization calls for reexamination of a whole set of linkages. Melville wrote long before Homestead, Gary, and the East Side sweatshops. Yet his words anticipated the indictment of industrialization a generation later, just as they echoed the much earlier trepidations of Mary Shelley and William Blake's still earlier forebodings about the dark, satanic mills defacing England's pleasant land. The sequence of connections is faulty if Shelley, Melville, and Chaplin voice the same protest, though regarding very different worlds.[22]

21 H. G. Wells, *First Men in the Moon* (London, 1901), 144, 145; "Man Who Could Work Miracles," *Tales of Space and Time* (New York, 1899). His ambivalence appears also in *Time Machine; Invisible Man;* and *Empire of the Ants.* See also Mark R. Hillegas, *Future as Nightmare: H. G. Wells and the Anti-Utopians* (New York, 1967); Jack Williamson, *H. G. Wells: Critic of Progress* (Baltimore, 1973).

22 Blake's line, conventionally read as a reference to the Industrial Revolution, actually applies to England before the Fall; alludes to the phrase in Milton's *Samson Agonistes,* where Samson is eyeless at the mill with slaves; and refers to "Satan's enslavement of the mind, the beginning of human error." See William Blake, *Poems,* ed. W. H. Stevenson (London, 1971), 489; Robert Nisbet, *Sociology as an Art Form* (New York, 1976), 56 ff.

Evidence at hand permits the reordering of some elements; at least one remains unclear. It is almost a truism to point to the misleading implications of the term "industrial revolution." The process to which that phrase applies extended over a very long period, almost two centuries, in Britain, the United States, France, and Germany. Its beginnings reached back toward the middle of the eighteenth century; its full extent only became apparent by the close of the nineteenth. Sharp breaks in continuity and notable changes in course marked the generations-long transition from the traditional forms of handicraft manufacture to mechanized factory production. To link any cultural or social phenomenon with industrialization requires a precise sense of timing and of actual relationship.

For a long time industrialization operated in a rural rather than in an urban environment. In 1854, when Melville wrote, London, Paris, Berlin, New York, and Boston housed no factories in significant number. The new form of production appeared in rural places, like Lowell, Webster, and Franklin, Massachusetts, like Vienne, Essones, and Carmaux in France. In the 1870s Lawrence, Massachusetts, a modern industrial community, still was close to the countryside. In the 1970s in Britain, Witney (Oxfordshire), seat of an old long-established mill, retained a rustic appearance. The factories originated in the fields, not in the metropolitan centers; and this phase of industrialization implied no break with nature, no sense of alienation. The destitution that Melville observed in Liverpool, and others saw in London, Manchester, Paris, and New York emanated from entirely different sources, which had been there long before the factory appeared.[23]

Fear of the machine originated in anxieties unconnected with the factory, although sometimes projected onto it. There is no evidence that the men, women, and children who tended the iron animals felt aggrieved by their work or by the devices which spared them labor. Their complaints, like their problems, cen-

---

23 Donald B. Cole, *Immigrant City: Lawrence, Massachusetts* (Chapel Hill, N.C., 1963). Manchester was unique and, therefore, the subject of frequent comment— occasionally by intellectuals, like Disraeli or Carlyle, who approved or disapproved of the machines, but more often by social observers, like Engels, who noted not the conditions of factory labor, but the conditions of life in the slums. See Steven Marcus, *Engels, Manchester and the Working Class* (New York, 1974), who does not quite understand the distinction.

tered not in alienation, but in low wages, long hours, and the hazards of life and work.

The trepidation about the machine and the concern with alienation were perceptions of bystanders. The dread articulated by intellectuals such as Melville was their own. The question that remains is why they transposed ancient fears (which were of the knowledge and the progress to which they gave ostensible loyalty) onto the machines and the workers who attended them.[24]

[24] David F. Noble, *America by Design* (New York, 1977) , illustrates the fear which also leads into factual, conceptual, and interpretive errors.

# 13
## *Good Guys and Bad*

THE BRITISH FASCINATION with Richard III and the little Princes in the Tower is evidence that other countries suffered from similar distortions in their view of the past. But the very circumstances of their origin as a people rendered Americans particularly susceptible to the pervasive Manichaeanism, which interpreted history as the battlefield between the forces of light and those of darkness—the good guys against the bad guys. In this drama the honest, the altruistic, and the patriotic constantly battled the greedy and the corrupt in defense of national virtue. This formulation had the virtue of simplicity and of clear identification of heroes and villains; its drawback lay in its slight correspondence with actuality.[1]

Once upon a time, the good guys were the capitalists who built the nation and the bad were their socialist detractors. In 1954, for instance, a book edited by F. A. Hayek argued that an academic conspiracy on the part of the socialists, who controlled the teaching of history, had propagated "the legend of the deterioration of the position of the working classes in consequence of the rise of 'capitalism.' " Hayek's charge did not have a shred of substance; he did not quote a single historian who maintained the position he claimed all historians held.[2]

The evidence, insofar as the volume contained any, appeared in an essay, "The Anti-capitalist Bias of American Historians" by

1 See Chapter 3 at note 39.

2 F. A. Hayek, ed., *Capitalism and the Historians* (Chicago, 1954) ; Oscar Handlin, "Capitalism, Power, and the Historians," *New England Quarterly*, XXVIII (March 1955) , 99 ff.

Louis M. Hacker. His errors resulted from both misquotation and ignorance. It revealed unfamiliarity with the literature to maintain that American historical writing before the 1920s "gave little attention to economics," or that it was then composed "almost entirely in nationalist (i.e., isolationist) terms," or that historical interest in Jefferson was slight before 1930.

When Hacker left the popularizers outside the historical profession, and approached the academics proper, he outdid himself in distorted logic. American historians, he held, acquired their anti-capitalist bias "from their espousal of Jeffersonian as opposed to Hamiltonian ideas." This led "leveling historians" to count Hamiltonianism an evil and to pass "a moral and not an economic judgment . . . on his extraordinary achievements." The same viewpoint dominated writing on the Jacksonian period. "Enough to say that the historians sympathetic to Jackson are also anti-capitalist." Revisionist writers on the Civil War earned the same condemnation. The defenders of the farmers of the postwar period were also anti-capitalist. (Here there was a curious lapse: the historians cited were J. C. Ransom and Herbert Agar and Allen Tate!) As for the New Dealers, their "anti-capitalism" was political and moral." (The historian cited: J. N. Frank, *Save America First!*) Yet, while Hacker's wild charges labeled as anti-capitalist any Jeffersonian or agrarian, he himself (p. 74) spoke of an "agrarian slave-capitalist group." The slaveholders were thus respectably capitalist, but the "revisionists," charged with having defended them, were anti-capitalist by virtue of that defense.

Given the climate of ideas of the early months of 1954, when this volume appeared, no scholar could view with equanimity its irresponsible and false assertions that a whole generation of historians was anti-capitalist. Few academics spoke out in criticism; it took as much fortitude to defend the bad guys in 1954 as in 1978, although the labels applied at different points in the political spectrum. Nevertheless, the essays had little effect. Capitalists after all did not fear the threat; and the status and attitudes of the historical profession were altogether middle-class.

The greater damage was done to the study of "capitalism" itself. Whether the institution was a good thing or not, whether the captains of industry were moral or not, were the wrong questions to ask. The continual raising of these queries by self-constituted defenders of "capitalism" obscured the much more vital issues of the means by which "capitalism" transformed the economy, the forms it took, and its effects upon the whole society.

⌒

Allan Nevins' study of John D. Rockefeller was an illuminating example.[3] This distinguished historian was not guilty of the sins of the essayists in the Hayek work. As always, Nevins was meticulously careful in his use of sources, his efforts at accuracy were obvious, and his judgments were fair-minded and temperate. On points of detail he was thoroughly reliable. It was only on the large, important issues involving interpretation that he went astray.

In these matters the work was apologetic. Nevins did not distort his evidence, and on occasions even rendered a verdict against his hero. But the author became deeply involved in the defense of his subject, so deeply that he flinched at every aspersion on Rockefeller or his family (for example, I, 4). Respect for the protagonist endowed his very calling with preeminence; business was "the central field for usefulness" of the period, drawing the most ambitious and most able men of the nation. Rockefeller thus acquired a special virtue by his vocation that set him above such of his contemporaries as, say, O. W. Holmes, Jr., or Henry James, or Willard Gibbs. It was hardly surprising to encounter the suggestion that without Rockefeller the nation would not have survived the two world wars (I, viii, ix).

Yet these two volumes offer no satisfactory definition of the nature of Rockefeller's achievement. He was not an innovator. Nor did he have the vision to anticipate long-term economic development. He had, nonetheless, been intimately associated with the crucial process of industrial consolidation since the Civil War. Yet, how he directed or conditioned that process was never made clear.

Nevins' account, for instance, did not recognize that the heart of the Standard Oil enterprise was its consistent and continuing illegality throughout the whole period of Rockefeller's active connection with it. It profited from preferential transportation

3 Allan Nevins, *Study in Power: John D. Rockefeller, Industrialist and Philanthropist*, 2 vols. (New York, 1953).

rates, which were sometimes though not always of critical importance in its growth (for example, I, 249). Now, conspiring to secure such exceptional treatment, whether in the form of rebates or otherwise, was not merely a matter of bad manners or of abstract ethics, as Nevins incorrectly implied (I, 267). It was a crime. The law had made it so, even before it supplied the means for governmental review of rates. The railroads and other carriers were quasi-public bodies, chartered by the states and endowed with extraordinary powers, under certain limitations, among which was the rule that they extend equal nondiscriminatory treatment to all those they served. The fact that the machinery of enforcement was weak and the provisions for redress imperfect did not make these rules any less binding as law.

Furthermore, Standard Oil in its growth early took a path that involved illegal forms of consolidation. Aversion to monopoly was not just an amiable quirk of the American temperament, as Nevins casually described it (for example, I, 297; II, 155) ; it was aversion to a crime. Conspiracy to effect a monopoly in restraint of trade was illegal long before the Sherman Act. Statutes in the states derived from the common law were as old as the Republic. Yet Rockefeller's tactics, repeatedly resorted to, consistently flouted the law in the furtherance of the interests of his own enterprise (I, 253, 365; II, 58, 335).

Thus, the combination of transportation and refining activities was itself in the nature of a conspiracy, as the reaction to the development of the pipeline graphically illustrated. As a refiner, Standard Oil should have welcomed the appearance of a device which enabled it to lower costs. It did not, because the new means of transportation threatened to deprive it of advantages it enjoyed over the remaining independent refiners. It met the new situation by encouraging the railroads in a rate war to destroy the pipelines (I, 237). When that failed, it attempted to eliminate the independents served by the pipelines. Only as a last resort did it acquire a pipeline system of its own, which it later used against the independents (I, 298 ff., 345 ff.).

The illegality of these combinations was plainly known to all those involved in them. In a confidential letter of 1880 that explored the various potential forms of company organization, S. C. T. Dodd advised Rockefeller: "In regard to the question which plan renders the parties least liable to the charge of forming an illegal combination, I do not think it makes any difference unless the combination is specially legalized by a special charter in the mode above stated. *It is not the mode of combination which makes it illegal, but the extent, purpose, and tendency of it"* (I, 391; italics mine).

When the courts had an opportunity to pass upon the combination, they did not hesitate to find it criminal. Hence the eagerness of Standard Oil to deprive the courts of that opportunity. Hence also the evasiveness of officials in testimony, their perjury, the destruction of records, the secrecy of proceedings, and the inability to reply to attack (for example, I, 304, 305, 307, 386; II, 133 ff., 230 ff.). All these tactics were not simply poor public relations, as Nevins considered them; they were rather the necessary response of men whose activities could not stand judicial scrutiny (I, 179, 210; II, 148).

The heart of the problem—how this truly religious and, by his own lights, honest man could for decades break the law of the land —evaded Nevins. Instead, his full energies went into elaboration of an intricate web of justifications for Rockefeller's actions.

Standard Oil was constrained to adopt the tactics it did, because everyone else was doing so; and because if it had not, its rivals would have (I, 63, 65, 94, 267). "To have been ultra-moral would have invited ruin" (II, 35). If Nevins meant by this to condemn a whole generation of businessmen, he opened up but did not explore an interesting line of speculation with regard to the relationships of business and law. But he could hardly wish to be taken literally. Perhaps he meant that some industries in their development offered tempting opportunities to men willing to bypass the law. But in that case, he might better have devoted his attention to the question of why, than to special pleading on his hero's behalf.

A more seductive argument was inevitability. "An irresistible business law" left the Standard no alternative (I, 401; II, 429). Excessive competition in the industry unavoidably led to concentration of control. By 1872 too many wells and "too much refining capacity" plagued the overexpanded industry. The result, a fall in prices, brought everyone to the verge of chaos (I, 78, 81, 130, 266). Rockefeller acted out of love of order. His fears of depression were not personal but almost altruistic as the industry moved toward its days of trial. Nevins painted a touching picture of Rockefeller and

Flagler sauntering home in 1873, distressed in spirit and uncertain about what to do. "The prospects . . . were dark" (I, 96, 97, 177).

The pathos faded from the picture, however, for readers who turned back a page to the profit statement of Standard Oil in the difficult year of 1872: 15 percent, in addition to a surplus (I, 176, 211). And the prospects remained equally "dark" for the Standard and for many of its persistent independent competitors. This, despite the fact that prices continued to fall steadily, so that the level of the "disastrous" year 1872 was not once regained in the next thirty years! (See table, II, 477.) The lower prices continued to yield a profit because of the enormous and steady rise in the volume of production.

What, then, did Nevins mean when he spoke of "overproduction" in 1872? Here he swallowed whole the arguments of those —Rockefeller among others—anxious to cut production in the interest of an immediate increase of profits. Certainly if one considered the rate of growth of the population, of industry, of urbanization, and of other relevant factors in consumption, the whole argument of overproduction collapsed. Or to put it another way, since the demand for petroleum products for illumination and for lubrication was not being fully met, it might even be that measures which prevented the price from falling impeded the expansion of potential markets.

For Nevins, however, efficiency was the ultimate justification for Standard Oil's tactics. Large-scale production was more economical than small-scale, and thus socially defensible. Whether this proposition held in the abstract or not, a more important question should have occupied Rockefeller's biographer: Were or were not the particular forms of organization devised for Standard Oil conducive to increased efficiency? That is, would a well-run refinery or pipeline function more or less effectively within the business complexes—pools, trust, holding company—Rockefeller helped contrive? Nevins never confronted the question squarely. Yet occasional clues, such as resistance to innovations like the pipeline, showed that efficiency was not the purpose of combination.

Interesting evidence also emerged after 1911 in the aftermath of the Standard Oil Case. The dissolution of the holding company raised profits and increased prosperity for the industry and the constituent companies. This Nevins regarded as an indication "that

the dissolution had in large part been a failure" (II, 382), for to
him the issue had been not one of law, but "whether the Standard
Oil combination or the Department of Justice was the stronger"
(II, 362). But those who had prosecuted the trusts had not done
so with the intention of ruining the industry or destroying the
profit system. On the contrary, they had persistently argued that
the trust itself had been a source of inefficiency, had limited profits, and had raised costs. The results of dissolution supported their
contention fully. For the oil industry thrived, avoided cutthroat
competition, and expanded without the monolithic monopoly for
which John D. Rockefeller labored all his life as an active businessman.

The impulse toward apologetics drew the attention of this able
author away from the far more important tasks of analyzing Rockefeller's exceptional qualities as an entrepreneur and estimating his
deep influence upon the American economy. Now and then per-
tinent sections dealt with these matters, but all too soon, Nevins
was off in the pointless and deceptive advocacy of his subject's
virtue—pointless because these were not the critical issues and deceptive because the advocate's role blunted the historian's power
of judgment.

The historian should approach business as he does politics or
literature or religion or the other important areas of social action.
The place in history of a poet or a politician, a painter or a
preacher, does not hang upon his personal probity. Whether he
was honest or a hypocrite may be important insofar as that influenced his work. But the interpreter who insists upon defending
his subject's good name at whatever cost will again and again
wander away from the topics that should properly absorb his
attention.

That truism applied to business history as to any other kind,
and a turn of the wheel of intellectual fashion in itself brought
writers no closer to a dispassionate yet critical evaluation of the
development of American industry. A quarter-century later a
study of the Rockefeller family reversed Nevins' judgments about
who was hero and who villain. The founder of the family fortune
was a "flinty industrialist who had terrorized his competitors and
bent the country's economic system to his iron will." His son dedicated his life "to changing the adverse view of the family created
by the excesses of the Standard trust." The third generation held

"power of a kind their grandfather never could have hoped for."
The story unfolded in the fashion once used to treat history as
the will of kings, only now dangerous or wicked ones.[4]

⌒⌒

The inability to deal with the past other than as a conflict of
good guys and bad totally distorted the understanding of American Populism in the scholarship of the years after 1945. The writing of the next three decades revealed the extent to which history
was still far from a cumulative science, which steadily refined the
understanding of the past through successive discoveries. If any
figure of speech was appropriate, it was that of the treadmill, with
regressions and standstills as frequent as advances.

The heated emotions the Populist movement aroused among
contemporaries extended into the historical literature. Well before
the New Deal, the Populists had captured the sympathy of the
American historian.[5] Their agrarianism, their advocacy of the
cause of the oppressed poor, their situation as game independents
facing up to the entrenched and powerful, and their spontaneous
grassroots origins gave them a heroic cast in the accounts of
writers influenced by progressive ideas. Charles A. Beard summarized the prevailing attitude in *The Rise of American Civilization:* the Populists were the culmination of the long history of
agrarian protest and an integral element in the struggle for American democracy. A more definitive academic statement of this
position came from John Hicks in 1931. "Thanks to this triumph
of Populist principles, one may almost say that, in so far as political devices can insure it, the people now rule . . . the acts of
government have come to reflect fairly clearly the will of the
people."[6]

---

[4] Peter Collier and David Horowitz, *Rockefellers: An American Dynasty* (New York, 1976).

[5] C. Vann Woodward errs in the chronology of the shifts in attitude toward the Populists ("Populist Heritage and the Intellectual," *American Scholar,* XXIX [Winter 1959–60], 55 ff.). See also Oscar Handlin, "Reconsidering the Populists," *Agricultural History,* XXXIX (April 1965), 10 ff.

[6] Charles A. and Mary R. Beard, *Rise of American Civilization,* 2 vols. (New York, 1927), II, 278 ff., 556 ff.; John D. Hicks, *Populist Revolt* (Minneapolis, 1931), 422, and "Persistence of Populism," *Minnesota History,* XII (March 1931), 3 ff., and "Legacy of Populism in the Western Middle West," *Agricultural History,* XXIII (October 1949), 225 ff.

Such firm commitments impeded every effort to interpret the movement. Each bit of fresh evidence had to meet the test of whether it cast the Populists in the role of heroes or villains.[7] The result was a sterile round of argument that added little to the understanding of the subject.

The extended—and pointless—discussion of whether the Populists were anti-Semitic was a glaring illustration. In 1951, when I attempted to assess the attitude of Americans toward Jews at the end of the nineteenth century, I found that by 1900, "the favorable prevailing temper of tolerance had produced a great willingness to accept the Jew as a desirable and equal participant in the emerging culture of the nation." But, I added, widely held stereotypes, which in the 1890s were not derogatory in intent, provided the materials which anti-Semites would use after 1910. The attitudes of the Populists did not differ from those of any other group, except that their insistence upon a bankers' conspiracy deepened the popular image of the mysterious international Jew. Nothing in the subsequent literature in the least challenged those conclusions.[8]

Instead, it was necessary to ascribe to me views I did not express, so that they could be refuted. When Walter T. K. Nugent asserted that I wrote that the Populists "swum with the racist current of the period" and "were personally guilty of some degree of overt anti-Semitism," it was not from anything he read in my text, but from the exigencies of his own argument. Nevertheless, the label stuck, not simply through the misrepresentation of my position, but more generally from the suggestion that I held the Populists to be no more pure of heart than their opponents.[9]

7 See the candid account in Walter T. K. Nugent, *Tolerant Populists: Kansas Populism and Nativism* (Chicago, 1963), 3 ff.

8 Oscar Handlin, "American Views of the Jew at the Opening of the Twentieth Century," *Publications of the American Jewish Historical Society*, XL (June 1951), 323 ff. To keep the chronology accurate, it is well to point out that this essay was written before the onset of the McCarthyite hysteria. See also Oscar Handlin, "How U.S. Anti-Semitism Really Began," *Commentary*, XI (June 1951), 541 ff., and *Adventure in Freedom* (New York, 1954), 174 ff.; Samuel T. McSeveney, *Politics of Depression: Political Behavior in the Northeast, 1893–1896* (New York, 1972), 186 ff.; Stanley B. Parson, *Populist Context: Rural versus Urban Power on a Great Plains Frontier* (Westport, Conn., 1973), 101 ff.

9 Nugent, *Tolerant Populists*, 15, 16. By the 1970s the erroneous idea of a "Pollack-Handlin debate" had become embedded among the clichés which substituted for thought—e.g., review by David J. Pivar, *American Historical Review*, LXXXII (October 1977), 1089.

The need to cast the Populists as either heroes or villains turned the discussion about the false question of whether they were proto-Nazis or tolerant. Richard Hofstadter, using essentially the same evidence as I, added the pejorative designation "anti-Semitism"—although he qualified his characterization more carefully than his critics thought. The choice of that term was unfortunate, for it stirred up a hornet's nest. C. Vann Woodward, Norman Pollack, John Higham, and Nugent in their zeal to defend the Populists thoroughly befogged the issue.[10]

The tortuous apologetics of the defenders were wider of the mark than Hofstadter's blanket indictment. Higham, for instance, clamped the whole subject into a dubious cyclical device. To relieve the agrarians of blame, he argued that the patrician intellectuals and the underprivileged masses of the Eastern cities "were more deeply engaged in ethnic conflict" and, therefore, more venomous and fierce in their anti-Semitism than the rural radicals or rustic pamphleteers of the West. But, in any case, he argued, decisive internal forces could not have activated anti-Semitism, which "ebbed and flowed on an international level," rising everywhere in the 1880s and 1890s and declining between 1900 and 1918.[11]

It took utter disregard of the evidence to contrive this apologia. There was no advance in anti-Semitism in the last two decades of the nineteenth century; and the period in which Higham asserted that "anti-Semitism made no significant advances" was uncomfortably marked by the East Side riots, the Leo Frank case, and the first overt discrimination in employment. Actually, anti-Semitism slowly took form in the first decade of the twentieth century, gained strength in the second, and reached its peak of intensity in the 1920s and 1930s. There were no cycles—however useful to Higham in obscuring the "American traditions, circumstances, or

10 Richard Hofstadter, *Age of Reform* (New York, 1955), 61 ff., 76 ff.; Woodward, "Populist Heritage and the Intellectual," 55 ff.; Norman Pollack, "Hofstadter on Populism," *Journal of Southern History,* XXVI (November 1960), 478 ff., and "Myth of Populist Anti-Semitism," *American Historical Review,* LXVIII (October 1962), 76 ff.; John Higham, "Anti-Semitism in the Gilded Age," *Mississippi Valley Historical Review,* XLIII (March 1957), 559, and "Social Discrimination against Jews in America," *Publications of the American Jewish Historical Society,* XLVII (September 1957), 1 ff. Michael Paul Rogin, *Intellectuals and McCarthy* (Cambridge, 1967), 173, parrots the line.

11 Higham, "Anti-Semitism," 571, 572 ff.; Woodward, "Populist Heritage and the Intellectual," 64.

habits of mind" by which Populists and others prepared the ground for anti-Semitism in the United States.[12]

The supererogatory task of refuting the charge of Populist anti-Semitism led to other extraordinary perversions. To demonstrate the benign intentions of Ignatius Donnelly's *Caesar's Column,* Nugent explained that, "The idea that the Jewish nation was reborn out of the revolution's chaos . . . showed Donnelly's admiration for the ancient chosen people." Reference to the passage in question revealed the quality of that admiration. Donnelly had the revolutionary Jew abscond with "one hundred million dollars that had been left in his charge . . . He took several of his trusted followers, of his own nation, with him" and proposed to "revive the ancient splendors of the Jewish race, in the midst of the ruins of the world." Those who sought—needlessly—to rehabilitate the Populists could even believe that an author "used the word 'Shylock' about a dozen and a half times but never made it specifically Jewish." What a mass of error would have been avoided by recognition that the Populists were neither exceptionally tolerant nor exceptionally prejudiced. They shared the attitudes of most other Americans before 1900 as after. At Tom Watson's death in 1922, Eugene V. Debs and the Ku Klux Klan joined in tributes to the old Populist—no incongruity. On this issue there was "consensus."[13]

The same defensive attitude confused his critics with reference to a much more important element in Hofstadter's account: the incisive analysis of the irrational element in Populist thought. The idea that politicians were subject to other than rationally calculated drives was not in itself startling; Populists, like Democrats and Republicans, were human beings. Yet the suggestion that the Populists' agrarianism, or their belief in an Anglo – Wall Street conspiracy, did not rest on pure reason alone evoked an instinctive response that justified them as farsighted men essentially correct in the analysis of the problems of their time. Pollack, for instance,

---

12 Higham, "Anti-Semitism," 571; Higham, "Social Discrimination," 13 ff. See also Oscar and Mary F. Handlin, "Acquisition of Political and Social Rights by the Jews in the United States," *American Jewish Year Book,* LVI (1955) , 65 ff.

13 Nugent, *Tolerant Populists,* 113; Ignatius Donnelly, *Caesar's Column,* ed. W. B. Rideout (Cambridge, 1960) , 283. Pollack similarly misstates the case when he asserts, "Donnelly never attacked radical Jews" ("Myth of Populist Anti-Semitism," 78) . See also C. Vann Woodward, *Tom Watson, Agrarian Rebel* (New York, 1938) , 486.

felt compelled to demonstrate that they were progressive (or radical or socialist) in order to prove that they were not a "source for later proto-fascist groups, McCarthyism, anti-Semitism, xenophobia, and anti-intellectualism."[14]

The techniques of defense were significant. The standards of judgment applied to the Populists differed from those used for their opponents. The apologists assumed that the reforms proposed were self-evidently valid and wrote off indefensible ideas as irrelevant eccentricities.

Protestations of concern for the interests of the people and for the general welfare were part of the common rhetoric of politicians and businessmen in the last quarter of the nineteenth century. John D. Rockefeller was not a hypocrite when he described himself as steward of God's gold, nor was James G. Blaine when he proclaimed his intention "to elevate and dignify labor—not to degrade it."[15] Nevertheless, however sincere these statements, no historian could overlook personal ambition or class and sectional motives in accounting for the actions of the men who made them. By the same token, the scholar ought not have explained the behavior of the farmers, editors, and lawyers who became Populists, by their expressions of belief in "the brotherhood of man." No party was free of politicians who sought passes from the railroads, or who took flyers in mineral lands, or who proved corrupt and inept, or who were able to "work both sides of the street," or who balanced tickets and sought the votes of Negro and immigrant groups while opposing the entry of nonexistent contract laborers and condoning segregation.[16] Uncritical acceptance of professions of virtue and of disinterestedness in the case of any of them, whether Wall Street bankers or Populists, drew the unwary into a quagmire of misunderstandings.

[14] Norman Pollack, *Populist Response to Industrial America* (Cambridge, 1962) , 6. See also the review by Herbert Shapiro, *American Journal of Economics and Sociology*, XXVII (July 1968) , 321 ff.

[15] James G. Blaine, *Words on the Issues of the Day* (Boston, 1884) , 285.

[16] Pollack, *Populist Response,* 14; Nugent, *Tolerant Populists,* 78, 131, 150, 203 ff.; Hicks, *Populist Revolt,* 71; Roscoe C. Martin, *People's Party in Texas* (Austin, 1933) , 94 ff., 111 ff., 226 ff.; Jack Abramowitz, "Negro in the Agrarian Revolt," *Agricultural History,* XXIV (January 1950) , 95, n. 47; Francis B. Simkins, *Tillman Movement in South Carolina* (Durham, 1926) , 140 ff.; Martin Ridge, *Ignatius Donnelly* (Chicago, 1962) , 305. On the contract laborers, see Charlotte Erickson, *American Industry and the European Immigrant* (Cambridge, 1957) .

Too often also the defenders gullibly assumed that the Populists were correct in the assessment of problems and in the reforms
advocated. Certainly in the periods of falling prices and depression
of the 1880s and 1890s American farmers, like American laborers,
had genuine grievances. But it did not follow that they understood
their own situation or that their "folk wisdom" provided them
with simple solutions to complex philosophical and economic
questions.[17]

"What really irked them," Nugent wrote, "was not commerce
but the abuse of commerce, not loans and interest but usury, not
banking but special privilege, not enterprise but speculation"—as
if those differentiations were clear and precise, as if he knew where
interest and enterprise ended and usury and speculation began. He
easily paraphrased Populist literature in denounciations of "monopoly" and in demands for the "equitable distribution of wealth";
he never determined or explained just what those concepts meant.[18]

When it came to specifics, the failure of analysis was glaring.
"More and more wealth of all kinds was concentrating in fewer
and fewer hands." "Who does not know that no man can be nomi-
nated for president by either party who is not approved by the
money power of New York and Boston? Who does not know that
the railroad barons, democrats and republicans though they be,
are ONE in the halls of Congress?"[19] The Senate was a corrupt,
rich men's club; political machines perverted democracy; not overproduction, but plutocratic monopoly, deflation, and excessive distribution costs caused the farmer's difficulties. The apologists accepted these judgments as statements of fact with scarcely any
effort to go beyond the data presented by their advocates. Nor was
there any more careful scrutiny of the remedies proposed. The
direct election of senators and the primary would reform politics;
monetary inflation, cooperatives, and government ownership
would save the yeoman, raise farm incomes, and lower consumer
prices.[20]

17 Pollack, *Populist Response*, 7, 9.

18 Nugent, *Tolerant Populists*, 95 ff.

19 Nugent, *Tolerant Populists*, 103; Pollack, *Populist Response*, 79.

20 James C. Malin, "Mobility and History," *Agricultural History*, XVII (October
1943), 178; Pollack, "Hofstadter on Populism," 490; Lawrence Goodwyn, *Demo-*

The experience of the decades after 1900 revealed that the advocates of those changes were not wiser, more enlightened, more concerned with the public welfare than their opponents. Direct election did not alter the character of the Senate, and the primary did not weaken the political machine. Agricultural surpluses did not disappear, and subsidies did not save the small family farm. Nor did the agricultural cooperatives, about which Lawrence Goodwyn seemed not to know, but which flourished in New York, Wisconsin, and California, with only a negligible effect on distribution costs. And government ownership, to the extent that it was adopted, brought no cures. The discrepancy between results and expectations was not decisive—conditions changed after the 1890s —but it raised an unheeded warning against the passive assumption that the Populists understood what ailed them or knew what was good for them. It certainly left open the possibility that the Populists may have clung to their nostrums for reasons that were as nonrational as those which attached the goldbug or Bourbon to his own.

Finally, the defensive accounts obscured, or wrote off as harmless eccentricities, the inexplicable peculiarities of some of the Populists. Thus, Mary Ellen Lease's racist visions of world conquest and Ignatius Donnelly's belief in the lost continent of Atlantis or in the Baconian authorship of Shakespeare's plays seemed altogether irrelevant. Nugent shrugged when the Populist legislature of Kansas, elected in 1896, failed to enact a railroad regulation bill and launched into a debate on a measure "to give statutory force to the ten commandments." Vann Woodward argued that the two parts of Tom Watson's life were unconnected

*cratic Promise: The Populist Movement in America* (New York, 1976). For studies which cast doubt upon these propositions, see Chester M. Destler, "Agricultural Readjustment and Agrarian Unrest in Illinois," *Agricultural History*, XXI (April 1947), 107 ff.; Theodore Saloutos, "Agricultural Problem and Nineteenth-Century Industrialism," *Agricultural History*, XXII (July 1948), 162 ff., 166 ff.; Ralph A. Smith, "'Macuneism' or the Farmers of Texas in Business," *Journal of Southern History*, XIII (May 1947), 242, 244. On money, see Milton Friedman and Anna J. Schwartz, *Monetary History of the United States, 1867–1960* (Princeton, 1963), 91 ff., 113 ff., 119 ff.; Charles Hoffman, "Depression of the Nineties," *Journal of Economic History*, XVI (June 1956), 164. The useful summary of national data in Fred A. Shannon, *Farmer's Last Frontier* (New York, 1945), 291 ff., takes for granted such assumptions as that ton-mile rates should have been the same throughout the country. Paul W. MacAvoy, *Economic Effects of Regulation* (Cambridge, 1965), is relevant on the railroads.

and found no meaning in his subject's worship of Napoleon. The
felt need to justify the Populists reduced these aberrations to
negligible dimensions.[21]

Apologia obscured the genuine problems that the scholars ought
to have addressed. Had they ceased to worry about whether the
Populists were more farsighted and more virtuous than their contemporaries and recognized that, as in Alabama, the agrarians were
neither backward-looking nor revolutionary, merely provincial,
historians could have confronted the really distinctive characteristics of the movement.[22]

Populism drew together many discontented elements in American society: farmers, laborers, social reformers, and intellectuals.
The very diversity of these groups rendered futile the quest for a
single ideology among them, either at the time, or retrospectively.
Socialists and currency men, Bellamy Nationalists and Knights of
Labor could unite in complaints against contemporary capitalism
and in resentment of the moral deficiencies of the new wealth, but
not in their vision of the future. Significantly, Pollack, who sought
to define such an ideology, dealt with criticism of existing conditions, not with proposals for the future. His book achieved such
coherence as it had by excluding the South, just as Goodwyn's did
by excluding the West. James Youngdale, dazzled by Adlerian
paradigms, discerned three varieties—Tory Populism, Socialist Populism, and radical neomercantilism—although neither he nor the
other partitionists could explain why all the people who in the
1890s used the common name somehow thought they formed a
single movement.[23]

21 Nugent, *Tolerant Populists*, 204; Woodward, "Populist Heritage and the Intellectual," 67.

22 Sheldon Hackney, *Populism to Progressivism in Alabama* (Princeton, 1969),
79 ff.

23 Pollack, *Populist Response;* Destler, "Agricultural Readjustment," 115; Chester
M. Destler, *American Radicalism, 1865–1901* (New London, Conn., 1946), 15 ff.;
Goodwyn, *Democratic Promise;* James M. Youngdale, *Populism: A Psycho-Historical
Perspective* (Port Washington, N.Y., 1975), 13, 128 ff. Karel D. Bicha, *Western Populism* (Lawrence, Kans., 1976) makes another set of exclusions. Rogin, *Intellectuals
and McCarthy,* 64 ff., 283 ff., evades the problem by equating Populists, progressives,
and radicals and by statistical devices which assume the constancy of constituencies,

The process of voicing grievances produced not a common set of ideas but a common style. Populist literature and oratory bristled with rhetoric that appealed to the emotions. Again and again it summoned the audience to "put on the bright armour of chivalry, ride forth to the rescue and smite the dungeon-door with the battle-axe of Lionheart." It therefore responded with "impulsiveness and emotionalism" to "anything from an economic doctrine to a political platform." What was true of Kansas was often true elsewhere. The election of 1890 could "hardly be diagnosed as a political campaign. It was a religious revival, a crusade, a pentecost of politics in which a tongue of flame sat upon every man, and each spake as the spirit gave him utterance." Senator Peffer once explained that "the Alliance is in a great measure taking the place of the churches." He was correct in more ways than he knew; the style had recognizable antecedents as far back as the Great Awakening. And it was particularly compelling for those in the audience reared in evangelical denominations.[24]

Sensational revelations of conspiracies which threatened the safety of the Republic spiced the treatises on money or on the trusts. The authors and speakers were of course sincere; they believed absolutely in the gospel for which they sought converts. But the villainies they exposed did not become known through research or investigation. Although some of the authors worked industriously to compile their data, in the end they could only infer the conspiracy of the gold gamblers. But it had to be true, because only thus could believers reconcile the discrepancy between events and faith.[25]

The Populist faith rested consistently upon one article: the competence of the common man—in whom a divine spark dwelt—to deal adequately with all the problems of life. Control by the mass of the people could solve every difficulty; direct election of Senators, the primary, cooperatives, and government ownership

1886–1960. See also George B. Tindall, *Ethnic Southerners* (Baton Rouge, La., 1976) , 163 ff.

24 Woodward, *Tom Watson,* 41, 138, 139; Hicks, *Populist Revolt,* 159.

25 Norman Pollack is himself the victim of the same faulty logic, "Hofstadter on Populism," 493; Paul W. Glad, *Trumpet Soundeth: William Jennings Bryan and His Democracy, 1896–1912* (Lincoln, Neb., 1960) , 49 ff. No evidence of conspiracy has emerged in scholarship since the 1890s.

were ultimately means of establishing that control. The voice of the people was the voice of God, even when, later, sounded by a lynch mob.[26]

Most Populists in the 1890s, however, learned to accept a distinction between the people as they were and as they should be, if for no other reason than because the majority voted incorrectly. "The very fool workingmen who are deprived of the means of subsistence will continue to vote for the perpetuation of the system which is constantly adding to the number of unemployed just as often as they get a chance," wrote the Topeka *Advocate*.[27]

The Populist explained away the failure of the people to elect those who would best serve them by references to the corrupting power of conspiracy. And he had no doubt about who were the unregenerate and who the redeemed. "The government is the *people* and *we* are the people," announced Jerry Simpson. "Old man Peepul is on top. Aunt Sarah Jane is on top. We country folks are on top, and everybody is going to be happy." Virtue was safe on the farm, in danger in the urban setting. An agrarian promised land was the true home of the people; the apocalyptic visions of *Caesar's Column* exposed the alternative. Hence the hostility to the city, the resentment of its power to draw men from the farms, and the mistrust of the strange populace clustered there.[28]

Awareness that the people as they were were not the same as the people as they should have been also turned many Populists against the institutions which deceived and misled as well as oppressed the common man. The business corporations, entrenched in Wall Street, were an obvious target; but mistrust and hostility spilled over to the hireling subsidized press, to the universities, and occasionally to the churches—all tools of the capitalists and unresponsive to the popular will.

One can neither accept these categorizations at face value as valid nor dismiss them offhand as aberrations. Properly viewed,

26 Woodward, *Tom Watson*, 445; R. C. Miller, "Background of Populism in Kansas," *Mississippi Valley Historical Review*, XI (March 1925) , 469 ff.; Glad, *Trumpet Soundeth*, 35; Kenneth Barkin, "Case Study in Comparative History: Populism in Germany and America," in Herbert J. Bass, ed., *State of American History* (Chicago, 1970) , 373 ff.

27 Pollack, *Populist Response*, 62.

28 Nugent, *Tolerant Populists*, 77; Woodward, *Tom Watson*, 428.

Such explanations told only half the story. Why did some agriculturalists yield to temptation and not others? Why was the incidence of debt high, not in the poorest sections, but in those in which land values rose rapidly? Studies like those of Allan Bogue revealed that interest rates were falling, and that it was by no means simple to attract Eastern or European funds into the West. And the farmers were by no means reluctant victims. Tillman himself recalled that, "My motto was, 'It takes money to make money, and nothing risk nothing have.' " Denunciations of the competitive system rose to the heavens in hard times, but a speculative, acquisitive atmosphere suffused many regions just before they turned Populist and just after they left the faith. It would help to know to what extent the farmers—and editors, lawyers, doctors, and small-town businessmen—who became Populists remained spiritually boomers and sooners.[33]

We catch only fragmentary glimpses, beneath the definable economic grievances, of more pervasive causes of discontent. However idyllic the images of the happy husbandman, the audience knew well enough the isolation of the Great Plains, the dreariness of life in the rural South, the debilitating effects of illness, the devastation of climatic disasters. No change in railroad rates or cotton prices could transform these harsh conditions. The alliances, like the granges earlier, were social before they were political organizations. Perhaps the intensity of the emotions of their members owed something to the repressed consciousness that some problems were utterly beyond their control.[34]

The Populists were neither saints nor sinners, but men responding to the changes that remade America in their time. So, too,

33 Allan G. Bogue, *Money at Interest* (Ithaca, N.Y., 1955) , 83 ff., 263 ff., 269 ff., and *From Prairie to Corn Belt: Farming on the Illinois and Iowa Prairies in the Nineteenth Century* (Chicago, 1963) , 177; Malin, "Mobility and History," 181 ff.; Simkins, *Tillman Movement*, 51 ff.; Pollack, *Populist Response*, 18, 27; Nugent, *Tolerant Populists*, 54 ff.; Hofstadter, *Age of Reform*, 42, 58; Ridge, *Ignatius Donnelly*, 17 ff.; Glad, *Trumpet Soundeth*, 46; Woodward, "Populist Heritage and the Intellectual," 62; B. H. Wilcox, "Historical Definition of Northwestern Radicalism," *Mississippi Valley Historical Review*, XXVI (December 1939) , 394; E. C. Blackorby, *Prairie Rebel: The Public Life of William Lemke* (Lincoln, Neb., 1963) , 1 ff.

34 Hicks, *Populist Revolt*, 128 ff.; William D. Sheldon, *Populism in the Old Dominion* (Princeton, 1935) , 40 ff.; Theodore Saloutos, *Farmer Movement in the South, 1865–1933* (Berkeley, 1960) , 69 ff.

were Rockefeller and his contemporaries, although after their own fashion, which sometimes paralleled that of the Populists, sometimes diverged, and sometimes conflicted with it. And so, too, were abolitionists and slaveholders, freedmen and redeemers. In politics, at least, goodness was not all of a piece. Benevolence of intentions sometimes masked dangers; and the good that men hoped to do was often buried with them, while unattended consequences lived long after.[35]

To compress the exceedingly complex relations among individuals and groups into a formula of polarity vents prejudices, but impedes understanding. Only a few books display willingness to regard actuality as something other than a projection of their authors' wishes. Genuine moral commitment requires at least a comprehension of the real world. Enlistment on the side of the angels, while reserving the right to afix halos at will, calls for neither intelligence, nor skill, nor ethical sensitivity. Only recognition of the actual men and women revealed by the evidence permits valid judgments of goodness and evil, weakness and strength.[36]

[35] Oscar Handlin, "Slave and Freedman," *Commentary*, III (June 1947) , 599 ff.

[36] Clifton K. Yearley, *Money Machines* (Albany, 1970) , is an example of the ability to escape crippling polarities.

# 14

## The Two-Party System

FOR A CENTURY or more, students of American politics, regarding the highly structured electoral and legislative organizations of their time, tried to discern antecedents back in the earliest days of the Republic. John Fiske found "the seeds of all party differences" thereafter to bear fruit in the United States "sown and sedulously nurtured" in Washington's first administration. Charles A. Beard and V. L. Parrington, from other perspectives, advanced the same theme and pushed the same interpretation back into the revolutionary period. They seemed thus to have uncovered the key that put order and coherence into the evolution of democratic government in the New World.[1]

The idea continued to entice those eager for easy answers. In 1953 Wilfred E. Binkley's natural history gave it thoughtful expression, using the data collected by a generation of research.[2]

His preface stated the theme: "The fact that almost from the beginning of the national period two major interests, the mercantile-financial on the one hand and independent farming on the other" had contended for supremacy "undoubtedly provided the basis of our two-party alignments" (viii). This division, Binkley believed, extended back to Bacon's Rebellion, although his detailed study began with the American Revolution (6). The emergence of one party was relatively simple. The patriots of 1770 became first anti-Federalists, then Jeffersonian Democrats; and, after a period of one-party government, Jacksonian Democrats,

---

1 John Fiske, *Essays Historical and Literary* (New York, 1902), I, 170.

2 Wilfred E. Binkley, *American Political Parties* (New York, 1943); review by Oscar Handlin, *New England Quarterly*, XVII (March 1944), 117 ff.

whose strength for nearly a century "depended primarily upon the maintenance of an entente between Southern and Western agrarians on the one hand and Northern metropolitan masses on the other" (57 ff., 373). The evolution of the other party was more complex. The merchants, supporters of the Constitution, became Federalists until after the War of 1812. Out of sight for a while, they reappeared as Whigs, drawing votes from the Black-Belt planters and Clay farmers, became Constitutional Unionists when the slavery issue disrupted the old alignments, and finally captured the Republican Party after 1868.

The boldly stated theme could not be carried out. Since Binkley was thoroughly honest, the weight of evidence time after time forced him away from it. Complex qualifications and involved reasoning rendered many portions of the thesis nugatory, and startling contradictions emerged from the necessity of putting together evidence that did not fit. Thus, "the great planters of the South" supported both the Constitution and Hamilton's financial program for no substantial reasons (25, 38). The merchants could become Democratic-Republicans because "business interests were devoid of principle and would combine with any party" (98). Ex-Federalists were "a striking element" in the formation of the Jacksonian Democratic Party (118). New England Jacksonians were the party of the common man, but "the presence of a strong Whig—that is to say, conservative—opposition, amounting in most communities to a majority," conditioned their tactics and forced them to temper their radicalism; as a result, extremists, facing "conservatism in both major parties, turned to third parties," which naturally "ran rampant among the humbler folk of rural New England" (125). The soul of the Locofoco Party marched on in Jacksonian Democracy, though its most effective accomplishments were in alliances with Whigs (143). A majority of the anti-Nebraska congressmen elected in 1854 were Know-Nothings, but that party evaded the slavery issue (194, 195). Republicans received the "labor vote" in 1860 (213, 230 ff., 246), although the foreign-born, especially the Irish, who made up much of that vote, opposed them (232, 267). The captains of finance, industry, and commerce were Grant Republicans, although Belmont, Hewitt, and McCormick were Seymour-Tilden Democrats (271, 279, 305). In the West, in the "zone of New England colonization," environment transformed Federalists into Jeffersonians; but Whigs and

Republicans retained their allegiance, although the debt-ridden small farmers who migrated were Jacksonian Democrats anyway (73–75, 165, 187, 283). When 59 percent of the farmers favored Franklin Delano Roosevelt in 1936, it was "reasonable to assume that they appreciated the benefits of Agricultural Adjustment Act" and other New Deal legislation, though the 41 percent opposed benefited similarly from the same measures (380).

That the work bore the burden of an untenable thesis was unfortunate because it contained another, more valid and more useful, generalization. Cutting through the overgrowth of attempts to identify parties with specific, continuous, and opposing combinations of interests was the acute perception that these organizations were frequently multigroup entities, consisting of diverse and often incoherent interests, led by "astute opportunists free from petrified ideas," and guided by "expediency" (ix, 230). That is, the major parties constituted only loose confederations of local parties (78). This understanding was in accord with that of John Adams, who wrote Thomas Jefferson (June 20, 1813) : "The real terrors of both parties have always been, and now are, the fear that they shall lose the elections, and consequently, the loafs and fishes, and that their antagonist will get them." As for differences, "Put them in a bag and shake them, and then see which will come out first."[3]

Scholarly research after 1945 cut the ground out from under the theme of party continuity. On the crucial period between 1787 and 1800, three decades of investigation destroyed the link between radical anti-constitutionalists and Jeffersonian Democratic-Republicans, on the one hand, and conservative constitutionalists and Hamiltonian Federalists, on the other. Other scholars raised serious questions about the persistence of the party system in the first half of the nineteenth century; and efforts to extend the radical-conservative scheme through the Civil War failed.[4] The

[3] John Adams, *Works*, ed. Charles Francis Adams, 10 vols. (Boston, 1850–56), X, 48.

[4] Claude Bowers, *Jefferson and Hamilton* (Boston, 1925) stated the older view. For the early republic, see Joseph E. Charles, *Origins of the American Party System* (Williamsburg, Va., 1956) ; William N. Chambers, *Political Parties in a New Nation* (New York, 1963) ; Paul A. Varg, *Foreign Policies of the Founding Fathers* (East Lansing, Mich., 1963) ; Paul Goodman, *Democratic-Republicans of Massachusetts* (Cambridge, 1964). For the early nineteenth century, see Roy F. Nichols, *Invention of the American Political Parties* (New York, 1967) ; Richard McCormick, *Second*

argument for continuity in the twentieth century was stronger; but Arthur M. Schlesinger concluded that even for the 1920s there was "no basic disagreement between the old parties as to the theory of government." Neither took issue with the existing economic organization of society; and such differences as existed were largely in point of view and in temperament.[5]

〜〜

The curious power of survival of the two-party, radical-conservative syndrome for the revolutionary decades owed little to the evidence, much to Carl L. Becker's acute analysis of New York politics before independence. He argued that the conflict between colony and empire concealed a significant cleavage among the Americans themselves, that an internal struggle for power coincided with that against England.[6]

Exploring the issue in four preliminary articles, Becker at first cautiously treated colonial politics as "factional contests," in which the personal element predominated until 1769. He then slipped into use of the terms "court party" and "popular party," although referring as late as April 1775 to the "conservative faction."[7]

Becker's book, however, was unambiguous; and its forceful statements inspired further research into the nature of the domestic divisions and their connection with the causes of the revolt against the mother country. Impressive studies showed that in New Eng-

---

*American Party System* (Chapel Hill, N.C., 1966) ; David H. Fischer, "Myth of the Essex Junto," *William and Mary Quarterly*, XXI (April 1964) , 199 ff., and *Revolution of American Conservatism* (New York, 1965) . On the Civil War, see Oscar Handlin, review of *Lincoln and the Radicals* by T. Harry Williams, *New England Quarterly*, XV (June 1942) , 381 ff.

5 Arthur M. Schlesinger, "Radicalism and Conservatism in American History," *New Viewpoints in American History* (New York, 1922) , 103 ff., and "Riddle of the Parties," *ibid.*, 294. See also William N. Chambers and Walter D. Burnham, *American Party Systems* (New York, 1967) .

6 Carl L. Becker, *History of Political Parties in the Province of New York, 1760–1776* (Madison, 1909) .

7 Carl Becker, "Nominations in Colonial New York," *American Historical Review*, VI (January 1901) , 267, 269, and "Growth of Revolutionary Parties and Methods in New York Province, 1765–1774," *American Historical Review*, VII (October 1901) , 59, and "Nomination and Election of Delegates from New York to the First Continental Congress," *Political Science Quarterly*, XVIII (March 1903) , 17, 18, 36 ff., and "Election of Delegates from New York to the Second Continental Congress," *American Historical Review*, IX (October 1903) , 85.

land, by and large, two groups contested the control of the struggle with Britain. The merchants and their allies, harried by the new colonial policy, turned for assistance to elements lower in the social scale, to "their natural enemies in society."[8] The men of substance and property were concerned primarily with the adjustment of their own grievances. They calculated on limiting the conflict and moderating its pace and were apprehensive lest in the excitement of the contest the machinery of state slip into the hands of those whose aid they courted. More cautious and more moderate as the crisis approached, more aware of the benefits of remaining within the Empire, the group contained a substantial number who would not tolerate the course of events that precipitated the break and so became Tories. But though split at the crucial moment into moderates and loyalists on the question of relations to the mother country, the merchants and their satellites had, during the preceding fifteen years, acted as a coherent conservative party.

The opponents arrayed against them saw in the Revolution a strategic opportunity for wresting political privilege out of the hands of the wealthy, who had long dominated colonial government. The urban artisans and laborers, the small farmers, and the frontier settlers, underrepresented and underprivileged and aggrieved against England on their own score, used collaboration with the conservatives as a lever with which to gain power in the state. With only a slight stake in the old order, the radicals had little patience with moderation and wished to bring the issue to a boil, for therein lay their main chance to profit from the dilemma of the merchants.[9]

The same party division, Becker suggested, persisted beyond 1776. "The differentiation of loyalist and revolutionist had not yet been completed before" the beginnings of new party alignments were visible. "These new alignments were merely the revival, in a slightly different form, of the fundamental party divisions which had existed from the time of the stamp act. The fear of British oppression was transformed into the fear of oppres-

8 A. M. Schlesinger, *Colonial Merchants and the American Revolution, 1763–1776* (New York, 1918), 307.

9 The general position is summarized in Curtis P. Nettels, *Roots of American Civilization* (New York, 1938), 621 ff.

sion by the national government, while the demand of the un-
franchised classes for recognition . . . was to find its ultimate
answer only in the achievements of Jefferson and Jackson."[10]

This concept, pushed further implicitly and explicitly by successive writers, and restated by Merrill Jensen, entered into much
of the historical thinking on the early national period. Jensen
found the same division into radicals and conservatives after 1776
as before. "The basic social forces in colonial life were not eliminated by the Declaration of Independence. There was no break
in the underlying conflict between party and party representing
fundamental divisions in American society."[11]

The thesis that revolutionary parties continued into the post-
revolutionary era supplied a comfortable link with their putative
descendants of the end of the century. But, whatever the nature
of the connection of Federalists and Democratic-Republicans with
conservatives and radicals, the two decades after 1775 presented
problems which this simple explanation could not solve. A reexamination of this thesis, even from material in commonly available sources and standard accounts, revealed serious deficiencies.[12]
As applied to Massachusetts, at least, it was misleading and inaccurate and failed to explain the most significant developments in
the twenty years between the outbreak of war and the emergence
of the parties of Jefferson and Hamilton. It did not account rea-
sonably for the activities of the leading personalities in the Commonwealth between 1775 and 1795; it did not square with the
political reactions of economic groups; it left no place for changes
in class structure and composition; and it failed to explain the
impact of new issues.

The significant statesmen of the period did not fit into a consistent two-party system reaching back before 1774.[13] By 1790 John

10 Becker, *History of Political Parties,* 274 ff.

11 Merrill Jensen, *Articles of Confederation: An Interpretation of the Social-
Constitutional History of the American Revolution, 1774–1781* (Madison, Wisc.,
1940) , 7.

12 Oscar and Mary F. Handlin, "Radicals and Conservatives in Massachusetts after
Independence," *New England Quarterly,* XVII (September 1944) , 343 ff.; also Van
Beck Hall, *Politics Without Parties: Massachusetts, 1780–1791* (Pittsburgh, 1972) .

13 In this and succeeding paragraphs reference is made, in the absence of other
citations, to biographical accounts in the *Dictionary of American Biography,* and
Alden Bradford, *Biographical Notices* . . . (Boston, 1842) .

Hancock and James Bowdoin had emerged as leaders of two opposing groups; by 1797 Elbridge Gerry and Samuel Adams had become Republicans of sorts, while John Adams was a Federalist of sorts. Yet, on the revolutionary issues, on questions arising out of relations with England, they had taken identical radical positions. And what was true of the brightest luminaries was likewise true of the lesser, younger lights; Timothy Pickering and James Sullivan, Caleb Strong and Benjamin Austin divided later, but on revolutionary questions they had been united.[14]

Nor was this a surface unity only, concealing fundamental differences under the pressure of an emergency which demanded cooperation. For even the crisis did not create concord everywhere. Although all the men here mentioned were radicals, there were conservatives before independence, and the course of the struggle heightened rather than abated differences. The Continental Congresses before 1776, for instance, had divided over the extent of legitimate British authority and over the measures proper to meet the coercive acts. But all the Massachusetts delegates had acted in accord. In Philadelphia all New Englanders shone as democrats; John Adams was a radical fully as "arch" as Sam, when compared with Joseph Galloway, John Dickinson, or even John Jay.[15]

But although all the leaders prominent after 1775 were radicals, they had conservative opponents in Massachusetts before that date. The Bay State approximations to Jay and Dickinson were Thomas Hutchinson, Francis Bernard, and Andrew Oliver, the respectable established merchants of the provincial metropolis. Some merchants, particularly those like Hancock and Bowdoin from newly risen families, were radical for individual reasons. Others, like John Andrews, chose independence when the issue was clearly drawn. But the most prominent and the most important colonists cherished the advantages that came from their position in the

[14] See also Charles W. Akers, "Sam Adams—and Much More," *New England Quarterly*, XLVII (March 1974), 120 ff.; George A. Billias, *Elbridge Gerry* (New York, 1976), 153 ff., 218 ff.

[15] Schlesinger, *Colonial Merchants*, 244, 410 ff., 433; Nettels, *Roots of American Civilization*, 646; Becker, *History of Political Parties*, 253; Jensen, *Articles of Confederation*, 118, 127.

British trading system and preferred unity with the mother country.[16]

In Massachusetts sooner than elsewhere the conservatives perceived the true character of the struggle. They had of course organized to resist the trade laws after 1763; but they did not, as did their counterparts in New York and Pennsylvania, pursue the chimerical hope of tempering or controlling the radicals. There were no moderates in Massachusetts, no Friends of Liberty and Trade to counterbalance the Sons of Liberty. The conservatives recognized the potential power of those beneath them in the social scale, feared it, and would have no truck with it. By 1766 they were already distrustful. Three years later Governor Bernard noted that he had "the generality of respectable Men on his Side," while in New York they were "more generally against Government."[17]

After 1770, as prosperity returned, many more refused to participate in the protest movement any longer. They made up their minds earlier than did the New York conservatives, who eventually became Tories but still, in 1776, participated in the Third Provincial Congress. Long before then, the loyalist character of Massachusetts conservatives was clear; their conversion "occurred earlier than in the other provinces."[18]

When the break came the most prominent emigrated. The Hutchinsons, Vassalls, and Brattles went, and with them more than two hundred others in 1775 alone. Diverse personal considerations induced some to stay, but they played no part in the politics of the new state. Loyalty to the mother country, conviction of her ultimate success, and the difficulty of effacing the taint of toryism kept those who remained on the sidelines, at least until the

16 Schlesinger, *Colonial Merchants*, 103 ff., 281 ff., 434; Adams, *Works*, II, 215 ff.; Bernard Bailyn, *Ordeal of Thomas Hutchinson* (Cambridge, 1974) ; and, in general, C. M. Andrews, "Boston Merchants and the Non-Importation Movement," Colonial Society of Massachusetts, *Publications: Transactions, 1916–17* (Boston, 1918), XIX, 159 ff.

17 Edward Channing and A. C. Coolidge, *Barington-Bernard Correspondence* . . . (Cambridge, 1912), 142; Schlesinger, *Colonial Merchants*, 60 ff., 92; Becker, *History of Political Parties*, 86 ff., 112 ff., 195, 264.

18 Andrews, "Boston Merchants," 243; Schlesinger, *Colonial Merchants*, 240 ff., 260, 604; Becker, *History of Political Parties*, 207, 274; Virginia D. Harrington, *New York Merchant on the Eve of the Revolution* (New York, 1935), 348 ff. Thomas C. Barrow, "American Revolution as a Colonial War for Independence," *William and Mary Quarterly*, XXV (July 1968), 456 ff., suggests the importance of timing.

peace. The original division between radicals and conservatives in Massachusetts did not persist beyond 1775. By then the only participants in the struggle for independence were the radicals. Since the other side disappeared completely, either physically or by a withdrawal from politics, all subsequent divisions and alignments originated from within the once-united radical group.[19]

Supporters of the thesis that the same divisions were always present and persisted unchanged rested their case upon the contention that the break with England was not the true test of radicalism and conservatism, that opposing ideas about the nature of the state and divergent social attitudes determined fundamental party groupings, which emerged into the open once the obscuring issue of independence cleared away.[20] Actions—in this period almost the only available index to men's ideas—did not reveal such a dichotomy for the leading figures. The state constitution of 1780 and Shays's Rebellion, issues laden with social import, failed to divide the prominent Massachusetts men; the two Adamses, Hancock and Bowdoin, Gerry and Strong shared the same attitudes. Even the antagonisms raised by the federal Constitution did not produce a lasting and open break among these men. The proposed amendments largely met the limited objections to the document, summarized by Mercy Otis Warren. In any case, immediately after ratification, Strong and Gerry, the delegates who had refused to sign at Philadelphia, cooperated with groups which had fought bitterly for adoption. Both Ames brothers welcomed the new instrument of central government, although they later fell into sharp disagreement.[21]

[19] Schlesinger, *Colonial Merchants,* 604; Lorenzo Sabine, *Biographical Sketches of the Loyalists of the American Revolution,* 2 vols. (Boston, 1864), I, 25. There are more complete lists in James H. Stark, *Loyalists of Massachusetts* (Boston, 1910); and in Justin Winsor, *Memorial History of Boston,* 4 vols. (Boston, 1881), III, 175 ff. See also A. E. Morse, *Federalist Party in Massachusetts to the Year 1800* (Princeton, 1909), 11.

[20] For example, Jensen, *Articles of Confederation,* 10, 57.

[21] Even Beard acknowledged that in 1790 "the Federalist-Republican schism" was not yet "clearly developed." Gerry was not a Republican until after 1796 (Charles A. Beard, *Economic Origins of Jeffersonian Democracy* [New York, 1915], 10 ff., 43, 62, 73). For the state of parties in 1790, see Gerry's illuminating letter to Bowdoin, June 25, 1790, Massachusetts Historical Society *Collections, Seventh Series* (Boston, 1907), VI, 196; also Noble Cunningham, *Jeffersonian Republicans*

The rare occasions on which social ideas found formal expression failed to furnish a firm basis for party divisions. When John Adams outlined a system of government in 1776, he was, at one and the same time, condemned for being too popular and too aristocratic. A period that could take him for the author of *Common Sense* could hardly have been aware of deep party differences, based on abstract political theory.[22] Nor did the historian's perspective simplify the task of pigeonholing Adams on the basis of such divisions; attempts to do so plunged into contradiction. In Jensen's monograph, for instance, the Braintree lawyer appeared at least six times as a conservative, eight times as a radical, and on one page as a radical in the text and a conservative in its footnote.[23] At the root of this confusion was the inescapable obligation to draw specific instances of party division either from questions arising out of the imperial problem[24] or from anticipated party affiliations which arose twenty years later, identifying those who became Federalists as conservatives and those who became Democrats as radicals.[25]

When the focus of attention shifted from individuals to broad social groupings it revealed that the thesis of continuous party development did not conform to actual alignments in the Commonwealth of Massachusetts.

The notion that the radical and conservative parties persisted beyond independence rested upon the assumption that the state's

---

(Chapel Hill, N.C., 1957) ; Stephen G. Kurtz, *Presidency of John Adams* (Philadelphia, 1957) . See also Charles Warren, "Elbridge Gerry, James Warren, Mercy Warren and . . . the Federal Constitution in Massachusetts," Massachusetts Historical Society *Proceedings* (Boston, 1932) , LXIV, 162; Charles Warren, *Jacobin and Junto* (Cambridge, 1931) , 44. On the state constitution, see H. A. Cushing, *History of the Transition from Provincial to Commonwealth Government in Massachusetts* (New York, 1896) ; Oscar and Mary F. Handlin, *Commonwealth* (Cambridge, 1969) , ch. 1.

22 Patrick Henry to John Adams, May 20, 1776, Adams, *Works*, IV, 201 ff.; see also II, 507 ff.; IV, 193 ff.

23 Jensen, *Articles of Confederation*, 13, 57, 90, 144, 167, and 173; 44, 46, 52, 62, 65, 83, 95, and 118; 85.

24 *Ibid.*, 41, 55, 59, 88, 89, and 115.

25 That is clearly the case, for instance, when it was said of John Adams in 1775 "that while he was a conservative, he was never really a Federalist" (*ibid.*, 85) .

society throughout this period remained divided into two coherent and consistent parts—the merchants on one side, the artisans and farmers on another. This assumption was untrue. The misconception that "the masses in the towns and on the frontier" voiced the same economic and political demands fathered numerous errors. That those people had worked together for independence was no guarantee of future collaboration. On such vital questions as price-fixing, commodity control, and representation in the General Court, urban areas—artisans and laborers included—were bitterly hostile to the rural sections.[26]

Far from voting automatically with the farmers, the poorer urban elements frequently supported the merchants against the agriculturists. Thus, the commercial towns rejected the state Constitution of 1778, but accepted that of 1780 almost unanimously. Paul Revere and the mechanics meeting at the Green Dragon applied the pressure that helped swing the ratifying convention of 1788 in favor of the federal Constitution. And a committee of manufacturers and tradespeople as well as a committee of merchants congratulated Bowdoin on his election in 1786. In the very nature of the case, the merchants were not numerous enough to control the state or even the towns in which they lived without the support of substantial numbers drawn from the "masses."[27]

The farmers themselves were far from a single coherent unit. Nearness to market, character of husbandry, and length of settlement—often more important in this period than the common roots in the soil—created serious divisions and struggles for control, even within purely agricultural towns. Unsettled conditions of government sometimes permitted "Poor People, that had no whare Else to go" and had pitched "upon the ungranted Lands" to oust from the town meeting, not the remote land speculator or investor, but the settled inhabitants who also tilled the soil.[28] Furthermore, the

[26] *Ibid.*, 10; Nettels, *Roots of American Civilization*, 660. On the question of representation, for instance, Plymouth pointed out that the Constitution of 1778 would "opperate to the disadvantage of the Towns bordering on the Sea Coast whenever any Commercial Question may be agitated" (Massachusetts Archives, CLVI, 426). Oscar and Mary F. Handlin, "Revolutionary Economic Policy in Massachusetts," *William and Mary Quarterly*, IV (January 1947), 3 ff.

[27] Massachusetts Historical Society *Collections, Seventh Series*, VI, 50–53; Winsor, *Memorial History of Boston*, III, 196.

[28] Hancock petitions, Massachusetts Archives, CLXXXI, 102, 206.

farming regions in the state rarely acted together; against the unanimity of the commercial towns on the two state constitutions, for instance, the agricultural communities offered only diversity. The vote on the ratification of the federal Constitution also revealed a striking division among the rural towns. Those close to urban areas tended to favor it, but Worcester County opposed it, while Berkshire, Hampshire, Bristol, Essex, and the Maine counties showed no meaningful pattern at all.[29]

Social mobility complicated the realignment of the various groups in the revolutionary years and made difficult the perception of interests or the delineation of policy. Emigration created great gaps in the trading communities. Fragmentary statistical evidence and other indications, no less valuable, point to substantial displacement. Of nineteen prominent members of the Merchants' Club in Boston between 1764 and 1770 only two remained through the Revolution: one had left in 1768, two had died before 1775, one was insane, and fully thirteen had become Tories.[30] Economic changes shook the position even of the merchants who stayed. Depreciation presented serious problems to creditors. The closing of the port of Boston transformed the conditions of trade. The old order never returned, for independence ended the state's role in the British trading system. Such men as Bowdoin and Jonathan Jackson lost heavily until the end of hostilities. Old, established merchants had difficulty maintaining their position, unless able to adjust to untried new methods.[31]

Into the vacuum created by emigration and by the lack of adaptability of the old merchants rushed a host of newcomers. Some were traders from the outlying towns. Enterprising young

---

[29] Votes as given in *Debates and Proceedings in the Convention of the Commonwealth of Massachusetts Held in the Year 1788, and Which Finally Ratified the Constitution of the United States* (Boston, 1856) ; Hall, *Politics Without Parties*, 256 ff., 294 ff., 321 ff. For other interpretations, see R. A. East, "Massachusetts Conservatives in the Critical Period," in *Era of the American Revolution*, ed. R. B. Morris (New York, 1939) , 365; O. G. Libby, *Geographical Distribution of the Vote of the Thirteen States on the Federal Constitution, 1787–8* (Madison, Wisc., 1894) , 12 ff.; S. B. Harding, *Contest over the Ratification of the Federal Constitution in the State of Massachusetts* (New York, 1896) , 99 ff.

[30] The figure in R. A. East's *Business Enterprise in the American Revolutionary Era* (New York, 1938) , 219 ff., is far too low. See also Andrews, "Boston Merchants," 164.

[31] Cf. Winsor, *Memorial History of Boston*, IV, 154 ff.

men who saw and seized opportunities rose from petty retailing, or even from off the farms. Privateering shipowners and aggressive newcomers with contacts in the government reaped profits from speculation, contracting, and the purchase of loyalist property. All thrived in a fluid economy which often bewildered the traditional merchant.[32]

The new men were ever more important in the activities of the Commonwealth. Rough quantitative measurements, such as the high percentage of newcomers among the purchasers of loyalist estates, substantiated conclusions from social and political data.[33] All the evidence pointed in the same direction. Revolutionary conditions produced the new merchant, so different in experience, origins, and interests that in 1785 the Senate, stronghold of property and wealth, refused to permit the return of the banished Tories because of "the clamours of a few who have plundered their Effects," even though the more popular House had agreed to this.[34] North Shore traders like George Cabot, whom straitened family finances had driven from a Harvard hall to a ship's cabin; former mechanics and the sons of mechanics, like Nathaniel Gorham and Christopher Gore; former ship captains, like Mungo Mackay in Boston; the tanner Timothy Dexter in Newburyport; William Gray, son of a shoemaker in Salem; and, in the west, poor newcomers like Theodore Sedgwick and John Chandler Williams were characteristic figures of the new era.[35]

---

[32] East, *Business Enterprise,* ch. 2.

[33] Using as a test election or appointment by the town meeting to any town office or committee between 1758 and 1774 (cf. *Boston Town Records, 1758–1777, Record Commissioners Reports* [Boston, 1886, 1887], XVI, XVIII), a comparison on the same basis of ninety-one Suffolk County absentees for whom agents were appointed with those who acquired their estates reveals that 48 percent of the absentees had held office as compared with only 27 percent among the purchasers. (The absentee lists are given in Massachusetts Historical Society *Proceedings, Second Series,* X [Boston, 1896], 162 ff.) See also Richard D. Brown, "Confiscation and Disposition of Loyalists' Estates in Suffolk County, Massachusetts," *William and Mary Quarterly,* XXI (October 1964), 548.

[34] J. F. Jameson, ed., "Letters of Stephen Higginson, 1783–1804," *Annual Report of the American Historical Association, 1896* (Washington, 1897), I, 727.

[35] East, *Business Enterprise,* 65; Stephen W. Williams, *Genealogy and History of the Family of Williams* (Greenfield, Mass., 1847), 43; M. C. Crawford, *Famous Families of Massachusetts* (Boston, 1930), I, 160–161; Winsor, *Memorial History of Boston,* III, 191; *Volume of Records Relating to the Early History of Boston, containing Miscellaneous Papers, Record Commissioners' Report* (Boston, 1900), XXIX, 272, 289.

To assume the continuous development of a merchant class under these circumstances was to argue that membership in an economic group automatically and immediately shaped political and social points of view. In this transitional period, when all the problems of government were new, such oversimplification falsified a complex process. Even excluding such prominent individual deviators as Hancock and Gerry, the merchants had not had time to acquire and consolidate control, or to become conscious of their own identity and interests in the unclear, rapidly changing, and confused condition of the state's economy. The young, the strangers, the newly risen had not severed old ties and established new ones, or ascertained their interests and learned how to protect them. That is, they had not discovered that they formed a class.

⟡

The confused reactions of new social groupings to new problems became evident on many levels of state policy. Nowhere did colonial experience furnish a simple precedent. Rarely was status in 1775 a determining influence, for positions changed continually under the pressure of new conditions and of the very acts of government. In the economic sphere the earlier decades of the paper-money controversy offered no guide through the mazes into which revolutionary finance plunged the state. Those who had repeatedly sought the cure-all of an adequate circulating medium found the presses, once started, uncontrollable. While everyone scampered for safety, the flood of paper converted many hard-money men into advocates of official inflation and many soft-money men into defenders of the sanctity of contract. When the Province Charter of 1691 proved ineffective, some who had defended it in 1775 found attractions in the idea of a new state constitution, which they had once fought, while some of those who had earliest demanded a constitution became the bitterest foes of the one adopted. The exigencies of a defenseless commerce after independence persuaded many who had at first opposed centralizing tendencies most vigorously that a greater measure of authority had to be vested in the national government.

The groupings that emerged from these issues were not simple. Most important, groupings on any one issue were not coterminous with those on another. The state's politicians did not align themselves in two clear-cut camps, nor did the old radical and conservative divisions extend into the years after independence.

Later the parties of Jefferson and Hamilton attempted to establish a prerevolutionary ancestry. But it was not theirs legitimately. The new forces which arose in the two decades after Lexington were products of the problems of those years. The economic and social conditions in which they evolved were the keys to their understanding. By the same token, the general interpretation of American political history as the continuing contest of radicals and conservatives—to which Becker, Beard, and Binkley lent their authority—reflected efforts to deal with party problems after 1876, particularly in the opening decade of the twentieth century, when those issues became the subjects of fresh analysis by political scientists.

If the same tired two-party carriage continued to lumber along, conveying the same tortured evidence and parroted ideas, it was largely because the mossy conception of continuity, smooth-seeming and attractive at first sight, preempted the most fertile areas of historical thinking and stifled more fruitful interpretations.[36]

[36] Stephen E. Patterson, *Political Parties in Revolutionary Massachusetts* (Madison, Wisc., 1973), clings to the old view. Among the works which illuminate the turn of the century context are: Moisei I. Ostrogorskii, *Democracy and the Organization of Political Parties* (New York, 1902); James Allen Smith, *Spirit of American Government* (New York, 1907); Arthur F. Bentley, *Process of Government* (Chicago, 1908), 400 ff.

# The Uses of History

IF I TUNE OUT when colleagues plead for relevance, it is despite the fact that I profited greatly by application of that standard.

The General Catalogue of Harvard University for 1945 contained the following notices:

Sociology 10b.     The Boston Community. Dr. Handlin
Sociology 15.      Peasants in Urban America: Immigrant Culture in Transition. Dr. Handlin
Sociology 32.      Seminar: Group Prejudice and Conflict. Professors Allport and Parsons and Dr. Handlin

For some years thereafter I continued to offer those courses in Sociology and in its successor, Social Relations. Enrollments were gratifyingly large. Yet I could not help but agree with the suggestion that subjects such as these were not relevant to the 1950s. The work of a generation of Chicago urban sociologists had settled the outstanding issues of that field. With immigration ended and the race problem on the way to solution, those matters would not attract the attention of up-and-coming social scientists. (And indeed they did not.) Those old topics were properly the province of historians—a judgment which resolved my identity crisis and put me where I belonged.

Still, in the intervening years, I could not help wondering about relevance. Perhaps dispassionate, analytical study of race, ethnicity, and the city in the placid 1950s would have furthered understanding in the turbulent 1960s. Perhaps not. Then, too, how was an aspiring scholar to know what would be relevant by the time his work reached the public? The timetable troubled me. An excellent, hard-working doctoral student could complete his dissertation, revise it, and see it into print in perhaps eight years from the start of graduate study. Take two years, with luck, for reviews to appear and the word to spread. The total was a decade from the point of decision to that of any possible influence. In the 1970s urban historians were at a premium—hyperrelevant—

but not in the 1950s, when they might have been trained. It is safe to predict that those being trained in the 1970s will glut the market by the time their first fruits appear.

Hence the historian must resist all pleas to solve the world's immediate problems. By the time this particular type of equipment is ready, the fire has moved elsewhere.

Besides, this particular equipment, which generates cautious tentative statements about complex relations, only encumbers people in action. Men and women make decisions on the basis of interest, bias, or calculation. In doing so, they want either a formula that will help them predict the outcome or a myth that will permit them to believe in the correctness of their choice. They draw upon the past for formula or myth or both, but not through the history written by historians.

The information historians purvey provides a long view. It opens opportunities for reflection and understanding; it encourages reasoning from analogy, rather than from the application of equations or the acting out of articles of faith. The uses of history, that is, are not those of immediate relevance. Efforts to compete with novelists in mythmaking or with scientists in devising formulas not only doom history to failure but also prevent it from serving its proper function.

Look first at what mythmakers did to the historical novel. Then regard the misapplication, in one area, of a social science formula. Then consider a statement of the utility of history.

# 15

## *The Diet of a Ravenous Public*

HISTORICAL NOVELISTS, Georg Lukács argued, showed "artistically the concrete *historical genesis* of their time." His definition was unduly restrictive, excluding as it did writers interested in the past for its own sake whom he denominated mere antiquarians. Furthermore, since Lukács held a particular understanding of historical development, he also excluded those who saw the past differently. *A Tale of Two Cities* thus was deficient for the same reason as *Salammbo:* their authors' "purely moral" negative views of mass violence.[1]

I prefer to treat as historical any novel that draws material from the remote or recent past rather than to assume that any single theory explains a genre within which many types of fiction fall.

Stylistic considerations, intellectual assumptions, and market preferences always shaped the nature of these works. But by the 1970s one form had crowded to the head of the best-seller lists in the United States in response to the insatiable appetite of a public hungry for a taste of the past.

In the great nineteenth-century novels—whether categorized as historical or not—the concreteness of place and circumstances, although incidental to the author's ultimate purpose, nevertheless usefully advanced the narrative or helped develop character. The scenes of Parisian life served Balzac as London did Dickens. When a discussion of railroads intruded into *Brothers Karamazov,* it

[1] Georg Lukács, *Historical Novel,* trans. Hannah and Stanley Mitchell (London, 1962), 199, 243, 344 ff.

cast light upon the response of the gentry to change, as Melville's description of Liverpool in *Redburn* illustrated the effects of environment upon conscience. The use of such material accorded with the requirements of the novel *meublé*, equipped in full with detail.

From Thackeray onward, other writers described the setting as a way to delineate the society within which their characters moved. American local-color novelists and, later, Edith Wharton and Henry James relied heavily on that method; and various forms of realism—Thomas Hardy and Emile Zola in Europe, Frank Norris and William Dean Howells in the United States—lent the technique additional emphasis.

The settings described were contemporaneous with and, in a sense, reflective of the authors' experiences. But it did not demand a drastic alteration of point of view to shift into the past tense in novels more narrowly defined as historical. The account of the Gordon riots in *Barnaby Rudge,* of Waterloo in Stendhal, of the Civil War in *The Red Badge of Courage,* and of the Napoleonic invasion of Russia in *War and Peace* drew upon incidents from the past; but they did so in a fashion that served the purpose of the novel, as a means of developing plot and character. The writers from Walter Scott to Zoe Oldenbourg, who portrayed the whole of a bygone society, looked back through the same lenses which, for others, brought their own times into focus.

Writing was not a license for invention about the past any more than about the present. Accuracy, integrity, and authenticity were the standing concerns of the great novelists, as they were for Americans like Conrad Richter, who wrote in that genre, or for John Dos Passos, who adapted it to his own technique. Even books with explicit polemic purposes, like *Uncle Tom's Cabin,* displayed a determined effort at veracity. The research, however faulty, was conscientious and earnest; for the end served required that the facts be accurate. Borrowings from the past helped the truth-telling novelist only when they amplified the understanding of reality about people, societies, and ideas.

The wedge of imagination did keep the door open to fantasy into which even the talented slipped from time to time, sometimes within the confines of a volume otherwise respectful of fact. In *The Heart of Midlothian* (1817) Scott approached but did not yield to the temptation; in *Ivanhoe* (1819) he could not resist the dramatic possibilities of the Templar's fatal passion for the beautiful dark Jewess or of Ivanhoe's chivalrous gesture that freed her of the charge of sorcery so that she could flee unwed to Spain. *The Spy* (1821), James Fenimore Cooper's account of patriots and British, moved along nicely—until the denouement (chapter 34) revealed, beneath the guise of the ever-helpful Mr. Harper, the majestic figure of George Washington.

The important test the characters Scott and Cooper invented fail to pass is not that of accuracy, but of plausibility. There is no evidence that Rebecca or George behaved in the storybook fashion; and, even considered purely as figures of fiction, they never come alive as medieval woman or Virginia gentleman. They are the products not of imagination, which seeks understanding of real people, but of fantasy, which gratifies the moods of author and reader. Such wish-fulfilling stock figures, whether or not adorned with the names of actual personages, offer the novelists an escape from the responsibilities of their craft by softening the task of persuasion. A myth shared with the audience—of the mysterious dark beauty or of the Father of His Country—wins acquiescence and draws attention away from the problems of plot.

The hacks who churned out popular novels in the nineteenth and twentieth centuries had less regard than did Scott and Cooper for either literary or historical accuracy and yielded more readily to the languorous temptations of myth. This was not a certain means of entry to the best-seller lists, but it was more likely to win rewards than painstaking craftsmanship; witness Lew Wallace's *Ben Hur* (1880). In the 1930s and 1940s Margaret Mitchell, Kenneth Roberts, and Howard Fast, in their various fashions, demonstrated the profitability of work of this sort.[2]

Although they differed widely in political orientation, literary quality, and size, as well as in subject matter and distance from the truth, these books shared common defects so that almost any one was representative of the others. *The American* was run-of-the-mill Howard Fast—not his best book, not his worst.[3] Its central

---

[2] Kenneth Roberts, *Arundel* (Garden City, N.Y., 1933), *Rabble in Arms* (Garden City, N.Y., 1933), *Northwest Passage* (Garden City, N.Y., 1937), and *Oliver Wiswell* (New York, 1940).

[3] Howard Fast, *American: A Middle Western Legend* (New York, 1946); Oscar Handlin, "Fake," *Commentary* II (September 1946), 295 ff.

figure was John Peter Altgeld, whose career followed the traditional American scheme of success. Immigration as an infant,
youth on a harsh, marginal farm, and a start in life through
desultory, debilitating day-labor were the somber background;
ultimate prosperity as a corporation lawyer and real estate op-
erator, public popularity as a politician, and the crowning reward
of high office—governorship of the state of Illinois—were the
luminous relief.

The significance of the man, however, lay not so much in the
extent of his conformity to the expected pattern as in three devia-
tions from it: an enlightened and progressive study of criminality;
a pardon, granted in the face of violent disapproval, to the An-
archists unjustly convicted of the Haymarket riot; and leadership
in the movement that temporarily took control of the Democratic
Party away from the conservative Grover Cleveland. Altgeld's life
was well worth examination for the light it shed on the development of American personality and for its reflections on the general
character of politics in the United States at the end of the nineteenth century.

Fast's book satisfied in neither respect. He did not intend it to
be a biography of course. The jacket referred to it as a novel; the
subtitle, with unconscious humor, as a legend. However considered, it failed, because it coasted along on the commonplace myth
of hero against the interests, and thus passed by the opportunity
to examine Altgeld's uniqueness as a subject, for fiction or for
history.

The same rigorous canons of evidence that fetter a history do
not bind a work of fiction. The novelist is free to make substantial changes in the order of events. He may omit what does not
fit; here, for instance, there is no mention of the court case in
which the Haymarket judge earned Altgeld's hostility, or of the
macabre foundation for the hysteria after the riot—the bomb sent
by the anarchist August Spies to a newspaper editor as a lunatic
joke. Similarly, the author may alter incidents, as when the suicide of one of the condemned men is turned into a murder by
prison guards. Again, there is no reason why the characters should
stand in the same relationship to each other as they did in actual
life: thus, Altgeld is made to despise rather than to court Samuel
Gompers.

By labeling his work fiction, Fast claimed immunity for such liberties with the factual past. But he could not so readily evade another order of obligations.

Even a novel should display a sense of the time and the place in which its incidents occur. *The American* lacks that quality in its most rudimentary forms. It shows no feeling at all for decor. The characters walk about without clothing, in unfurnished rooms, and speak a neutral, colorless language. Occasional half-hearted attempts to satisfy that deficiency lead to egregious blunders. In a conversation on literature, Altgeld expresses admiration for Tolstoy and Mark Twain and contempt for Dickens—a preference extremely improbable in a man of his period and position, and one that runs counter to Altgeld's own remarks on the subject. When it comes to broader social issues, such as immigration, industrialization, and urbanization, or to political problems, such as those posed by populism or free silver, there is only pathetic and transparent ignorance.

More important, Fast's characters lacked character; they acted without motivation and without meaning. In the case of the protagonist, there was no insight into the forces that drove a successful lawyer and politician into unconventional and unpopular measures. In the case of the opposition, there was not even a pretense of understanding. Cleveland behaved as he did because he sold out "to monopoly." But why he, and why not Altgeld? The monopolists themselves—Pullman, Armour and Field—were simple, demoniacal powers, shivering, between orgies in the Union League Club, at the very hint of painfully innocuous reform proposals. There was no need to account for the motions of lay-figures; their joints moved in response to the simple will of their creator.

Other stories in the same genre displayed similar failings, to a greater or lesser extent, depending upon the skill and the conscientiousness of the authors. Willingness to let actuality yield to myth was the key to their conceptions of the historical novel. The novelist who knew the craft, who understood the feelings of men and women, had no need to endow characters with the names of actual people. The characters themselves were real people: Andrey Bolkonsky as much so as Kutuzov, Conte Mosca as much so as Prince Metternich. But in a work whose every page screamed fake, the names of men who once lived were essential, because only the names were real.

The most important cultural and social forces of the 1960s and 1970s pressed novelists away from depictions of reality, toward mythical expression. The general loosening of narrative forms diminished the value of rationality and coherence; the critical standards that accepted William S. Burroughs and Thomas Pynchon were not such as to put a premium on older concepts of causation and motivation. In a world entirely askew, distortion was the rule. With every perception partial and erroneous, with actuality as phantom as fantasy, it mattered not in the least for purposes of expression whether or not some abstract, real, truth existed beyond the haze.

Not truth, but the appearance of truth, mattered, for it legitimized the qualities most salable in a sensate society. The brutal sexual shocks and the physical violence, for a time unacceptable as ends in themselves, lost the taint of forbiddenness when attached to historical personages. And, since American law in effect excluded any redress for slander and libel, writers felt free to make any association they desired as a way to wash down the hot stuff. Adolescents of ordinary intelligence would have recognized the absurdity of Alan Lelchuck's incident which sent a bullet through the anus of a rival author, but for the arbitrary ascription of the buttocks to Norman Mailer, a joke so chuckle-worthy as to obscure the ludicrousness of the whole account.[4]

The worth of an appearance of truth also accounted for the strenuous effort to equip the novels with enough furnishings, accurate in detail and brand, to conceal the sleight of hand in the treatment of more important matters—the progression of events and the development of character. E. L. Doctorow's readers learn that the Boston and Maine Railroad ran Baldwin 4-6-0 locomotives, and the Army, Reo pagoda-hooded trucks; they meet names known from headlines and history books; their vigilance drops, and they accept the fraudulent concoction as an approximation of reality. It was an old trick of journalists to throw in all

4 Alan Lelchuck, *American Mischief* (New York, 1973) , 292.

the little stuff—color of socks, flowers in the neighbor's garden, reaction of the kid across the street—so that even subscribers who never learned what happened at least got the feeling of being there.

On the other hand, there was no worth at all to the truth, as such, whatever that was. The past, as in Martin Duberman's drama of 1970 *The Memory Bank,* became a vast mechanical force in the background manipulable by the dominant actors in the foreground. The modern author had tasted enough of anthropology, at first or second hand, to have acquired a liking for relativism. Every culture had its myths, one as good as another. Each had its uses; and the historical novelist, having decided what he wished to say, needed only to lace the narrative with enough sex and violence to move his puppets along toward the chosen goal. An academic audience listened placidly in 1977 while Doctorow announced that he knew things "in an intuitive manner," so that whatever resonated within him was a fact, while "any such thing as truth in the factual sense" was very destructive. "Politicians, journalists, and historians" had "always made up history." The right belonged to novelists as well.[5]

The myth chosen after 1960 accorded with the temper of the times. Gone was the celebration of the United States as symbol of democracy, liberty, equality—a symbol so compelling only a generation earlier that, for the then-radical, Communism had been twentieth-century Americanism. Now the guiding theme more likely was Amerika, land whence every evil flowed, home of lust and exploitation. That simple notion provided Gore Vidal with the material for a succession of empty stories, perverse in their view of the past and empty of all emotion but spite. *Burr* (1973), he claimed, "was history and not invention," although he claimed also the privilege of keeping Edward Livingston alive for two months, for convenience's sake. But it was not history to endow Aaron Burr with two illegitimate sons, one imaginary, one Martin Van Buren; nor was there evidence historians accepted that Jef-

5 "Ragtime Revisited: A Seminar with E. L. Doctorow and Joseph Papaleo," *Nieman Reports,* XXI (Summer/Autumn 1977), 4, 49.

ferson had fathered a brood of mulattos, or that Washington was a bungling incompetent. The inventions disguised the poisonous portrayal of the early Republic in a fantastic tale of corruption, greed, and sex. A no-more-plausible rerun, *1876,* celebrated the bicentennial (1976).

With the fashion set, younger writers trailed along—no need for holding back on any target in an unending open season on any game, and truth the universal victim. Tyler Bowen, *The Last Best Hope* before everything fell apart, moves from the McCarthy campaign of 1968 to Kent State, waiting for some divine hero, while Peter Tauber's novel (1977) drags from wisecrack to wisecrack, with a little rape here and a little violence there. Racial prejudice is the crutch on which Doctorow's *Ragtime* (1975) limps along. Robert Coover's *The Public Burning* (1977) heaps the whole fraudulent pile together: Uncle Sam Slick the Yankee Peddler; Richard Nixon, plagued by sexual and digestive inadequacies, who falls in love with Ethel Rosenberg; and the orgy at the public execution of the two innocent idealists. Never mind the absolute factual inaccuracy—it really did not happen that way —but consider the mindlessness of the fantasy which dreams it did, the literary pauperism which stoops to shoveling it up, and the critical gullibility which swallows it.

By the 1970s such novels competed with the avowed trash— John Craig's *In Council Rooms Apart* (1971), or R. M. Koster's *Dissertation* (1975), or Jeffrey Archer's *Shall We Tell the President?* (1977)—riots of James Bondish conspiratorial derring-do, embellished with real names but with no pretense to authenticity. On paperback racks they struggled for space with *romans à clef* by Harold Robbins and Jacqueline Susann, which made a pretense to authenticity although unembellished with real names. Disaster films shared the same market. Blazing infernos, sinking vessels, macroscopic or microscopic creatures let loose upon the earth raised the shock threshold to ever higher levels, so that the harried hucksters, driven to escalation, could cling to shreds of credibility only by costuming their monsters in borrowed historical garments.

Perhaps this reaching for the new-model myth of evil Amerika responded to the longing of people in a time of stress and terror to hold to something from the past, a longing of a piece with the fitful waves of nostalgia that periodically swept the country. And in their ignorance of the past, while straining to forget the lackluster present, with the future too horrible to ponder, such people found only ghosts, whispers, and shadows to absorb their longing. Perhaps so, although that was probably only part of the explanation. Another part originated in the pervasive anti-Americanism of the fashion-setting intellectuals of the second half of the twentieth century. The balance emanated from the marketplace to which the vendors brought their books.[6]

Writers for whom fame and fortune were the spurs typed away in vain so long as they imagined that some benevolent process would convey their words to a reader who would appraise their worth. Not words, but pictures, lay at the end of the rainbow; and for a chance at the jackpot, editors, publishers, and agents knowledgeable about subsidiary, residual, and rerun rights involved themselves from the germ of an idea to its maturation. The mechanism which made Peter Benchley the author of *Jaws,* or which converted Mario Puzo from the sensitive author of the *Fortunate Pilgrim* (1964) to the manufacturer of the shiny *Godfather,* effaced the line between truth and untruth and nurtured the current myth.[7]

A new commodity—not fact, not fiction—preempted the market, with the pretense of historicity concealing every deficiency of plot and character, and the storyteller's license justifying departures from the record. Truman Capote's *In Cold Blood* (1965) wandered off from the evidence at the will of its author, although ostensibly it treated an actual incident, just as John Ehrlichman's *The Company* (1976) compensated for its worthlessness as a story by the credentials of a compiler cognizant of the events and personalities in the narrative. Puzo candidly described how he fabricated *The Godfather* "to make money" and toward that end calculatedly built "Vietnam and big business parallels" into the story. The faction genre accorded well with the television medium, which edited brief discontinuous segments into attention-grabbing sequences that left viewers drained of emotion but lulled by vague general, though incoherent, impressions. The labyrinthine plots of *Washington behind Closed Doors* (1977) or *Truman at Potsdam* (1977) and other TV docudramas were

[6] See William Styron, *Set This House on Fire* (New York, 1960), 18; Oscar Handlin, "Liberal Democracy and the Image of America," *Freedom at Issue,* no. 43 (November 1977), 11 ff.

[7] Ted Morgan, "Sharks," *New York Times Magazine,* April 21, 1974, 10 ff. (62 ff.).

no more drawbacks than was their historical inaccuracy. In 1978 Young Joe Kennedy, Lee Harvey Oswald, and the Lincoln Conspiracy were on the way.[8]

༄

The time had long since been right for application of the same techniques to ethnicity. The market cried for a book as laden with sex and violence as *Godfather,* like it, fiction suggested by fact and validated by history, but heated with a little racial spice.

Take a family, black not Italian. Trace it back to Southern origins, back to slavery days, back indeed to African progenitor. Your family, actual, recalled from grandmother's tales of suffering, striving, becomes the narrative none will dare question because you, the author, are its living witness.

Margaret Walker's *Jubilee* (1966) had been a premature and inadequate response to the opportunity. She had industriously recaptured her great-grandmother's stories, and she had conscientiously worked up the historical background. From Lukács she knew the appropriate models, and she had read Tolstoy and Scott. She wrote an honest, earnest novel about half devoted to life under slavery, about half to the problems of freedom.[9]

Alex Haley was the cleverer writer; and the advantage of time gave him critics whose faculties faction had dulled and an audience habituated to sensation, which the market apparatus of a *Reader's Digest* enterprise was prepared to deliver. In *Roots* (1976) he put together "a novelized amalgam of what" he knew took place and what his "researching led" him "to plausibly *feel* took place" (686). Claiming both the mantle of veracity and exemption from its rules, he disposed of space in a way that permitted him to devote about 85 percent of his attention to the period before the Civil War, the time least subject to reader verification, the time most readily freighted with nostalgia and fantasy for their benefit. Success in print and on the tube was the ample reward.

*Roots* and *Jubilee* share a good deal of material. The details of nineteenth-century plantation life—the slave celebration of Christ-

8 Mario Puzo, *Godfather Papers and Other Confessions* (New York, 1972), 33 ff., 250 ff.

9 Margaret Walker, *How I Wrote Jubilee* (Chicago, 1972).

mas, the food, the cries for gifts, and the relationships among the bondsmen are remarkably similar. Vyry, the bastard of her master, who became a companion to Miss Lillian, bears a striking resemblance to Lil Kizzy; and the artisans Randall Ware and Tom are much alike, although one is slave, the other free. The role of the cook, the contempt of the house people for the field hands, the poor whites, and the attitudes toward religion are the same in both books.

The respects in which the two differed no doubt accounted for the greater popularity of *Roots*. By foreshortening the recent past, Haley escaped the difficulties of explaining plausibly the century just before he wrote. For the period before the Civil War his narrative edged away from historical evidence. The black characters used twentieth-century jargon, were literate, politically oriented, abreast of world affairs, and rebellious, while the whites, described from the perspective of the slaves, were inhuman caricatures. Walker's account was truer to the record, her people better rounded and more credible, her plot less violent and more plausible—all attributes which diminished marketability.

Because Walker knew little about their antecedents, *Jubilee* began with the arrival of her family in America. Haley had no such scruples; he invented an idyllic homeland and described it in elaborate detail, that proved inaccurate wherever evidence was available. The people of his village did not raise rice or practice monogamy; they did not use place names later invented by imperialists; they had no concept of "Africa," nor did they regard all "Africans" as brothers. Nor was bondage a status inflicted by whites upon blacks. Slaves were the most lucrative export of indigenous traders and the people of Juffure were active middlemen in the business. Haley's Kunta Kinte is not a man of the eighteenth-century West African coast, but a twentieth-century civil-rights activist. And the pages devoted to him falsify actuality to capitalize on the sense of guilt and grievance of the potential audience. The television version took substantial liberties with the original text—but not in the direction of correcting it.

Few critics were so obtuse as to fail to note the defects of *Roots*. Historians and anthropologists pointed out its crude errors of fact. Literary types conceded that it was "romantic and melodramatic, its characters . . . in many ways unconvincing and unreal." But, they hastened to add, none of that disturbed "its larger

human truth."[10] It was not an American but an English reporter
who took the trouble to follow Haley's tracks back to Gambia
and to reveal the deceptive nature of the account of Kunta Kinte's
origins. Even then, historians shrugged the revelations off: every
people deserved a myth. And indeed, in 1977 Atlanta bookstores
displayed *Roots* and *Gone with the Wind* side by side, giving
buyers their choice of fantasy.[11]

Truth and understanding are the first casualties of this happy-
go-lucky manipulation of the facts. To compare *Roots* with *Uncle
Tom's Cabin,* as some commentators did, was to miss the point:
Harriet Beecher Stowe stayed within the record's limits because
she had absolute faith that the facts honestly told would make
her case, and more than a century of research has not faulted her
in detail. Even in the case of Styron's *Nat Turner,* the failings
were less those of historicity than of imagination and of characterization.

The myth never does justice to the real people of the past.
Along the coast of eighteenth-century Africa the trade in slaves
involved blacks and whites very different from their descendents
two centuries later, just as the nineteenth-century American plantation bound masters and slaves not at all the same as the men
and women who bore their names generations later. The victims
of wish-fulfilling impulses who dress up their ancestors in borrowed garments deny the dignity of those who really then lived
and died but remain unrecognized.

Call it fiction, call it history, such a book does not further, but
impedes, the understanding of both past and present. Better the
novels with no pretense of historicity which tell the truth by an
honest stretch of the imagination, as John Hersey's *White Lotus*
(1965) does about slavery, or Joseph Conrad's *Heart of Darkness*
(1902) and E. M. Forster's *Passage to India* (1924) do about race
prejudice.

---

10 Meg Greenfield, "Uncle Tom's Roots," *Newsweek,* 89. (Feb. 14, 1977), 100.
See also R. Grann Lloyd, "Defining the Situation," *Negro Educational Review,*
XXVIII (April 1977), 58 ff.; Russell Warren Howe, "An Elusive Past," *New
Leader,* LX (Jan. 3, 1977), 23 ff.; Benjamin DeMott, "Culture Watch," *The At-
lantic,* CCXXXIX (May 1977), 88 ff.; Marvin Kitman, "Mighty Miniseries," *New
Leader,* LX (Feb. 14, 1977), 25.

11 Mark Ottaway, "Tangled Roots," *Sunday Times,* April 10, 1977, pp. 17, 21;
*New York Times,* April 10, 1977; Renato Berger, "Der 'Roots'-Mythos im afrika-
nischen Kontext," *Neue Züricher Zeitung,* Dec. 31, 1977 (Nr. 307), 4.

# 16

## *Ethnicity and the New History*

THE ABILITY to treat problems of ethnic development in the United States tested the aptitude for relevance of scholars who enlisted under the banner of the New History and consciously dedicated themselves both to the service of society and to description of the common people.

In the twentieth century the term "New History" became the rallying cry of historians who sought to analyze the interplay of economic, social, and geographic factors with politics, institutions, and ideas. Although they did not form a unified school, and although they pursued a variety of interpretive schemes, they shared a general tendency to emphasize the experience of the ordinary men and women of the past. The approach was stimulating, not only because it brought scholars into contact with fresh material and forced them to develop novel techniques of research, but also because it seemed by stripping away surface forms to reveal the naked reality of life.[1] By 1920 the practitioners of the New History not only had gained academic respectability; they were well on the way to the professional dominance which they long retained. They produced exciting monographs and moved into commanding posts in the leading universities.

Detached from its own rhetorical manifestos, however, the New History was neither so new as it claimed to be, nor as linked to the assumptions of a particular era as its critics charged. It still exercised influence in the 1970s, and its antecedents reached far back to the first efforts to chronicle the American past. Its practitioners, like other students of American social history, had to describe the

[1] Oscar and Mary F. Handlin, "New History and the Ethnic Factor in American Life," *Perspectives in American History,* IV (1970) , 5 ff.; Chapter 3 at note 40.

character of the people, that is, they had to revert to the issue of national identity. Preoccupation with that subject nurtured a belief in the unique purpose of the New World as a field for the contest of good and evil, of heroes and villains.

Twentieth-century scholars, confident that they had made an altogether new start, were unaware of the intellectual assumptions they shared with remote predecessors. Differences in style and technique concealed thematic continuities. The New Historians believed that professionalization, precise research standards, and incorporation among the social sciences had carried them far from their literary forerunners. Their subject was a counterpart of the laboratory, a source of data by which to test the theories of economists, political theorists, and sociologists and thus serve society.

The ethnic elements in the American experience deserved a central place in the New History. Voluntary and involuntary immigration, along with the frontier and urbanization, produced a constant shifting in the country's population; and the consequences endured far beyond the lifetimes of the men and women who made the crossing to the New World. Operating within the distinctive patterns of political and economic organization in the United States, immigration emphasized the pluralism of American society and, at the same time, contributed to the continuing instability and fluidity of family, cultural, and communal life. These topics had special interest for the New History; they received considerable attention in *The History of American Life* series, and they appeared frequently in the hortatory catalogues of needs and opportunities with which scholars urged themselves and their students onward. Moreover, rapid changes within their society presented them with an opportunity for reconsidering basic judgments about race and nationality, long a part of their canon. A few rose to the occasion. Yet, as a group, they faced up to the challenge only partially and inadequately. Inertia, derived from the hesitation to cast loose from traditional approaches, and excessive preoccupation with utility prevented them from making greater contributions.

The obstacles to success were not inherent in the discipline. Unlike European scholars, who then only rarely ventured to deal with the recent past, Americans were acutely sensitive to the issues of their own times. Unfortunately, present-mindedness and an orientation toward social science were as often impediments as aids.

Research into migration and group life had a bearing on the understanding of prejudice, one of the great problems of the twentieth century. The United States was, after all, a nation of nations, already in the nineteenth century a microcosm of the tense world of the 1950s or 1970s. In treating this set of issues, historians stood in a strategic position. Handling specific cases in diverse situations, they could consider the variables which produced conflict or cooperation and evaluate the consequences of differences in the context, thus adding depth to the concept of prejudice. Yankees of the 1790s expressed hostility toward Yorkers, Englishmen, Frenchmen, Papists, Jews, Indians, and Negroes, but found intermarriage more tolerable with some groups than with others, for significant distinctions controlled the salience and intensity of sentiments, all of which might vaguely be denominated prejudice. Social and cultural forces produced differences in attitude and in permissible degree of contact.

Historical analysis could also reveal the elements of dynamic change. The Quakers, once hounded out of Boston, in time became respected citizens there. The Quadroons, prominent in New Orleans society early in the nineteenth century, in time became figures of shame. Communities which eagerly sought to convert and assimilate Jews in the 1850s, as eagerly sought to exclude and segregate them after 1900. Race for Bancroft had a meaning entirely different than for Burgess. Attitudes were not fixed or immutable, but responded to pressures subject to historical analysis.[2]

The historical context could open a view of intergroup hostility unobstructed by the observer's need to identify with either victim or agent. Treating the past, the scholar could discern the unrevealed motives, the ambiguities, the shortsightedness, and the errors that consciously or unconsciously subjected heroes as well as villains to the pressure of prejudice, which was not an attribute of the evil or weak, but a human failing to which many yielded. American history was full of examples of conflict in which the issues were defined along no clear Manichean line.

American history was also replete with examples of the resolu-

2 See Chapter 7 at note 21.

tion of conflict. In the long run, the multitude of peoples in this society achieved a basis of understanding and cooperation more important than the disputes that marked the way to it. It required no commitment to any particular ideology of pluralism to grasp the potentialities of investigation into the nonpathological aspects of intergroup relations which abated tension, furthered tolerance, and created the conditions of cooperation.

These subjects cried unheeded for attention by social historians, who diverted their attention to other matters of more immediate concern. Down through the first quarter of the twentieth century they concentrated upon two issues of group life—Reconstruction and immigration restriction—that had agitated Americans since the 1890s, that is, precisely in the period of historical professionalization. Both problems receded slowly from the public consciousness in the 1920s, but each occupied the attention of scholars for two decades more.

The tragic failure of Reconstruction had raised the question of whether Negroes as a group were capable of acting as equals and citizens in a democracy. Before the turn of the century, the dominant historical interpretation explained the inability to bring the Civil War to an end that justified its costs by racial inferiority, drawing upon the then current theories of the social and biological sciences. To the reader of the 1970s the writings of John W. Burgess, of William A. Dunning, and of their followers conveyed a curious, antique impression. It seemed scarcely credible that a sincere racist commitment swayed their authors. But it did, no doubt in part out of the persistent Manicheanism of American thought. Since history was a contest of heroes and villains, failures followed from someone's sin; and the Negro was cast as sinner. Yet the works that expressed these views were products of serious scholarship, had respectable scientific underpinnings, and earned respect as useful contributions to the solution of current problems.

The first generation of professional historians converted judgments about the outcome of the Civil War into questions about its causes. The undesirable outcome suggested that perhaps the conflict was needless. The Negro not fit for freedom after Appomattox certainly did not deserve it before Sumter. Some reinterpretations treated the abolitionists as reckless agitators disruptive of social order, while slavery became an institution appropriate to the capabilities of black men. Others traced the effort of an aggressive Northern capitalism to eliminate Southern agrarianism.[3]

In the 1930s some scholars had difficulty reconciling the covert racism in these interpretations with the empirical evidence. Yet the only open attack in that decade, W. E. B. DuBois's Marxist interpretation, evoked little response among academic historians. Racist overtones still ran through the most widely used account in that period, that of J. G. Randall.[4]

Directly and indirectly, racism also affected the historiography of American immigration. In a world of biologically distinct species, the natives of Sicily were as distinct from those of Norway as either were from those of the Gold Coast. Impure blood, whether from Europe or from Africa, threatened the Anglo-Saxon stock. The restrictionist argument had immediate import in the agitation for immigration restriction and also markedly influenced academic historians. Casual assumptions about innate Anglo-Saxon superiority and about the racial differences between the old and new immigrants uncritically penetrated the writing of the period. Scholars who adopted the racist interpretations were not simply yielding to personal prejudice, but had the support of the best-informed science of their times.

Even those who challenged the dominant tendency generally accepted its premises. The dissenters usually sought to justify a particular group, or immigrants in general, by pointing to their constructive contributions to American society. Implicitly A. B. Faust and the authors of similar works subjected the newcomers to the test of merit, though differing from the restrictionists in rendering a positive rather than a negative verdict. Historians who came to the defense of Negroes formulated the issue in the same way.[5]

Those who argued the merits of a favored ethnic stock did not

---

[3] Avery O. Craven, *Repressible Conflict* (Baton Rouge, La., 1939); Arthur M. Schlesinger, Jr., "Causes of the Civil War," *Partisan Review*, XVI (October 1949), 969 ff.; Thomas J. Pressly, *Americans Interpret Their Civil War* (Princeton, 1954).

[4] James G. Randall, *Civil War and Reconstruction* (Boston, 1937).

[5] Edward N. Saveth, *American Historians and European Immigrants* (New York, 1948), 202 ff.; George W. Williams, *History of the Negro Race in America*, 2 vols. (New York, 1882); Carter G. Woodson, *Negro in Our History* (Washington, 1922); A. B. Faust, *German Element in the United States,* 2 vols. (Boston, 1909).

describe the mass of Negroes, or of German, Scotch-Irish, or Jewish immigrants as they really were, but ascribed to them, or to
exceptional individuals among them, the characteristics of the
dominant image of the ideal American: patriotism, individualism,
love of liberty, and the ability to get ahead. The authors of such
books portrayed the ancestors they wished they had rather than
those of actuality.

In the 1920s political decisions settled the question of restriction, and the discussion moved to a somewhat higher plane. The
academics who then turned to the subject did so with more skill
and more control than their predecessors. But A. M. Schlesinger
and Carl Wittke, though properly critical of earlier efforts, still
worried about immigrant contributions. The scholars of their
generation rarely commanded the languages with which to approach the sources of neglected elements of the population; and
the felt obligation to refute a previous generation's racism locked
them into concepts of assimilation tested by contributions. The
ascendancy of the New Historians, therefore, did little to alter
familiar habits of thought. Restriction, like Reconstruction, remained deeply embedded in the writers' consciousness long after
the issues had lost relevance.[6]

The 1930s offered historians an opportunity to escape from the
treadmill of inherited issues. Corrective elements in their own
discipline and the loss of immediate public interest freed them to
explore neglected aspects of the ethnic past. Already, monographic
research on the experience of Negroes under slavery and Reconstruction had cast doubt upon the dominant general interpretive
assumptions, not enough for any large revisionary synthesis, but
leverage for a subsequent review of the old position.[7]

Furthermore, a fresh generation of scholars, reared on the New
History, refused to view Reconstruction and immigration simply
as subjects of governmental decision, but sought to trace the broad

---

[6] Arthur M. Schlesinger, *New Viewpoints in American History* (New York, 1922) ;
Carl Wittke, *We Who Built America* (New York, 1939) .

[7] See Howard K. Beale, "On Rewriting Reconstruction History," *American Historical Review,* XLV (July 1940) , 807 ff.

range of forces that played upon the character of the whole population. The crucial questions for them did not concern the wisdom of the policies of radical Reconstruction or immigration restriction, but rather their social, economic, and cultural context. In the 1930s also the racism of earlier writers lost academic standing; and the very term "race" dropped out of fashion.

Once the innate deficiencies of the Negroes and the new immigrants ceased to explain the failure of Reconstruction or the need for restriction, then the possibility opened that the causative elements might lie not in the groups discriminated against, but in those that discriminated. In other words, historians arrived at a point at which they could begin to examine the meaning of prejudice and of group life in America. The results were evident in the work of two young scholars just before the Second World War. Paul Herman Buck dealt with the difficulties of post-Civil War adjustment in the light of a wide array of social and cultural factors. And Marcus Lee Hansen subordinated the immigrant contributions to a larger consideration of the major elements in the transfer of cultures.[8]

The New Deal and the Second World War heightened awareness of the diversity of the American population. It should, therefore, have stimulated fresh investigations into its past. Changes in the discipline of anthropology should have had the same effect. But, although self-congratulatory chronicles of contributions remained popular, few studies yielded satisfying information or insights. Occasional racist slurs in the 1940s and 1950s were less troubling than the failure of scholars during those decades fully to apply the techniques of the New History to the ethnic element in the American past. Not even the students of the borderlands— H. E. Bolton and his successors—grasped the opportunity to examine the regional mingling of cultures.[9]

The most satisfactory results appeared in monographs focused

---

[8] Paul H. Buck, *Road to Reunion* (Boston, 1937) ; Marcus L. Hansen, *Atlantic Migration* (Cambridge, 1940) ; Caroline F. Ware, ed., *Cultural Approach to History* (New York, 1940) , 62 ff.

[9] F. J. Brown and J. S. Roucek, *One America* (New York, 1945) ; Louis Adamic, *Nation of Nations* (New York, 1945) ; E. M. Coulter, *Confederate States of America* (Baton Rouge, La., 1950) ; Henry Pratt Fairchild, *Race and Nationality as Factors in American Life* (New York, 1947) .

on specific issues, which held closely to the materials and dealt empirically with concrete problems. Broad treatments that called for more extended analysis were less successful. Examinations of the interplay of personal and group interests, of ideology and social instability, and of conflicts of personality revealed the subtle development of prejudice. Barbara M. Solomon thus treated the Boston Brahmins and Charlotte Erickson, the organized labor movement at the end of the nineteenth century. David Levin, William Stanton, and C. Vann Woodward threw light on hostility toward Catholics and on segregation as an instrument of Negro debasement; detailed descriptions of various urban communities isolated areas of conflict and sources of tension; and studies of particular ethnic groups traced the adjustment by newcomers to the American environment. Such works outlined the elements conducive to cooperation as well as to hostility and yielded perceptive insights into both long- and short-term forces capable of modifying habits and beliefs. The coverage was fragmentary, however. Apart from accounts of the Greeks by Theodore Saloutos and of the Slavic miners by Victor R. Greene, the best of them dealt with the older immigrants. For the Poles and the Italians it long was necessary to look back to contemporary analyses by sociologists and economists. The past of black people remained virtually unknown; indigenous Indians stayed in the province of anthropologists; Gunther P. Barth's was an isolated investigation of the Orientals; and no Southern or Western cities received a treatment comparable to those of New York and Boston.[10]

⁓

In the mid-1960s the situation changed. The civil rights movement and the revival of ethnicity called attention to long-neglected aspects of the American past and unloosed a flood of books, both general and specialized. Early in the 1970s black and ethnic history

[10] Gunther P. Barth, *Bitter Strength* (Cambridge, 1964); Charlotte Erickson, *American Industry and European Immigrants* (Cambridge, 1957); Victor R. Greene, *Slavic Community on Strike* (Notre Dame, Ind., 1968); David Levin, *History as Romantic Art* (Stanford, 1959); Theodore Saloutos, *Greeks in the United States* (Cambridge, 1964); Barbara M. Solomon, *Ancestors and Immigrants* (Cambridge, 1956); William Stanton, *Leopard's Spots* (Chicago, 1960); C. Vann Woodward, *Strange Career of Jim Crow* (New York, 1955). See also Oscar Handlin, "Twenty Year Retrospect of American Jewish Historiography," *American Jewish Historical Quarterly,* LXV (June 1976), 295 ff.

were the most popular fields of teaching, publication, and research. The tide of print that mounted steadily after 1965 contained much of value, but also a good deal twisted out of shape by the circumstances of composition. Far too often the imperative to relevance obstructed the channels of thought and prevented scholars from making the most of their material.

The sense of ethnocentric grievance that suffused the real world of these decades spilled over into scholarship. All past historiography victimized the underprivileged, just as all past experience had. Robert Berkhofer demanded an "Indian-centered history," and Robert Starobin a Negro-centered one. Some writers campaigned for a "usable black past," while a panel of respectable scholars, historians among them, asserted that the United States was "not so much 'a nation of immigrants' as . . . a nation of immigrant groups."[11]

The blanket indictment blinded many writers to earlier sympathetic treatments of Indians and Africans. Yet, without understanding why an eighteenth-century historian of South Carolina, condemning slavery, explained that nature gave "the people of one continent no superiority over those of the other," it was not possible to understand the later claim to that very innate superiority.[12]

11 Shirley Teper, *Ethnicity, Race, and Human Development: Report on the State of Our Knowledge* (New York, 1977), 14; Robert Starobin, "Negro: a Central Theme in American History," *Journal of Contemporary History*, III (January 1968), 37 ff.; Robert F. Berkhofer, Jr., "Native Americans and United States History," in William H. Cartwright and Richard L. Watson, Jr., *Reinterpretation of American History* (Washington, 1973), 37 ff.; John W. Blassingame, "Afro-Americans: From Mythology to Reality," *ibid.*, 53 ff.; Rodolfo Acuña, "Freedom in a Cage: The Subjugation of the Chicano in the United States," *ibid.*, 113 ff. Rudolph J. Vecoli, "Ethnicity: a Neglected Dimension of American History," in Herbert J. Bass, ed., *State of American History* (Chicago, 1970), 70 ff. For a variety of expressions of the general revival of ethnicity and race consciousness, see Geno Baroni, "America Needs Ethnicity," *Perspectives*, VII (1977), 321; "Rewrite of the American Experience," *Journal*, VII (1969); Michael John Arlen, *Passage to Ararat* (New York, 1975); John Gregory Dunne, *True Confessions* (New York, 1977); Richard Gambino, *Blood of My Blood* (New York, 1974); Andrew Greeley, *Why Can't They Be Like Us?* (New York, 1969); Irving Howe, *World of Our Fathers* (New York, 1976); Dan Rottenberg, *Finding Our Fathers* (New York, 1977). See also Nathan Glazer and Daniel P. Moynihan, *Ethnicity* (Cambridge, 1975); Oscar Handlin, "Nationhood, Self-Identity, and Ethnicity: An American Dilemma," *Cultures*, V, no. 2 (1978).

12 Alexander Hewatt, *Historical Account of the Rise and Progress of the Colonies of South Carolina and Georgia*, 2 vols. (London, 1779), I, 24; Samuel Williams, *Natural and Civil History of Vermont* (Walpole, N.H., 1794), 133 ff.; Robert Beverley, *History of Virginia* (Chapel Hill, N.C., 1947), 38 ff., bk III.

The result frequently was a slide into apologetics, compounded of pride and a false claim to uniqueness and expressed in a reversion to the boastful catalogue of contributions—only now not so much by great, as by common men and women. The crowning injustice to people of the past who had suffered much was to falsify their history to gratify the passions of their descendants. A practical claim sustained the impulse; the greater the victimization and services of the past, the greater the right to future reparations. But the stance had consequences damaging to scholarship.

It identified ethnicity with underprivileged minority status, thereby obscuring its significance among other elements of society, which also cherished an ancestral culture, tended toward endogamy, and preserved the recollection of common antecedents. Thus, John Higham distinguished the founders or settlers from later immigrants. The former established the core culture to which the latter, the ethnics of common usage, had to adapt. A German, Indian, or Mexican was an ethnic in Wisconsin, Minnesota, and California of 1850, but a Yankee was not, although all behaved in much the same way in transferring inherited behavior patterns from their places of origin. The newcomers simply assimilated with or blended into the core, which, however, unaccountably itself changed. For instance, Protestantism was certainly one of the salient elements in colonial culture; but in the nineteenth century "Americanism ceased to be Protestant." This point of view made necessary the obdurate insistence that all pluralistic views, from Crèvecoeur and Paine onward, were visions of the foreign-born.[13]

Had the image of the core not blinded them, historians might have found many clear statements of the process of adjustment—in a speech to an ethnic organization in 1915, for instance. Addressing the Daughters of the American Revolution, President Woodrow Wilson, always conscious of his own ethnicity, explained that the United States had not grown by the mere multiplication of the original stock, but also by the addition of strangers. "Men of all sorts . . . came to our shores with . . . a hunger for it such as some of us no longer felt." Strangers "came to remind us of what we had promised ourselves." The many and the one meshed

13 John Higham, *Send These to Me* (New York, 1975) , 5, 6, 21, 59 ff.

in the United States, not by virtue of any particular attributes of either the founders or the newcomers, but by virtue of the principles of liberty and of hope built into American institutions.[14]

An easy alternative to the polarity of core and ethnic was that of black and white, which historians accepted all the more readily after the civil rights struggle focused the concern of social scientists on the problems of color. The fact that most statistical data after 1940 fell into the categories of white and non-white, as well as the tactics of current controversy, eased acquiescence in the proposition that American population, past and present, fitted neatly into two distinct racial groups.

The fantasies of Staughton Lynd, who gratuitously made color the central issue of the last quarter of the eighteenth century, were less distressing than the tendency that flawed the more valuable efforts of serious scholars such as Gilbert Osofsky and Allan Spear. It may or may not have been correct to speak of "whites" or of the "white community" in New York or Chicago of the 1960s; it was grossly inaccurate to do so for those cities before 1930. In the repeated use of those terms, the historian forgot that they applied not to homogenous groupings, but to congeries of populations sharply divided among themselves.[15]

Historians who treated every group as static hopelessly distorted their analyses by the assumption that each of the differentiated categories had enough consistency to set it off from its contrast— non-Jew and non-Negro, as well as Jew and Negro. That formulation trapped the unwary. Lulled by the belief that black and white consistently carried the same connotations, Winthrop Jordan overlooked the significant changes of the seventeenth and eighteenth centuries. The unreliability of statistics and the fragmentary social evidence about mulattoes and about "passing" did not exempt historians from the obligation to recognize the existence of mis-

14 Woodrow Wilson, *Selected Literary and Political Papers* (New York, 1926), II, 132. George B. Tindall, *Ethnic Southerners* (Baton Rouge, La., 1976), is one of the few such treatments of a predominantly native group. However, see also the treatment of Yankees as ethnics in Sydney G. Fisher, *Making of Pennsylvania* (Philadelphia, 1896); Dixon Ryan Fox, *Yankees and Yorkers* (New York, 1940); also Dietmar Rothermund, *Layman's Progress* (Philadelphia, 1961), 113 ff.

15 Staughton Lynd, "Beyond Beard," in Barton J. Bernstein, ed., *Towards a New Past* (New York, 1968), 54 ff.; Gilbert Osofsky, *Harlem* (New York, 1966); Allan H. Spear, *Black Chicago* (Chicago, 1967).

cegenation or from taking account of black class and regional distinctions present through the nineteenth and twentieth centuries.
Nativity was always important, whether in Alabama, Oklahoma,
or Massachusetts, whether on the mainland or the West Indies,
whether in Haiti or Puerto Rico. Careful monographs did reveal
the difficulty of mobilizing group consciousness; yet few accounts
showed a due regard for the qualifications on the appropriateness
of considering blacks a coherent whole community.[16]

The same difficulty arose in allowing the terms Indian or Native American to hide profound tribal differences; or Jew to conceal Galicians and Syrians; or Italian, Sicilians and Venetians; or
non-Jew, ethnic and Wasp—to cover up the vast diversities of actuality. All these aggregative terms had some utility, greater or
lesser depending upon circumstances, but the amount should have
been the conclusion, not the starting point of scholarly inquiry. As
it was, they obscured the extent to which individuals moved across
or between lines, shared multiple identities, or remained totally
unaffiliated.

These complex, unstable, constantly changing groupings became
comprehensible only in their own context. Efforts to drag them
out of their past to serve some present purpose were self-defeating.

Disaster followed the tendency to read later definitions back
into the past. Perhaps it was not surprising, in the light of the
problems of their own times, that twentieth-century writers
treated the exclusionary practices of the 1880s and 1890s as the
first stage of anti-Semitism, particularly since the blame thereby
fell upon the bad guys. Yet the designation "non-Jews" said
nothing about the character of the group that sought to shut the
outsiders out of its clubs and hotels. The Brahmin society of Boston built its walls not to bar Israelites but to keep out such
Yankees as Silas Lapham; and the patrons of Saratoga's Grand
Union Hotel, which refused to admit Joseph Seligman, themselves

16 For the difficulties of defining black identity, see, e.g., Floyd J. Miller, *Search
for a Black Nationality: Black Emigration and Colonization, 1787–1863* (Urbana,
Ill., 1975); Tony Martin, *Race First: Ideological and Organizational Struggles of
Marcus Garvey and the Universal Negro Improvement Association* (Westport,
Conn., 1976), 273 ff., 344 ff.

found no welcome in the circles of New York's Four Hundred. The attitude toward Jews was incidental to a broader, unde-scribed, social adjustment.[17]

The laudable impulse toward informing public policy added to conceptual vagueness by shifting attention to the categories of the present and away from those of the past. Thus, an important study of the black family, intent upon testing and disproving the welfare propositions advanced by a government official in 1965, compiled a fascinating array of data reaching from 1750 to 1925. The quality of its samples and the validity of its interpretation received little critical attention. The book probably showed what it set out to show; but in doing so it neglected other, ultimately more impor-tant and significant, questions about the effects of migration, emancipation, mobility, and class upon the family.[18]

Present-mindedness, unfortunately, distorted the whole subject of slavery in the 1970s as in the 1870s. The true value of *Time on the Cross* and of *Roll, Jordan, Roll* lay neither in the statistical sophistication of the one, nor in the putative Marxism of the other, but in the extent that both approached an understanding of the social concommitants of a forced labor system; and both suffered from the compulsion to speak to the issues of the moment. Most of the vast published outpouring on blacks and slavery after 1965 was worse—faulty in research, poor in expression, and, for interpretation, decked out in the fashionable rags of the moment. By conflating race and bondage, by collapsing three hundred fifty years of history into a static present, they befogged the vital dy-namics of important human problems. Only the few scholars able to factor out the elements of guilt and wishfulness began to under-stand American slavery, racism, and the relation between them.

Slavery was African, and to some extent European, before it reached the New World. Yet it differed from one continent to another and from one century to another. The specific nature of black bondage in the pre-Civil War South is comprehensible only in the context of the evolving economy of the region and of its labor system, white as well as colored. Nevertheless, only a handful

---

17 Oscar and Mary F. Handlin, "Acquisition of Political and Social Rights by the Jews in the United States," *American Jewish Year Book*, LVI (1955) , 70 ff.

18 Herbert G. Gutman, *Black Family in Slavery and Freedom* (New York, 1976) .

of studies looked at the seventeenth and eighteenth centuries; and even they, by narrowing their vision to the blacks, tended to identify later with earlier forms, so that the relation of bondage to color, prejudice, and race remained unclear. For the nineteenth century the few fresh studies on slavery and on the urban Negro did not ease the difficulty of reasoned judgment about the degree of black rebelliousness, about the relation to abolitionism, about divisions among slaves, freemen, and freedmen, and about group cultural identity. Some, though not all, of the best work on the subject was the product of earlier years—or of foreigners able to maintain some distance from immediate issues.[19]

After 1965 the ambiguities of the civil rights movement, which won the allegiance of most historians, hindered understanding of the development of racism. The prevailing belief of the decade in the equality of rights of all persons carried the corollary assumption about the equal natural endowment of all. Given identical opportunities, all would behave in the same way, feel the same ambitions, and array themselves in callings proportionate to their total number. From that belief and assumption, it followed that any deviation from the general pattern which left some groups underrepresented in some endeavors was evidence of inequality of opportunity and of discrimination. But at the very same time, blacks, and later other ethnics, insisted upon their own particularity and distinctiveness and struggled determinedly to preserve their identities as against the homogenizing forces about them. The question resolutely evaded was, whether some particular life styles, attitudes, or cultural traits furthered or impeded social mo-

---

[19] Harmannus Hoetink, *Slavery and Race Relations in the Americas* (New York, 1973), 130 ff., 166 ff., struggles with the problems of unfree labor and with the influence of changing numbers on perceptions and prejudice, but gets tangled in needless theoretical complications. See also W. Kloosterboer, *Involuntary Labour since the Abolition of Slavery* (Leiden, 1960). Among the best works on these subjects are: Charles H. Nichols, *Many Thousand Gone* (Leiden, 1963); Willie Lee Rose, *Rehearsal for Reconstruction* (Indianapolis, Ind., 1964); John L. Eighmy, *Churches in Cultural Captivity* (Knoxville, Tenn., 1972); T. H. Breen, "Changing Labor Force and Race Relations in Virginia, 1660–1710," *Journal of Social History*, VII (Fall 1973), 3 ff.; Peter H. Wood, *Black Majority* (New York, 1974); and Robert Higgs, *Competition and Coercion: Blacks in the American Economy, 1865–1914* (New York, 1977). For *Time on the Cross*, see Chapter 8. Eugene Genovese, *Roll, Jordan, Roll* (New York, 1974), has value as a study of the system despite the paternalism with which it endows the masters and the collective consciousness of a black nation it imposes on the slaves.

bility and contributed to the disparity among occupational and income distributions.

In the context of the battles of the 1970s over place and privilege, the question was explosive. Politicians and activists understandably shied away from it, as did black and other ethnic intellectuals, who used the suffering of the masses as leverage to improve their own status. But scholars had other obligations; and their readiness to burrow away in the same unreflective fashion deprived them of the ability to cast light upon the problem. Instead they simply read present meanings into the past.

In the 1960s victimization explained everything; deprivation, failures to achieve, cultural inadequacies, and personal maladjustments, past as well as present—all ultimately originated in the society that corrupted its members. Differences in status were evidence of differences in degree of victimization. These terms most readily described the American Indians, earliest in the land and superficially at least the longest deprived; but slavery gave blacks a claim, as economic exploitation did Chicanos and the descendents of immigrants.

The result spoiled the fruit of potentially valuable research. Dee Brown and other popular writers perpetuated the old cowboy (cavalry) and Indian stories—though with the roles reversed. More important, serious scholarly efforts suffered from the same distortion. Berkhofer's study of Protestant missions disavowed any intention of passing moral judgments on the subject, yet it imputed low motives to the whites and condemned any interference with tribal organization. Francis Jennings in 1971 called for a turn away from legend to history, "from heroes and demons to conflicting persons," entangled in "a single process involving plural cultures and societies." The intention was admirable, the execution less so; and widespread acclaim measured not the worth of his book, but the masochistic impulses of its reviewers. Jennings' evidence would have sustained a portrayal of the Puritans as confused, well-intentioned, and incapable of adapting to differences a universalistic faith could not recognize. Instead they became pious hypocrites, their ideas "cant," who all along wanted to do the original inhabitants out of their land. Jennings made much of a change in terminology from settlement to conquest or invasion, although neither the new nor the old population thus conceived of the migration. And King Philip's War was not the culminating tragedy of the contact of clashing cultures, but a fiasco for the victors who had provoked it in hope of easy plunder. Since the atonement books pivoted on hostility to the whites, the portrayal of aboriginal culture varied with the preference of the author. For Jennings, the Indians were virtuous Yankee yeomen, who out-did the Puritans in frugality, industry, prudence, humanitarian-ism, cleanliness, peacefulness, and reasonableness. For Gary Nash, the tribesmen were California countercultural rebels, defenders of women's rights, and communist egalitarians—to say nothing of their anticipations of Freudianism.[20]

A few works rose above the polemic level; they recognized the tragedy of Indian defeat, displacement, and assimilation, but also the complexity and ambiguity of motives of those who forced them out. Bernard W. Sheehan understood that pressure on the tribes-men in the early nineteenth century stemmed not from racism, but from belief in the unity of mankind and in the equality of the Indians. A study of the reaction of three Cherokee leaders to the Jacksonian threat revealed the fallacy of treating removal in sim-ple good guys, bad fashion. Of course these judicious and unsen-sational books had no hope of winning such popular attention as rewarded Jennings, Nash, or Rogin, any more than Robert M.

20 Dee Brown, *Bury My Heart at Wounded Knee* (New York, 1970); Robert F. Berkhofer, Jr., *Salvation and the Savage* (Lexington, Ky., 1965); Francis Jennings, "Virgin Land and Savage People," *American Quarterly*, XXIII (October 1971), 541, and *Invasion of America* (Chapel Hill, N.C., 1975). Gary B. Nash, *Red, White, and Black* (Englewood Cliffs, N.J., 1974), made the same profession of impartiality and plunged into the same pit of partisan hostility to the Europeans. Louise K. Barnett, *Ignoble Savage: American Literary Racism 1790–1890* (Westport, Conn., 1975), made no professions and lashed out indiscriminately. Richard Slotkin, *Regeneration through Violence: The Mythology of the American Frontier, 1600–1860* (Middletown, Conn., 1973), sinks into a Jungian morass. G. E. Thomas, "Puritans, Indians, and the Concept of Race," *New England Quarterly* XLVIII (March 1975), 3 ff., wrote without comprehension either of the concept of race or of seventeenth-century warfare. Wilbur R. Jacobs, *Dispossessing the American Indian* (New York, 1972), was more sober, but still tilted in favor of the redmen. Atonement cast a shadow even across serious efforts to revise estimates of pre-Columbian aboriginal population; William M. Denevan, ed., *Native Population of the Americas in 1492* (Madison, Wisc., 1976), 289 ff. By contrast, see Richard R. Johnson, "Search for a Usable Indian," *Journal of American History*, LXIV (December 1977), 623 ff.

Utley's sober account of plains warfare could match Dee Brown's.[21]

Whirl as they would, the presses produced little in the decade after 1965 that did more than replicate current controversy about different degrees of victimization, epitomized by disputes over the legitimacy of ethnicity.[22] The dynamic qualities of intergroup relations remained unclear. Indian tribes as often fought with one another as with whites—and the whites with whom they dealt might well include blacks, and certainly included Yankees, Scotch-Irish, English, Germans, and other Europeans. So, too, blacks encountered not whites, but a variety of different peoples. And color was not always the only or even the most decisive element in these contacts; migrants to Northern cities brought with them a heritage that was rural and Southern, as well as African and black. Religious prejudice arrayed German, Irish, and Polish Catholics against one another, as well as against Protestants and Jews. Stereotypes distorted reality, but often reflected a view of self as well as the view of others. Language maintenance was not just a matter of ethnic solidarity, but was also part of the process of acculturation. Social distance as often displaced as evoked conflict.[23]

21 Bernard W. Sheehan, *Seeds of Extinction: Jeffersonian Philanthropy and the American Indian* (Chapel Hill, N.C., 1973) ; Thurman Wilkins, *Cherokee Tragedy: The Story of the Ridge Family and the Decimation of a People* (New York, 1970) ; Ronald N. Satz, *American Indian Policy in the Jacksonian Era* (Lincoln, Neb., 1975) ; Robert M. Utley, *Frontier Regulars: The United States Army and the Indian, 1866–1891* (New York, 1973) ; Chapter 3 at note 60.

22 Orlando Patterson, *Ethnic Chauvinism* (New York, 1977) , labels every voluntary manifestation of group identity reactionary; Michael Novak, *Rise of the Unmeltable Ethnics* (New York, 1971) , labels every deviation from ethnicity an assault from outside the group.

23 Among the books which treat these questions are: Philip Gleason, *Conservative Reformers: German-American Catholics* (Notre Dame, Ind., 1968) ; Jay P. Dolan, *Immigrant Church: New York's Irish and German Catholics* (Baltimore, 1975) ; Humbert S. Nelli, *Italians in Chicago* (New York, 1970) , and *Business of Crime* (New York, 1976) ; Victor R. Greene, *For God and Country: The Rise of Polish and Lithuanian Ethnic Consciousness in America* (Madison, Wisc., 1975) . For shared stereotypes, see William J. Schafer and Johannes Riedel, *Art of Ragtime* (Baton Rouge, La., 1973) , 161 ff.; Daniel J. Leab, *From Sambo to Superspade* (Boston, 1975) , 59 ff.; Thomas Cripps, *Slow Fade to Black: The Negro in American Film, 1900–1942* (New York, 1977) , 219 ff., 263 ff.; Oscar Handlin, *Adventure in Freedom* (New York, 1954) , 174 ff.; Richard Stivers, *Hair of the Dog: Irish Drinking and American Stereotypes* (University Park, Md., 1976) . For language and culture, see Jules Chametzky, *From the Ghetto: The Fiction of Abraham Cahan* (Amherst, Mass., 1977) . Good new community studies include: Thomas Kessner, *Golden Door:*

The American social historians of the 1960s and 1970s, although more sophisticated than earlier scholars, too often still brought together under such vague rubrics as racism, anti-Catholicism, nativism, or anti-Semitism, a variety of different manifestations of hostility. They still drifted into schematic interpretations, and they still allowed eagerness to identify the saints and sinners of the past to blow them off course.

The causes of this uneven performance were embedded in patterns of thought firmly fixed in the writing of American social history. Both the claims to scientific status by the practitioners of the New History and the traditional assumptions they inherited proved handicaps.

To the extent that history was a science, the monograph was the means of adding to knowledge of the past. But the most impressive monographs stood each a lonely monadnock, without links to any larger design—in ethnic studies as in other fields of social history.

The difficult academic situation of American historians was not enough to explain the sporadic and intermittent character of their achievements. Granted, burdensome teaching obligations and the attraction of more remunerative forms of writing explained why few produced more than one monograph in a lifetime. But the historian did not differ in that respect from colleagues in economics and sociology. Different factors accounted for the discontinuity of historical research. Even the most challenging monographs lacked resonance, because the questions they raised and the answers they gave failed to stir scholarly attention.

The assumptions which guided the judgment of the New Historians about the topics worthy of attention deprived their work of continuity. Although history was a science, its subject matter

*Italian and Jewish Immigrant Mobility in New York City, 1880–1915* (New York, 1977) ; and Kenneth L. Kusmer, *Ghetto Takes Shape: Black Cleveland, 1870–1930* (Urbana, Ill., 1976) . Among the thoughtful studies of ethnicity and politics are Frederick C. Luebke, *Immigrants and Politics: The Germans of Nebraska, 1880–1903* (Lincoln, Neb., 1969) ; John M. Allswang, *House for All Peoples: Ethnic Politics in Chicago, 1890–1936* (Lexington, Ky., 1971) ; Richard Jensen, *Winning of the Midwest: Social and Political Conflict, 1888–1896* (Chicago, 1971) ; Paul Kleppner, *Cross of Culture* (New York, 1970) ; and the general statement of the problem in Oscar Handlin, "Immigrant in American Politics," in David F. Bowers, ed., *Foreign Influences in American Life* (Princeton, 1944) , 84 ff.

was not autonomous but instrumental. Questions unfolded, not from the materials of the past, but from analytical social science or, even more, from contemporary social problems. The obligation to make history useful, that is, relevant to immediate issues, in the 1940s and 1950s pointed the attention of scholars away from race, ethnic groupings, and immigration, matters settled in practice and, therefore, of antiquarian interest only. The meaningful questions defined by social scientists had in those decades revolved about international affairs, underdeveloped countries, and totalitarianism. Only a handful of scholars glanced at ethnic problems between 1940 and 1960.

The discovery after 1962 that race was scarcely settled as an issue of public policy suddenly revealed to innocent explorers a vast new world waiting to be cultivated. The difficulty was that decades of neglect had prepared few for the task, and the imperatives of relevance demanded instant conclusions, adaptable to formulas that would promptly solve the problems of the day.

The dependence upon social science was deleterious in another sense. It kept alive the belief inherited from early in the century that all issues could ultimately be reduced to an economic base. In the United States that notion was less a product of Marxist thought than of the operational logic of social scientists committed to formulating practical action programs. Since 1930, at least, the bias toward solutions which involved the expenditure of funds profoundly influenced interpretations of the social system. Undoubtedly the sources of prejudice, criminality, and disordered family life were not only material. But, because the economic factors were, or seemed to be, most readily subject to treatment, historians and other social scientists stressed them, thereby obscuring the ethnic elements in the American past or reducing them to dollars-and-cents consideration, a tendency that persisted into the less sanguine 1970s.

The uneven performance of the social historians stemmed also from the belief that the distinctive character of the American people imparted a moral, if not a providential, quality to their experience. Few scholars remained detached enough from their subjects to hold back from the persistent quest for villains and heroes. If the immigrants were no longer sinister undermen, or the Negroes childlike savages, or the Indians barbarians, then they were saintly victims, whose difficulties stemmed from the evil intentions of individual or group antagonists.

Insofar as the New History and its descendants dissolved the formal restraints against which it rebelled, they pointed the direction in which scholars must move to treat adequately the development of the population of the United States. Freed of the older formulations derived from Reconstruction and immigration restriction, historians could confront the rich materials of the American experience with the reactions of dissimilar men in contact with one another. But those inadequately conscious of the confining heritage of a historiography subject to the inconstant gusts of immediate utility and susceptible to pleas for a diet of fantasy, will not produce the epic—tragic, comic, heroic—the subject deserves. They will grind out the familiar endless, pointless, vacuous soap-operas, useless as history, as formula for action, or as a source of faith.

# 17

# The Uses of History

WHY RESIST the temptation to be relevant? The question nags historians in 1978 as it does other scholars. The world is turning; it needs knowledge; and possession of learning carries an obligation to attempt to shape events. Every crisis lends weight to the plea: transform the library from an ivory tower into a fortress armed to make peace (or war), to end (or extend) social inequality, to alter (or preserve) the existing economic system. The thought boosts the ego, as it has ever since Francis Bacon's suggestion that knowledge is power. Perhaps authority really does lie in command of the contents of books![1]

In the 1960s the plea became an order, sometimes earnest, sometimes surly, always insistent. Tell us what we need to know—straight answers. Thus, students to teachers, readers to authors. The penalties for refusal ranged from mere unpopularity to organized boycotts and angry confrontations—in a few cases even to burning manuscripts and research notes. Fear added to the inducements for pleasing the audience, whether in the classroom or on the printed page.

To aim to please is a blunder, however. Sincere as the supplicants generally are, it is not knowledge they wish. Having already reached their conclusions, they seek only reassuring confirmation as they prepare to act. They already know that a unilateral act of

1 Oscar Handlin, "Living History," *New York Times,* March 6, 1971, p. 27. For an instance of the lust for spurious relevance, see Herbert Blau, "Relevance: The Shadow of a Magnitude," *Daedalus,* XCVIII (Summer 1969), 654 ff. For hunger for a mass audience see John E. Wills, Jr., "History and Its Audience," American Historical Association, *Newsletter,* XVI (February 1978), 5 ff.

404 The Uses of History

will could stop wars, that the United States is racist, and that capitalism condemns the masses to poverty. The history of American foreign policy, of the failure of post-Civil War Reconstruction, and of industrial development would only clutter the mind with disturbing ambiguities and complexities.

At best, the usable past demanded of history consists of the data to flesh out a formula. We must do something about the war, the cities, pollution, poverty, and population. Our moral sense, group interest, and political affiliation define the goals; let the historian join the other social scientists in telling us how to reach them. At worst, the demand made of the past is for a credible myth that will identify the forces of good and evil and inspire those who fight with slogans or fire on one side of the barricades or the other.

The effort to meet either demand will frustrate the historian true to his or her craft. Those nimble enough to catch the swings of the market in the classroom or in print necessarily leave behind interior standards of what is important and drop by the wayside the burden of scrupulous investigation and rigorous judgment. Demands for relevance distort the story of ethnicity as they corrupt the historical novel.

Whoever yields, forgoes the opportunity to do what scholars are best qualified to do. Those who chase from one disaster to another lose sight of the long-term trend; busy with the bandaids, they have no time to treat the patient's illness. The family did not originate yesterday, or the city, or addiction to narcotics; a student might well pick up some thoughts on those subjects by shifting his sights from the 1970s to Hellenistic society.

Above all, obsession with the events of the moment prevents the historian from exercising the faculty of empathy, the faculty of describing how people, like us, but different, felt and behaved as they did in times and places similar to, but different, from our own. The writer or teacher interested only in passing judgment on the good guys and the bad will never know what it meant to be an Irish peasant during a famine, or the landlord; an Alabama slave in the 1850s, or the master; a soldier at Antietam, or a general.

༄

The uses of history arise neither from its relevance nor from its help in preparing for careers—nor from its availability as a subject which teachers pass on to students who become teachers and in turn teach others to teach.

Nevertheless, again and again former pupils who come back for reunions after twenty-five years or more spontaneously testify to the utility of what they had learned at college in the various pursuits to which life's journey had taken them. Probing usually reveals not bits of information, not a general interpretation, but a vague sense that those old transactions of classroom and library had somehow expanded their knowledge of self. The discipline of history had located them in time and space and had thereby helped them know themselves, not as physicians or attorneys or bureaucrats or executives, but as persons.

These reassuring comments leave in suspense the question of why study of the past should thus help the individual understand himself or herself. How do those who learn this subject catch a glimpse of the process of which they are part, discover places in it?

Not by relevance, in the competition for which the other, more pliable, social sciences can always outbid history. Nor by the power of myth, in the peddling of which the advantage lies with novelists. To turn accurate knowledge to those ends is, as C. S. Peirce noted, "like running a steam engine by burning diamonds."[2]

The use of history lies in its capacity for advancing the approach to truth.

The historian's vocation depends on this minimal operational article of faith: Truth is absolute; it is as absolute as the world is real. It does not exist because individuals wish it to anymore than the world exists for their convenience. Although observers have more or less partial views of the truth, its actuality is unrelated to the desires or the particular angles of vision of the viewers. Truth is knowable and will out if earnestly pursued; and science is the procedure or set of procedures for approximating it.

What is truth? Mighty above all things, it resides in the small pieces which together form the record.

History is not the past, any more than biology is life, or physics, matter. History is the distillation of evidence surviving from the

2 C. S. Peirce, "Notes for a Projected History of Science," *Collected Papers* (Cambridge, 1960) , I, 19–49.

past. Where there is no evidence, there is no history. Much of the
past is not knowable in this way, and about those areas the historian must learn to confess ignorance.[3]

No one can relive the past; but everyone can seek truth in the
record. Simple, durable discoveries await the explorer. So chronology—the sequential order of events reaching back beyond time's
horizon—informs the viewer of the long distance traversed and
of the immutable course of occurrences: no reversal of a step
taken; no after ever before. The historian cannot soar with the
anthropologists, who swoop across all time and space. Give or take
a thousand years, it is all one to them in pronouncements about
whether irrigation systems succeeded or followed despotisms, or
in linking technology, population, food, and climatic changes.
In the end they pick what they need to prop up theory. The discipline of dates rails off the historian and guards against such
perilous plunges. No abstraction, no general interpretation, no
wish or preference can challenge chronology's dominion, unless
among those peoples who, lacking a sense of time, lack also a
sense of history. And whoever learns to know the tyranny of the
passing hours, the irrecoverable nature of days passed, learns also
the vanity of all aspirations to halt the clock or slow its speed, of
all irridentisms, all efforts to recapture, turn back, redeem the
moments gone by.[4]

Another use of history is in teaching about vocabulary, the
basic component of human communication. Words, singularly
elusive, sometimes flutter out of reach, hide in mists of ambiguity,
or lodge themselves among inaccessible logical structures, yet
form the very stuff of evidence. The historian captures the little
syllabic clusters only by knowing who inscribed or spoke them—a
feat made possible by understanding the minds and hearts and
hands of the men and women for whom they once had meaning.
Words released by comprehension wing their messages across the
centuries. A use of history is to instruct in the reading of a word,
in the comprehension of speakers, writers different from the
listener, viewer.

And context. Every survival bespeaks a context. Who graved

[3] Herbert Lüthy, "What's the Point of History?" *Journal of Contemporary History*, III (January 1968) , 1 ff.; Ernst Cassirer, *Essay on Man* (New Haven, 1944) , 191 ff.; Rebecca West, *Black Lamb and Grey Falcon* (New York, 1943) , 55.

[4] For example, Mark N. Cohen, *Food Crisis in Prehistory* (New Haven, 1977) .

or wrote or built did so for the eyes of others. Each line or shape denotes a relation to people, things, or concepts—knowable. The identities of sender and recipient explain the content of the letter; the mode of transmission explains the developing idea, the passions of employers and laborers, the organization of the factory. A use of history is its aid in locating discrete events, phenomena, and expressions in their universes.

The limits of those universes were often subjects of dispute. Early in the nineteenth century Henry Thomas Buckle complained, in terms still applicable decades thereafter, of "the singular spectacle of one historian being ignorant of political economy; another knowing nothing of law; another nothing of ecclesiastical affairs and changes of opinion; another neglecting the philosophy of statistics, another physical science," so that those important pursuits, being cultivated, "some by one man, and some by another, have been isolated rather than united," with no disposition to concentrate them upon history. He thus echoed Gibbon's earlier injunction to value all facts. A Montesquieu, "from the meanest of them, will draw conclusions unknown to ordinary men" and arrive at "philosophical history."[5]

On the other hand, a distinguished scholar fifty years later pooh-poohed the very idea that there might be a relation among the Gothic style, feudalism, and scholasticism, or a link between the Baroque and Jesuitism. Nevertheless, the dominant thrust of twentieth-century historians has been toward recognition of the broader contexts; in a variety of fashions they have searched for a totality denominated civilization, culture, or spirit of an epoch, and which they have hoped would permit examination of enlightening linkages and reciprocal relations. Even those who deny that history is a single discipline and assert that it is only "congeries of related disciplines" would, no doubt, expect each branch to look beyond its own borders.[6]

[5] Henry Thomas Buckle, *History of Civilization in England*, 2 vols. (New York, 1858), I, 4; Hugh Trevor-Roper, "Other Gibbon," *American Scholar*, XLVI (Winter 1976–77), 94 ff. See also Leonard Krieger, "Horizons of History," *American Historical Review*, LXIII (October 1957), 74.

[6] For a contemporary expression of the narrow view, see Lee Benson, "Middle Period Historiography," in George A. Billias and Gerald N. Grob, *American History* (New York, 1971), 156 ff. For the broad view, see Johan Huizinga, *Wege der Kulturgeschichte* (Munich, 1930), 9 ff., 33 ff., 47 ff.; Karl Mannheim, *Essays on the Sociology of Knowledge*, ed. Paul Kecskemeti (London, 1952), 33 ff.; Cassirer, *Essay on Man*, 176 ff.

In the final analysis, all the uses of history depend upon the integrity of the record, without which there could be no counting of time, no reading of words, no perception of the context, no utility of the subject. No concern could be deeper than assaults upon the record, upon the very idea of a record.

Although history is an ancient discipline, it rests upon foundations laid in the seventeenth century, when a century of blood shed in religious and dynastic warfare persuaded those who wrote and read history to accept a vital difference in tolerance between facts and interpretation. The text of a charter or statute was subject to proof of authenticity and validity, whatever the meanings lawyers or theologians imparted to its terms. The correct date, the precise phrasing, the seal were facts which might present difficulties of verification, but which, nevertheless, admitted of answers that were right or wrong. On the other hand, discussion of opinions and meanings often called for tolerance among diverse points of view, tolerance possible so long as disputants distinguished interpretation from the fact, from the thing in itself. Scholars could disagree on large matters of interpretation; they had a common interest in agreeing on the small ones of fact which provided them grounds for peaceful discourse.

From that seminal insight developed the scientific mechanisms that enabled historians to separate fact from opinion. From that basis came the Enlightenment achievements which recognized the worth of objectivity and asserted the possibility of reconstructing the whole record of the human past.

True, historians as well as philosophers often thereafter worried about the problems of bias and perspective; and some despaired of attaining the ideal of ultimate objectivity. None were ever totally free of bias, not even those like Ranke who most specifically insisted on the integrity of the fact which he struggled to make the foundation of a truly universal body of knowledge. But, however fallible the individual scholar, the historian's, task, Wilhelm von Humboldt explained, was "to present what actually happened." It may have been a dream to imagine that history would become a science meaningful to all people, everywhere. If so, it was a noble dream.[7]

[7] Wilhelm von Humboldt, "On the Historian's Task" (1821), *History and Theory*, VI (1967), 57 ff.

By contrast, historians in the 1970s and increasingly other scientists regarded the fact itself as malleable. As the distinction between fact and interpretation faded, all became faction—a combination of fact and fiction. The passive acceptance of that illegitimate genre—whatever mixes with fiction ceases to be fact—revealed the erosion of scholarly commitment. More and more often, the factual elements in an account were instrumental to the purpose the author-manipulator wished them to serve. It followed that different writers addressing different readers for different purposes could arrange matters as convenient. In the end, the primacy of the fact vanished and only the authority of the author, the receptivity of the audience, and the purpose intended remained.

Whence came this desertion, this rejection of allegiance to the fact?

Chroniclers of the past always suffered from external pressure to make their findings relevant, that is, to demonstrate or deny the wisdom, correctness, or appropriateness of current policies. They resisted out of dedication to maintaining the integrity of the record; and long succeeded in doing so. In the 1970s, however, the pressures toward falsification became more compelling than ever before.

Although the full fruits of the change appeared only in that decade, its origins reached back a half-century. It was one of Stalin's most impressive achievements to have converted Marxism from its nineteenth-century scientific base to an instrument of state purpose, and it was not by coincidence that history was the first discipline to suffer in the process. The Soviet Union did more than impose an official party line on interpretations of Trotsky's role in the revolution of 1917; it actually expunged the name Trotsky from the record, so that the fact of the commissar's existence disappeared. What started in the domain of history led in time to Lysenko's invasion of the natural sciences. The Nazis, once in power, burned the nonconforming books; and after 1945 the assault spread to all countries subject to totalitarian control. Those developments were neither surprising nor difficult to comprehend; they followed from the nature of the regimes which fostered them.[8]

[8] On Nazi history, see Helmut Heiber, *Walter Frank und sein Reichsinstitut für Geschichte des Neuen Deutschlands* (Stuttgart, 1966); on Soviet scholarship, see Chapter 3 at note 50.

More surprising, more difficult to comprehend, was the acquiescence by the scholars of free societies in the attack on history,
first, insofar as it affected colleagues less fortunately situated, then
as it insinuated itself in their own ranks. External and internal
circumstances were responsible.

In a sensate society the commercial standards of the media
governed the dissemination of information. Since whatever sold
was news, the salient consideration was one of attracting attention; factual accuracy receded to the remote background. An
affluent and indulgent society also mistook flaccid permissiveness
for tolerance. Everything went because nothing was worth defending, and the legitimate right to err became the disastrous
obliteration of the difference between error and truth.

Difficult critical issues tempted the weak-minded to tailor fact
to convenience. In the United States, but also in other parts of
the world, the spread of a kind of tribalism demanded a history
unique to and written for the specifications of particular groups.
Since knowledge was relative to the knowers, it was subject to
manipulation to suit their convenience. The process by which
blacks, white ethnics, and women alone were conceded the capa-
bility of understanding and writing their own histories wiped
out the line between truth and myth.

That much was comprehensible; these forces operated outside
the academy walls and were not subject to very much control.
More important, more susceptible to control, and less explicable
was the betrayal by the intellectuals of their own group interests
and the subsequent loss of the will to resist. A variety of elements
contributed to this most recent *trahison des clercs*. Exaggerated
concern with the problems of bias and objectivity drove some
earnest scholars to despair. Perhaps they reacted against the excessive claims of the nineteenth century, perhaps against the inability of historians, any more than other scholars, to withstand
the pressures of nationalism in the early decades of the twentieth
century. In any case, not a few followed the deceptive path from
acknowledgment that no person was entirely free of prejudice or
capable of attaining a totally objective view of the past to the
conclusion that all efforts to do so were vain and that, in the end,
the past was entirely a recreation emanating from the mind of the
historian. Support from this point of view came from the philos-

ophers Benedetto Croce in Italy and, later, R. G. Collingwood in England. Support also came from a misreading of anthropological relativism, which drew from the undeniable circumstances that different cultures evolved differently, the erroneous conclusion that judgments among them were impossible.

Perhaps playfully, perhaps seriously, Carl L. Becker suggested that the historical fact was in someone's mind or it was nowhere, because it was "not the past event," only a symbol which enabled later writers to recreate it imaginatively. His charmingly put illustrations deceived many a reader unaware that serious thinkers since Bayle and Hume had wrestled with the problem. "No one could ever object to the factual truth that Caesar defeated Pompey; and whatever the principles one wishes to use in dispute, one will find nothing less questionable than this proposition—Caesar and Pompey existed and were not just simple modification of the minds of those who wrote their lives"—thus Bayle.[9]

The starting point in Becker's wandering toward relativism, as for others among his contemporaries, was the desire to be useful in solving "the everlasting riddle of human experience." Less subtle successors attacked neutrality "toward the main issues of life" and demanded that society organize all its forces in support of its ideals. "Total war, whether it be hot or cold, enlists everyone and calls upon everyone to assume his part. The historian is no freer from this obligation than the physicists." Those too timid to go the whole way suggested that there might be two kinds of history, variously defined: one, for instance, to treat the positive side of slavery to nurture black pride; another, the negative, to support claims for compensation.[10]

---

[9] "Projet d'un dictionnaire critique" (1692) in Pierre Bayle, *Dictionnaire historique et critique* (Paris, 1820), XV, 242; also Carl L. Becker, *Detachment and the Writing of History*, ed. Phil L. Snyder (Ithaca, N.Y., 1958), 11 ff., 47 ff.; Chapter 4 at note 27.

[10] See Chapter 3 at note 49; Carl L. Becker, "Some Aspects of the Influence of Social Problems and Ideas Upon the Study and Writing of History," *American Journal of Sociology*, XVIII (March 1913), 675, and *Everyman His Own Historian* (New York, 1935); Burleigh T. Wilkins, *Carl Becker* (Cambridge, 1961), 32; Conyers Read, "Social Responsibilities of the Historian," *American Historical Review*, LV (January 1950), 283; Stanley M. Elkins, "Slavery Debate," *Commentary*, LX (December 1975), 40 ff., and *Midstream*, XXIII (December 1977), 74; Arthur J. Vidich, "Ideological Themes in American Anthropology," *Social Research*, XLI (Autumn 1974), 721 ff. For another view, see also Ihor Ševčenko, "Two Varieties of Historical Writing," *History and Theory*, VIII (1969), 346 ff. For the sober version of a "sane

Historians who caved in to pressure and ordered the past to please the present neglected the future, the needs of which would certainly change and in unpredictable ways. Scholarship could no more provide the future than the present with faith, justification, self-confidence, or sense of purpose unless it first preserved the record, intact and inviolable.

History does not recreate the past. The historian does not recapture the bygone event. No amount of imagination will enable the scholar to describe exactly what happened to Caesar in the Senate or to decide whether Mrs. Williams actually lost two hundred pounds by an act of faith. History deals only with evidence from the past, with the residues of bygone events. But it can pass judgment upon documentation and upon observers' reports of what they thought they saw.

Disregarding these constraints, Becker concluded that, since objectivity was a dream, everyman could be his own historian and contrive his own view of the past, valid for himself, if for no one else. He thus breached the line between interpretation, which was subjective and pliable, and fact, which was not.

Internal specialization allowed historians to slip farther in the same direction. The knowledge explosion after 1900 made specialization an essential, unavoidable circumstance of every form of scholarly endeavor. No individual could presume to competence in more than a sector of the whole field; and the scope of the manageable sector steadily shrank. One result was the dissolution of common standards; each area created its own criteria and claimed immunity from the criticism of outsiders. The occupants of each little island fortress sustained the illusion that the dangers to one would not apply to others. Lines of communication, even within a single faculty or department, broke down so that, increasingly, specialists in one area depended upon the common mass media for knowledge about what transpired in another.

The dangers inherent in these trends became critical as scholarship lost its autonomy. Increasingly reliance on support from external sources—whether governments or foundations—circumscribed the freedom of researchers and writers to choose their own

---

and reasonable" relativist, see Leo Gershoy, "Some Problems of a Working Historian," and Ernest Nagel's comments on it, in Sidney Hook, ed., *Philosophy and History* (New York, 1963), 59 ff., 76 ff.

subjects and to arrive at their own conclusions. More generally, the loss of autonomy involved a state of mind which regarded the fruits of scholarship as dependent and instrumental—that is, not as worthy of pursuit for their own sake, not for the extent to which they brought the inquirer closer to the truth, but for other, extrinsic reasons. Ever more often, scholars justified their activity by its external results—peace, training for citizenship, economic development, cure of illness, and the like—in other words, by its usefulness. The choice of topics revealed the extent to which emphasis had shifted from the subject and its relation to the truth to its instrumental utility measured by reference to some external standard.

The plea from utility was dangerous. In the 1930s it blinded well-intentioned social scientists and historians to the excesses of totalitarianism. It was inevitable in creating the omelette of a great social experiment that the shells of a few eggs of truth would be broken, so the argument ran. So, too, in the avid desire for peace, in the praiseworthy wish to avoid a second world war, Charles A. Beard abandoned all effort at factual accuracy. Yet the errors to which the plea for utility led in the past have not prevented others from proceeding along the same treacherous path in pursuit of no less worthy, but equally deceptive utilitarian goals.

Finally, the reluctance to insist upon the worth of truth for its own sake stemmed from a decline of faith by intellectuals in their own role as intellectuals. Not many have, in any conscious or deliberate sense, foresworn their allegiance to the pursuit of truth and the life of the spirit. But power tempted them as it tempts other men and women. The twentieth-century intellectual had unparalleled access to those who actually wielded political or military influence. And few could resist the temptation of being listened to by presidents and ministers, of seeing ideas translated into action. Moreover, a more subtle, more insidious temptation nested in the possibility that possession of knowledge may itself become a significant source of power. The idea that a name on the letterhead of an activist organization or in the endorsement of a political advertisement might advance some worthy cause gives a heady feeling of sudden consequence to the no-longer-humble professor. Most important of all is the consciousness that knowledge can indeed do good, that it is a usable commodity, not only capable of bringing fame to its possessor but actually capable of causing beneficent changes in the external world.

All too few scholars are conscious that in reducing truth to an instrument, even an instrument for doing good, they necessarily blunt its edge and expose themselves to the danger of its misuse. For, when truth ceases to be an end in itself and becomes but a means toward an end, it also becomes malleable and manageable and is in danger of losing its character—not necessarily, not inevitably, but seriously. There may be ways of avoiding the extreme choices of the ivory tower and the marketplace, but they are far from easy and call for extreme caution.

In 1679 Jacques Bossuet wrote for his pupil the Dauphin, heir apparent to the throne of France, a discourse on universal history. Here certainly was an opportunity to influence the mind of the future monarch of Europe's most powerful kingdom. Bossuet understood that the greatest service he could render was to tell, not what would be pleasant to hear, but the truth about the past, detached and whole, so that in later years his pupil could make what use he wished of it.[11]

Therein Bossuet reverted to an ancient tradition. The first law for the historian, Cicero had written, "is never to dare utter an untruth and the second, never to suppress anything true." And, earlier still, Polybius had noted that no one was exempt from mistakes made out of ignorance. But "deliberate misstatements in the interest of country or of friends or for favour" reduced the scholar to the level of those who gained "their living by their pens" and weighed "everything by the standard of profit."[12]

In sum, the use of history is to learn from the study of it and not to carry preconceived notions or external objectives into it.

The times, it may be, will remain hostile to the enterprise of truth. There have been such periods in the past. Historians would

11 Jacques-Bénigne Bossuet, *Discourse on Universal History*, ed. Orest Ranum (Chicago, 1976), xxviii, xxx, 3.

12 Cicero, *De Oratore*, II, xv, 62 (Loeb Classical Library, Cambridge, 1942), I, 242 ff.; Polybius, *Histories*, XVI, xiv, 7–10, trans. W. R. Paton (Loeb Classical Library, London, 1927), V, 29.

do well to regard the example of those clerks in the Dark Ages who knew the worth of the task. By retiring from an alien world to a hidden monastic refuge, now and again one of them at least was able to maintain a true record, a chronicle that survived the destructive passage of armies and the erosion of doctrinal disputes and informed the future of what had transpired in their day. That task is ever worthy. Scholars should ponder its significance.

# ACKNOWLEDGMENTS

COMPLETION OF my earlier books was usually the occasion for acknowledging assistance received in composition, a simple, sometimes hurried, but always pleasurable and easy duty. This time, the task of enumerating intellectual and scholarly debts is difficult, for this volume draws together threads spun over a period of more than forty years. The initial drafts of some of the pages that appear here go back to 1934, when my scholarly career began. Some chapters draw upon articles earlier published though now revised; and I am grateful to the journals, referred to in the notes, for permission to reprint, and to their editors for vigilant and stimulating criticism.

More generally, accumulated obligations have left me heavily in arrears and beyond my capacity for repayment. The unlikely combination of circumstances that made this book possible depended heavily on luck in timing and in attracting assistance. Had I turned up a decade earlier, some doors would have been closed to me; a decade later they would have opened upon rooms either empty or crowded. I can only express awareness of my good fortune and gratitude for aid and opportunity.

Access to books has never ceased to be important to me. In my youth, desperate expedients verging upon illegality enabled me to lay hands upon volumes their custodians deemed inappropriate or unnecessary to one my age. From high school, I learned to range the vast Brooklyn spaces to exploit the collections on Montague Street and in the Pratt Free Library. From college, I wiggled around inconvenient rules to use the magnificent resources of the New York Public Library. My arrival in Cambridge and exposure to the Widener stacks opened a way to learning that enriches me still. Not a page I have written but has profited thereby. If, almost a half-century later, I am more inclined to complain than previously, it is not simply out of the crotchetiness of advancing age or in protest against present custodians, but in response to the increasing magnitude of the task of maintaining such a collection.

The dedications of earlier books named the teachers with whom I worked most closely and who helped advance my scholarship. But thinking about this book reminded me of other, less readily defined, obligations. I do not know how to convey to the anxious young men and women who enroll in the 1970s what excitement it brought to a first-year graduate student to take seminars with William Leonard Langer and Abbott Payson Usher and to learn to read a text with Charles McIlwain and Harry Wolfson, in addition to work in American history. The insight into method of analysis, as well as the substance acquired, sustained me for years.

In time, I acquired a collegiate relationship with these and younger colleagues. Harvard then was a small university; and the Department of History enjoyed an intellectual intimacy that Gaetano Salvemini celebrated when he dedicated one of his post-retirement books to that Department. It means a good deal to me still to be able to talk in those terms with Donald Fleming.

Leverett House was another intellectual and personal setting. There I got to know Salvemini well in the days after the War and before his return to Florence, when he was a rather lonely figure residing in an available suite in the House. There also I counted among my friends David Owen, Perry Miller, Kenneth Murdock, Benjamin F. Wright, and Mark DeWolfe Howe; and association with them added a textural richness to involvement as a scholar in the Harvard community.

I was more fortunate also than I can say in the time and the circumstances which shaped my teaching career. The mature, purposeful, and knowledgeable graduate students who returned from the War after 1945 immediatedly rewarded those with whom they worked. Teaching then was largely a matter of listening, involving more a process of mutual instruction than the transmission of knowledge; and the narrow difference between their ages and mine added to the value of the experience. The accidents of later propinquity bring the names of Bernard Bailyn, Morton Keller, Barbara M. Solomon, Stephan A. Thernstrom, and Sam Bass Warner, Jr., first to mind. To enumerate all those from whom I learned would demand a long and overly sentimental recital.

I recall, too, the undergraduates I knew when tutorial was one to one. Some, like John M. Blum, Class of 1943, themselves went on to scholarly careers. Others, from Joseph S. Stern of the Class of 1940 to Eric Mandelbaum of the Class of 1978, went on to a variety of callings, leaving me the reminder that the world beyond made demands of its own upon the academy. Facing generation after generation of those young men and women kept me aware that what I knew had to be meaningful in terms comprehensible to those not themselves historians.

∽

This book, like others, consists of words on paper. Between the idea and its physical expression lie a succession of processes that are more than mechanical. That Ann Louise McLaughlin saw this manuscript through the Press, as she did another for me twenty-five years ago, reminds me of my luck in that regard also.

Without the assistance of Debby Beardsley I would have had a tangle of tapes, a jumble of old proofs, and a heap of scribbled inserts. To her and her predecessors who worked on portions of manuscript which entered into this book I am immensely grateful. I cannot explain the good fortune which providentially brought her to my assistance and, before her, Nancy Evans, Phyllis Frost, Alicia Zintel, Katharine Top, Evelyn Bender, and Cecily Tourtellot—each a unique and distinctive person, yet each, for the time we worked together, applying a dedicated intelligence to ease all the tasks of composition, so that I was never disappointed in an expectation and often surprised by help beyond my expectations.

∽

I owe the meticulous index that follows to the efforts of Ruth Cross.

Some chapters of this book drew upon work performed in collaboration with Mary Flug Handlin.

Other chapters, and the book as a whole, were the products of collaboration with Lilian Handlin.

O.H.

June 8, 1978

Portions of some of the chapters in this volume are reprinted with permission from the following journals: *Agricultural History,* "Reconsidering the Populists," XXXIX (April 1965), 10 ff. (Chapter 13). *The American Scholar,* "History: A Discipline in Crisis?" XL (Summer 1971), 447 ff. (Chapter 1); "Living in a Valley," XLVI (Summer 1977), 301–312. (Chapter 2); "Man and Magic: First Encounters with the Machine," XXXIII (Summer 1965), 408 ff. (Chapter 12). *Freedom at Issue,* no. 15 (September–October 1972), 2 ff. (Chapter 6). *Journal of Economic History,* "Laissez-Faire Thought in Massachusetts, 1790–1880," *Tasks of Economic History,* 1943, pp. 53 ff. (Chapter 7). Massachusetts Historical Society, "James Burgh and American Revolutionary Theory," *Proceedings,* XXIII (1961), 38 ff. (Chapter 11). *New England Quarterly,* "Capitalism, Power, and the Historians," XXVIII (March 1955), 99 ff. (Chapter 13); "Radicals and Conservatives in Massachusetts after Independence," XVII (September 1944), 343 ff. (Chapter 14). *Virginia Quarterly Review,* "History in Men's Lives," XXX (Autumn 1954), 534 ff. (Chapter 10).

# Index

Abernethy, T. P., 72
Acton, Lord, 18
Adams, Brooks, 91
Adams, Charles Kendall, 59
Adams, George Burton, 60
Adams, Henry, 59, 61, 66–67, 91, 118
Adams, Herbert Baxter, 59, 63
Adams, James Truslow, 74
Adams, John, 11, 50–51, 53, 119, 312; and Burgh's *Disquisitions,* 294, 308, 310, 312; and political differences, 355, 359, 361, 362
Adams, Samuel, 271, 359, 361
Adler, Alfred, 273; and Adlerian theory, 289, 346
Adorno, Theodor W., 288
A.F. of L. (American Federation of Labor), 199
Agar, Herbert, 333
*Age of Reason* (Paine), 85
Agricultural Adjustment Act, 355
Agriculture, U.S. Department of, 263
Albania, 173
Almanacs, 200
Altgeld, John Peter, 374–375
*America in Midpassage* (Beard and Beard), 102
*American, The* (Fast), 373, 375
American Council of Learned Societies, 7, 253
American Economic Association, 191
American Historical Association (A.H.A.), 20, 67; shift in standards of, 3, 23, 156–157, 158–159; Council of, 6; dual orientation of, 6–7; Needs and Opportunities for Research list, 17; formation of, 59

*American Historical Review,* 20, 150, 159; states "establishment doctrine," 156
American Institute of Public Opinion (Gallup poll), 264
American Iron and Steel Institute, 199
*American Life* series. See *History of American Life* series
American Medical Association, 199
American Nation series, 18, 61
American Revolution, 109, 142, 147, 190, 353, 357; historical treatment of, 5, 56, 293; as step toward worldwide republicanism, 51, 52–53
*American Spirit, The* (Beard and Beard), 102
American Statesman series, 58, 267
American Statistical Association, and *Journal* of, 201
Ames, Fisher, and Nathaniel, Jr., 361
*Analogy* (Butler), 86
Anderson, Eugene, 3
Andrews, Charles M., 61, 63, 268
Andrews, John, 359
*Annales* (journal), 7, 74, 80
*À nous la liberté* (moving picture), 322
*Anticipations* (Wells), 321
Anti-Semitism, 179, 340–343, 385, 394–395
Appleton, Nathan, 187
Archer, Jeffrey, 378
*Architects of Illusion* (Gardner), 154
Ariès, Philippe, 15
Aristotle, 94, 309, 314

*Armenische Grammatik* (Hübsch-
    mann), 254
Armour, Philip, 375
Arthur, Timothy Shay, 232
Ashley, W. J., 63
Atkinson, Edward, 191
Audubon, John J., 233
Austin, Benjamin, 359

Bach, Johann Sebastian, 119
Backus, Isaac, 65
Bacon, Francis, 255, 403
Bacon, Peggy, 244
Bacon's Rebellion, 353
Baer, George, 132
*Ballou's Monthly*, 234–235
Balzac, Honoré de, 371
Bancroft, George, 8, 57, 61, 385; and
    concept of mission, 55–56, 94; and
    "unity of human race," 107, 178
Bancroft, Hubert Howe, 70, 127
Barlow, Joel, 53
*Barnaby Rudge* (Dickens), 372
Barnes, Harry Elmer, 252, 255, 270,
    283
Barnum, P. T., 237
*Barron's* (financial magazine), 199
Barth, Gunther P., 390
Bartlett, William Henry, 234
*Basic History* (Beard and Beard),
    102–103
Bastiat, Frédéric, 186, 189
Bayle, Pierre, 85, 255, 411
Beach, Mrs. H. H. A., 247
Beale, Howard K., 3
Beard, Charles A., 10, 70, 74, 98; and
    "new history" concept, 69, 71, 90;
    and interpretation, 83, 101–103,
    252, 339, 353, 367, 413
Beard, Mary R., 69, 102–103
Becker, Carl L., 10, 61; and interpre-
    tation, 83, 91, 100–101, 252, 314,
    367, 411–412; analyzes colonial
    politics, 356–358
Beer, George Louis, 63

Belaney, Archie, 124
Belknap, Jeremy, 65
Bellamy, Edward, 321, 322, 346
Bellows, George, 243, 245
Belmont, August, 354
Benchley, Peter, 379
*Ben Hur* (Wallace), 373
Benjamin, Walter, 103
Bentley, Arthur F., 256
Benton, Thomas Hart, 130
Berkhofer, Robert F., Jr., 391, 397
Bernard, Francis, 359, 360
Beveridge, Albert J., 54
Beverley, Robert, 49, 50
Bierstadt, Albert, 239
Bigelow, Erastus B., 185
Billings, William, 247
Bingham, George Caleb, 234
Binkley, Wilfred E., 353–354, 367
Biography, 266–275; and study of
    Rockefeller, 334–338
Black, J. W., 241
*Black Reconstruction* (DuBois), 74
Blacks. *See* Negroes; Racism; Slavery
Blackstone, Sir William, 309
Blaine, James G., 343
Blake, William, 329
Blegen, T. C., 74
Bloch, Marc, 7, 10, 175
Blume, Peter, 244
Boas, Franz, 100
Bogue, Allan, 351
Bohr, Niels, 282
Bolingbroke, Viscount (Henry St.
    John), 309
Bolton, H. E., 389
Boorstin, Daniel, 95
Boosterism, 45, 50, 65
Booth, Charles, 261
Bossuet, Jacques, 48, 414
Boston, Massachusetts, 117, 330, 385,
    394; trade problems of, 183–184,
    185, 364; railroads of, 190–191, 376;
    aerial photograph of (1870), 241
Boswell, James, 298
Bowdoin, James, 359, 361, 363, 364

Bowen, Francis, 187–189, 191, 192
Bradford, Gamaliel, 271
Bradford, William, 46–47, 48, 53, 64, 90, 170
Brady, Mathew, 235
Brant, Irving, 269
Brattle family, 360
Braudel, Fernand, 78
*Brave New World* (Huxley), 322
Brezhnevism, 82
Bridgeport, Connecticut, 237
Bright, John, 105
Brinton, Crane, 11
*Britain's Remembrancer* (Burgh), 295, 299
Brodhead, J. R., 58
Brookings Institution, 201
*Brothers Karamazov, The* (Dostoevsky), 371
Brown, Dee, 397, 399
Brown, Norman O., 278
Brownson, Orestes A., 104
Brown University, 4
Bry, Théodore de, 233
Buck, Paul H., 72, 389
Buckle, George E., 268
Buckle, Henry Thomas, 89, 106, 407
Bullitt, William C., 14–15
Bunker Hill monument, 241
Burckhardt, Jakob, 68, 228, 259
Bureau of Foreign and Domestic Commerce, U.S., 197
Burgess, John W., 95, 385, 386
Burgh, James, life and writings, 293–314
Burr, Aaron, 377
*Burr* (Vidal), 377
Burroughs, William S., 376
Bury, J. B., 61
Bushnell, C. J., 261
Butler, Bishop Joseph, 86
Byron, Lord, 56

Cabet, Etienne, 321
Cabot, George, 365

*Caesar's Column* (Donnelly), 342, 348
Cage, John, 251
Calhoun, John, 170
Callender, John, 50
Calvert, Charles, 233
Calvinism, 46, 48
Cambridge Modern History series, 18
Campbell, Patrick, 235
Camus, Albert, 288
Canton, Maurice, 244
Čapek, Karel, 322
Capitalism, 96, 105, 316, 387; "finance," 104, 108; and "anti-capitalist bias," 330–334
Capote, Truman, 379
Carey, Henry, 186
Carlyle, Thomas, 9, 330n.23
Carr-Saunders, A. M., 14
Carver, Thomas N., 191
Cash, W. J., 72
Cassirer, Ernst, 16
*Cato's Letters,* 309
Catton, Bruce, 58
Census, U.S. Bureau of the, 173, 198, 199, 215
Chamberlain, Houston S., 107
Chambers, Ephraim, 255
Channing, Edward, 61, 268
Channing, William Ellery, 137
Chaplin, Charlie, 242, 244, 322, 329
*Charter for the Social Sciences, A* (A.H.A.), 7
Chase, Samuel, 308
Cheyney, Edward P., 60
Chiang Kai-shek, 160
Chicago, Illinois, 230, 393
Chomsky, Noam, 165
Churchill, Winston S., 161, 268
Cicero, 157, 309, 313, 314, 414
C.I.O. (Congress of Industrial Organizations), 199
*City Lights* (moving picture), 244
Civil rights movement, 81, 390, 393, 396

Civil War, 95, 109, 386; historical treatment of, 72, 269, 355, 372
Claghorn, Kate, 261
Clair, René, 322
Clap, Thomas, 49
Clapham, John, 225
Clark, John B., 256
Cleveland, Grover, 268, 374, 375
Clinton, Sir Henry, 272
Colden, Cadwallader, 50
Cold War, 153n.6; origins of, 105, 148–149, 155, 160
Cole, Thomas, 239
Coleman, Glenn, 244
Collingwood, R. G., 100, 411
Collinson, Peter, 299
*Columbiad: A Poem* (Barlow), 53
Columbia University, 70, 127, 256
Columbus, Christopher, portrayal of, 232, 238
Comic strips, 231–232, 239, 240, 251
Commons, John R., 98
*Common Sense* (Paine), 310, 362
Communist Party and communism, 82, 148, 159, 179, 377; spread of, 80, 153–154; and "anti-Communist" as reproach, 149, 160
*Company, The* (Ehrlichman), 379
Computerization. *See* Quantitative techniques
Comte, Auguste, 63, 89, 252, 255
Condorcet, Marquis de, 88
*Coney Island* (moving picture), 242
Congress, U.S., 131, 132, 198; Continental/Provincial, 52, 53, 359, 360; and direct election of Senators, 345, 347
*Congressional Record, The,* 121
Connecticut, 49, 230
Conrad, Alfred H., 13
Conrad, Joseph, 382
Constitution, U.S., 102, 197, 269, 361, 363, 364
Continental Congress. *See* Congress, U.S.

*Contours of American History* (Williams), 145
Cooley, C. H., 256
Cooper, James Fenimore, 373
Coover, Robert, 378
Copley, John Singleton, 231, 233
Cornell University, 59
Cotton, John, 174
Coxe, Tench, 200
Craftsmanship, decline of, 18–20, 23–24, 77–78, 149–150, 156–161 (passim), 225
Craig, John, 378
Credibility as issue, 124–130, 151–152, 376–379, 409–412. *See also* Revisionism
Crèvecoeur, J. H. St. John, 392
Croce, Benedetto, 100, 101, 411
Crystal Palace (London), 321
Currier and Ives, 231
Curti, Merle, 75, 99
Curtis, B. R., 184
Czechoslovakia, 148, 173

*Dædalus* (quarterly journal), 21, 209
Daley, Richard J., 158
Dallas, Texas, 230
Dana, Richard Henry, 228
Däniken, Erich Von, 254
Darwinian thought, 61–62, 63, 87, 91, 107, 191
Daughters of the American Revolution, 392
Dean, James, 138
Deane, Silas, 308
Debs, Eugene V., 342
Declaration of Independence, 34, 119; drafting of, 173, 176, 314; and party concept, 358
*Deep South* (Davis et al.), 262
DeForest, R. W., 261
Degas, Edgar, 235
Dehn, Adolf, 244
Delano, Jack, 235

Democracy: and U.S. achievements, 63; connotation of, 179
Democratic party, 131, 350, 362, 374; National Convention of (1968), 158; and Jeffersonian and Jacksonian Democrats, 353–355; Democratic-Republican, 354, 355, 358
DeThulstrup, T. (artist), 245
*Development of Modern Europe* (Robinson and Beard), 69
Dewey, John, 97
Dexter, Timothy, 365
Dialectic: as term, 94; Marxist, 96. *See also* Marx, Karl, and Marxism
Dickens, Charles, 371, 375
Dickinson, John, 308, 359
Diderot, Denis, 255
Diem, Ngo Dinh, 160
*Dignity of Human Nature, The* (Burgh), 295, 297, 300
Dillingham Committee, 122
Dilthey, Wilhelm, 15, 95, 142
Disraeli, Benjamin, 268, 330n.23
*Dissertation* (Koster), 378
*Dissertation on the Canon and Feudal Law* (Adams), 50
*Docks of New York* (moving picture), 242
Doctorow, E. L., 376, 377, 378
Dodd, S. C. T., 335–336
Dodd, William E., 72
Donald, David, 15
Donnelly, Ignatius, 322, 342, 345, 348, 349
Dos Passos, John, 372
Douglass, William, 51
Dow, Charles, 202
Draper, John William, 89
Draper, Lyman, 70
Dred Scott Decision, 121–122
Drumont, Edouard, 107
Duberman, Martin, 377
DuBois, W. E. B., 74, 387
Dulles, John Foster, 159
Dunbar, Charles F., 191
Dunning, John H., 108

Dunning, William A., 386
Durkheim, Émile, 10, 256, 262, 286
Dwight, Timothy, 260

Earl, Robert, 234
École Pratique des Hautes Études, 78
*Economic Interpretation of the Constitution, An* (Beard), 98
Eddy, Mary Baker, 124
Edwards, Jonathan, 48, 49
Eggleston, Edward, 67–68, 69, 71, 106
Ehrlichman, John, 379
*1876* (Vidal), 378
Eisenhower, Dwight, 152
Eliot, T. S., 9
Elkins, Stanley M., 15, 278–279
Ely, Richard, 98
Emancipation Proclamation, 131. *See also* Slavery
Emerson, Ralph Waldo, 94, 104, 138, 266, 328n.18
*Encyclopedia of Social Sciences, The* (Seligman, ed.), 7
*Ends of Power, The* (Haldeman), 128
Engels, Friedrich, 96, 330n.23
Engerman, Stanley L. See *Time on the Cross*
Enlightenment, the, 133, 248, 279, 408; influence of, on U.S. historians, 43, 49–50, 54, 85, 89
Erie Canal, 117, 235
Erikson, Charlotte, 390
Erikson, Erik, 14, 272–273
European history, 70, 78; influence of, on colonial historians, 50, 52–53, 68
Evans, Walker, 235, 237, 243
Everett, A. H., 184, 188

Farm Security Administration, 235, 237
Fascism, 179
Fast, Howard, 373–375

Faulkner, William, 9
Faust, A. B., 387
Febvre, Lucien, 7, 14
Federalism, 181
*Federalist, The* (papers) , 293
Federalist party, 354, 355, 358, 359, 361n.21, 362; and anti-Federalists, 353
Federal Reserve Board, 198
Field, Marshall, 375
Fischer, David Hackett, 19, 20
Fish, Hamilton, 268
Fisher, Sydney George, 56, 65
Fisk, James, 234
Fiske, John, 62, 64, 90, 353
Flagler, Henry M., 337
Flood, James C., 237
Fogel, Robert W., 13. See also *Time on the Cross*
Fogerty, J. J., 243
Force, Peter, 58
Ford, Henry, 137
Ford Foundation, 77
Forster, E. M., 382
*Fortunate Pilgrim, The* (Puzo) , 379
*Fortune* magazine, 154
Foster, Stephen C., 247
Fothergill, John, 299
Foucault, Michel, 15, 133
Fowles, John, 21
Fox, Charles, 143
Frank, J. N., 333
Frankenstein's monster, 327–328
Franklin, Benjamin, 61, 147, 324; biographies of, 272; visits England, 298, 299, 308
Franklin, Massachusetts, 330
Frederick, prince of Wales, 297
Freeman, Douglas S., 268, 269
Freeman, Edward A., 63
Freidel, Frank B., 268
French, Daniel Chester, 238
*French Lieutenant's Woman, The* (Fowles) , 21
French Revolution, 11, 177

Freud, Sigmund, 10, 14; and Freudian theory, 171, 239, 270–274, 289, 398
"Frontier interpretation," 70
Frye, Northrop, 287

Gabriel, Ralph H., 75
Gadsden, Christopher, 308
Galloway, Joseph, 359
Gallup, George, and Gallup poll, 264
Galpin, C. J., 261
Gardner, Lloyd C., 154
Garrison, William Lloyd, 116
Gay, E. F., 63
*General Evening Post, The* (London) , 295
*General History* (Hubbard) , 49
Genet, Jean, 288
Genovese, Eugene, 104, 148, 224, 396n.19
George, Henry, 91
George III, king of England, 14, 177, 178, 267
Georgia, contemporary history of, 50
Gerry, Elbridge, 359, 361, 366
Gibbon, Edward, 34, 90, 91, 407
Gibbs, Willard, 334
Gibson, Charles Dana, 238
Giddings, F. H., 261
Gilbert, Cass, 237
Gillette, J. M., 261
Glackens, William, 245
Gladstone, William E., 105
Glass, D. V., 14
Gobineau, J. A., 107
*Godfather, The* (Puzo) , 379, 380
Godwin, William, 35, 88
Goethe, Johann Wolfgang von, 93
Goldmann, Lucien, 104
Gompers, Samuel, 374
*Gone with the Wind* (Mitchell) , 382
Goodwyn, Lawrence, 345, 346
Gore, Christopher, 365
Gorham, Nathaniel, 365
Gould, Jay, 90
Government Printing Office, 122

Gramsci, Antonio, 103, 104
Grant, Madison, 108
Grant, Ulysses S., 354
Graunt, John, 201
Gray, Lewis C., 224
Gray, William, 365
*Great Plains, The* (Webb), 73
*Greed* (moving picture), 242
Greeley, Horace, 131, 234
Green, John Richard, 62, 64
Greene, Victor R., 390
"Grey Owl" (Archie Belaney), 124
"Grid" system, 25
Griffith, Mary, 320
Gross, Charles, 60
Gross National Product, 202

Hacker, Louis M., 333
Haldeman, H. R., 128
Hales, Stephen, 297
Haley, Alex, 126, 380–382
Hamilton, Alexander, 183; and Hamiltonian ideas, 333, 354, 355; party of, 358, 367
Hancock, John, 308, 359, 361, 366
Handel, George Frederick, 119
Handsome Lake, 289
Hansen, Marcus L., 74, 389
Hardy, Thomas, 372
Harlow, Ralph V., 271
*Harper's Weekly*, 232, 245
Harrington, James, 294, 309
Harris, Louis, and Harris polls, 260, 264
Hart, Albert Bushnell, 18, 61
Harvard, John, portrayal of, 232, 238
Harvard University, 59
Haskins, Charles H., 60, 61
Hayek, F. A., 332, 334
Haymarket riot, 374
Hayter, Thomas, 297
*Heart of Darkness* (Conrad), 382
*Heart of Midlothian, The* (Scott), 372

Hegel, Georg W. F., 57, 87, 93, 94; and Hegelian theory, 96, 97, 100, 259
Held, John, Jr., 238
Herder, Johann Gottfried, 93, 142
Hersey, John, 382
Hesselius, John, 233
Hewatt, Alexander, 50, 88
Hewitt, Abram S., 268, 354
Hicks, John D., 339, 349
Higham, John, 5, 341, 392
Hildreth, Richard, 57
Hine, Louis, 234, 235, 242
*Historians' Fallacies* (Fischer), 19
*Historical Statistics of the United States, 1789–1945* (U.S. Census Bureau), 198
*History of American Life* series (Schlesinger and Fox, eds.), 71, 72, 384
*History of the Five Indian Nations, The* (Colden), 50
Hitler, Adolf, 109, 148, 273
Hobson, John A., 105
Hofstadter, Richard, 341, 342
"Hogan's Alley," 251
Hogarth, William, 231
Hollingsworth, J. Rogers, 350
Holmes, Oliver Wendell, Jr., 334
Holst, Hermann E. von, 59, 95
Hoosac Tunnel, 190–191
Hoover, Herbert, 147
Hopper, Edward, 243
Horkheimer, Max, 74
Houston, Texas, 230
Howells, William Dean, 372
Hubbard, William, 49
Hübschmann, Heinrich, 254
Huizinga, Johan, 68, 228, 259
Humboldt, Wilhelm von, 93, 254, 408
Hume, David, 85, 124, 294, 304, 411
Humphrey, Hubert, 158
Hünig, Wolfgang K., 254
Huntington, Ellsworth, 107
Hutchinson, Thomas, 50, 359, 360
Huxley, Aldous, 322

Immigration (as subject), 74, 108, 390, 401; restriction of, 386, 387–389, 402

Imperialism, 55, 82, 109; definitions of, 105–106, 108, 180

"Imperial School," 63

*In Cold Blood* (Capote), 379

*In Council Rooms Apart* (Craig), 378

Indians, American, 124, 390, 391, 392, 394, 397–399

"Industrial revolution," 330

*Information Please Almanac,* 200

Ingraham, Joseph, 288

Intellectual history, 17, 64, 75, 156–157

Interior, U.S. Department of the, 197

*Iron Age* (journal), 199

*Ivanhoe* (Scott), 372

Ives, Charles, 249


Jackson, Andrew, 117, 130, 358; and Jacksonian Democrats, 55, 353, 354–355; historians and, 333

Jackson, Jonathan, 364

*Jacobins, The* (Brinton), 11

James, Henry, 288, 334, 372

James, William, 76, 97, 118

Jameson, J. F., 268

Japan, war with, 153–154

Jaspers, Karl, 89

*Jaws* (Benchley), 379

Jay, John, 234, 359

Jefferson, Thomas, 106, 119, 237, 274, 308, 377–378; studies of, 66, 98, 102, 147, 268, 333; and Jeffersonian democracy/Democratic party, 69, 98, 148, 333, 353–355, 358, 367; and Louisiana Purchase, 92, 109; and Declaration of Independence, 176–177, 314; readings recommended by, 293–294

Jennings, Francis, 397–398

Jensen, Merrill, 358, 362

Johns Hopkins University, 59, 63

Johnson, Edward, 46, 47–48, 53, 65

Jordan, Winthrop, 393

*Journal of American History,* 20

Joyce, James, 9

*Jubilee* (Walker), 380, 381

*Judge* (magazine), 232

Jung, Carl, 273, 278

Justice, U.S. Department of, 338


Kafka, Franz, 288

Kalm, Peter, 260

Kansas, Populism in, 345, 347

Keaton, Buster, 242

Kefauver Committee, 122

Kennedy, John F., assassination of, 119

Kennedy, Young Joe, 380

Kerner Committee, 122

Keynes, John Maynard, 10, 256

Khrushchev, Nikita, 152

Kimball, Warren F., 156–157, 159

Kim Il Sung, 160

King, Clarence, 91

King Philip's War, 398

Kippis, Andrew, 299

*Kirkus Review,* 113

Knights of Labor, 173, 346

Know-Nothing party, 354

Kojève, Alexandre, 103

Kolko, Gabriel, 108, 154

Kondratieff, Nikolai D., 205

Korea, 148, 159–160

Korzybski, Alfred, 165

Koster, R. M., 378

Kuczynski, R. R., 14

Ku Klux Klan, 342

*Kultur der Renaissance in Italien, Die* (Burckhardt), 68

Kuznets, Simon S., 202


Labor, U.S. Department of, 263

LaFeber, Walter, 108

Laing, R. D., 14

Laissez faire: Williams on, 145, 147; as (abused) concept, 181–182; re-

jection of doctrine of, 182, 184–190; redefined, 190–192
Lamprecht, Karl, 95
Lange, Dorothea, 235, 237
Langer, William L., 14, 163
Language, 15; and literary style, 8–9, 58; and choice of (quantitative) adjectives, 12–13, 222; and nomenclature of the mountains, 26–28; and rhetoric, 130–134; and articulacy/inarticulacy, 141–143; and meaning, 165–181, 192–193, 285–286, 313, 406
Lasch, Christopher, 20, 156
*Last Best Hope, The* (Tauber), 378
Laveden, Pierre, 14
Lawrence, Abbott, 185
Lawrence, Kansas, 261
Lawrence, Massachusetts, 330
Lease, Mary Ellen, 345
Le Bon, Gustave, 277
Lecky, William E. H., 89
Lee, Henry, 183
Lee, Robert E., biography of, 268, 269
Lee, Russell, 235
Leibniz, Gottfried von, 86
Lelchuk, Alan, 376
Lenin, V. I., 105, 109
Leslie, Cliffe, 191
*Letters on the Application of Probabilities . . .* (Quetelet), 203
Levin, David, 390
Lévi-Strauss, Claude, 15, 239, 287, 289
Lewinson, Paul, 3
Leyendecker, J. C., 238
*Liberator* (abolitionist newspaper), 116
Library of Congress Archive of Folk Song, 246
*Life and Letters of Martin Luther, The* (Smith), 271, 273
Lincoln, Abraham, 99, 102, 119, 147, 234, 380; and emancipation, 131, 132; biography of, 268

Link, Arthur, 269
Lippmann, Walter, 277
*Literary Digest* poll, 264
*Literary History, The, of the American Revolution, 1763–1783* (Tyler), 64
Livingston, Edward, 130, 377
Lloyd, Harold, 242
Locke, John, 293, 294, 309, 314; interpretations of, 146, 147; and meanings of words, 170, 176
Locofoco party, 354
Löher, Franz von, 65
London, Jack, 126, 179
London *Economist*, 202
London Exhibition (1851), 321
London *Gazeteer*, 295
*Lonely Crowd, The* (Riesman), 262
*Looking Backward* (Bellamy), 321
Loria, Achille, 10
Los Angeles, California, 230
Louisiana Purchase, 92, 109
Louis XVI, king of France, 177
Lovejoy, Arthur O., 16, 75, 176
Lowell, James Russell, 9
Lowell, Massachusetts, 317, 330
Luddites, 319
Ludwig, Emil, 270
Lukács, Georg, 103, 371, 380
Luks, George, 244
Luther, Martin, biographies of, 271, 272–273
Lynd, H. M., 260
Lynd, Robert Staughton, 5, 260, 393. See also *Middletown*
Lyon, Pat, 231
Lysenko, Trofim D., 409

Mabillon, Jean, 85
Macaulay, Thomas, 8, 9, 57, 65, 67
McCarthyism, 149, 343
McCormick, Cyrus Hall, 221, 354
McCulloch, Hugh, 188
McGee, Thomas D'Arcy, 65

McIlwain, Charles H., 5, 61
Mackay, Mungo, 365
McKean, Thomas, 53
McMaster, John B., 65–66, 67, 72
Macnie, John, 321
Maddox, Robert J., 150, 151, 154–156
Madison, James, 66, 177, 269
*Madness and Civilization* (Foucault), 133
*Magnalia Christi Americana* (Mather), 266
Mahler, Gustav, 248
Mailer, Norman, 376
*Main Currents in American Thought* (Parrington), 69
Malcolm X, 168; *Autobiography* of, 126
Malin, James C., 106, 108
Malone, Dumas, 268
Malthusian theory, 91, 188
Manifest Destiny, 54–55. *See also* Mission, concept of
Mannheim, Karl, 10, 100
Mao Tse-tung, 148, 160; and Maoism, 82
Marin, John, 244
Marsh, Reginald, 244
Marshall, Alfred, 256
Marshall, John, 53, 57
Marx, Karl, and Marxism, 96, 137, 179, 239; western historians and, 70, 78, 82, 96, 103–105, 148, 387, 395; U.S. attitude toward, 70, 73, 74–75, 82, 83, 96–97, 98, 401; and artistic genius, 248; Stalin and, 409
Massachusetts: laissez faire concept in, 181–187, 189, 190, 192; party division in, 358–361, 362–364
Massachusetts Bay, contemporary history of, 50
Massachusetts Bureau of Labor Statistics, 199
Massachusetts Society for the Promotion of Agriculture, 185

Mathematical Social Science Board, 208
Mather, Cotton, 49, 170, 266
Mathiessen, F. O., 79
Maurois, André, 270
*Meet General Grant* (Woodward), 270
Meinecke, Friedrich, 16, 99
Melville, Herman, 9, 321, 324; novels of, 54, 316, 372; social document of, 317–319, 323, 329, 330, 331
*Memory Bank, The* (Duberman), 377
Mendelsohn, Lev A., 105
Merk, Frederick, 5
Merrens, Harry R., 14
Merrimack River mill towns, 231
Meyer, John R., 13
Michelet, Jules, 57, 66
Michels, Roberto, 10
Middleton, Henry, 143
*Middletown* (Lynd and Lynd), 260, 262
Mifflin, Thomas, 308
Migration. *See* Immigration (as subject); Mission, concept of
Mikhailovitch, Draja, 160
Mill, John Stuart, 90, 105, 139
Miller, Perry, 16, 75
Minneapolis, Kansas, 261
Mission concept of: and "American experience," 43–44, 68; and "providential design" (of migration to America), 46, 47–51, 55, 85, 88; 19th-century, 53–57
Mitchell, Margaret, 373
*Moby Dick* (Melville), 316
*Modern Prometheus, The* (Shelley), 328
*Modern Times* (moving picture), 322
Moneypenny, William F., 268
Monograph (s): assessment of, 16; defined, 291. *See also* Specialization

Montesquieu, Charles Louis de, 90, 100, 106, 293, 294, 407
Moody's *Manual*, 199
More, Thomas, 214
Morgan, J. P., 234
Morison, Samuel Eliot, 5, 58
Morris, William, 322
Morse, J. T., 267
Morton, Charles, 297
Moser, J. J., 86
Motley, John L., 55, 57
Moving pictures, 232, 233, 234, 239–244 (passim), 322
Mozart, Wolfgang Amadeus, 248
Murnau, F. W., 243, 244
Music, 15, 246–251
Myers, Jerome, 245

Napoleon I (Bonaparte), 109, 346, 372
*Narrative and Critical History of America* (Winsor, ed.), 58
Nash, Gary, 398
Nast, Thomas, 232
*Nation*, 155
National Archives, 122
National Bureau of Economic Research, 201
National Industrial Conference Board, 201
Nationalism, 18, 102–103, 142, 346, 410
National Opinion Research Center, 264
National Socialists. *See* Nazis
*Nat Turner* (Styron), 128, 382
Nazis (National Socialists), 153, 179, 238n.20, 409
Neagle, John, 231
Nef, John U., 181
Negroes, historical treatment of, 74, 116–117, 385–391, 393–394, 395–397, 399. *See also* Slavery
Nekritsch, Aleksander, 151

Nevins, Allan, 58, 268; and Rockefeller study, 268, 334–338
New Amsterdam, 230
Newburyport, Massachusetts, Thernstrom study of, 12–13, 16
New Deal, 339, 389
New England: contemporary history of, 45–48; historical neglect of, 73; Burgh on, 307; party division in, 356–361
*New England Primer*, 231
"New History," 67, 69, 71, 90, 98, 383–402
*New History* (Robinson), 90
*New Ideas on Population* (Everett), 188
New Jersey, contemporary history of, 50
New Left historians, 81–82
New Orleans, Louisiana, 117, 385
*New Radicalism in America, The, 1889–1963* (Lasch), 20
Newspapers as evidence, 134–136
Newton, Isaac, 88, 255
*New Viewpoints in American History* (Schlesinger), 71
New World Records, 246
New York Central railroad, 190
New York City, 117, 230, 330, 393
*New Yorker* magazine, 20, 159
New-York Historical Society, 55
*New York Review of Books*, 155, 209
New York *Times*, 20, 149, 209; and Pentagon Papers, 135
*New York Times Magazine*, 159
Ngo Dinh Diem, 160
Nguyen Van Thieu, 160
*Niles' Weekly Register*, 200
*1984* (Orwell), 322
Nixon, Richard M., 82, 273, 378
Nomenclature. *See* Language
Norris, Frank, 372
*North American Review*, 187
Northwest Ordinance (1787), 190
Nugent, Walter T. K., 340, 341, 342, 344, 345

Oberholtzer, Ellis P., 61
*Of Plymouth Plantation* (Bradford),
46
Oldenbourg, Zoe, 372
Oliver, Andrew, 359
Olms catalogue, 254
Organization of American Histo-
rians, 157n.14, 158
Orwell, George, 322
Osgood, Herbert L., 61, 63
Osofsky, Gilbert, 393
O'Sullivan, John L., 54
Oswald, Lee Harvey, 129, 380

Paine, Thomas, 85, 102, 392. See also
*Common Sense* (Paine)
Palfrey, John G., 57
Palmer, Robert, 314
Panofsky, Erwin, 15
Pareto, Vilfredo, 10, 137, 256
Paris Universal Exposition (1867),
321
Park, Robert E., 256, 261
Parkman, Francis, 8, 9, 57, 58
Parrington, Vernon L., 69, 70, 353
Parsons, James B., 157
Parsons, Talcott, 256
Parton, James, 268
*Passage to India, A* (Forster), 382
*Passing of the Great Race, The*
(Grant), 108
*Past and Present* (journal), 78
Patten, Simon N., 256
Peffer, W. A., 347
Peirce, Charles Sanders, 5, 20, 97,
114, 405
Pennsylvania, contemporary history
of, 50
*Pennsylvania* (Fisher), 65
Pentagon Papers, 135
Perkins, Max, 130
Perroux, François, 103
Perry, A. L., 186
Petty, William, 201

*Phänomenologie des Geistes* (Hegel),
93
Philadelphia, Pennsylvania, 12, 117,
230, 324
Phillips, U. B., 108; and "Phillips
School," 223
Phillips, Willard, 186, 191
Pickering, Timothy, 359
*Pierre* (Melville), 316
Pilgrims, the, 44, 46
*Pit and the Pendulum, The* (Poe),
145–146
Pittsburgh, Pennsylvania, early views
of, 230
Pittsburgh Survey, 261
*Plainville* (West, pseud. for Withers),
262
Plato, 294, 309
Plumb, J. H., 20–21
Plutarch, 266
Plymouth, Massachusetts, 44, 363n.26
Poe, Edgar Allan, 145–146
Pokrovskii, Mikhail N., 74
*Political Disquisitions* (Burgh), 293–
294, 295, 306, 308, 310
*Political Economy* (Carey), 186
Politics, 74; past, history as, 63; two-
party system in, 350, 353–367
*Politics of War, The* (Kolko), 154
Polk, James K., 157
Pollack, Norman, 341, 342, 346, 350;
and "Pollack-Handlin debate,"
340n.9
Pollock, Jackson, 251
Polls, public opinion, 260, 263–265
Polybius, 414
Population studies, 201. *See also* Cen-
sus, U.S. Bureau of the; Quantita-
tive techniques
Populist movement, 74, 97, 339–352
Potsdam Conference, 154
Pound, Ezra, 9
Powderly, Terence V., and Knights
of Labor, 173, 346
Prendergast, Maurice, 245
Prescott, William H., 57

President's House, 241
Price, Richard, 51, 298, 299
Priestley, Joseph, 298, 299
*Princeton, U.S.S.,* 109
*Principles of Political Economy . . .*
(Bowen), 187
Pringle, Sir John, 299
Progressive era, 68; and progressive
historians, 68–69, 74, 97
Promotionalism. *See* Boosterism
"Providence," liberty as secular
equivalent of, 51. *See also* Mission, concept of
Psychology, 14, 16. *See also* Erikson,
Erik; Freud, Sigmund
*Public Burning, The* (Coover), 378
*Publishers Weekly,* 113, 199
*Puck* (magazine), 232
Pufendorf, Samuel, 86
Pullman, George, 375
Puritans, the, 52, 54, 68, 175, 397–
398; as historians, 46, 48, 83, 125,
170; experience of, in England, 48,
178
Puzo, Mario, 379
Pynchon, Thomas, 376

Quadroons, 385. *See also* Negroes
Quakers, the, 68, 385
Quantitative techniques, 11, 14,
315n.44; and computerization, 10–
12, 194, 206, 213, 222; and interpretation, 12–13, 208, 212–213, 225;
in population studies, 201
Quetelet, L. A. J., 203
Quincy, Josiah, 308

Race, as term, 107, 178, 389
Racism, 55, 82, 385, 390, 395–401; of
historians, 108, 116, 386–388, 389
Radosh, Ronald, 155
Rae, John, 187
*Ragtime* (Doctorow), 378
Ramsay, David, 52

Randall, James G., 387
Randolph, Thomas Mann, 293
Ranke, Leopold von, 87, 93, 94, 157,
408
Ransom, J. C., 333
*Reader's Digest,* 380
Reconstruction, 95, 107, 386, 388–
389, 402, 404
*Red Badge of Courage, The* (Crane),
372
*Redburn* (Melville), 372
Reformation, the, 38, 48, 51
Relativism, 259n.11, 411
*Republic, The* (Beard), 102
Republicanism, spread of, as historical theme, 51, 53
Republican party, 350, 354–355, 359,
361n.21; Democratic-Republican,
354, 355, 358
Research: discontinuity of, 17, 18;
and consciousness of continuities,
60
Revere, Paul, 231, 237, 363
Revisionism, 147–157, 159, 160–161,
333, 338
Rhee, Syngman, 160
Rhode Island, contemporary history
of, 50
Rhodes, James Ford, 58, 87
Ricardo, David, 188
Richards, I. A., 15
Richard III, king of England, 332
Richter, Conrad, 372
Riesman, David, 262
Riis, Jacob, 234, 242
*Rise of American Civilization, The*
(Beard and Beard), 69, 102, 103,
339
*Rise of the Dutch Republic, The*
(Motley), 55
Robbins, Caroline, 313
Robbins, Harold, 378
Roberts, Kenneth, 373
Robertson, William, 52, 106, 295
Robinson, James Harvey, 69, 70, 71,
90, 100

Rochester, New York, 230
Rochester Conference (1974), 208, 211
Rockefeller, John D., 132, 343, 352; Nevins study of, 268, 334–338
Roe, E. P., 288
Rogers, John, and Rogers groups, 231
Rogers, Samuel, 298
Rogers, Thomas, 298
Rogin, Michael P., 398
*Roll, Jordan, Roll* (Genovese), 395
Roosevelt, Franklin Delano, 102, 130, 138, 355; pro-British policy of, 132; and Soviet policy, 152, 153–154, 161; biography of, 268
Roosevelt, Theodore, 275; as historian, 58, 70
*Roots* (Haley), 380–382
Roper, Elmo, and Roper poll, 264
Rosenberg, Ethel, 378
Rosenberg, Hans, 3
Rosenman, Samuel I., 130
Ross, George, 308
Rossiter, Frank R., 248–249
*R.U.R.* (Čapek), 322
Russell, Bertrand, 15
Russia. *See* Soviet Union

St. Louis, Missouri, early views of, 230
*Salammbo* (Flaubert), 371
Salisbury, Harrison, 135
Saloutos, Theodore, 390
*Samuel Adams* (Harlow), 271
Sandburg, Carl, 268
Sapir, Edward, 287
Sargent, John Singer, 233
Sarony, Napoleon, 234
*Save America First!* (Frank), 333
Savio, Mario, 138
Say, J. B., 182
Schiller, Johann Christoph, 93
Schlesinger, Arthur M., 5, 7, 8, 71, 163, 356, 388
Schorske, Carl, 15

Schouler, James, 58, 65
Schumpeter, Joseph A., 10, 204
Scopes trial, 137
Scott, Sir Walter, 56, 372, 373, 380
Sedgwick, Theodore, 365
Seligman, Edwin R. A., 7
Seligman, Joseph, 394
Semiotics, 254
Seward, William H., 106, 321
Seybert, Adam, 200
Seymour, Horatio, 354
Shaler, Nathaniel S., 107
*Shall We Tell the President?* (Archer), 378
*Shape of Things to Come, The* (Wells), 322
Shattuck, Lemuel, 201, 260
Shays's Rebellion, 361
Sheehan, Bernard W., 398
Sheeler, Charles, 244
Shelley, Mary, 328, 329
Sherman, Roger, 234, 308
Sherman Anti-Trust Act, 335
Simpson, Jerry, 348
Skelton, Raleigh A., 25
Slavery, 117, 122, 131, 333, 397; studies of and writings on, 109, 207–224, 278–279, 380–382, 386, 388, 391, 395–396, 411; and slave rebellion, 128–129; meaning of word, 174–175
Sloan, John, 244, 245
Small, Albion, 63
Smibert, John, 234
Smith, Adam, 182, 187, 188, 293, 294
Smith, Gaddis, 159, 160
Smith, Henry Nash, 79
Smith, J. Allen, 69
Smith, John, 45, 232
Smith, Joseph, 124
Smith, Preserved, 271, 273
Smith, Samuel, 50, 51
Smith, William, 50
Smithsonian Institution National Collection of Fine Arts, 246
Smythe, Sir Thomas, 173

Snow, C. P., 325
Social Democratic party, 179
Socialism, 96, 97, 332; as term, 179
Socialist Party, 179
Social Science Research Council, 6, 252, 288; Committee on Research in Economic history, 164
Society for Political Education, 191
Solomon, Barbara M., 390
Solzhenitsyn, Aleksander I., 160
Sorokin, Pitirim A., 10, 92
Sousa, John Philip, 247
South, the, focus of history of, 72
South Carolina, contemporary history of, 50, 391
Soviet Union, 148–149, 151–154, 159, 172, 409
Sparks, Jared, 58, 59, 61, 266–267
Spear, Allan, 393
Specialization: and the monograph, 16, 61, 75, 291; dangers of, 17, 78, 84, 163, 412; institutional, 62–64, 66, 70–71, 114; 325–326; sectional (regional), 72–73, 79
Spencer, Herbert, 63, 89, 90, 255
Spengler, Oswald, 92
Spies, August, 374
Springfield, Illinois, 261
*Spy, The* (Cooper), 373
Stalin, Joseph, and Stalinism, 73, 82, 149, 153, 160; and destalinization, 103; brutality of regime under, 148, 152; and distortion of record, 154, 155; converts Marxism to state purpose, 409
Standard and Poor, 199
Standard Oil enterprise, 334–338
Stanton, William, 390
Starobin, Robert, 391
*Statement of Some New Principles* (Rae), 187
*Statistical Abstract of the United States* (annual), 198
Steel, Ronald, 155
Steichen, Edward, 234
Stendhal (Marie Henri Beyle), 372

Stephenson, George M., 74
Sternberg, Josef von, 242
Stevens, Thaddeus, 272
Stowe, Harriet Beecher. See *Uncle Tom's Cabin*
Strachey, Lytton, 270
*Streetcorner Society* (Whyte), 262
Stroheim, Erich von, 242
Strong, Caleb, 359, 361
Strong, Josiah, 54
*Strukturen des Comic Strip* (Hünig), 254
Styron, William, 128, 382
Suetonius, 266
Sullivan, James, 359
Sullivan, John, 308
Sumner, Charles, 272
Sumner, William G., 106, 277
Susann, Jacqueline, 378
Sydney, Algernon, 309, 314

Taine, Hippolyte A., 89, 106, 107
*Tale of Two Cities, A* (Dickens), 371
Taney, Roger, 130
Tarlé, E. V., 74
Tate, Allen, 333
Tauber, Peter, 378
Taussig, Frank W., 191
Taylor, Frederick W., 323
Taylor, John, 147
Television, 37, 134, 232, 234, 379
*Ten Nights in a Bar-Room* (Arthur), 232
Terkel, (Louis) Studs, 128
Thackeray, William M., 9, 372
Thernstrom, Stephen A., 12–13, 16
Thieu, Nguyen Van, 160
Third World, as term, 172
Thompson, E. P., 78
Thompson, J. Walter, Co., 200
Thompson, William ("Bill"), 137
Thomson, Charles, 308
Thoreau, Henry David, 104, 138

Thoresby, Mr. (rector of Stoke New-
ington), 298
*Thoughts on Education* (Burgh),
295
*Three Hundred Years Hence* (Grif-
fith), 320
Thucydides, 8
Thünen, Johann H. von, 189
Thwaites, Reuben G., 70
Ticknor, George, 58
Tilden, Samuel J., 354
Tillman, Benjamin, 350, 351
Tilly, Charles H., 11
*Time on the Cross* (Fogel and Enger-
man), 206–224, 395
Tocqueville, Alexis de, 177
Tolstoy, Leo, 66, 110, 375, 380
Tönnies, Ferdinand, 262
Topeka (Kansas) *Advocate,* 348
Tories and toryism, 357, 360, 364,
365
Toynbee, Arnold J., 92
*Tragedy of American Diplomacy,
The* (Williams), 154
Treasury, U.S. Department of the,
197
*Tribune Almanac,* 200
Trotsky, Leon, 409
Truman, Harry S, 160, 173; and
Soviet regime, 152, 153, 154
*Truman at Potsdam* (TV docu-
drama), 379
Trumbull, Benjamin, 65
Turner, Frederick Jackson, 10, 70–
71, 72, 73, 106, 268
Turner, Nat, 128–129, 382
Twain, Mark, 90, 375
Tyler, Moses Coit, 64


*Über die Verschiedenheit des
menschlichen Sprachbaues* (Humboldt), 254
*Uncle Tom's Cabin* (Stowe), 212,
372, 382
United Mine Workers, 239

United Nations, 160, 161
University of Chicago, 59, 256
Utley, Robert M., 399
*Utopia* (More), 214


Van Buren, Martin, 377
Vanderbilt, Cornelius, 237
Vanderbilt, George W., 237
Van Ingen, William H., 232, 233
Vanzetti, Bartolomeo, 125
Varga, Eugen, 105
Vasari, Giorgio, 266
Vassall family, 360
Veiller, Lawrence, 261
Velikowsky, Immanuel, 254
*Vendée, The* (Tilly), 11
Vesey, Denmark, 129
Victoria, queen of England, 170
Vidal, Gore, 377, 378
Vietnam war, 81, 135, 138
Virginia: migration into, 44, 45; con-
temporary history of, 45, 49, 50
Voltaire, François, 53
Von Däniken, Erich, 254
Von Stroheim, Erich, 242
Von Thünen, Johann H., 189
*Voyage en Icarie* (Cabet), 321


Walker, Amasa, 186, 191
Walker, Francis, 188, 191, 197
Walker, Margaret, 380, 381
Wallace, Lew, 373
Walzer, the, 37–38
*Waning of the Middle Ages* (Hui-
zinga), 68
*War and Peace* (Tolstoy), 372
Ward, Lester, 261
Warhol, Andy, 251
Warner, Lloyd, 262, 263
Warner, Sam Bass, Jr., 12, 16
*Warning to Dram-Drinkers, A*
(Burgh), 295, 297
War of 1812, 354

War of Independence. *See* American Revolution

Warren, Mercy Otis, 51, 361

Washburn, Emory, 187

Washington, George, 109, 308, 373; biographers and, 57, 61, 267, 268, 274, 378

*Washington behind Closed Doors* (TV docudrama), 379

Watson, Tom, 342, 345

Waugh, Samuel B., 235

*Wealth of Nations* (Smith), 34

Webb, Walter P., 73, 106

Weber, Max, 10, 74, 137, 139, 256, 277

Webster, Daniel, 183

Webster, John, 168

Webster, Pelatiah, 200

Webster, Massachusetts, 330

Weeden, William B., 66

Weems, Parson M. L., 53

Welch, W. H., 275

Wells, H. G., 91, 179, 321, 322, 329

West, the: focus of history on, 70, 73; study of attitudes toward, 79

Wharton, Edith, 372

Whig party, 109, 354

White, John, 233

*White Devil, The* (Webster), 168

Whitefield, George, 147

*White Jacket* (Melville), 54

*White Lotus* (Hersey), 382

Whitman, Walt, 54

Whitney, Eli, 275

Whyte, W. F., 262

Widger, William, 142–143

Williams, Mrs. Alvester, 124, 412

Williams, John Chandler, 365

Williams, Roger, 99

Williams, William Appleman, 145–147, 148, 154, 155, 156, 161

Williamstown Convention (1957), 208

Wilson, James, 308

Wilson, Woodrow, 125, 138, 392; as historian, 55; biographies of, 269, 271

Winckelmann, J. J., 68

Winks, Robin W., 19

Winsor, Justin, 58

Wise, John, 102, 147

Wittgenstein, Ludwig, 165

Wittke, Carl, 388

Wolfe, Thomas, 130

*Wonder-Working Providence* (Johnson), 47

Woods, Robert A., 261

Woodward, C. Vann, 72, 341, 345, 390

Woodward, W. E., 270

Woolson, Thomas, 85

Woolworth Building (New York), 237

*World Almanac*, 200

World War I, effect of, 71

World War II: effect of, 75–76, 78, 80, 389; cause of, 148

Wright, Carroll D., 199

Wright, Joseph, 234

Yankee City Series, 262

Yates, Francis, 15

Yorktown, battle of, 109

Youngdale, James, 346

*Young Man Luther* (Erikson), 272–273

Yugoslavia, 173

Zola, Emile, 372